Cities and crisis

Manchester University Press

Cities and crisis

JOSEF W. KONVITZ

Manchester University Press

Copyright © Josef W. Konvitz 2016

The right of Josef W. Konvitz to be identified as the author of this work has been asserted by him in accordance with the Copyright, Designs and Patents Act 1988.

Published by Manchester University Press
Altrincham Street, Manchester M1 7JA

www.manchesteruniversitypress.co.uk

British Library Cataloguing-in-Publication Data
A catalogue record for this book is available from the British Library

Library of Congress Cataloging-in-Publication Data applied for

ISBN 978 1 7849 9290 3 hardback
ISBN 978 0 7190 9964 9 paperback

First published 2016

The publisher has no responsibility for the persistence or accuracy of URLs for any external or third-party internet websites referred to in this book, and does not guarantee that any content on such websites is, or will remain, accurate or appropriate.

Typeset in Sabon and Gill by
Servis Filmsetting Ltd, Stockport, Cheshire
Printed in Great Britain
by Bell & Bain, Glasgow

For Isa, Eli, and Ezra

Contents

Preface and acknowledgments	*page* viii
Abbreviations	xv
Introduction: the difference a crisis makes	1

Part I If cities are like dynamos, why is the economy sputtering?

1	We are where we are, but how did we get here?	27
2	Housing and cities: toward what future?	51
3	Infrastructure and innovation: new limits to growth	75
4	Managing space better: the problem of shrinking cities and economies	103
5	Jobs to people: livability, governance, and strategic planning	134

Part II: Making cities safer

6	The vulnerability and resilience of cities	163
7	Regulatory governance, risk, and the new security economies	191

Part III: Cities and paradigms for economic governance

8	How the West overcomes crises, reduces risks, and copes with uncertainty	213
9	Paradigms for economic governance: how cities grew bigger and better	235
10	Cities and nation-states in the urban age: will inter-dependence reshape rules for the twenty-first century?	260

Index	289

Preface and acknowledgments

This book begins with a story. On 9 October 2009, a year after the crash of Lehman Brothers and with years of recession ahead of us, I met Prof. James Conroy, then Dean of the School of Education, in his office on the campus of the University of Glasgow. We discussed how ill-prepared countries are to give young people a sense of hope about the future because teachers are not sufficiently aspirational, and transmit their view of closed horizons. My reflections were sharpened a few minutes later when we discussed regulation. Jim spoke of how fear in society leads people to demand more, and unreasonable, levels of protection (a reaction corroborated by studies), and to accept rather than question the status quo and their place in it. Perversely, this leads many in school to under-invest in the skills they need to cope with rapid change. Our discussion resonated with my own thoughts not only on my professional work at the time as Head of the Regulatory Policy Division of the OECD, but also provoked by the Argentinian play *Paranoia* which I had seen two nights before at the Théâtre du Châtelet in Paris. Why are our well-educated societies, at peace, so risk-averse, so afraid?

In the upper right margin of the paper on which I was taking notes, I wrote down a couple of long-term trends which singly or in combination diminished hope and opportunity: territorial (desertification, abandonment in and of cities by the shrinking middle class); political-cultural (the circumscribed public realm, social erosion); and fiscal (ageing, social care, employment). Population growth, urbanization and the growth of the largest cities, reaching unprecedented size, innovation and scientific discoveries, and the expansion of political and social rights which enlarged the workforce and markets for the last half of the twentieth century had carried the economy forward, like currents in the sea, over peaks and troughs. Their impetus is now much reduced, leaving the economy on becalmed waters, directionless, with government-supplied liquidity and credit for buoyancy.

What struck me most in 2009, one year into the global crisis, was the incontrovertible evidence that the situation is not self-correcting by the usual operation of cyclical swings between extremes. In 2008, economists anticipated a sharp recession, followed by a return to growth and, a year, later, a fall in unemployment, with good news to report before many governments would have to face the electorate again. Instead, governments confronted the Euro-crisis (2010–11) and deadlines to lift the ceiling on the debt in the United States, continued high unemployment and low levels of investment, pushing back the date when a recovery would come until after 2012. After many false dawns, the timing of a recovery and its strength are still unpredictable.

The crisis of 2008, which has lasted far longer than almost anyone predicted, has shown how unprepared governments were when it erupted. As the crisis unfolded and deepened, my overall impression intensified that this is a crisis of operational culture which can be defined by the range of incompatible and conflicting advice given to decision-makers, by the predictive flaws of models based on the experience of recent decades, by the tension between economic and social trends on the one hand, and electoral calendars on the other. The hopelessness and frustration which have only amplified since 2009 in virtually all western countries and ignited demonstrations and uprisings in London, Athens, New York, Madrid and Tel Aviv show that renegotiating the social contract is no mere technical matter of ceilings on welfare payments or the minimum wage. This working out of imbalances and debt on a global scale is no ordinary crisis. Explanations which focus on finance and regulation are not enough to satisfy the public's need to understand; no wonder simplistic, nationalistic platforms appeal to so many who no longer identify with the political mainstream and the governments it has elected.

A fresh and clear-eyed assessment is needed of what has changed since 1990 and what has not, of assumptions embedded in policy about how cities grow and what to do when they do not, of lessons of experience relevant to the future. Even if there is a widespread recovery in 2016, the crisis has shown that macro-economic and sectoral policies are necessary but not sufficient to generate the growth of urban economies and nurture the sustainable development of cities on which so much rests. I began writing this book by asking why cities did not figure conspicuously in policies for recovery, as had been the case in the Great Depression when the percentage of the population living in cities was far smaller than it is today. Cities are critical to the transition to the economy of the future. Reflecting that the urban transformation covers what must change in cities, as well as their impact on larger systems, my focus shifted to consider economic governance to manage space better. Belief in prosperity as the solution for many if not most problems has been badly shaken; we need a paradigm better suited for the times ahead when the prospect is of more crises – environmental, economic, perhaps social. The reader looking for a wealth of data about the performance of cities and the impact of policies on them will have to wait for other books, to be written some years hence, assuming that the research needed to draw some conclusions will have been carried out. By the same token, references to specific cities illustrate general points; a multitude of examples showing how different cities can be one from the other would only strengthen the argument that uniform, top-down macro-economic and sectoral policies are not sufficient to help cities achieve their potential, including their capacity to survive external shocks and crises. Yes, a larger evidence base would enrich the analysis. But when so many are writing about the crisis and trends for the future from other perspectives, better, I thought, to add to the public culture now, to spur further research and debate.

This is a book with an argument, written with a sense of urgency in the hope that it will be as relevant after it is published, whatever the headlines in the press, as when it was written. A draft was finished by the fall of 2013, then revised between August and December 2014. The main structure and argument remained unaltered in the process, but Chapter 4 and the second part of Chapter 10 changed the most, reflecting the duration and depth of a crisis which has signally failed to provoke either a change in international economic governance or a significant re-evaluation of measures taken, or avoided, between 2008 and 2013.

Thoreau wrote that to walk in the woods in the dark, navigating the mile or so between the village and his hut by the pond, his feet felt the path which his eyes could not see. But of course he meant that the senses we rely on most can deceive us both literally and metaphorically. Thoreau's point was that 'we are constantly, though unconsciously, steering like pilots by certain well-known beacons and headlands, and if we go beyond our usual course we still carry in our minds the bearing of some neighboring cape …'. When we are lost, and maps and charts are of no use, we truly find ourselves.

Contemporary policy in historical perspective

In 1991–92, recession, combined with concerns about the emergence of an urban underclass, de-industrialization and the impact of the end of the Cold War, pushed urban issues to the top of the policy agenda. The historical experience of 1919–22 and of 1945–48 when unemployment skyrocketed and governments were overthrown in revolutions was a sobering point of reference. There was little I could do about any of these issues except explain them in my courses at Michigan State University, where I had joined the history faculty in 1973. In 1992 however I was recruited to the Urban Affairs Division of the Paris-based Organisation for Economic Co-operation and Development (OECD) in the weeks before a major conference on urban economic, social and environmental issues, for which I had to prepare the substantive agenda and background papers. The transition from university to intergovernmental organization, and from teaching and research in history to a second career in public and economic policy and diplomacy, was remarkably smooth. Years later, I understood how my life before I joined the OECD prepared me for it (but that is a story for another book, drawing on personal experience, to explore crises in history and diplomacy). I held several positions with responsibility for urban policies from 1992 to 2003 before becoming Head of Regulatory Policy, the OECD's only multi-disciplinary program (2003–11).

Governments come to the OECD not only to understand technical issues that complicate decision-making and to benefit from the evaluation of policies and practices, but also to look beyond the short term, over the horizon. The relevance of the OECD for current debates rests on its ability to analyse, draw conclusions about and make recommendations on macro-economic and sectoral policies, exploit its unique database, and support policy dialogue, including between its member countries and many emerging and developing economies. OECD reports and publications produced on the responsibility of the Secretary-General, some completed under my supervision or to which I contributed substantially, provide much of the evidence in this book and help inform the narrative and chronology. The Secretariat is committed to the practice of collective responsibility and to the principle of neutrality; reports, in draft or released for publication, reflect the intellectual rigor, evidence and objectivity with which they are prepared, not the opinions and views of individuals or of governments. Permission to use and cite all OECD reports and documents, for which the OECD retains copyright, is gratefully acknowledged. The analysis and contextual interpretation of OECD documents in this book are my own and do not represent the views of the Organisation or of its member countries. Unlike OECD reports and publications, which for the most part have been submitted in draft to a committee of delegates, the opinions expressed and arguments employed in OECD Working Papers are those of the authors.

Whether its advice was sound, whether governments followed its advice, are questions which call for research in many archives; more scholars should study the OECD, not just as a global institution, but for what can be learned about policy innovations, priorities, and failures, and about the conditions favorable to reform in different countries and contexts. Necessarily, mine is more of an insider's view of policy developments that historians with greater detachment may one day analyse, the better to understand decision-making and the tools and techniques which influence it.

History helps us understand the choices that others confronted in the past: historians judge how they acted, given what they knew and the means they had at their disposal; they try to understand why things happened as they did, or, put another way, what could have turned out differently. Decision-makers look for relevant historical analogies based on an informed view of the behavior of societies, economies, and states. But what history? The post-Cold War era showed how impermanent were the arrangements and borders between East and West which even in the late 1980s appeared likely to survive for decades, and, by contrast, how enduring were some other, older fault lines and unifying forces. The seventeenth century – my doctoral field at Princeton University – is strikingly relevant in 2014 when the Ukraine, Catalonia, Ireland and Scotland are on the front pages of the press, when the Westphalia settlement may be unraveling, when there are still struggles to impose the rule of law to check the arbitrary use of power, and when global climate change may lead to significant political as well as social disruption.

Acknowledgments

I was honored to work with many colleagues at the OECD on whose dedication, creativity, courage, discretion, and integrity I could rely. For their encouragement and support to eschew the conventional and the familiar, to take risks, and to keep the big picture in view, I am indebted to the late Jarl Bengtsson for our partnership on "the learning city region", and to Rolf Alter who nurtured the Directorate for Public Governance and Territorial Development from an idea on an organizational chart to a vibrant agency for reform.

James Moore helped me see that a transition from the university to the OECD was both possible and desirable. Thierry Bruhat foresaw the transition I would make to another form of action upon retiring from the OECD. William and Rosellen Monter, Michael and Paula Koppisch, Christopher and Rhoda Friedrichs, Steven Kramer, and Jay and Naomi Pasachoff gave me the strongest encouragement to find my way in a second career at the OECD, and continue their support in retirement. Peter Hall encouraged me to tackle big questions. Sadly, not all have lived to see this book in print. Amy Livingstone Thompson and her family, Gordie, Sam and Will, share our love of history, France, food, and the best literary and civic heritage of the Midwest. Mario and Inés Alanis, whose friendship is an enduring link for me with Mexico, are a special example of culture and compassion in public service and education. Australians Allan and Margaret Rodger, Jan and Mark Schapper, Lyndsay Neilson, Brian and Renate Howe, Chip Kaufman, and Wendy Morris always draw me back to what is at stake for the future.

My wife Isa always knew that cities are the subject I cared about more than others. Together with our sons Eli and Ezra, and Catherine, our daughter-in-law, Isa looked forward to the time after the OECD when I could write again in my own voice. With their questions and comments fresh in mind, I often returned to pen or keyboard, always with greater insight. The flaws that remain reflect my deafness to criticism and my impatience to finish.

The boy who goes to the city is one of the oldest leitmotifs in literature, but, as Thomas Wolfe noted in *The Web and the Rock,* often the great city is really within him before he gets there. I already knew something of large cities while growing up in Ithaca, New York, where my father, Milton R. Konvitz, began teaching at Cornell University a month after I was born in New York City. My interest in cities was formed in my father's library among books he had assembled for their relevance to his work as counsel in the Newark and then New Jersey Housing Authorities in the early 1940s, and for their literary and cultural importance. One of those, *Can Our Cities Survive?* by J. L. Sert (1942) inspired the title of this book: cities can survive more disorganization and destruction than thought possible, but that is no reason to ignore the benefits of strategic planning, the quality of design and of the environment, sound institutions, and far-sighted policies. While I was still in high school searching for an intellectual framework to understand contemporary civilization and a professional vocation to act on it, I was fortunate to read Lewis Mumford's *The Culture of Cities* (1938) and then *The City in History* together with *The Death and Life of Great American Cities* by Jane Jacobs when they appeared in 1961. I realized that the pattern of life I had known as a child in Forest Home, a village of some sixty families, was connected to a multi-faceted, multi-secular urban civilization. What mattered was to understand the unique mix of the particular and universal that described each place within the urban world. (In deciding whether to illustrate this book, I opted to follow Jacobs's example, for text only, rather than Mumford's with its rich portfolios of annotated illustrations.) From books I learned that the city was something one could think about, that no reflection on the city of the present could be undertaken without an understanding of history that includes politics and the economy, that planning and architecture are among the great arts of every epoch, and that the future of cities would be shaped by decisions and choices to be taken here and now.

Shortly before he died in 2003, my father, who lived through the worst and the best of the twentieth century, said that he was a meliorist: things could get better but probably will not. I told him that I remained an optimist. The meliorist, looking back, is probably closer to what happens. To get any change for the better, the optimist, looking ahead, must over-reach.

References

Jacobs, Jane (1961), *The Death and Life of Great American Cities* (New York: Random House).

Mumford, Lewis (1938), *The Culture of Cities* (New York: Harcourt, Brace).

Mumford, Lewis (1961), *The City in History* (New York: Harcourt, Brace and World).

Sert, Jean Luis (1942), *Can Our Cities Survive? An ABC of Urban Problems, Their Analyis, Their Solutions*, based on proposals by CIAM, the Congrès international d'architecture moderne (Cambridge, MA: Harvard University Press).

Thoreau, Henry David, *Walden* (1854), chapter on "The Village" (London: Everyman, 1903).

Abbreviations

APEC	Asia-Pacific Economic Co-operation
ECMT	European Council of Ministers of Transport, now the International Transport Forum
EU	European Union
GDP	gross domestic product
IMF	International Monetary Fund
NBER	National Bureau of Economic Research
OECD	Organisation for Economic Co-operation and Development

Introduction: the difference a crisis makes

In one single year, unemployment in the developed economies belonging to the OECD went from thirty-three to thirty-nine million, mostly concentrated in cities. A small country in Europe saw its economy plunge 10 per cent, several countries in Europe and North America suffered an unprecedented collapse of housing prices leaving many stranded with negative equity, their houses no longer worth financing; bank failures followed. De-industrialization – hollowing-out, offshoring, outsourcing – which went hand-in-hand with growth in developing countries (mostly in Asia), and with the rapid rise of the information-based knowledge economy, made it unlikely that many of those unemployed would ever find work again, or at least not in the factories where they had worked before. Delegates at a global conference on sustainable development in Rio tried to reconcile economic growth and environmental quality.

The year was not 2012, but 1992. Allowing for details – in 1992, Sweden and Finland suffered sharp recessions, in 2012, Portugal, Spain and Greece; the United Nations Conference on the Environment and Development in Rio in 1992 gave the world hope, which twenty years later gave way to frustration at a second Rio conference – the descriptions of 1992 and 2012 are superficially similar. But their context is different. Except for Japan, which began a two-decade period of deflation, 1992 was the second in a three-year recession; 2012 was the fourth year in an evolving crisis – now the second longest since 1929 – which shows no sign of ending soon.

The trigger for the crisis in 2008 – financial systemic risk – was misunderstood at the time. Having failed to anticipate how problems in the housing sector in the United States could lead to a global financial crisis, macro-economists in 2008–9 anticipated a recession with a "V" or "W" profile, with employment picking up a year after a return to growth. Political leaders in 2009–10 expected good economic news before they had to return to the electorate. By 2011, however, the United States was grappling with the problem of its budget, the famous "fiscal cliff," and

Europe with the prospect of a banking and fiscal union to strengthen the Euro. Neither problem, which dominated the news for months, had been anticipated in 2008. By the time the depth and duration of the crisis became apparent, the opportunity for radical reform, either of credit-driven housing markets in the United States or of Eurozone governance, had passed. Structural reforms that worked in the 1990s became more difficult to launch, and less likely to show short-term results. Clearly something outside previous experience happened.

Macro-economic and fiscal policies have yet to build a sustainable recovery. The loss of wealth and confidence will take years to make good. Policy is grounded on the assumption that the correct remedy depends on an accurate diagnosis. But economists disagree about what the problem is. Briefly, one school is largely focused on banks, finance, and debt; another argues that declining productivity, low levels of innovation and infrastructure investment, and blocked structural reforms are holding back growth. Both schools may be right at the same time, because each is focusing on different things. The problem is that the two schools are proposing incompatible remedies, austerity and investment, each with different impacts on cities.

No wonder people are disoriented and confused. When crises erupt, and people do not understand what is happening, they usually respond by:

- asserting that they have no control over external forces
- explaining that in any case they lack the power to act
- hoping that someone else will act, bringing the situation under control
- telling themselves that in any case a disaster may bring benefits, part of a normal process of change
- affirming a belief in the self–correcting tendencies of large, established systems.

When people do not understand what is happening, they fall back on their core values and beliefs to decide what is the threat or danger which they take most personally. No wonder politics are polarized around clusters of issues at the extremes rather than coherently at the center.

Just because there are cycles does not mean that things go back to where they were, restarting the clock. Unfortunately, the distinction between decline and growth in economies gives a false impression that the crisis is over when the recovery is under way. Historians are clearer about the causes of the Great Depression than about when it ended. Tellingly, the most insightful studies of the Great Depression were written only twenty years or more later: the monetary history of the US by Milton Friedman and Anna Schwartz with its trenchant analysis of the period 1928–33 appeared in 1963 (Friedman and Schwartz, 2008). Those of us who have seen the crisis unfold may perceive things differently from what others, with more hindsight, will see. But we have to act on the basis of the knowledge we possess and the wisdom we have, hopefully, acquired.

Cities have been missing from discussions of the crisis of 2008 and its aftermath. In a highly urbanized economy, national statistics and trends largely reflect what happens in cities. National economies suffer when cities under-perform, or, put another way, when cities do not reach their potential, neither do national economies. But cities themselves are invisible in national statistics. The dynamism of many cities – London, Berlin, Boston – has kept the crisis from being worse than it is. But the crisis has also revealed long-standing, widespread deficiencies in urban education, infrastructure, environmental quality and services, and much else, in well-performing and lagging cities alike. To this list of long-standing problems must be added looming problems, issues of growing importance which were in the distant future twenty years ago. These are the new limits to growth.

The crisis exposed basic problems in policy, governance, and institutions which have not been corrected: policy coherence in housing and infrastructure is compromised by the complexity of multi-level governance and of regulatory tools; cross-sectoral co-ordination remains difficult; the demands of the public for greater participation have spilled into the streets; disaster preparedness and risk reduction still reflect the primacy of the nation-state, not the reality of cross-border and global risks. A belief that economic growth will in due course solve urban problems ignores the fact that many problems will remain even if growth accelerates and will certainly worsen if growth falters. Benign neglect is not a sane alternative to a constructive, proactive and visionary urban policy. Years of very low growth will make it difficult to reduce deficits of urban innovation and of infrastructure investment; the outlook of more crises to come, environmental, health, and even economic, makes these deficits more alarming.

The economic facts matter, to be sure, but so does the psychological impact of a crisis – a depression is, well, depressing. People can endure a lot for a cause or a purpose; some economists will argue that a recession can actually do good, by eliminating inefficient firms, bursting an asset bubble and clearing the way for major reforms. But an economic crisis of this order of magnitude seems good for nothing. With less to spend on social welfare, health, education, the environment, infrastructures and pensions, but more demands for those services, there will be sharper political contests over who gets how much and for what, and perhaps lower levels of protection against major risks and catastrophes. There are populists on both the Left and on the Right telling people they are innocent victims of external forces over which they have no control, a message not easily confounded by reasoned, evidence-based debate. The fact is that most people are not prepared to cope with crises at all, or, if so, not for very long.

Cities belong at the center of concern about the crisis, recovery and future global challenges. No state has ever reversed the trend to urbanize except through violent means. What other social body is as central to humanity, now that more than half the world's population is urbanized? How will the damage caused to cities by the crisis be repaired? And how will they function in a very low growth economic environment, providing services to growing numbers of retired people and coping with the long-term unemployed, often people whose workforce skills are inadequate? The stakes are high. Will urban change promote democracy, rule of law, economic growth, social cohesion, and environmental quality? Or will it encourage demagoguery, autocracy, social instability, environmental collapse, and economic decline? Utopia? Or dystopia? Urbanization can be productive, or sterile: each outcome is plausible, and neither is inevitable.

Cities needed attention in the 1990s – the infrastructure deficit

The recession of 1990–92 highlighted the problem of co-ordinating urban development with technological innovation, environmental pressures, regulatory reform, and global economic change. Three disasters in 1992, coincidentally all in the United States, dramatically framed how ill-prepared even the most advanced economies of the world were at that time to meet these challenges. We are perhaps less well placed today.

The year 1992 was that in which a break in the wall of an abandoned utility tunnel under the Chicago River flooded the Chicago Loop (the central business district), when the Rodney King riots which began on 29 April 1992 and left fifty-three dead and over two thousand injured in Los Angeles put questions about the resurgence of an urban underclass on the front page, and when Hurricane Andrew hit Florida on 23–6 August 1992, leaving an estimated $30 billion in damages. Like the recession of 1990–93 itself, each of these events in Chicago, South Florida and Los Angeles is over, but they have had after-shocks.

Of these, the Chicago leak is perhaps the least well known. Work on the Kinzie Street Bridge on 13 April 1992 put pressure on an old, abandoned tunnel wall under the Chicago River. Water – some 250 million US gallons or 950,000 cubic metres – flooded the basements of office buildings, leading to the evacuation of the central business district for three days and including two of the world's most important nodes for buying and selling contracts, the Chicago Board of Trade and the Chicago Mercantile Exchange, disrupting global business. The cost was estimated at nearly $2 billion. This event is called a leak because insurance covers damage from leaks but not floods, making this a very expensive broken pipe. This is not just playing with words. When riots in a few Parisian suburbs in 2005 were called *émeutes* in the press, the implication was that the violence was premeditated and directed against the state, in which case the state and not insurance companies would have to settle claims; if the events were a *manifestation*, a demonstration, then the state would not be liable. In September 2014, the National Railroad Passenger Corporation, known as Amtrak filed claims against insurers to recover damages from Hurricane Sandy which forced the closure of tunnels, interrupting service between New York and Boston for nine days and between New York and New Jersey for five in 2012. The insurers argue that their liability from a flood is limited to $125 million; Amtrak argues that its losses of over $500 million were the result of several events, and that a storm surge is not a flood (*Financial Times*, 2014).

The Chicago leak is emblematic of a huge deficit in infrastructure investment in the western world. On 9 April 1992, just days before the leak, Peter F. Drucker published an op–ed piece in *The Wall Street Journal* entitled "Where the new markets are," highlighting infrastructure, which he defined as "facilities that serve both producers and consumers." Drucker identified information and communication markets, markets for air and water quality and for non-chemical agriculture, for efficient and renewable energy, and to "repair, replenish and upgrade physical infrastructure, especially transportation systems – roads, railroads, bridges, harbors and airports," all on any list today. His recommendation for more privatization, which was very much in the air at the time, underscored that neither government nor business had the resources or the strategic vision to handle this agenda on its own. Much was indeed privatized in the 1990s, but this kind of structural reform – a means to an end – has been a poor substitute for the strategic vision which Drucker, rightly, demanded.

Particular events contain general warning lessons. Hurricane Andrew showed how urbanization in coastal areas magnified the cost of deadly storms. Increasing awareness of global climate change has not yet slowed the migration of people to vulnerable coastal regions; time will tell whether Hurricane Sandy will have this effect. The reconstruction of South Florida since 1992 led to greater segregation and polarization by income, race, and ethnicity. (In 2014, police killings in Ferguson, Missouri, Cleveland, Ohio, and New York City generated in-depth news articles diffused worldwide about persistent racial and class patterns in the United States.) Alarming studies of widening income disparities and high unemployment among young people today show a scary resemblance to Los Angeles' problems of inclusion in the past; the riots in London in August 2011 – or massive street demonstrations in Athens or Madrid – should not have taken so many people by surprise. Nevertheless, single catastrophic events in faraway places give people a false sense of security: they think "it can't happen here."

Two lessons, one obvious and the other less so, can be taken from the comparison of the recession of 1992 and the post-crash crisis since 2007. The first is that economic crises and other catastrophes cannot be disentangled. Managing in a crisis often means responding to many different crises at the same time. It might be optimal to concentrate on one thing at a time, but life is not like that. Ask the Japanese who have had to face the tsunami in Fukushima, tensions with China in the South China Sea, and the consequences of two decades of economic stagnation and deflation. The second is that the experience and memory of a disaster are sufficiently intense to change behavior and have an impact on policy only for a limited time, usually not more than a decade. By 2000, the events of 1992 were no longer having much effect; today they have been forgotten. The years between 1990, say, and 2007, seem remote to people whose parents or grandparents remember the coming down of the Berlin Wall. By 2018 if not sooner, many people will no longer remember what the future looked like before the crisis began. Is this why historian Chris Andrew called "Historical Attention Span Deficit Disorder … the distinguishing intellectual vice of the late twentieth and early twenty-first centuries" (Andrew, 2010: 858)?

The observations of street activity in Jane Jacobs's classic *Death and Life of Great American Cities* (1961) continue to inspire urbanists. Her focus in that and in her later books however was on how experts – economists, educators, policy-makers, and administrators – did so many of the wrong things, and why things should be done differently. Better decision-making was her constant preoccupation. The problem, as Jane Jacobs forcefully articulated in *The Economy of Cities*, is not that cities have problems – cities, by their very nature, generate problems – but that cities are dysfunctional if problems persist and solutions are not sought. "Practical problems that persist and accumulate in cities are symptoms of arrested development," she wrote (Jacobs, 1969: 105). Evidence

Introduction

of past policy failure however often discourages leaders to try again. Defeatism is not only a condition of life for some people in disadvantaged neighborhoods; it is also a political attitude when decision-makers assume that urban policies are a waste of public money.

The well-being of cities and the wealth of nations: America and Europe

Another look at contemporary Chicago highlights (1) the cost to everyone when cities neglect undervalued – and often unique – assets, (2) the need to manage space better and how, and (3) the challenge to apply best practice and find creative solutions. Once locally specific conditions are accounted for, the mix of problems facing Chicago is broadly similar to what many other cities face.

Chicago, together with Osaka, Shanghai, Hamburg, Milan, and Glasgow, was one of the most famous "second cities" in the world in the twentieth century. During its rapid growth after the fire of 1870, Chicago established leadership in engineering and architecture, becoming the manufacturing capital of the United States. At the junction of rail routes connecting the east and west coasts and the Gulf of Mexico, and at the foot of Lake Michigan with access to the resources of the Great Lakes, Chicago provided logistics and market functions with international ramifications. As the city grew along transit routes, it absorbed immigrants, becoming the largest Irish, Greek, and Polish city outside Europe. Newcomers to America enjoyed civic rights including freedom from repression and foreign domination; the great migration of Blacks who moved to Chicago in the 1930s and 1940s enjoyed rights denied them in segregated states. A new civic and social culture enlarged the provision of public services. Pioneering studies of international significance of urban housing, social structures, land use, and political institutions were undertaken in and about Chicago in the twentieth century. And the famous Chicago Plan of Daniel Burnham for the Commercial Club in 1908, a marvelous civic initiative that showed that being visionary in business is practical, set a standard of excellence to communicate in words, maps and drawings how the city could be reshaped to respect the lake front, accommodate the huge demands of transportation on space, and provide people, regardless of class and status, a sense of belonging to a well-ordered metropolis where they could aspire to something more than just a job.

Today however the tri-state Chicago region with 9.5 million people – a mid-size European country – ranks lower in terms of gross domestic product (GDP) per capita than several smaller American centers as well as Los Angeles and New York. Significantly, its real annual GDP growth at 1.6 per cent was lower than the OECD average of 2.6 per cent for metro regions between 2001 and 2007, ranking sixteen out of twenty-nine US metro regions. Had its rate of growth in employment merely been average, it would have generated 600,000 more jobs than it had in 2012 (OECD, 2012: 19, 69–70). There are not enough jobs for the large numbers of high school drop-outs (38.3 per cent in the City of Chicago in 2011, a level among the highest in the United States). "Large numbers of youths and young adults in the region are neither working nor studying, particularly those who are black" (OECD, 2012: 20). A critical handicap for young Blacks is transport: most of the jobs in demand are in places which are poorly connected to where unemployed young people live. Long commuting journeys by car, responsible for nine of ten journeys to work, generate higher costs to business and households, increasing the negative and depressing the positive effects of agglomeration economies (size, density, complexity). Not only is there a mis-match between the public transport infrastructure and suburbanization for workers; road and rail movements for freight are highly congested as well.

The 2012 OECD report on the tri-state Chicago region focused on two problems which make Chicago less able to create jobs and lift incomes: the skills mis-match at the low, medium, and high ends of the workforce spectrum due to uncoordinated and incoherent education and training programming fragmented across state lines and de-linked from business across the region, and an underfunded transit system that needs integrated multi-modal region-wide planning to maximize the seamless, fluid movement of goods, services, and people into, within, and out of the region (OECD, 2012: 21–31). How then can the 20 per cent of the region's population living in high-poverty neighborhoods improve their prospects? And if the level of poverty, strongly linked to race and gender, remains high, how can progress on other fronts improve the region as a whole?

Chicago's economy is at risk in fields which it once dominated. Fifty per cent of US rail freight transits through the region, but the rail infrastructure has been congested for years, and the region is at risk of losing its advantages as other inter-oceanic routes are developed. The region ranks fourth among US metropolitan areas in educational achievement, but it ranks much lower on indices of the skills associated with innovation, a trend illustrated by the fact that it ranks only eleventh among US metro regions in terms of patents per capita. With 1,700 local governments, agencies, and other jurisdictions, the most of any US metropolitan area, the tri-state Chicago region has significant challenges to co-ordinate programs, set priorities, direct funding to the sectors where it will lift productivity and growth; indeed many of the services which had helped the region develop and which benefited millions are no longer sustainable fiscally.

Both the United States and Western Europe face the urban agenda of the twenty-first century with advantages and constraints, but they are not the same ones. Europe, with the world's oldest and densest urban network, is an urban civilization to a greater degree than the United States. After 1990, and for reasons which only partly have to do with the end of the Cold War, Europe took the lead from the United States in many aspects of urban development. In Europe, many cities antedate nation-states as the oldest form of democracy. In no other civilization are there as many cities; nowhere else are people in one city so near to their neighbors in other cities; in no other civilization has the level of urbanization been so high for so long. To learn how to manage better in a highly urbanized world, there is no going around the European experience. Here are three examples:

- De-industrialization in both Europe and the US liberated vast swaths of land, often contaminated, in dense urban areas; insurance and regulatory practices in Europe, combined with novel forms of public–private partnership and imaginative design, returned many sites to new commercial and residential uses more quickly than in America. Rotterdam, for example, has undergone its second rebuilding since its destruction in 1940.
- Since the mid-1990s, most European countries (including France and Germany) increased their stock of knowledge workers in research and development at a faster rate than the US; in less than two decades, several (including Denmark and Finland) have reached a higher percentage than that of the United States of people working in research and development.
- The spatial shape of the European economy has been transformed by the construction of high-speed train lines along the great axes from Hamburg to Rome, London to Munich, Paris to Amsterdam, expanding local labor markets and creating new opportunities for firms: the whole can be bigger than the sum of the parts when connectivity compensates for the smaller size of individual cities. In this respect the Old World has more in common than the New with the Far East – China, Korea, Chinese Taipei, Japan. Trains in Europe at up to four hours are competitive against planes. By contrast, inter-city travel times in the United States are unchanged over decades.

Many of the programs to achieve change in Europe may look technocratic, but in fact they were highly political. On 19–20 November 1993, Jacques Delors devoted one of a series of high-level symposia about the future of Europe to "The City in European Society." Looking ahead thirty years, Delors posed several questions to the participants:

- how cities, with their historical presence, can help shape our identity in today's world
- what value is added by cities to economic development and how networks between cities help
- whether contemporary cities can meet the needs of people and enhance their well-being, while also reducing societal problems
- how public–private partnerships and other forms of co–operation can help cities reclaim greater autonomy
- how individual citizens can contribute to the development of their cities. (based on *En quête de l'Europe*, 1994: 154)

There was not then, nor is there today, anything uniquely European about these questions; Americans have been asking them too. The same concerns about the rise of an urban underclass are felt in Brussels, Berlin, and Milan, as in St Louis, Los Angeles, and New York. But in Europe after the Cold War, the substantive role of the Commission through regional policy, research, and the environment, and the creation of the single market (as well as, in due course, the Euro), forced national governments, as well as cities and regions in the member states, to develop policy frameworks through which European initiatives, regulations, and funding could flow – and this in addition to specifically national urban policies. In the United States, cities are, literally, incorporated entities in the separate states; the Constitution does not mention the city at all. Subsidiarity, meaning that decisions should be taken at the level closest to the citizens affected, could imply that the institutions of the European Communities should have little to do with cities. But there remains a legitimate role for both national and supra-national institutions in urban affairs: subsidiarity, after all, implies a linkage between the European, national, and sub-national levels because transport and labor mobility on the one hand, and inequality and regional disadvantage on the other, affect the functioning of the single market.

Bringing cities into the European agenda helped span the gaps between centrally controlled and market economies, across generations, between the industrial and the knowledge economy, and between formerly totalitarian and long-standing democratic systems. With the passage of time it is difficult to recollect what it was like to travel or do business in a world divided into First, Second, and Third World categories, resembling the standard of comfort and the level of respect accorded the passengers in three classes on pre-1945 trains. It is not just that 1989 introduced a new periodization in western history, demarcating a new "before-and-after" date similar to 1914 or 1945; the reunification of Europe meant that much twentieth-century history had to be revised in the light of what could be learned and understood after 1989 about the period between 1933 and 1989. For example, the history of architecture in the twentieth century written in the postwar era gave far greater emphasis to the transatlantic connections between Western Europe and the United States, at the expense of developments in Central and Eastern Europe which until 1939–45 were part of the same exploration of how to build and house people in the contemporary city. For decades, Mies's Barcelona House could be seen; the Tugendhat House in Brno could not. This reconnection through urban history is as important in those parts of Europe that always remained free as in Portugal and Spain (fascist until 1974–75) or in Central and Eastern Europe. During the 1990s, older buses from Poland and the Czech Republic brought visitors to Paris for the first time; thousands from the West went to Prague, Krakow, and Warsaw. Until reunification, Berlin was divided not only by a wall but by two different logics of mobility. In the East people could ride to the top of the radio tower at Alexanderplatz and survey the vast, flat expanse of both Berlins, but they did not have cars to get around on the ground. People in the West had cars – fast cars – but could only drive to the edge of their zone and back. Mobility and the infrastructures to facilitate it have political and cultural as well as economic significance for post-1990 Europe.

It is not a question of saying that one continent – Europe or America – is superior to the other. Their respective handicaps – the dysfunctional budget reform process in the United States and the imperfect monetary union in the European Union (EU) – highlight similar problems of political reform. When it comes to how to manage cities and create economic and social benefits on the basis of the connections between cities, their network effects, Europe and the United States begin the twenty-first century from different starting positions. Chicago does have Millennium Park. If Chicago were in the Ruhr, the Netherlands, Sweden, or France, however, its brownfields would have been converted to housing and facilities for small to medium enterprises (SMEs) in expanding sectors serving as a link between the region's universities and its manufacturing base and attracting inward investment for research and development; new rapid rail routes and tramways would connect suburbs to suburbs and older urban districts through new networks; more museums and cultural centers would have been built both downtown and in other parts of the region; the city-region would have a strong image internationally based on its lakeside setting, its architectural heritage, and its promise as a design center to help cities worldwide find a better balance between land and water; its multi-jurisdictional patchwork would have been simplified; it might even have won the bid for the 2016 Olympic Games.

When cities around the world are inter-dependent, urban policy is no longer exclusively domestic

The Organisation for Economic Co-operation and Development (OECD) broadened the focus of its work on urban policies in the 1990s to include both global competitiveness and sustainable development. The OECD was created in 1960 to succeed the Organisation for European Economic Co-Operation, established in 1948 to administer the Marshall Plan. In contrast to the twin Bretton Woods institutions, the International Monetary Fund and the World Bank, the OECD is not a lending institution; its assets are intellectual. The OECD has a kind of genetic code based on historical experience: that economic policy errors in the interwar era contributed to the rise of fascism and the resort to military aggression. Contemporary concerns about widening inequality, amplified by electorates which are increasingly alienated from government, are the latest sign that a focus on the economy is not an end in itself but an essential dimension of peace, democracy, and human development. Yes, there is an element of idealism in this.

The OECD is frequently misrepresented in the press as a think tank or as the club of rich (or mostly rich) countries; as an intergovernmental organization, neither label is satisfactory. The average GDP of member countries of the OECD was US$33,023 in 2009, but this average included Mexico at $14,388, Poland at $18,925 and Turkey at $14,218 as well as Luxembourg, Switzerland, Australia, and the United States, well above the average. The country whose GDP came closest to the OECD average in 2009 was Italy, at $32,413 – hardly an average country then or since, in economic or political terms. As an intergovernmental organization, its agenda is set in capitals, not by the Secretariat. Governments can be surprisingly open to take a critical look at what they are doing. The diplomatic challenge lies in creating a confidential arena where governments discuss, evaluate and compare domestic policies (with the exception of culture, defense, and justice as regalian rights) in light of longer-term trends as well as of short-term forecasts. With a focus on structural reform and using its unique peer review process, the OECD helps its member governments (twenty-four in 1992, thirty-four in 2014) to discuss and compare domestic policy amongst themselves in committees which bring together experts and senior officials from capitals, not as an academic exercise, but as leverage to set priorities and implement reforms. The general public is more aware of its macro-economic forecasts than of its work on global risks, environmental issues, regulatory policy, innovation, urban and regional development, agricultural subsidies, fisheries, health policy, pensions, employment, trade, investment, development assistance, fiscal policy, or corporate governance – a list that cannot be exhaustive. As the amount of data has expanded together with evidence of what works in policy and what doesn't, benchmarking and indicators have taken on greater importance. In principle, the OECD has nothing to say about the constitutional or administrative arrangements of its members; over the years, however, it has paid more attention to institutions and governance arrangements that have a positive effect on the design and implementation of reforms. By providing data, often on topics which have never been compared internationally, the OECD questions conventional wisdom and challenges governments to pursue options which they might not have considered. Weighing the costs of doing nothing against the benefits of change, the OECD helps officials and politicians understand the consequences of policy choices, but the choice of policies remains that of the governments (Woodward, 2009; Carroll and Kellow, 2011; Bocquet, 2012; Pal, 2012).

The role of the United States in past decades to put urban issues at the top of the agenda of the OECD has been all but forgotten. Cyrus Vance as Secretary of State took this initiative in the annual Ministerial meeting in 1977. Vance was concerned that governments were not paying enough attention to the decline of manufacturing in major cities and its legacy of environmental and social problems, and to the potential of new technology as a basis for future urban development. A comprehensive approach to urban issues was necessary, he argued, to help sustain the positive contribution of cities to economic welfare. The American position recognized that when urban problems are simply absorbed into sectoral economic, political, and environmental categories, the overall outcome "may well be worse than the status quo. As opposed to what may be called a sector-by-sector approach, the advantage of an 'urban' approach to such issues is its comprehensiveness; this presumably allows for an effective consideration of their essential interrelationships and mutual interactions" (OECD, 1978).

The Vance initiative met with favorable attention on the part of many members of the OECD. The Council, composed of ambassadors to the OECD, set up the Group on Urban Affairs as a Committee in the Environment Directorate; work continued in the 1980s focusing on urban land markets, innovation and infrastructure in industrial centers, and environmental problems including pioneering work on urban noise, and on ageing in cities. (There is always a question whether urban issues are best in the hands of experts who know a lot about how cities function but less about separate policy areas such as education, health, environment, communications technology, etc., or in the hands of experts in fields which have an impact on cities but who know little about how cities function.) The Reagan administration, which took office in 1981, did not share the belief that national governments had much to do with an urban agenda; a bias in favor of market-based, state, and local solutions continued through the administration of George H. W. Bush. When Bill Clinton was elected in 1992, a year that put Chicago, Los Angeles, and Miami on the front pages of the world press, there was high expectation that his administration would renew the interest of the federal government in urban issues.

The depth of the crisis in 1992 was alarming. The hopes for a peace dividend from the end of the Cold War having vanished, governments were eager to find a strategy which would buy time in expectation of a recovery. But they also needed to assess, soberly, the damage the crisis was causing to society and the economy. Perhaps it was the reunification of Berlin, perhaps the Los Angeles riots, perhaps the Barcelona Olympics, perhaps the impact of the Rio summit on sustainable development: urban issues rose higher on the policy agenda.

In November 1992, the Secretary-General of the OECD, Jean-Claude Paye, chaired a two-and-a-half-day conference on urban economic, environmental, and social problems. Two points received widespread assent: that urban policies have failed to keep pace with urban change and with the growth of the global economy; and that a well-rounded national economic strategy cannot ignore the spatial structure of the economy, or the qualities and characteristics of cities that affect environmental conditions, social cohesion and economic performance (OECD, 1994, 1995). The implications were clear: national governments need policies for cities, not in a remedial effort to correct their shortcomings and deficiencies, but proactively, to enhance their assets and develop their potential; and policies must take account of the size, complexity, and rapid rate of change of cities, their exposure to external shocks and global and local risks, and their ability to generate and absorb innovation.

To champion the integration of cities into the mainstream sectoral and macro-economic work of the OECD – an institution focused on and governed by central governments – required the support of many countries. In 1994, the Urban Affairs Division (in the Environment Directorate since its inception), together with other units in the OECD on regional and rural policy and on local initiatives for employment, were brought together to compose the Territorial Development Service (since 2002, part of the Directorate for Public Governance and Territorial Development). In the mid-1990s, the OECD was the premier arena where governments reached consensus on key urban priorities, using case studies, thematic analyses, and indicators to understand trends and target policy interventions. The OECD Australia Conference on Cities and the New Global Economy, in Melbourne, 1994, was the largest world meeting between the two United Nations (UN) summits on human settlements, Vancouver 1976 and Istanbul 1996, and arguably one of the first at which western countries engaged with emerging economies such as China and Indonesia to discuss the future of urban development. ("Cities and the New Global Economy," 1995). At the Habitat II Summit on Human Settlements in Istanbul in 1996, when many developing countries argued for growth first before investing in environmental quality, OECD countries offered their experience to make the point that in the long run it is better to reduce high environmental costs while going for growth – knowing that, in the short run, the economic trumps the social. OECD reports on sustainable urban development steered by Germany, Denmark, and Sweden (OECD, 1996) and on distressed urban areas (OECD, 1998) led by the United States under Peter Edelman, Counsellor of the Department of Health and Human Services, highlighted how data and indicators could help public officials co-ordinate different forms of intervention such as education, health, spatial planning, and employment to reduce social and environmental costs, and how unconventional, innovative policies could be tested, proved, and mainstreamed. Some of the issues raised in the 1990s remain on the international agenda: housing, environmental degradation, new technology; others have risen in importance: regulation and governance, transparency and anti-corruption, education, population ageing, natural disasters.

The last decade of the twentieth century ended on a more optimistic tone than it had started, when books were written about the decline of America, and debates about whether the middle class in western countries had a future filled the newspapers. "Many Americans fear US living standards have stopped rising; they believe their children face a tougher future", ran the headline of the *Wall Street Journal*, in 1989. In an ironic twist, and perhaps an unconscious one, the article appeared on the first of May – a day celebrated worldwide except in the United States and Canada as Labor Day. Eighteen months later, *The Economist* published a survey on American living standards, "Running to stand still," which is pretty much what has happened for a generation, as echoed by Edward Luce writing about the end of the American dream (*The Economist*, 1990; *Financial Times*, 2010).

The world welcomed the twenty-first century with hope, and, a year later, the introduction of the Euro demonstrated how Europe could manage one of the most extraordinary logistical feats in modern history successfully. The return to growth in the mid-1990s took much of the pressure off fundamental policy reform, at least in respect of urban issues – with the notable exception of regulatory reform to accommodate privatization in public services. (Regulatory reform benefited from strong support from finance ministries and the private sector but also encountered opposition from the public and criticism from the media.) When the OECD Territorial Development Committee met in July 2003, it endorsed an American proposal to change the emphasis in the program of work away from a focus on sustainable urban development and toward the factors of competitiveness.

Crises as the new normal

The growing frequency and severity of disasters is perhaps the most important line of continuity between the 1990s and the second decade of the twenty-first century. Forest fires or earthquakes may occur naturally, but how cities are built and organized, and where, has a lot to do with their vulnerability to disasters of different kinds. How societies and states respond will have a significant bearing on the kind of urban growth we will have.

Crises are as normal as their absence. Carmen Reinhart and Kenneth Rogoff (2009) made the point that people are deluding themselves when they believe that crises are the result of some malfunction which can be corrected so that they will not recur. Reinhart and Rogoff were referring to economic cycles driven by high levels of debt, but their point applies to many other types of crisis and catastrophe. Yes, there is nothing new in history: spectacular financial crashes occurred in the eighteenth, nineteenth and twentieth centuries as well as dramatic natural disasters – floods, earthquakes, crop failures, droughts, floods – some more costly in life and larger in territorial impact than anything we have recently known. Once we accept that they are not freak events, or signs of divine punishment, it is possible to study crises like other phenomena that have certain normative characteristics. Crises can be analysed for what they reveal of how well societies cope with the unexpected, and for what needs to be done to reduce costs and damages in the future.

What makes an event a crisis? The scale of the event, for one thing: beyond deaths and injuries, beyond physical destruction, there are three parameters: what needs to be done outside normal channels and procedures to cope with it, or in other words, the extent to which it upsets conventional life; whether the event reveals anomalies and flaws in systems which were known but had gone uncorrected, or brings to light new problems which must be addressed to reduce the impact or frequency of a crisis in the future; and the time and effort needed to resolve it. Some events are of such a magnitude as to place the future of the state and society in question; others of a lesser scale can have a similar effect if they discredit segments of society or the government. The human, social dimensions of a crisis matter, well, critically to their political and cultural impact; the lines of transmission have interested sociologists and psychologists since the nineteenth century in efforts to define the modern city and the crowd. It can be difficult to determine when a crisis ends because the aftershocks have long-lasting effects: crises lead to investigations which help us understand better how we live, in what kind of institutional and legal framework, and whether we have the resources – mental, social, cultural as well as material – to cope with the unexpected. Thus, crises which ended decades ago may still generate research: think of the French Revolution, or the Great Depression, which are often reinterpreted in the light of current events. When several crises reveal a pattern that explodes conventions and assumptions about how things should work, the expectation of future disasters only adds to an underlying anxiety. We may be at a point of rupture or discontinuity when, to bring the level of uncertainty and distrust down to manageable levels, a fundamental change in paradigms for public policy and urban development becomes the task of a generation.

Just looking at natural disasters, one major category of crisis, Swiss Re, the insurance company, recorded forty-six major events between 1970 and 1999, each with damages in excess of $1 billion; of these thirty-two occurred between 1989 and 1999 (Swiss Re, 2000). In the last year of the twentieth century, seven catastrophes involved damages of more than $1 billion. Gales in northwest Europe, 25 January to 26 February 1990, took 120 lives and cost $10.5 billion in damages. In February 1995, floods in northwest Europe – the worst in the Netherlands since 1953, when two thousand drowned and thirty thousand were displaced – raised questions about land-use changes and planning practices. Floods in the Mississippi Valley of the US which cost $12 billion made 150,000 homeless and changed settlement patterns. The Northridge California earthquake of 17 January 1994 killed fifty-six people, left 25,000 homeless, and disrupted water and transport networks at a cost of $30 billion.

The Great Hanshin earthquake which devastated Kobe a year later killed over six thousand (mostly elderly) people, far many more people than had been anticipated in forecasts of earthquake damages; three hundred thousand were made homeless; maritime and industrial activity was interrupted, and, in some cases, shifted permanently elsewhere. Property costs reached $100 billion, the most costly disaster of the 1990s. At the end of the decade, an earthquake in Turkey on 13 March 1999 killed four thousand and left 180,000 homeless; the August 1999 earthquake in the Izmit region killed over fifteen thousand and cost over $20 billion in property losses.

The greater frequency and intensity of disasters over the last two decades is now beyond dispute. Of course, there are more insured assets in wealthier countries and prosperous cities. Nevertheless, greater population density, often in vulnerable areas such as coastal zones, highlights a factor that most people prefer to ignore: governments are reluctant to restrict development in vulnerable regions if people, for whatever reason, want to live there. And earthquakes, floods, fires, and similar natural catastrophes are but one of a list of crises ranging from industrial accidents to systemic risk in finance and global epidemics which will shape the urban policy agenda for decades. Well might *The Economist* begin 2012 with a leader on "The rising cost of catastrophes" and a policy brief on natural disasters, highlighting the exposure of cities. The newspaper cited evidence from Munich Re that the cost of natural disasters in 2011 of $378 billion broke the previous record of $262 billion in 2005. Cities can survive more disorganization and destruction than thought possible, but that is no reason to neglect or under-invest in preparedness. Governments are advised to get priorities right, put more emphasis on pre-disaster preparedness, resist private interests when they want to promote development in vulnerable areas, and forswear measures such as subsidies and implicit insurance protection which reduce the incentives for individuals and firms to act more responsibly. All very sensible; will it happen?

For decades, if not centuries, war has been the biggest threat to cities: sieges, bombardment, starvation, epidemics in time of war mark the popular consciousness and historical memory. In the past century, the destruction of Leuven and Rotterdam, the siege of Leningrad, the fire bombing of Tokyo and Hamburg, the occupation and battle of Warsaw, the wartime famine of Calcutta and the nuclear apocalypse of Hiroshima and Nagasaki stand out. The defense of cities against attack is pre-eminently a matter for nation-states, which monopolize weapons of mass destruction. But, as current fighting in Syria and Iraq shows, forces which lack nuclear weapons can still capture cities. Other threats fit less well into international law and relations, which historically have been shaped by concerns about military aggression and stability. National borders no longer define where the responsibility of governments ends. When the tsunami in Indonesia in 2005 killed Swedes and Swiss on vacation, their governments, which had the legal means to act in an emergency within their borders, had to improvise to extend help to citizens in a foreign country. In fact it was the government of Stockholm and not the national administration which mobilized the Swedish relief effort. What may happen to city–state relations and to collective security in an era when cross-border, non-military risks are the greatest threat to cities?

There are two new economies in the 1990s, both heavily concentrated in cities. The new economy everyone refers to is the global economy of innovation, communications technologies, falling barriers to global trade and investment. The growth economy puts pressure on government to reduce the size of the public sector, decentralize, carry out structural reforms, remove non–tariff barriers to trade and competition, and improve public services. In the past, economies that are more open, more innovative, more global, recovered from crises better than those that were less so. The new economy that people ignored, at least until 11 September 2001, is the economy of security, marked by tougher policing and a larger prison population, the spreading use of CCTV and other forms of surveillance, efforts to control money laundering, identity checks for travel, "enclaves" or privately owned and protected residential and commercial sites with restricted access, and improved measures to respond to disasters, all involving rising public expenditure as well as greater costs and regulatory burdens on citizens and the private sector (at significant, non-discretionary cost), and greater centralization. Both new economies of growth and security are necessary to cope with risk. The problem is that the two economies can get in each other's way: the growth of the security state can compromise the very forces of adaptation and resilience which have enabled cities to overcome challenges in the past. Cutbacks in public services which appear unavoidable in many countries will only aggravate this trend.

The future is dominated by the prospect of crises and knowledge of how damaging they could be to cities. There is no sense in pretending they won't happen; they will, even if we cannot predict when and where. Preparedness is a state of mind, a latent capacity in social and economic systems. Our ability to anticipate the likelihood of any particular catastrophe is greater, our knowledge of past disasters is better, but our understanding of how to reduce risks to cities and the costs of disasters if they occur is still very elementary. The Candide effect tells us that we are living in the best of all possible worlds; the Micawber effect however is more insidious, lulling us into a false sense of security in the belief that a solution will turn up in time. We know what won't work: a series of incremental measures that postpone costly and unpopular measures in the hope that "the big one" will miss us, or will come decades hence, or will be diminished in impact by some wondrous technological invention.

The crisis agenda has to be seen in the light of demographics. The world's population of 200 million in the Year One reached a take-off point of one billion around 1800. Doubling by 1927, global population, when marked on a graph, swept upward on a steep curve. In 1987, the world's population reached five billion, double the number in 1950, and seven billion in 2011 with forecasts of nine billion in 2050. In a parallel trend, more than half the world's population lived in cities by 2007, with developing countries accounting for 95 per cent of new urban growth. Every year, the number of people living in cities increases by sixty million, approximately the population of France. To put this in perspective, in 1995 there were only a few mega-cities with more than ten million people in OECD countries, of which two were in Asia (Seoul and Tokyo). By 2025, Asia alone will have twenty mega-cities. In 1800, only London and Beijing, and perhaps Paris, had more than one million inhabitants. There were seventy-five cities of this size in 1950, and over four hundred in 2008.

We are in new territory. It has been conventional to say that there has been a compression of time: coping with the short term takes up so much energy and time that there is little of either to devote to agendas for the medium and long term. Another oft-cited phenomenon is the extent to which historical landmarks and figures which once served as clear signposts have receded from view, making it more difficult to find our way forward. What has not received as much attention is the acceleration of spatial change. The fixed quality of national borders gives the misleading impression that the wealth and population of a nation may increase or decrease but not its territory. (One is reminded of how Louis XIV reacted with equanimity when, at his request, maps of a superior quality were made which showed that France was in fact smaller than previously believed.) Two key variables of spatial change have shifted in recent years. The first is linked to urbanization, which alters the distribution of people and land uses, often dramatically and at a rate that rapidly makes policy frameworks obsolete. The second, also linked to urbanization, concerns the impact of global warming on glaciers, the polar ice caps, sea coasts, the distribution of rainfall, and more. Our culture and indeed our politics have yet to adjust to the acceleration of spatial change. Although change is global, this book focuses on cities in OECD countries because their history and the dynamics of policy-making are distinctive. The problems facing countries in Africa, Latin America and Asia with rapid urban growth merit separate study. The problem-solving efforts in OECD countries to improve and adapt cities, promote urban strategies which contribute to overall growth, and reduce the amplitude and cost of crises in the future are issues of wider interest because leadership in urban innovation and policy probably still rests with developed countries in Asia-Pacific, Europe and North America. A sustainable recovery depends on getting these right.

A word about words is in order. In English and in French, cities are distinguished from suburbs even though some suburbs are as old as many cities, and most have the same legal status. But we recognize that cities and suburbs have different connotations in culture. Some of the suburbs of Paris – *banlieues* – are associated with intractable social problems, others are richer on a per capita basis than Paris itself, but the word *banlieue* is misused as a blanket label as if all suburbs were dangerous, when the reality is of great heterogeneity and diversity. Suburbs are a natural phenomenon associated with urban growth when density reaches certain limits, consistent with the desire of many people to enjoy low-rise living with gardens, and with the zonal segregation of some economic and social activities from others. The same people who may prefer to live in suburbs when raising children want to move closer to the city center in retirement; children raised in suburbs may want to live in cities, or in suburbs – the trends are not unilinear over time, making predictions about who will want to live where, taking account of changes in family demographics, hazardous. Both cities and suburbs have their place. Size does not tell us much: there are small cities and populous suburbs. The negative features of most suburbs are often the same as those of some parts of many cities: mono-functionality, unmanageably small jurisdictions given their responsibilities, dependency on one mode of transport. Suburbs can be rebuilt to have many of the benefits of cities – greater economic and social diversity, better public sector management and accountability, and transport-oriented development. What matters to both cities and suburbs is connectivity – between places, and for people. Ultimately, cities and suburbs alike survive because people have created assets in them that give them added value, and help them survive through adaptation. In this book, the word "city" covers both center cities and different kinds of peri-urban expansion, stretching from suburbs which, like many in the first ring of Paris, are visibly indistinguishable from Paris itself, to industrial and residential suburbs, satellite cities within a metropolitan region, and edge cities or ex-urban places. Each type has its own specificity but for the purposes of the arguments made in this book about cities, nation-states and economies and economic governance, the distinctions among them are implicit, not explicit.

Books about cities either adopt a pessimistic or an optimistic point of view, a pattern extending back in time at least to the early nineteenth century. Henry G. Cisneros, former mayor of San Antonio, Texas, and Secretary of the US Department of Housing and Urban Development in President Clinton's first term, edited a book the year after the Rodney King riots in Los Angeles called *Interwoven Destinies: Cities and the Nation* (1993) with an optimistic view about the potentially positive impact of federal legislation combined with local initiatives to deal with transportation, education, employment and other issues. Two years later, Jonathan Barnett, professor of urban design at the City College of New York, published *The Fractured Metropolis* (1995) whose concluding chapter, a national agenda for action, reads today as a list of things that were not done. These two tropes continue to shape the study of the city: Edward Glaeser's *The Triumph of the City* (2011) and Leo Hollis's *Cities Are Good for You: The Genius of the Metropolis* (2013) are defined by their titles; many academic works influenced by postmodernist theory and criticism argue that cities contain polarizing, irreconcilable extremes, generating the sources of their problems. How we think about cities is inseparable from values and judgments about the role of government to secure individual freedom and social justice. People who favor less government intervention may be more likely to emphasize how well cities perform, implying that specific policies are not necessary; those advocating more intervention may highlight how overwhelming urban problems are. Both points of view focus on people, emphasizing how cities nurture or frustrate their personal development. When we ask what kind of city we want in the future, we are in fact asking what kind of society to we want to live in.

References

Andrew, Christopher (2010), *The Defense of the Realm: The Authorized History of MI5* (London: Penguin).
Barnett, Jonathan (1995), *The Fractured Metropolis* (New York: Harper Collins).
Bocquet, Dominique (2012), *Pour une mondialisation raisonnée: les révolutions discrètes de l'OCDE* (Paris: La Documentation française).
Carroll, Peter and Aynsley Kellow (2011), *The OECD: A Study of Organisational Adaptation* (Cheltenham and Northampton, MA: Edward Elgar).

Cisneros, Henry G. (1993), *Interwoven Destinies: Cities and the Nation* (New York: W. W. Norton).

"Cities and the new global economy: implications of the OECD–Australia Conference" (1995), prepared by the Australian Housing and Urban Research Institute for the Commonwealth Department of Housing and Regional Development (Canberra: Australian Government Publishing Service), linked to "Urban Futures: Issues for Australian Cities," *Urban Futures*, 19 (August 1995).

The Economist (1990), "American living standards running to stand still," 10 November.

The Economist (2012), "The rising cost of catastrophes" and a policy brief on natural disasters, 14 January.

En quête de l'Europe (1994), Cellule de Prospective, Commission Européene, in the series Les Carrefours de la science et de la culture (Rennes: Editions Apogée, 1994); "La ville dans la société européene," pp. 151–81.

Financial Times (2010), Edward Luce, "Goodbye, American Dream," 31 July–1 August.

Financial Times (2014), "Amtrak fights insurers over superstorm fallout," 25 September.

Friedman, Milton and Anna Jacobson Schwartz (2008), *The Great Contraction, 1929–1933*, with a new preface by Anna Jacobson Schwartz and a new introduction by Peter L. Bernstein (Princeton: Princeton University Press).

Glaeser, Edward (2011), *The Triumph of the City: How Our Greatest Invention Makes Us Richer, Smarter, Greener, Healthier and Happier* (London: Penguin).

Hollis, Leo (2013), *Cities are Good for You: The Genius of the Metropolis* (New York and London: Bloomsbury Press).

Jacobs, Jane (1961), *The Death and Life of Great American Cities* (New York: Random House).

Jacobs, Jane (1969), *Economy of Cities* (New York: Random House).

Mumford, Lewis (1938), *The Culture of Cities* (New York: Harcourt, Brace).

Mumford, Lewis (1961), *The City in History: Its Origins, Its Transformations and Its Prospects* (New York: Harcourt, Brace and World).

OECD (1978), Secretary-General of the OECD, Note, "Urban Concerns," 12 May; copy in the author's possession.

OECD (1994), *Cities for the 21st Century*, includes most of the oral statements and written papers of the 1992 conference (Paris: OECD). ISBN: 92-64-14287-8.

OECD (1995), "Urban issues: a priority for the political agenda," DT/UA (95)7, 4 September, note prepared by the Secretariat for the 27th Session of the Group on Urban Affairs.

OECD (2012), *The Chicago Tri-State Metropolitan Area* (Paris: OECD), box 1.3, pp. 69–70. DOI: 10.1787/9789264170315-en.

OECD (1996), *Innovative Policies for Substainable Urban Development: The Ecological City* (Paris: OECD).

Pal, Leslie A. (2012), *Frontiers of Governance: The OECD and Global Management Reform* (London: Palgrave Macmillan).

Reinhart, Carmen and Kenneth Rogoff (2009), *This Time Is Different: Eight Centuries of Financial Folly* (Princeton: Princeton University Press).

Swiss Re (2000), "Catastrophes naturelles et techniques en 1999," *Sigma*, 2.

Wall Street Journal (1992), by Peter Drucker, "Where the new markets are," 9 April.

Woodward, Richard (2009), *The Organisation for Economic Co-operation and Development* (New York: Routledge).

PART I

If cities are like dynamos, why is the economy sputtering?

1

We are where we are, but how did we get here?

If cities are the motors of the economy, how are they powered?

Dynamo, motor, generator: if cities are the motors of the economy, why are they neglected in policy agendas for a sustainable recovery? That cities are underperforming is beyond dispute at a time when unemployment remains high and the economy is running well below capacity. Wait for the problems in finance and credit to be resolved and for deficits to go down, the logic goes, and urban economies will start to expand again, adding jobs. To avoid a complete collapse and a long depression in 2008–9, the priority had to be on the financial sector and banking. That phase of the crisis is over, but not the crisis itself. Something else is happening.

Like many metaphors, the image of the city as generator oversimplifies an important truth. Because electricity cannot be stored, supply and demand must be balanced continuously in a system of inter-connected networks. This calls for monitoring within a range of variations which can be predicted on the basis of past experience. The highly centralized and bureaucratic system of control at the center where vast networks are co-ordinated came to represent the transformation of knowledge and work through science and technology – the expert or professional who can process information, react or anticipate as the circumstance dictates exercises considerable authority over the rest of society. This activity or function is an example of regulation in the form of interventions to keep a system operating normally.

Applied to urban economies, the regulatory function has become largely a matter of macro-economic settings, including fiscal and monetary policy and the stock of regulations that affect what can be built and where, competition in markets, standards of goods and services, and much else. Macro-economic indicators reinforce the importance of temporal change in the things that economists measure such as GDP, unemployment, investment, trade, etc. These policy frameworks however are space-blind; they do not take the needs and opportunities of specific cities into account, reflecting a map of the world divided into nation-states as if space is fixed and stable. But it is not. During the half century since the most recent division of Europe at the end of World War Two, national borders may not have not changed much but the physical world has, and rapidly, as the effects of global warming under the influence of industrial activity and urban growth have melted glaciers and the polar ice caps. And cities have evolved, too, some becoming more compact, others spreading out over a larger area and, in both cases, altering in the process the agglomeration effects which matter for productivity and specialization. To ignore space is to overlook both the benefits and costs associated with spatial change. Economic governance as we know it is ill-equipped to help decision-makers in the private and public sectors manage space better, which has become imperative.

The image of the dynamo came to symbolize the importance of electricity and other services in the modern city. These invisible services, a form of modern labor-saving magic, run virtually automatically, or at least without the need for those who use them to intervene in their production: we do not haul water or wood, put coal in furnaces, carry out chamber pots, or run our own generators, but set dials, turn knobs, flick switches, and pull levers. Gone the equally graphic image of smokestacks in the nineteenth century, or earlier, of towers for churches or the houses of nobility. The sound of smooth motorized traffic superseded the bang and din of steam engines or the ring of bells. But each of these images – dynamo, piston – took on deeper symbolic meaning because each corresponded to a different power structure, or, more to the point, alluded to the source of power and authority in the city. Electricity and other essential public services are available reliably and uninterruptedly without our need to request them. Big data, albeit with greater measures for public participation, are merely the latest version of an asymmetric system in which information confers power to manage cities.

The metaphor of the city as a machine which does not stop and go but performs almost on its own is a key to understanding why in a highly urbanized economy governments pay so little attention to cities. To be clear at the outset: the city that runs 24/7 may fit New York and Tokyo as the embodiment of a perpetual machine. The visitor has the impression of a stressful environment, of frenetic activity, of extremes in wealth, behavior, and style, the sense that anything can happen anywhere, phenomena which express the modernity of large, dense cities since Paris and Istanbul achieved unprecedented size in the late Middle Ages. Very few cities in any age actually function in this way; in any case, most residents in the world's most glamorous mega-cities lead lives which are not so different from the experience of ordinary people elsewhere. What is at stake here is something else: the use of the metaphor of cities as the motors of the economy raises the question where the driving power comes from.

Cities, as economic motors, need two critical inputs – innovation and infrastructure. These do not flow smoothly through macro-economic policy, but come in spurts, making it difficult for those responsible for the regulation of national economies to adjust, and all the more so since both innovation and infrastructure tend to induce changes – so-called dynamic effects – whose consequences are difficult to predict. Both are at levels which are insufficient to modernize and adapt cities for the twenty-first century. There were not enough "shovel-ready projects" in 2009, and certainly not enough today, to fill these deficits which reflect a different kind of hole, an inability to generate long-term visions with plans for the future of cities. If we seem stuck it is because we are.

As this section was being written, Jeffrey Sachs commented that "We must look beyond Keynes to fix our problems." Criticizing the "Keynesian model that assumes a stable growth path hit by temporary shocks," Sachs highlighted deep structural challenges for which a strategy based on change, not continuity, is needed. After the American labor market, Sachs took up the infrastructure sector, where investments

> are mostly paralysed. Every country needs to move to a low-carbon energy system. What is the US plan? There isn't one. What is the plan for modernized transport? There isn't one. What is the plan for protecting the coastlines from more frequent and costly flooding? There isn't one. Trillions of dollars of public and private investments are held up for lack of a strategy. The Keynesian approach is ill-suited to this kind of sustained economic management, which needs to be on a timescale of 10–20 years, involving co-operation between public and private investments, and national and local governments. (*Financial Times*, 2012)

Perhaps Sachs over-simplified Keynes to make a point. The question that Keynes would have raised is why, if the answers are so glaringly obvious, is there a paralysis of decision-making and leadership.

The metaphor of the city as generator or dynamo powering economies directs attention to the controlling agency at the national level, presumably regulating many different variables to keep growth sustainable. A moment's reflection on the crisis however tells us that something has gone badly wrong in the control room. Those entrusted with the power to keep the economy going did not have a sufficiently clear and accurate model in 2007–8 of how economic systems are inter-related to understand and account for the consequences of the crash of Lehman Brothers; they have been confused by the signals they receive, leading to contradictory strategies and debates about priorities; and they have failed – the word is not too strong – to articulate a vision of a more sustainable future in a highly urbanized world, a vision which could release investment.

Were it only easier to adopt an urban perspective in economic, social and environmental policy-making. Governmental programs, regulations, and budgets operate on the basis of measurable boundaries. The corporate boundaries of cities are often decades or centuries old, but the functional areas of cities are inherently unstable, spilling over jurisdictional lines and zoning patterns within and sometimes across national frontiers. Lyon became a metropolitan government in 2014 but this amalgamation will hardly dent the figure of over ninety thousand local government units in the European Union with over four hundred million people; by comparison there are 39,000 in the United States. The OECD uses fifty thousand as the threshold population size of a functional urban area, defined as an urban core and adjacent jurisdictions with high levels of commuting around it. Metropolitan areas are at least ten times larger, with a minimum size of half a million people. (How these areas are governed – and to what degree they are fragmented or centralized – affects not only the efficiency of the public sector, but the strategic reach and coherence of what it does.) The more than 275 metropolitan areas in OECD countries generate more than half of OECD GDP (OECD 2013: 17–20). But altogether, in the same thirty-four countries, there are 140,000 municipalities and local governments.

Data are needed for the purposes of international comparisons. Density is a key variable in the construction of inventories to understand how to reduce greenhouse gases, but different cities define the sectors to include and establish the boundaries of the area to be studied differently, impeding comparisons over time as well as an aggregate picture of what is happening on a wider scale. How can local or national leaders take decisions or assess progress? And this is just one example, albeit one pressing heavily on policy agendas (Corfee-Marlot et al., 2009).[1] For analytic and comparative purposes, common guidelines will help integrate spatial information, using GPS, and statistical sources (OECD, 2013). To get a better picture of the 1,148 urban areas in OECD countries, the OECD is promoting "a more systematic use of geographic data on population, land cover and use, transport networks and service infrastructure and air quality ... from different sources (censuses, registers, geographical information system)" (OECD, 2012: 22). Regional development policy and municipal initiatives "would benefit from a clear measure of the functional economy of these areas" (OECD, 2012:18). Changes in land use as well as population, the consumption of resources as well as of production, and information about housing quality, population density and migration, educational activity, crime, health, etc. should be cross-referenced. Moreover, data are not neutral: many laws and policy programs allocate resources or collect taxes on the basis of what happens in specific, delimited localities.

To macro-economists, cities are a kind of black box: because they do not know enough about why some cities perform better than others, they are loath to propose interventions. This may seem to be a caricature. But in fact what gives the national policy framework its strength is precisely its capacity to simplify many of the variables that account for why some cities perform better than others. The cohesion of nations is partly a function of the redistributive mechanisms by which the most productive cities – New York, Paris, London, and Tokyo – contribute more to the national budget than they receive. The unit of analysis and intervention is the nation-state: only in city-states such as Hong Kong, Singapore, or Luxembourg is there a close overlay between the urban and the national, and, even then, there are micro-scale regional variations which call for policy intervention by sectoral ministries.

That our knowledge of cities is inadequate has been known for decades. An *Economist* survey on cities "argued that cities are not passively shaped by the economy around them, but ... they themselves help to shape it" (*The Economist*, 1995). "If cities are able to confer a competitive advantage on the businesses operating within them, understanding how cities work and how to solve urban problems becomes all the more important. Yet we do not know much about what makes cities tick." Not much has changed in twenty years. Given the importance of location, it is surprising that business schools do not do more to teach students and executives about how cities function, what affects their development, how they cope with growth and recover from shocks. Governments may have spatially blind policies, but surely businesses do not.

Getting inside the black box that is the urban economy in national statistics is not easy. No mayor knows how much is being spent by all levels of government within their jurisdiction, a sum much larger than their own budget. "Each city," wrote Nigel Harris, "is economically peculiar, with, at a disaggregated statistical level, a unique output of goods and services. Aggregated data – like aggregated geographical areas – normally conceal this uniqueness, this degree of specialization." He concluded that it is no surprise that "the city economy is unknown terrain for most city officials," hampering their ability to adjust quickly to change. The growth of the service sector, much of it involving goods and services that are not traded beyond a city's borders, complicates data collection enormously (Harris, 1997: 1702). Harris wrote that a "city can only attain the capacity to adjust quickly, to increase the degree of flexibility in response to external changes, if it possesses accurate and timely information – otherwise, people learn of a changed structure only long after it has happened (or through the by-product of rising unemployment, increased in-or out-migration, or urban dereliction." At about the same time, and after carrying out a survey of the range and quality of data on different aspects of the London economy covering its export sectors, supply factors such as transport, utilities, education, health, property and demography, and the flow of funds to and from the national economy, Rosemary Scanlon concluded that London "lacks a source of consistent and regularly available research that produces comprehensive analysis and forecasts of its economy" (Scanlon, 1998). Data collection, analysis, and use have improved. Even without better and more timely data, long-term planning, particularly committing significant infrastructure investment and public capital, must still proceed.

Finding out a gross city product for any city is a challenge, but the results, however approximate, are striking: greater Tokyo has a GDP slightly smaller than that of the UK, which is twice as populous; the metropolitan area of New York covered by the New York–New Jersey Port Authority produces more than Brazil; Los Angeles, Seoul, Paris, London, the Ruhr – all mega-cities – would be among the richest countries in the world if they were independent city-states. Large cities can continue to prosper if they are well managed, and if infrastructure investment continues to sustain and enlarge their labor markets by making it possible for more people, offering a greater array of specializations, to find work. If city size does matter, then larger countries, with more big cities – the United States, France, Germany, the United Kingdom, and of course China, Indonesia, or Brazil – should have a competitive advantage over Switzerland and the Netherlands. To some extent this seems to be the case; however networks linking cities in the Netherlands and in Switzerland help those countries to compensate. If the link that matters is between above average urban GDP and national GDP, then a different set of comparisons emerges: Seoul and Tel Aviv do not lead in their respective countries as much as the experience of large metropolitan centers suggests they should; but the Randstad in the Netherlands and the metropolitan cities of Switzerland perform very well indeed, suggesting that there are network effects and complementarities for systems of cities that compensate for the smaller size of a national territory. As their strongest advocates and sharpest critics recognize, successful cities of whatever size are places where the benefits of agglomeration – a higher level of public services, institutions of justice, health, culture, and education – exceed the costs – substandard or unaffordable housing, health inequalities, congestion, pollution. The argument about cities hinges on how the costs and benefits are measured. Three conclusions are inescapable: the vast amount of data on financial markets and macro-economic performance did not help policy-makers avoid a crash; projects for smart cities and big data need major programs to build capacity to collect, interpret, and use more information of better quality; and guiding the future of cities cannot wait for better data about cities to become available.

Although national policies for housing, innovation, the environment, energy, education, competition, transport, food safety, trade, health, even defense affect both urbanization and individual cities and their regions, their impacts are either not calculated in advance or calculated only with limited models. Laurent Davezies has tellingly scoped the scale of the problem: there have been thousands of studies on the effects of globalization on cities and regions, but hardly any on the impact of public and social budgets on inter-regional solidarity or equity; and what studies there are focus on explicit programs and budgets which are authorized as part of an urban or social agenda, whereas by far the most important territorial effects come from implicit programs and budgets, that is, for research, defense, the environment, transport, etc. "The public policies with the most powerful territorial effects, curiously, are those which are non-spatial" (Davezies, 2012: 52; translation mine).

Specific urban policies framed around urban objectives matter less to the development of cities than other fiscal and sectoral policies which were drafted with other objectives in mind. This is not news to experts. Urban policies are a kind of residual; they matter much less than other sectoral policies or macro-economic settings. Strong political factors reinforce and perpetuate this state of affairs. The arguments against a city-centered policy agenda for growth have not changed much over the years: constitutional restrictions that subordinate municipalities to higher-level units and limit their competences; evidence that municipal departments are less efficient and city halls more likely to tolerate petty corruption than national administrations; concern that mayors will pander to special interests and promise to spend money they cannot raise in taxes; the memory of budget-busting projects which never had an adequate rate of return. A city-centered agenda could lead governments to become involved in picking winners, with all the problems attendant with industrial policy in the past; Treasury officials fear that sub-national governments would spend and borrow too much, compromising fiscal and debt management at the national level with implications for exchange and interest rates. The lack of better data about how urban economies perform then becomes an argument against changing the role of central government in determining what gets spent, and on what, at the sub-national level.

Governments especially at the sub-national level are already significant economic actors. Sub-national governments account for half of public procurement, and 63 per cent of public sector employment. In 2012, OECD countries spent US$1.17 trillion in public investment, or 2.7 per cent of OECD GDP and 15 per cent of all public and private investment. Of this, sub-national governments were responsible for an average of 72 per cent across the OECD, somewhat more in federal systems (in Canada, the sub-national share is about 90 per cent). How was this money allocated? Economic affairs (transport, communications, economic development, energy, construction, etc.) absorbed 37 per cent; education, an investment in human and social capital, took 23 per cent; 11 per cent went on housing and community amenities. In EU countries, around 70 per cent of public investment is used to maintain the current stock of infrastructure. Not only are these figures below the level needed to maintain what already exists; the creation of new capital stock is inadequate as well.

It is however difficult to know either how public spending, which covers virtually half of the national economy, affects different cities and regions, or how the money spent by cities and regions, which covers more than half of public spending, affects national economies. Between 2007 and 2012 per capita public investment fell in fifteen of thirty-three OECD countries: deficit reduction, and the husbanding of resources on welfare, health, and education may have represented sound fiscal decisions but at the expense of future growth and well-being. A few countries (Canada, Denmark, Finland, and Sweden) bucked the trend, but the overall level is down: in the twenty-seven countries of the European Union, public investment in 2012 was one-fifth lower than in 2009. "Do better with less" is not the whole answer when the long-term consequences of under-investment in cities and urban regions should ring alarm bells not only in city halls but in parliaments, corporate headquarters, investment funds, and citizen organizations (OECD, 2014b: 101–3).[2] Economic recovery depends more on how well cities and regions perform. A polarization between austerity – which reduces the funding available to all, or gives advantages to those which are less indebted – or a Keynesian stimulus – which encourages consumer spending, itself uneven territorially – is simplistic: neither strategy tells us very much about how best to improve the economic performance and make best use of the specific assets and potential of different cities and regions. The financial crisis of 2008 has evolved into a crisis of urban decision-making.

That governments do not pay enough attention to cities is one of many lessons of the crisis competing for attention. The urban agenda is not easy for national political leaders to get hold of. The portfolio is often given to a junior minister, or assigned to a ministry with low prestige and limited resources. The wider public culture of ideas about cities is an aggravating factor. Academic critics of urban development usually refer to the dysfunctional aspects of a city which breed pollution and poverty as well as wealth, and to the sheer unmanageability of large, dense places where economic success comes at huge environmental cost, where labor is exploited, where resentments accumulate. This negative view of cities can be counter-productive politically because decision-makers, facing many demands on their time, will choose to tackle other issues with higher chances of success and greater political rewards.

Urban policy as we know it is essentially remedial because it tries to correct distortions that have accumulated; a national policy for cities – not the same thing – would focus less on the problems inherited from the past and more on the opportunities that cities hold and the risks they face. Policies to unlock the potential of cities belong at the center of concern about the crisis, recovery, and future global challenges. No country can do without an urban strategy to harness the capacity of cities to generate and absorb innovation and investment.

Is it too late to adopt an urban strategy if it will take time to show results, first in construction (project design, demand for labor, and materials), and later in dynamic terms as people and businesses take advantage or and benefit from it? Certainly not: first of all, the crisis will continue, favoring conditions for precisely this kind of investment; and, second, it makes sense anyway because as Lawrence Summers noted, by increasing the capacity of the economy to grow, infrastructure investment will reduce rather than increase government debt burdens (*Financial Times*, 2014). Put another way, without more investment, growth will remain below potential. If only investors and citizens knew what the strategy for the next quarter century is! No wonder, as we shall see, efforts to restart economies through stimulus packages intended to lift infrastructure investment have been so limp.

If cities matter, so do better policies for cities. Monetary and fiscal policies are constrained, limiting the room for maneuver of governments which have more scope to exploit, improve, and develop their cities as assets. My starting point is not the level of government intervention as such, but its nature: the what for, not the how much. What can each sector – education, innovation, transport, housing, environment, health, energy – as well as core policies such as competition and trade – contribute to improve how cities function? An urban strategy sounds like a bottom-up approach to economic development: in fact it means turning the hour glass upside-down, so that the bottom is on top, receiving more attention and higher priority in national macro-economic and sectoral policy.

Facts and figures: are they enough to shift policies?
Innovation and infrastructure imply major investments in and for cities, usually involving significant spatial and social impacts. This is another way of saying that innovation and infrastructure build the city of the future. When people talk of a vision of the future, they often mean a vision of how things could be different and better. When infrastructure investment is coupled with innovation and efforts to increase human capital and new jobs, there are positive externalities, which is why integrated strategies are essential. The OECD's 2014 *Regional Outlook* seeks to boost national economies by applying a better understanding of "how cities work as engines for innovation, prosperity and growth," citing the "agglomeration benefits" of cities in the form of higher productivity and the resulting wage premia of between 2 and 5 per cent (OECD, 2014b: 18). But in the world of sectoral policy, innovation and infrastructure are disconnected from the urban arena where their impacts are the greatest. The strategies for investment simply bring together various projects from telecommunications, transport, environment, housing, and so on, without consideration of their dynamic effects, that is, the spillovers from one to the other. This is a complete nonsense: infrastructures have to go someplace and affect how well cities exploit their advantages of size, density, specialization, and complexity – the positive effects of agglomeration; many innovations help direct creative energy toward new and better ways of making cities livable. This exercise should be turned inside out, using the objective of making cities better, more productive and safer to generate a long-term supply of sectoral projects, lifting the supply side of the economy.

Three sets of figures – "killer facts" because they are so difficult to refute – speak volumes. The first is the sum in excess of *$50 trillion – 3.5 per cent of global GDP – which should be invested over the next twenty years to rebuild, expand, and upgrade the infrastructures and power systems on which cities depend*, two-thirds of this sum in developed countries. This eye-blinking figure from the OECD makes the reader wonder whether there has not been a typographical error: surely billions, not trillions (OECD, 2006). McKinsey, using a different methodology, reached the same conclusion in 2012, adding that this omits what it may cost to take account of global climate change. If financing was going to be difficult before 2007, consider how much more difficult it will be now that so much wealth has been destroyed in the crash (McKinsey, 2013).

Why has the bill exploded, decoupling infrastructure from growth in GDP or in capital formation? *Many infrastructure systems are coming to the end of their useful life-cycle at the same time.* The demands of the security agenda since 9/11 have only underscored the cumulative effect of under-investment over decades; routine maintenance and repair were never enough. Water and sewer systems built in 1850s, the extension of network utilities across metropolitan regions in the period 1890–1914, the modernization of infrastructure in the post-1945 era, and the last phase of building in the 1980s and early 1990s were all on different life-cycles. Older systems built to last hundred or 150 years, and newer ones built to last for twenty-five or fifity years have all come to the end of their useful life-cycle at the same time. Nothing like this has ever happened before.

There is more to be done to make cities more efficient, sustainable, and inclusive, but less in public budgets to do it with, which is why borrowing at today's low interest rates makes sense to so many economists. Years of lost output, high unemployment, and under-investment will not be made good, maybe for decades, and will in fact generate higher demands on social services because millions of people who have been unemployed are likely to be employed less often, and at lower levels of compensation, in the years to come. The rate of growth is expected to remain lower than what is was in the two decades before the crisis, returning to a level closer to the very long-term historical trend (Piketty, 2013). Adjustment to a lower rate of growth as the norm is as much a socio-cultural challenge for the population as an intellectual challenge for policy-makers (OECD, 2014c).

How can there be *urban projects* (a noun) when efforts to *project the future of the city* (a verb) are so weak? Yes, there are obstacles: the OECD cites co-ordination challenges across sectors and jurisdictional boundaries; capacity challenges to design and implement investment strategies which reflect the quality of government at all levels; and practices in budgeting, procurement, and regulation which are not always adequate or efficient across levels of government. It will take time – and money – to overcome the barriers to more and better investment for cities. During the years of crisis since 2008, governments and the private sector have been talking past one another: governments have been waiting for business, cash-rich, to invest; the private sector has been waiting for government to articulate a medium-term strategy for urban development. The quality of projects however is a matter not just of design and management, but of their potential impact on urban economies, an agenda which implies bolder efforts by governments to lead civil society and the private sector in generating strategies for urban futures. Some would argue that a recovery will come before the obstacles to more and better urban infrastructure investment can be corrected. But for six years this hope has not borne fruit. Betting on a recovery to solve urban problems is becoming a lottery, on the grounds that sooner or later there will be one; this is not a rational basis for policy and planning.

As the economy fluctuates in a narrow low-growth band in 2013–14, as the fear that deflation will stifle a recovery, as concerns about deficits depress public investment, economic commentators, politicians, and world bodies such as the IMF and OECD call for more to be spent on infrastructure: six years after 2008, they see nothing else left in the policy toolkit. Critically, they have been slow to acknowledge the lead time needed to design, approve, and begin construction on projects on a sufficient scale to leverage infrastructure investment into making cities more productive and sustainable. In the short term, the call for greater infrastructure investment is only likely to lead to arguments about how much should come from the private and how much from the public sector, and particularly how much from which level of government. The G20 meeting in November 2014 in Brisbane led to the creation of a Sydney-based infrastructure "hub" to help reduce barriers to investment, and match investors with projects through a database. Realism implies that the benefits of this investment on the economy will only be visible in two or more years, a challenge for central bankers and macroeconomists who must cope with things as they are, and especially if there is a further deterioration in the interim: the accumulated effect of more short-term policies linked to austerity compromises the prospects for long-term growth.

As Carmen Reinhart and Kenneth Rogoff have pointed out, crises are normal. People are deluding themselves when they believe that markets and institutions can be reformed to make them crisis–proof. The title of their book, *This Time Is Different: Eight Centuries of Financial Folly* (2009) captures their criticism of those who believe that crises are abnormal, the result of some malfunction which can be cured, and then prevented through progress. Crises, they assert, are normal too.

The crisis of 2008 is different, however, because policies and conditions for a resumption of growth were already compromised when the crisis began. This bold claim rests on the assertion that demographic, institutional, and urban factors of growth which helped the West overcome war and depression in the twentieth century have lost much of their potency. The effects of massive stimulus packages have been so short-lived because governments, overlooking fundamental structural changes in the factors of growth and neglecting cities where these are concentrated, have been pushing on a wet string.

Much could happen quickly; there is ample scope for innovation in the public sector especially if internal government regulations and personnel practices are realigned to promote it: creative talents in finance can propose ways to raise funds; planners, systems specialists, and experts on innovation can elaborate bold, transformational projects; economists, geographers, environmental scientists, energy and transport specialists can identify targets for investment which promise to lift productivity and reduce negative externalities. The example of "Le Grand Paris", to build a ring of fast, automated trains circulating around Paris and connecting to the radial routes being improved between the suburbs and the center (200 km of new lines, sixty-nine new stations), shows how difficult but important it is to tie these three things together: what should be done, how should it be resourced, and who should lead. In the final analysis nothing much will happen without a sense of urgency.

We are where we are

Billions of dollars and euros have been transferred from the United States and Western Europe to rapidly emerging economies enjoying extraordinary surpluses (only twenty out of 118 emerging market economies went backwards in 2009), the virtual equivalent of a loss of credit and capital normally associated with defeat in war. But there has not been a war.

The global crisis that begin in the American financial sector in 2007 is not over; we just think it is. Each phase, each set of problems since 2007 has lengthened the chain of causality, making the connections between one problem and another more obscure, less relevant to immediate concerns. There have been many false dawns. In the meantime, people adjust.

Growth of per capita GDP in Western Europe in the period 1000–1500, then dominated by the rural world, was 0.13 per cent; between 1500 and 1820, arguably the first age of globalization and the early industrial revolution, the rate was 0.15 per cent. In the fifty years from 1820 to 1870 marked by rapid urbanization, GDP per capita grew at the rate of 0.95 annually, a radical break from a past which stretched over centuries. The decades before World War One which saw the transformation of the economy through petroleum, electricity, and steel witnessed a further increase, to 1.32 per cent. After a decline to an annual rate of 0.76 per cent in what is often called the Second Thirty Years War, from 1913 to 1950 (still well above pre-1800 rates notwithstanding wars and depressions which destroyed capital), growth leaped to 4.08 per cent in the "Trente Glorieuses," the fabled postwar era that lasted from 1950 to the first oil crisis of 1973. From 1973 to 1998, the rate fell back to 1.78 per cent, still well above the pre-1914 level. In 2000, the twenty-seven countries of the European Union achieved a rate of 3.9, and in 2007 of 3.0; the figures for the United States were 4.2 and 1.9 per cent respectively. Then came the global financial crisis: GDP fell by 2.7 in the United States and by 4.2 per cent in the EU twenty-seven countries in 2009 (OECD, 2011: 55; Maddison, 2001: 126).

According to the OECD, disparities in wealth between regions widened in half of OECD countries as a result of the crisis of 2008, usually due to a greater drop in performance in the poorer regions relative to the wealthiest. Declining disparities by contrast are generally due to poorer performance in wealthier regions (OECD, 2014b: 26). Neither is a good way to go. Under the heading "Advanced economies have gone backwards by a decade as a result of the crisis," *The Economist* (2012) scanned figures on unemployment, equities, income and GDP to provide a composite picture which showed that GDP per person was lower in 2011 than in 2007 in every G7 economy but Germany, in thirteen out of thirty-two countries in Latin America and the Caribbean, and in twenty-two out of twenty-seven EU countries. For Britain, Spain, Hungary, 2012 felt like 2004; but for the United States and Portugal, it felt like 2002. Adjusted for the impact of inflation on property values, "the average American homeowner is living in 2001" in 2012. The US Federal Reserve Board reported in 2012 that US wealth fell 38.8 per cent in 2007–10, led by the collapse in house prices. This loss cost the median American household eighteen years of growth, or $77,300 in 2010. This will have long-term effects on future decisions about what to buy, when to accumulate debt, and how to plan for retirement. The output gap between 2007 and 2013 ranged from less than 5 per cent in Germany and Australia and about 5 per cent in the United States, to over 10 per cent in Britain and Portugal, more than 15 per cent in Spain, and 30 per cent in Greece (*The Economist*, 2014). Unemployment alone does not account for these gaps: lower capital investment, productivity, and labor-force participation matter more.

It seems unlikely that growth rates will be as high during a recovery as before 2008; it will be decades before economies make good the wealth that has been lost. When the economy is growing, projections are more likely to get the trend right than when the economy is contracting. Economists misunderstood or under-estimated "the unusually high speed and depth of cross-country interconnections between real and financial developments" as well as the timing and impact of debt reduction measures, and the impact of housing asset bubbles and private credit growth. Data lagged, models were superseded by events, and a lack of experience with anything similar hampered experts as they tried to provide governments with forecasts (Pain et al., 2014: 6).

The OECD'S Working Group on Short Term Economic Prospects (STEP), preparing the Economic Outlook for 2009, met on 27–8 October 2008, soon after the crash of Lehman Brothers. Projections previously released to governments were updated for this meeting, indicating a sharper decline than governments expected. The pessimism of the OECD may have accelerated more expansionary and dramatic measures, thus helping to avert even more dire outcomes. But even the OECD still considered it likely that financial markets would start to recover in late 2009, such that growth would resume by late 2010. A deep recession is often propitious to the introduction of major structural reforms to enhance competition, reduce trade barriers, strengthen competition and reform regulatory frameworks. The widespread belief early in the crisis that the recession would be over before many governments including in the United States, France, Germany, and the United Kingdom had to go to the polls (2011–13) lulled decision-makers into thinking that politically painful structural reforms could be avoided or postponed, thereby delaying and dampening the recovery. What was advisable or even imperative from a policy viewpoint in 2009–10 was one thing; what was politically feasible, especially given the polarized legislatures in many countries, was another.

Some of the most recent findings of the OECD about the unprecedented nature of the global financial crisis have untested implications for policy advice for growth (Pain et al., 2014; OECD, 2014a). Larger forecasting errors at the OECD correlated with international trade openness and the presence of foreign banks in an economy, factors which usually help countries recover from external shocks more quickly and remain on the list of reforms governments should pursue. Some forecasting errors relate both to assumptions about the behavior of political leaders (e.g. that the euro crisis would abate sooner) and to the market (e.g. a narrowing of sovereign bond yields); these two are clearly inter-related.

Better forecasting is only part of the problem, and hence only part of the solution. Prof. Catherine Schenk, in line with Reinhart and Rogoff and others who have looked at a succession of financial and currency crises, argues that

> As the 1990's drew to a close ... it was clear that the economic lessons of previous decades had not been learned. The fundamental causes of the

2007 crisis can be clearly identified in previous rounds of turmoil. It wasn't that policy makers were unaware of the problems, but rather that they could not conspire to resolve them ... Understanding how lessons were not learned from one crisis to another is fundamental to creating a sustainable framework for international banking and finance for the future. (Schenk, 2010: 10)

Solutions to the problems of transparency, resilience, supervision, compliance, regulatory competition, and the skills gap between regulators and the market have not been found at the international level; years after 2008, different national systems remain, well, different (Schenk, 2010). Why do these arguments about whether the knowledge and models were deficient, or whether the leadership was unable or unwilling to save the system from collapse, seem oddly reminiscent of the debates in 2014 about whether World War One could have been avoided at the brink? Were leaders unconscious of the danger? Over-confident of their ability to cope with a crisis? Or was the system of sovereign nation-states inimical to the kind of reforms that could enable it to survive?

States possess three powerful levers: monetary, fiscal, and regulatory. In the immediate aftermath of the crash of Lehman Brothers in October 2008, central banks injected liquidity, as they can, very quickly. The return of the state in 2008 was a salutary reminder of just how essential – and easily taken for granted – institutions are. But the financial crisis which restored the state to the center of decision-making in 2008 has turned into a political crisis, whether about taxation, immigration and the national debt in the United States and the United Kingdom, or about structural reform, banking regulation and austerity in the Eurozone. Countries with their own currencies (Sweden, the United States, the United Kingdom) are as polarized as countries which share a currency (Spain, France, Finland, Germany). The long decline in the level of trust in government has sunk to new levels. To summarize, states are worse off than before: they face the bill to repair the damage measured in deferred education, lost experience, health problems, and early retirement when people should be working longer. And they must cope with more problems with reduced resources because the recession has cut into the apparatus of the state itself; the level of debt may come down but so will the tax base insofar as the economy for years to come will be smaller than had there been no crisis. Our complex society needs public goods but the ability of the state to provide them is constricted. Doing without is one option but the thin veneer that is civilization will then begin to crack. There will be a revolution in public services as states try to find a way to reconcile demands and needs against capacities and resources. A more limited state – long the goal of many political movements – may be at hand, but perhaps with consequences that its proponents will not welcome.

Thomas Piketty, in his recent book on capital in the twenty-first century which has provoked interest because of its argument about widening income inequality, argues that the rate of economic growth will revert to its long-term level of between 1 and 1.5 per cent (Piketty, 2013). This may be the more important point. Expectations and policies have not yet adjusted to this lower level. More restrictive policies are no more likely to depress the trend than greater liberalization is likely to lift it; deep-rooted structural trends are not easily corrected by policy measures in the short term. Decline is not the inevitable outcome. Even a level of growth above 1 per cent depends on the growth of productivity in rich countries at a similar rate (possible if there is considerable technological innovation especially in the use of energy), and continued convergence in emerging economies, without political or military upheavals (which is possible but perhaps not probable). Fatalism will block the kind of creative thinking and adaptive policy-making which may prove to be the only way forward. Is it possible to improve investment and lift employment if the prospect is for very low growth for the foreseeable future? How will cities function in a low-growth economy? Are statesmanship and stewardship possible in such conditions, taking steps in the short term that bring benefits in the future? What is the policy mix for cities in a world of excessively low interest rates, high unemployment?

With less confidence that a recovery will restore prosperity, with more anxiety about the future, and with good reason to be concerned lest future crises bring unacceptable and avoidable levels of material destruction and social dislocation, the level of uncertainty – if such a thing can be measured – is high and still rising. In the history of the West since the Renaissance, new paradigms for collective living and governing evolve rapidly during a crisis. Crises of this order of magnitude, as will be argued in Part III, have happened before in the West at roughly eighty to a hundred year intervals. When the governing paradigms for society and the economy have been revised, radically, problem-solving becomes easier at least for a few decades. Questions about the long term usually deflect attention away from the strengths of Europe and North America and focus on the high rate of growth of China and of other emerging economies. I argue instead that the survival of the West has been assured in the past by a unique capacity for intellectual and political reinvention, that Europe has much to contribute to this process, and that interdependence, which is central to the post-war European experiment, could be the foundation stone for the next major paradigm.

A major paradigm is always future-oriented, promising to fulfill collective aspirations at a time when a crisis – or series of crises – raise the level of uncertainty and insecurity, undermining credibility in the previous paradigm. Belief that a leap toward a new paradigm of economic regulation and decision-making to benefit cities is possible is grounded in evidence that the current paradigm for urban development is struggling to deliver results, and in logic that it is ill-suited to cope with the challenges of the twenty-first century. Anglo-American empiricism is often contrasted to Cartesian rationalism, the former rooted in evidence, the latter in logic. This is of course an exaggerated distinction: both are needed, and are complementary. The best defense against speculation is to keep one's feet firmly on the ground. The problem is that where we stand, we cannot see very far, not far enough when actions taken today – including the decision to do nothing – can have long-term consequences.

A new paradigm for economic governance to bring down the level of uncertainty and give people confidence again in themselves and trust in their leading institutions must deal with three issues: (1) risk – what risks are reasonable to accept, what restrictions on individual or social behavior are necessary to reduce vulnerability and costs; (2) responsibility – who does what and is accountable; and (3) regulation, in the form of policies and practices which we can reasonably assume will be efficient and effective, consistent with priorities, and can be enforced and complied with.

More questions than answers: coping with uncertainty

It is likely that the secular trend in the twentieth century which saw successive increases in the scope of national governments over the things that matter for cities and regions has peaked; greater autonomy for cities and regions is the inevitable consequence of the erosion of sovereignty experienced by every nation-state. Consider the far-reaching shifts in international power and domestic governance as we are now witnessing:

- the loss of wealth, jobs and output that years of growth cannot make good
- fiscal deficits that constrain the public sector at a time when problems which are the unique responsibility of the state to address are intensifying
- the inability of western military power to do more than contain and control aggression through limited war, carried out at a distance from homelands

- rising insecurity, from the level of individual concerns about jobs and family, to national and global disturbances which fester.

We are living through one of those rare moments of transition between one era and another. How countries, great economic and social systems, recover from shocks and crises tells us a lot about their hidden strengths and weaknesses. These meta-events appear incomprehensible at first: there are too many dimensions and variables to form a coherent pattern. That people have questions is understandable: familiar landmarks are no longer reliable guideposts; the recovery promised for 2010 or 2011 has often receded; the future is not promising.

People want to know whether the places where they live will be better in ten years than they are today. Each of the following nine pairs of questions, organized in a hierarchy from the material and social to the political and intellectual, contains both a general and a city-specific question:

- Where will the jobs of tomorrow be? And in a globalizing economy growing more slowly, how can cities create jobs?
- Are networks of social relationships fraying, especially among young people, leading to an implosion of public culture and a loss of identity? And how can cities restore a life rich in connections and opportunities, conducive to family life?
- Are competitiveness and sustainability, equity and efficiency compatible? And what changes for economic and social life in cities are likely if these goals are to be pursued?
- What can be done to strengthen democratic institutions across all levels of government? And how can cities take more initiative without compromising the integrity of the nation-state?
- How will pressures on resources, including water and energy, affect regions which developed when resources were abundant and affordable? And what form, structure and appearance might characterize the city of the future?
- What regime of public spending is appropriate to a post-industrial, knowledge-based – and ageing – society? And how can the needs of people in cities be met in an era of declining public resources?
- How can peace be kept in the world when economic change increases mobility and migration, testing the limits of tolerance? And what does the new economy of security mean for cities?
- Will we have the ideas relevant to contemporary challenges? And how can cities develop the institutional and professional competences to make best use of available knowledge?

- Does it take a crisis to initiate change? Or can a constituency be found for incremental, proactive, and forward-looking urban policies and strategies?

These questions are the stuff of international conferences and academic research projects; several even keep political leaders awake at night. Answers are more likely to take the form of inferences from current trends, and educated guesses based on experience. Waiting for more data to become available is not likely to change the options in front of decision-makers who often have to act now, taking calculated risks because inaction is itself costly. Academics and public intellectuals speculate; politicians and decision-makers must make choices.

No free society has ever reversed the path toward urbanization. The future of the city is at the center of the debate. We can say about urbanization what de Tocqueville argued about democracy: that the trend is irreversible but its consequences for good or evil are not predetermined. There are today, and not for the first time, competing views about the status of communities in global social systems, and widespread concern about the role of the democratic process in making rules. A revival of anti-urban views has not emerged – plutocrats continue to be attracted to the pleasures of cities, and the competition to build taller and more spectacular skyscrapers keeps the image of urban modernity alive – but the possibility cannot be entirely dismissed either, as revealed by the electoral dynamics in most Western democracies of some parties with socially conservative and anti-immigrant views whose electoral base is in small towns in regions dominated by a metropolis. This is often manifest in images which express polarizing extremes, between a relatively stable present and a frightfully anarchic future, the result of trends and circumstances that make people feel that they are vulnerable to forces that they do not understand and cannot control. We are where we are.

Ever since the Renaissance, critics of the city have argued that because urban conditions are difficult to predict and control, cities – or at least very large cities – are a threat to economic, social, and political stability. There is no escaping the twin-faced nature of urban policy debates: viewed from one perspective, cities generate unmanageable social, and environmental problems that take years to remediate – if solutions can be found; at the same time, cities capture innovations and concentrate the talent and resources that open new trading opportunities and allocate resources more productively and raise living standards. On balance, the history of cities shows that people learn to resolve problems that are as difficult to anticipate as they are complex. The city is where people enjoy greater freedom, indeed, where many people enjoy a large measure of freedom for the first time in their lives: this has been essential to the distinctive role of cities in the emergence of capitalism in early modern Europe and to the growth and spread of the capitalist economy since the Industrial Revolution. Contemporary policy must be anchored in this history.

We need, all at once, a better understanding of what is actually happening; short-term strategies to repair the damage of years of recession; and a medium-to-long term strategy to invest and innovate for the future. These are not consecutive measures, but measures to be undertaken simultaneously. No wonder it is so hard to get a consistent, coherent view of what should be the central subject of our age, the dramatic, peaceful growth of cities, or to use the title Barbara Ward gave to her book at the time of the first UN Conference on Human Settlements in 1976, as *The Home of Man.* Sometimes, she taught, citing the global effort to eradicate smallpox in a lesson I have never forgotten, it can be better to under-estimate the scale of what must be done in order to mobilize the international community to tackle a major problem. It is however difficult to under-estimate the scale of what must be done to sustain urban civilization in the twenty-first century.

The argument of this book is developed in three parts.

First, cities are weaker after the Great Recession because innovation and infrastructure investment are insufficient, aggravating a medium-term trend which began before 2008; these are the new limits to growth. To adjust cities as they are and the pattern of their growth calls for more innovation and infrastructure investment, but there is no vision of the future of the city to translate into strategies and projects. Drawing on examples of declining and growing cities, and on OECD studies to explore the practical and theoretical advantages of place-based development, this first part argues that all cities have untapped potential. Policies do not develop the full potential of cities, in part due to a bias in favor of macro-economic and fiscal tools which, although spatially blind, are easier for governments to manipulate, and in part due to the lack of co-ordination across sectoral silos and jurisdictions; housing is an outstanding example of how things go wrong. Putting cities at the center of policy for a sustainable recovery will challenge how governments, structured by levels and sectors, work. Piecemeal changes are unlikely to add up to wholesale reform. A re-conceptualisation of policies around the needs and potential of cities is required.

Second, we are sailing into headwinds. In the twenty-first century cities face social, environmental, and economic risks qualitatively different from and perhaps of an order of magnitude greater than in the twentieth. Cities can withstand a lot but the growth of the security state could compromise the very forces of adaptation and resilience which have enabled cities to survive crises in the past; fear is driving the increase in regulations, an ineffective response to some risks. It seems improbable that a domestic regulatory system, including its emerging shape in the form of international agreements and delegated governance, can cope with a bigger, less stable, more complex agenda of "external" risks to cities stretching across many borders and challenging the Westphalian principle of non-intervention in the domestic affairs of other countries.

Third, the West has always resolved once-in-a-century crises with a paradigm shift. Every great paradigm speaks to our collective fears and hopes: prosperity embodied hopes in the twentieth century just as high unemployment, our fears. In the twenty-first century, when overwhelming catastrophes and social fragmentation threaten, a new mode of economic governance could emerge around the hope that we can reduce the impact of disasters and crises through greater inter-dependence, and the fear that crises otherwise will shatter social systems. The needs of cities alone, however compelling, will probably not provoke a paradigm shift in policy; instead a new paradigm which could guide urban development over this century is more likely to emerge *after* a series of shocks. The ability of governments to protect their citizens and territories is already a factor in the low level of trust in government; things may get worse before they get better. Are we prepared for a period of heightened uncertainty and instability?

Notes

1 The urban inventory challenge is discussed on pp. 67ff.
2 The difficulty of integrating an economic perspective in a field which has been dominated by questions of constitutional prerogatives and governance can be illustrated by the fact that the bibliography for chapter 2, "Drivers of city performance: the evidence" has 29 references, whereas that for Chapter 5, "a national strategy for cities: taking ownership of urban policy" has 97.

References

Corfee-Morlot, Jan, Lamia Kamal-Chaoui, Michael G. Donovan, Ian Cochran, Alexis Robert, Pierre-Jonathan Teasdale (2009), "Cities, climate change and multilevel governance," OECD Environmental Working Paper no. 14.

Davezies, Laurent (2012), *La crise qui vient: la nouvelle fracture territorial* (Paris: Editions du Seuil).

The Economist (1995), "A survey of cities: turn up the lights," 29 July.

The Economist (2012), "Lost economic time, the Proust index," 25 February.
The Economist (2014), "Counting the long-term cost of the financial crisis," 14 June.
Financial Times (2012), Jeffrey Sachs, "We must look beyond Keynes to fix our problems," 18 December.
Financial Times (2014), Lawrence Summers, "'Why public investment really is a free lunch,'" 7 October.
Harris, Nigel (1997), "Cities in a global economy: structural change and policy reactions," *Urban Studies*, 34: 1693–1703.
McKinsey Global Institute (2013), "Infrastructure productivity: how to save $1 Trillion a Year."
Maddison, Angus (2001), *The World Economy: A Millennial Perspective* (Paris: OECD). DOI: 10.1787/9789264189980-en.
OECD (2006), *Infrastructure to 2030: Telecom, Land Transport, Water and Electricity* (Paris: OECD), p. 29. DOI: 10.1787/9789264023994-3-en.
OECD (2011), *OECD Factbook: Economic, Environmental and Social Statistics, 2011–2012* (Paris: OECD), "Real GDP Growth," p. 55. DOI: 10.1787/factbook-2011-2-en.
OECD (2012), *Redefining "Urban": A New Way to Measure Metropolitan Areas* (Paris: OECD). DOI: org/:10.1787/9789264174108-en.
OECD (2013), *Regions at a Glance* (Paris: OECD); chapter one is a "Special Focus on Metropolitan Areas." DOI:org/10.1787/reg_glance-2013-en.
OECD (2014a), "OECD forecasts during and after the financial crisis: a post mortem," OECD Economics Department Policy Note no. 23, February.
OECD (2014b), *OECD Regional Outlook: Regions and Cities: Where Policies and People Meet* (Paris: OECD). DOI:orh/10.1787/9789264201415-1-en.
OECD (2014c), *OECD Economic Outlook*, 89 (May). DOI10.1787/eco_outlook-v2014-1-en.
Pain, Nigel, Christine Lewis, Thai-Thanh Dang, Yosuke Jin, Pete Richardson (2014), "OECD forecasts during and after the financial crisis: a post mortem," OECD Economics Department Working Papers no. 1107. http://dx.doi.org/10.1787/5jz73l1qw1s1-en.
Piketty, Thomas (2013), *Le capital au XXIe siècle* (Paris: Editions du Seuil), esp. Ch. 2.
Reinhart, Carmen and Kenneth Rogoff (2009), *This Time Is Different: Eight Centuries of Financial Folly* (Princeton: Princeton University Press).
Scanlon, Rosemary (1998), "Observations of economic report in London in the 1990s," a report prepared for FOCUS Central London and London Transport and published by the Greater London Group, London School of Economics, December.
Schenk, Catherine R. (2010), "Are we bad students or do we have poor teachers: why don't we learn the lessons from previous crises?" *Corporate Finance Review*, 15:2: 5–10.
Ward, Barbara (1976), *The Home of Man* (New York: W. W. Norton).

Selected additional references on the crisis of 2008

Blyth, Mark (2013), *Austerity: The History of a Dangerous Idea* (Oxford: Oxford University Press).

Cowen, Tyler (2011), *The Great Stagnation: How America Ate All the Low-Hanging Fruit of Modern history, Got Sick, and Will (Eventually) Feel Better* (New York: Dutton).

Ferguson, Niall (2012), *The Great Degeneration: How Institutions Decay and Economies Die* (London: Allen Lane).

Gorton, Gary (2012), *Misunderstanding Financial Crises: Why We Don't See Them Coming* (New York: Oxford University Press).

King, Stephen D. (2013), *When the Money Runs Out* (New Haven: Yale University Press).

Morris, Ian (2010), *Why the West Rules – For Now* (Stanford: Stanford University Press/Profile Books).

2

Housing and cities: toward what future?

Housing policy, the crisis and the factors of growth

We all saw it coming. "Close to bursting; house of cards" (*The Economist*, 2003a); "Shaky foundations: the higher house prices climb, the more they are likely to fall" (*The Economist*, 2003b); "After the fall: soaring house prices have given a huge boost to the world economy. What happens when they drop" (*The Economist*, 2005); "Cracks in the façade; America's riskiest mortgages are crumbling. How far will the damage spread?" (*The Economist*, 2007). Writing in the *Financial Times* in 2006, Martin Wolf asked whether higher house prices make a country richer. "The answer is simply 'no'." Were the pessimists wrong? Clearly not. Was their timing accurate? Clearly not. Lulled into complacency by storms that did not materialize, and oblivious to the problem of systemic risk, people adjusted to the bubble.

The crisis of 2008 in the United States, Ireland, Spain, and Iceland started in housing markets which were exposed to easy credit and innovation in the financial sector. Deregulation in financial services – where much of the innovation affecting housing appears to have been concentrated in recent years – contributed to the rise in house prices by as much as 30 per cent in the average OECD country between 1980 and 2005. In 2001, only 8 per cent of home purchases in the United States had a down payment of zero, but by 2007 this figure had risen to 22 per cent (OECD, 2011: 186). People believed that prices would continue to rise, even after the conditions to sustain such a belief began to come undone (André, 2010). No one foresaw the connection between housing and systemic risk: the problem had been contained when housing market asset bubbles burst in 1992 in Japan, Israel, Sweden, Finland, Australia, and the United Kingdom. Bricks and stone have long been an investment of choice for wealthy merchants to protect their gains: the plutocrats investing in property in New York or London have this in common with the eighteenth-century Bordelais or sixteenth-century Venetians. As the crisis intensified, many people considered housing a safe investment, as long as the mortgage can be paid. Meanwhile millions of people trapped with negative equity, or unable to get credit, cannot get the housing they need; many young people do not believe that they will ever own their own homes (Mian and Sufi, 2014). Those who are priced out of housing markets in cities where they want to study, work, and live do not need huge surveys or authoritative books to tell them that disparities are widening. The social and economic costs are not confined to the major cities where housing markets are the most distorted; the political costs are amplified nationally by the media and through elections.

Problems in urban housing markets were not just a matter of badly regulated financial markets that were poorly understood by people who had the responsibility to know better. There were other factors: planning, infrastructure capacity, housing, and regional development were also regulatory policy issues in multi-level mis-alignment in the United States, the United Kingdom, Spain, Ireland, Greece, and Iceland where local and regional jurisdictions contributed to an asset bubble in housing through planning and land use permits, etc. In places where new construction declined but housing prices rose sharply, regulatory procedures appear to have reduced supply by restricting large-scale development, perhaps due to pressure from homeowners fearful that new construction would reduce the value of existing properties. Housing has been regulated for centuries, but the accumulation of environmental, land-use and safety regulations affecting what can be built, how, and the administrative procedures and building codes that builders and owners need to comply with has had unintended consequences for housing markets and urban development (Glaeser et al., 2005). It was the combination of problems in two regulatory systems, one in the banking sector, the other in housing and urban development, that proved so damaging. But the fiscal and regulatory adjustments which seemed imperative in 2008-9 at the time of the crisis have been slow in coming, and concentrate mainly on finance.

The fact that the construction, maintenance, and renovation of urban housing help to sustain both capital (for investors and owners) and capitalism (in the form of a market system which co-ordinates supply and demand through private ownership) makes the current crisis even more important. The expansion that preceded the crisis was nearly twice as long as the average of six years; real house prices increased by 120 per cent on average in a survey of eighteen OECD countries (as against around 45 per cent in previous expansions). Construction is the largest sector in employment: 7 per cent of the EU workforce; more than forty million people in the EU, the US and Japan before the crash of 2008 (André, 2010). Defended as a stimulus for consumption with a multiplier effect generating business for decorators, manufacturers of white goods, repair workers, gardeners, plumbers etc., national statistics give prominence to new housing starts (and ignore renovation). If housing markets remain flaccid, labor will be reallocated to other sectors, local authorities will have to find other sources of revenue than licensing and permits associated with construction and land-use change, financial institutions will have to diversify further from lending for property development and from holding property as collateral. Does recovery mean returning to the volume of new housing starts in 2008, when housing markets were already disturbed by the perverse incentives and rising expectations of an asset bubble? Is it reasonable for an economy to see such levels of employment in construction? Can housing lead a recovery when new housing starts and property investment are usually a lagging indicator? These questions, while important, are like looking through the wrong end of a telescope. The challenge is not only or just the survival of the housing industry, notwithstanding its political weight; it is to maintain and even increase the positive agglomeration effects of cities and their metropolitan regions, which depend on their ability to attract and retain the widest diversity of people: inclusive growth.

The situation is unprecedented, an inversion of the 1930s. At that time, the accumulation of overcrowded and unsanitary housing mobilized politicians and generated massive public and charitable campaigns. In the nineteenth century, the population had grown and the percentage of people living in cities increased. The vast internal migration in most developed countries from rural to urban regions, and from city to city, often across hundreds of kilometers, did not accompany a growth in personal income sufficient to give many urban workers, still unskilled, supporting large families, a decent place to live. The end of World War One and the Great Depression conflated the urban crisis, the housing crisis, and the economic crisis. Fascist and democratic governments alike made the rebuilding of cities – and even the creation of new towns – into the centerpiece of programs for recovery.

The crisis of 2008 was an opportunity to change the model of housing for cities which in many countries contributed to an unsustainable asset bubble: suburban greenfield development of car-dependent single-family houses, a reliance on ownership for personal wealth appreciation, and insufficient leverage by which central governments can influence land-use and building decisions at the local level. Fixing the banks and finance for housing was critical in 2008, but no substitute for a broader reassessment of housing policy, if only to limit the factors that shape asset bubbles. In both country and thematic studies, the OECD recommends reforms to make housing markets work better by increasing housing supply and residential mobility through regulatory and fiscal reforms. But structural reforms which are spatially blind or neutral are at odds with the challenges cities face for inclusive and sustainable growth. When housing affordability is compromised by stagnant real incomes for most households, policy should tackle the barriers to greater productivity and higher levels of human capital to raise incomes, rather than promote subsidized mortgages or housing finance reforms which fit the short-term agendas of governments.

Housing and the factors of growth
The factors which sustained the housing sector and supported the upward mobility of millions in the urban middle class in the post-1945 era have either weakened considerably or gone into reverse. To continue to address problems in the sector without taking account of what has changed in our economies and societies – and to assume that these problems are self-correcting, without policy intervention – is to hold back the transition to the economy of the future. Four factors are highlighted: population trends, the formation of new cities, individual rights, and innovation.

First, population is no longer growing in many OECD countries (France, Mexico, the UK, and US are exceptions). New housing starts remain a key economic indicator, suggesting that more is better. But they do not tell us how much housing needs to be constructed or renovated, or where, or whether the proportion of households in sub-standard housing is increasing or declining. Figures about the gap between demand and supply mask the fact the locational aspects of housing demand for families facing divorce, for people living alone, or for ageing households, are quite different than for families with children moving from the countryside to the city, or setting up a household in a community where jobs are expanding.

Today the drivers are as much social as demographic: more people live in one- or two-person households (sometimes as much as 50 per cent of a large city). The number of people in France living alone increased by 21.5 per cent between 1982 and 1990. More than one dwelling in four in France is already occupied by only one person; some regions – southwestern France, Corsica, Brittany, and the Loire Valley – are more affected by this trend than others (*Le Monde*, 1995). The trend toward single living is increasing twice as fast among men than among women. In the United States, the number of people living alone has increased from 13.3 per cent in 1960 to 27.7 per cent in 2011, amounting to thirty-two million Americans (7.9 million older women – almost half of all women living alone – and 3.3 million older men). This percentage will grow as the population ages (Klineberg, 2013). Average household size has fallen in most OECD countries over the past three decades; the percentage of one-person households has risen to 35 per cent in Austria and the Netherlands, 40 per cent in Finland and Germany, and even higher in Sweden, and spectacularly from 5 to nearly 25 per cent in Korea (OECD, 2012).

Ageing creates a different dynamic, especially when people can remain independent but need a safer environment indoors and out and a different mix of services than may be found in the dwelling or community where they had lived for many years. This will be even more evident as housing and urban services are adapted to an unprecedented increase in the number of people over sixty-five. France enjoys one of the highest fertility rates in the western world, accounting for an estimated increase of 11.8 million people in the next half century when the country will grow to 73.6 million inhabitants. The age mix however will be unprecedented: by 2035 one-third of the population will be sixty years of age or older; the average age will increase from thirty-nine in 2007 to forty-three; and the number of centenarians, expected to be two hundred thousand, will be thirteen times the level of 2010 (*Le Monde*, 2010c). In Scotland, the number of people over sixty-five living alone in 2037 could be 488,200, as many as the population of Edinburgh in 2012. Ageing changes the nature of demand, even in countries such as Italy where the population is likely to decline but where the housing stock is already in excess to the number of households. Clearly a quantitative approach to housing which measures new housing starts and the number of square meters per occupant tells us only that, in a tight housing market, people will take what they can get.

Second, new cities are not under development in western countries, and cannot be initiated as easily as in the past. The conversion of rural land to urban uses is occurring at a rate greater than population growth, but in an inchoate manner, with overall results less optimal than if planning had been used on a greater scale. Some cities are still growing, many are mostly stable, but some are declining (a trend unheard of in the western world in the twentieth century). Housing policies and indicators continue to favor new construction on greenfield sites over intra-urban renewal. Policies to promote "compact cities" (OECD, 2012) can demonstrate practical results in metropolitan areas which are already built-up to make better use of vacant or damaged land. The overall building stock in cities changes at the rate of 1–2 per cent annually, meaning that it takes decades to remake a city through the process of demolition and construction. Incremental change may be good; it also has the effect of making planning rather too much of a theoretical exercise – by the time a ten-year or twenty-year plan has reached its use-by date, many of the variables that went into its development will have changed, perhaps significantly.

Cities once threatened with decline, such as Melbourne, Australia, after the crash of 1990, are growing so fast that efforts to channel the construction of new housing are attacked by the development industry. Indeed, any effort to get ahead of the pattern of growth raises political debates about who will win and who will lose. A fragmented pattern of land use will raise the cost of public service delivery and weaken the positive effects of agglomeration for labor markets; the challenge is to price access to land such that site selection is compatible with other public policy objectives (Siedentop and Fina, 2010). There is evidence that the market does not reflect consumer preferences well enough. A recent report from Australia's Grattan Institute highlights that people value both housing type and location, and that there is a mis-match, suggesting that there is greater potential for apartment buildings of four levels or more, and for semi-detached houses in the already-built up areas of central Melbourne and its inner suburbs. But financing for single-family dwellings on greenfield sites is easier to secure; lenders prefer a standard to an innovative product; and building and material costs will be lower for the house on a previously undeveloped land parcel (Kelly, 2011). Moreover, the cost of infrastructure in already-built up areas is much higher than on the outer edge. In Dublin, infrastructure lagged behind housing, meaning that new housing starts occupied land in areas where public services became even more inadequate, adding to inefficiency and congestion throughout the built-up area. This form of under-investment by the public sector was emblematic of the Irish asset bubble.

Although new cities are not being planned, urban activities are taking up more land at a rate greater than the rate of population growth. Between 1990 and 2000, the increase of artificial surfaces for housing, urban parks, industry, commerce, and transport was around 1,000 square kilometers per year within the twenty-seven states of the EU, or about 275 hectares per day, rising from 176,150 square kilometers to 186,200 square kilometers; by 2006, total figures had increased to 191,200 square kilometers. As an order of magnitude, this is equivalent to the making of a city exceeding the size of Berlin in a single year. The rate of conversion between 1992 and 2004 in France was 20 per cent when population growth was only 6 per cent. In France, the growth of forests, which had been increasing for a century, has actually been reversed: 16,974,000 hectares in 2008, or 28,000 hectares less than the previous year (*Le Monde*, 2010a).

The rate of increase may be slowing, but the trend to convert greenfield land into urban space, based on the financial gain when property can be converted from rural use to housing or a non-agricultural activity, continues. Agricultural land is converted to urban uses in France at the rate of 74,000 hectares (740 square kilometers) annually, a total of seven million hectares since 1960. This is indicative of a spreading out of population at overall lower density, often into villages on the edge of towns of at least ten thousand inhabitants, thus transforming villages into towns with an above-average pattern of individual houses but lacking many of the services and public goods traditionally associated with cities of any size. A similar study of the impact of urban growth on open space in and around cities in the United States concluded that 1.4 million hectares of open space was lost between 1990 and 2000 (McDonald et al., 2010). In contrast to the US, where large settlements combining housing and businesses have grown in recent years on greenfield sites, often in non-municipal jurisdictions, in France small towns or villages with high rates of growth do not transform themselves into city-like entities. These are largely residential, car-dependent districts which have benefited from lower land values than in many large communities, but are more exposed to increases in fuel costs. Many projects which absorb a lot of land such as logistics and shopping centres generate relatively few jobs, and correspond to a pattern of commercial property development subject to over-building, with attendant consequences in the form of under-utilised facilities (*Le Monde*, 2010b).

It is one thing to provide forecasts of the overall population of a country, and another to anticipate where they might live. The distribution of population across France has been changing in recent years in ways which are broadly similar to what can be seen in other developed countries e.g., Germany, Poland, the United States. Some French regions are expected to decline absolutely (Champagne–Ardenne) and others will grow more slowly than the national average (Nord-Pas-de-Calais, Lorraine, Bourgogne, all in the north–northeast quadrant of France). Paris–Ile de France will increase by 10 per cent, but the Loire region, Bretagne, Poitou–Charentes, Midi-Pyrénées, and Languedoc–Roussillon can expect higher growth rates of between 18 and 28 per cent. And the fastest growing regions will also have the larger share of people under twenty. These internal shifts have significant implications for the distribution of and access to core public services, urban design, and transportation connections within, between, and beyond (*Le Monde*, 2011). Given current trends, only a portion of this growth will benefit existing cities, whose size and spatial organization often make a critical difference not only to the location of major infrastructures, but to their financial viability as well. The urban periphery, where change is easier to start but more difficult to channel, will be under more pressure than town centers, where urban management stands a better chance of success. The conclusion is inescapable that undeveloped land is being urbanized *without necessarily gaining the benefits of agglomeration effects* associated historically with urban development.

Third, rights are often linked to housing. Property rights, including the right to privacy within one's dwelling and to transfer title, have been fundamental elements of the social and political structure, in some regions for centuries, conveying both voting rights and fiscal obligations. Agrarian societies often limited physical mobility through tenure arrangements that tied people to estates. Since the end of feudalism, the market economy and the relative absence of legal restrictions on movement gave rise to the impression that the settlement pattern is based on freely negotiated choices by individuals and families. The reality is a bit more complicated: people may wish to live in places where their chances of finding work happen to be low, or where the cost of living is too high given their income, or where they do not have a legal right to work. Migration in the early twenty-first century – even for those who are legal residents – is often a mix between constraint and opportunity filtered through tax laws, residency requirements, and other regulatory measures more often designed to deter rather than to attract newcomers. Policy objectives to promote home ownership in the twentieth century were inspired by the belief that, by giving even the lower middle class a financial stake in an asset and in a community, the attraction of socialism, or, worse, of communism, would be weakened. This has had unintended consequences, generating the politics of NIMBY-ism, "not in my back yard": people understandably defend acquired rights when housing tenancy often correlates with exclusive access to better schools and environmental amenities.

It is hard to anticipate what new right people will enjoy that is linked to the ownership of real property. Civic rights, which in the past had been linked to ownership of property above a certain value, are now universal, irrespective of wealth or mode of tenure. Tenants, for example, can often vote on the same issues as property owners even though their respective interests may be affected differently by the outcome. Anti-discrimination laws also affect access to and therefore demand for housing. (In many emerging economies, however, the issue of rights is still alive: services linked to residency in China, *hukou*, could be the hottest political issue in that country in the near future.) Whether states must provide housing at least under certain conditions proved to be divisive during the Habitat II UN Conference on Human Settlements, in Istanbul, 1996. Several OECD countries (e.g., Spain) took the position that housing is a basic right, to be enshrined in law and even in a constitution; others, including the United States, could not concur, out of concern to create a new entitlement for citizens.

Fourth, innovation is less apparent in the housing sector – discounting, of course, recent innovations in housing finance which turned out to cause unprecedented losses. We live in houses where people have lived before: the sanitary plumbing, methods for heating, cooking and cooling, lighting, and the like inside have changed – but within a physical structure which can still be used much as it had been generations ago. Many vernacular modes of building have virtues which are of considerable value for risk reduction (houses on stilts that survive flooding) or climate extremes (extreme heat in Yemen, heavy snow in northern Michigan). But innovation in the form of research on construction methods, building materials, land-use development, renovation and conversions, better ways to control risks and environmental externalities, and so on is under-funded, compromised by the large number of small home-builders, the complexity of building and design codes and zoned land uses which fragment markets and inhibit the adoption of new techniques, and community resistance based on fear of change. Innovation in governance to improve social, cultural and political acceptance for new ways of constructing, renovating and using housing, must be a priority on the way to sustainability.

Infrastructure investment and planning are critical to any change in what kind of housing is built, and where. Peter Newton, writing about the potential to add housing to and transform the pattern of development in the older, ageing ring of suburbs around Australian cities, called for "a new wave of urban innovation ... for a twenty-first century transition to sustainable metropolitan development" (Newton, 2011: 101). The key elements involve a new governance approach for what he calls a "transitions arena ... to stimulate and coordinate innovation and action around 'wicked' public policy issues"; a project planning and design system capable of rapidly assembling virtual models for regenerated precincts; new business models; and new businesses to deliver construction, fitting between the traditional subcontract producing houses on greenfield sites and commercial operators building multi-storey structures on dense sites. Alongside these, admittedly not very glamorous, needs are the stuff of technology dreamers who are enthralled by new lighting and cooling systems, new materials, and the application of information technology to control and manage the built environment.

Innovation is often greater in sectors more open to competition. But competition in construction is handicapped by a number of factors including regulatory barriers associated with licensing skilled labor and the division of work by craft-based skills on sites, restrictions in the trade of imported materials and products, and building codes themselves (OECD, 2008). Local building firms, which tend to be small, therefore have market advantages which also reflect the size of local markets. Successful large firms, which tend to work on large projects, are also favored by a proven record which may be a precondition for tendering. The business of house-building has more in common with nineteenth-century commercial practices, including debt financing and estate development, than other twentieth-century industries. Fragmentation has deterred research into new construction methods or materials; the postwar pursuit of mass production and large-scale site assembly, which reconstruction and mass migration made imperative, has reverted to earlier forms of housing supply. Innovation at the technical level to improve energy efficiency and reduce carbon emissions, and to adapt the current and future housing stock to climate change and the impact of natural catastrophes, will have to be synchronized with financial, social, and planning instruments to deliver a higher level of sustainability, a tall order.

To summarize, housing is linked to other factors that affect growth, but in ways that show how much more conservative it is than many other sectors, less open to innovation, more strongly linked to codes, contracts, and other legally binding instruments. The changing demographics of society – more one- and two-person households, a doubling of the over-sixty-five age group – are more important factors affecting the housing stock than the size of the population. Urban housing policy was aligned with the factors of growth for much of the twentieth century; policies shaped by that period however have not been revised for the twenty-first century. If the factors of growth linked to housing have changed, perhaps it is also time to reassess some of the macroeconomic assumptions that underlay policies in recent decades.

Questioning assumptions about housing and economic growth

Five years after the onset of the crisis, with few reforms in place in finance and virtually none on the stock of regulations affecting housing and land use at the sub-national level, two basic assumptions in housing policy about markets and growth should be subject to critical scrutiny: (1) that homeownership helps to stabilize social conditions in cities where people from different places and of different origins come together, and gives them an incentive to remain employed so as to keep their mortgages, and (2) that housing policy should promote labor mobility from regions of higher unemployment to places where firms are hiring. Both contributed to housing policies that steered governments toward treacherous financial shoals; both need to be re-examined in the light of experience.

Does homeownership strengthen social stability? Measures justified by the policy objective of promoting home ownership contributed to the crash which in turn has left millions out of the housing market, perhaps for their lifetime. Home ownership was embedded in policies earlier in the twentieth century when competing socialist and communist ideologies exploited the fear that capitalism would keep workers in a permanent underclass, ill-housed, ill-fed, ill-clothed. The bias in favor of home ownership continues to justify tax benefits for interest on mortgage payments, subsidies for low-income groups, and the massive influence of Fannie Mae and Freddie Mac in the United States. Now that social unrest is once again claiming the attention of politicians, measures to promote social stability must look attractive.

In fact the measures used by governments to promote home ownership may not even be efficient in achieving that objective, as the OECD noted in its 2007 survey of the economy of the United States. This survey cited four tax breaks to homeowners: the income derived from housing service (net imputed rent) is not taxed; homeowners can exclude up to $250,000 ($500,000 for a married couple filing jointly) of capital gains on the sale of real property; mortgage interest payments on debt for a primary or secondary residence on up to $1 million in acquisition debt and up to $100,000 in home equity debt are fully deductible; and local real estate taxes are deductible from federal income tax. As a result, the rate of taxation of housing is close to zero, and in some cases negative. These tax expenditures come at a large cost to the budget: the President's Tax Reform Panel identified incentives for homeownership as the second largest tax expenditure (after health deductions), with a total cost of over $700 billion during financial year 2006–7 excluding the non-taxation of imputed rent (another $185 billion). (In early 2012, the *Financial Times* reported that the mortgage interest tax deduction was estimated to cost the Treasury $107 billion annually). The US Treasury may need between $121 billion and $193 billion to bail out Fannie Mae and Freddie Mac; even if those institutions recover after receiving such injections, the question can be asked whether that money could have been spent to better effect if the housing sector had been healthier in the first place (André, 2010: 33, 41–2).

Tax breaks and credit facilitation measures put in place by law for the express purpose of promoting homeownership have little effect on the propensity to own; moreover, the wider social benefits of homeownership are probably exaggerated, and in any case are difficult to disentangle from other factors such as educational opportunities that affect social mobility and lifestyle. After decades of housing development in the United States (and elsewhere) based on owner-occupied single-family houses, access to particular schools, recreational facilities, and even shopping is often a matter of "buying in," acquiring a house within a given district. This is self-perpetuating: people may have no choice but to become owners, because other forms of tenancy do not provide equivalent access to the services and amenities they want. In many cities the right mix of services and amenities is available only to homeowners: the rental offerings are simply not comparable to individually owned properties. The roll-over of capital gains from the sale of a primary residence further reinforces homeownership, limiting consumer choice. Clearly this has consequences for labor mobility.

Has the bias toward ownership produced a more stable and cohesive society? A more resilient economy? And how would one know? Many countries with relatively low rates of homeownership – Switzerland, Germany, Sweden – are not associated with anti-capitalist or radical social movements. Negative equity problems and a huge volume of foreclosures in the United States did not provoke marches on Washington; there are no tent cities between the Capitol and the White House. Spain and Greece, with higher levels of homeownership than in the United States, have had to cope with serious unrest. Homeownership does not bring with it the wider social benefits that made it a keystone in social policy for generations (*The Economist*, 2009).

The assumption that housing mobility reduces unemployment and improves resource allocation probably held true in the past, at least in large economies with sufficient regional variation to make mobility attractive in labor markets when the nature of work changes, and when unemployment rises. Applied to urban development in the nineteenth and twentieth centuries, economic theory favored labor mobility by making it easier for people to move to live where their chances of employment are greater. This neo-classical approach removed obstacles to individual mobility. It assumed, furthermore, that an attachment to a place is not rational in economic terms if one can do better by relocation (OECD, 2011: 184–204). A fluid housing market, one in which supply corresponds to demand and in which the sale, purchase, or lease of housing is unimpeded by red tape and high conveyancing costs, supposedly promotes the redistribution of labor from places of high unemployment to places where there are jobs.

Building urban areas on the assumption that relocation or settlement should be easy has implications for the design of housing and for housing markets. In the logic of mobility, the more places resemble each other, with similar housing, schools, retail facilities, and the like, the easier it is for people to relocate. Space in the old Fordist economy could be developed wholesale on the basis of standardized models and zoned land-use patterns. In an economic version of classical geometry, this model assumes that space has no irregularity or qualitative features, or at least none that matter. This makes it easier to transform space into uniform units of measurement against which profit and loss, tax, and investment can be calculated. And it assumes that personal preferences can be accommodated in a large, fairly homogeneous average middle. This is the way urban areas grew in many parts of the western world in the twentieth century, and this is how many cities in emerging economies are growing today.

Clearly migration on this scale is not possible today. Moreover, even before the crisis of 2008, relocation for employment ranked only third after housing-related and family-related reasons. Many places which in the past had generated new jobs and attracted migrants, such as California and the South West US, suffered high unemployment and some of the worst housing market problems in the 2008 crisis. The places which are adding jobs are not necessarily calling for the skills which people who are unemployed are offering. Economists recognize an implicit contradiction between promoting homeownership or rental markets with long leases when it comes to the dynamics of labor markets. People who own houses where housing costs are high are unwilling to move to places where costs are low (an acute problem in the UK and in Spain), in part because the better labor market in more expensive localities (meaning that the chances for someone of finding a job are better) is reflected in housing prices. And this leaves to one side the inconvenient fact that people may want to remain where they are because of family connections, community life, the quality of schools, a spouse's career prospects, or other factors that make life complicated. People often live where they have family and community ties, even when their economic prospects would be better if they moved to someplace else: many other factors trump economic logic.

The assumption that people move to jobs is under pressure in the face of evidence that increasingly, employers want to locate where the people they employ want to live. And these are very often cities where the cost of housing is affordable only for the best-paid or foreigners seeking safety. For everyone else, the high cost of housing gives rise to different strategies, the trade-off being privacy at a greater distance from the center, or less space but better daily transport. The old manufacturing economy which absorbed low-skilled rural migrants and integrated them into cities has been eclipsed by the rise of the service sector with a wider range of specializations and high percentages of dual-income households, and whose employees make greater demands for urban amenities than the blue-collar workers of past decades. The shift to jobs that call for higher levels of education and skills is good for the economy as a whole. Housing policies however remain shaped by the old industrial economy which assume that people will move for work. The point is not to make housing markets less fluid, but to question how much they contribute to adjusting labor markets and reallocating resources in an economy which is turning toward a "jobs-to-people" paradigm.

What can be done in the short term to reform housing policy? Had leaders known then that the crisis would last four more years, they might have been more willing to adopt policy reforms and capacity-building measures. Today, when nothing else seems to be able to get the economy started, there is talk of what to do about housing. Macro-economists, asked how to generate a recovery by lifting housing construction, call for regulatory reforms of real estate markets, reductions in transaction costs to increase turnover, relaxed planning requirements to expand the supply of land, revised building codes to reduce costs, increased infrastructure investment to enlarge the areas available for housing and retail facilities, and better transport to enhance mobility – all supply-side measures which take time to implement and, to be coherent, compel a degree of planning at city and regional scale that has not exactly been in evidence in recent years. Had more been done a few years ago, the results might already be visible. But housing markets do not turn on a dime: it takes many months to release land, secure credit, assemble materials and labor, and, in the meantime, other factors are likely to have more influence, either depressing markets or accelerating sales.

There is a regulatory governance gap in housing policy which makes rapid government action unlikely, perhaps unwise. Fiscal and monetary policies evolve relatively quickly at the national level and can affect housing by changing the interest rate for builders and buyers. But the linkages between monetary policy and construction are not smooth. Policies and practices relevant to land use and transport planning, utility networks and the authorizations to connect properties to utilities, building codes, environmental regulations applied by local and regional authorities evolve relatively slowly and are difficult to co-ordinate; regulatory procedures are often inefficient at the local level, where they matter the most. Housing starts – a critical economic indicator – are subject to regulatory uncertainty whenever it is difficult to anticipate the outcome of an administrative procedure such as a permit application or occupancy permit. Central governments can do only so much when many micro-reforms are more a matter of local and regional or state authorities. Conveyancing requirements and their associated costs, rental regulations, building codes and inspections, land-use planning and environmental permits are embedded in professional practice and administrative structures. And because sub-national jurisdictions have an interest to maintain or increase the value of properties for purposes of collecting taxes on immovable assets, they may try to "cherry-pick" housing, to attract or retain property owners who will be net contributors to the local treasury. Equally, local jurisdictions facing significant budgetary pressures rely on revenue from the kind of transaction fees that central governments might wish to reduce or eliminate. Property developers can easily afford to bring lawyers to the negotiating table with local governments, which often lack the capacity to meet on anything like equal terms. Attention must be paid to the tools that local governments need to make appropriate decisions, ranging from cadasters and data about environmental conditions and risks to the facilities to process permit applications and handle appeals.

The fact remains that the bundle of regulations affecting housing and land use which contributed to the asset bubble remain unreformed. As a process, reform would have to bring together the credit system, land use and regional development, the construction, design and property professions, and all the sectors responsible for local service provision, from transport and waste management to health and education. In other words, a multi-level, whole-of-government approach would be needed, one sufficiently broad and flexible to take account of extreme local variations and sufficiently transparent to avoid regulatory capture and opportunities for corruption. This is not a quick fix to the economic consequences of the crisis, the fall in construction activity, and the problem of negative equity.

A wholesale review of housing policies, from credit and banking to building codes and land-use permits, was overdue in the run-up to the crisis. Sometimes a crisis makes policy reform easier: this was the case in 1990–92 when housing imploded in several countries with recessionary consequences (Sweden, Germany, Canada, etc.). At that time, however, few jurisdictions had adopted regulatory policies calling for evidence-based decision-making, consultation, and indicators for evaluation. Progress has been made in recent years to improve multi-level regulatory coherence, to strengthen public participation and transparency, to simplify administrative procedures, to integrate environmental and regulatory impact assessments, and to carry out both *ex-ante* and *ex-post* regulatory impact analysis – but the full set of regulatory tools and institutions has yet to be brought to bear on the housing policy agenda.

(See Chapter 7 for more background on regulatory policy.) There can be no progress if experts on regulatory reform are not engaged from the beginning, bringing both their technical knowledge of how to revise bundles of regulations and improve regulatory governance, and years of experience with the practical implementation of a complex package of reforms.

To be clear: land-use planning and infrastructure planning and expenditure may be devolved onto local and regional governments in both centralized and federated systems on the grounds that decision-making should be brought closer to the people who are most affected, and who in many cases will be asked to finance and pay for public investments. But increasingly, issues about the future are like nesting boxes: the smaller boxes must fit into the larger ones, and the larger ones have to make room for the smaller ones. Regional and local plans must take account of national programs and objectives for energy, clean air and water, pollution and remediation, and disaster reduction, to mention just the usual suspects, and issues of trans-border co-operation, inward investment, competitiveness, and sustainable agriculture often come into play.

The constituency for reform – those who would benefit – has probably shrunk as economic insecurity and fiscal consolidation squeeze the middle class further. The electoral dynamics for reform were already weak in the first years of the twenty-first century, when reforms might have been easier. Deficit-conscious governments for the foreseeable future have to make the trade-off between alienating home owners who have not lost financially in the crisis, and gaining votes from voters who stand to gain in a recovery. The temptation is great to hand the portfolio to experts. And here the usual problems appear: the experts who dominate the agenda often over-simplify; all the relevant experts are not consulted; experts do not agree among themselves. In the end the key decisions have to be taken by politicians.

What could be the future of housing policy?

Changes in assumptions in response to economic, social, and environmental trends should shape a new set of goals and visions for housing. But any changes in housing policy – or in policies that affect housing – will have to alter the existing stock of regulations in several sectors. What would a regulatory reform program for the housing sector look like? Regulatory reform in housing must address three challenges: risk management, cross-sectoral co-ordination, and multi-level coherence:

- Regulatory risk management is needed: for the financial sector; to reduce the vulnerability of housing to natural disasters; to control corruption at the local level, and to anticipate moral hazard problems due to government intervention and implicit guarantees.
- Regulatory multi-level coherence covers high administrative costs, unnecessary and time-consuming delays for land-use or occupancy permits, the impact of fees on local government budgets, competition in construction, problems of weak enforcement, obsolete or excessively costly building codes and regulatory barriers to innovation, zoning, and, in general, the misalignment between national and local demands and objectives.
- Regulatory policy coherence addresses the problem of co-ordinating housing trends and solutions with health, education, transport, and the environment. Regional and local decisions related to housing will be affected by national sectoral policies, and will in turn affect outcomes in those sectors.

This is a huge undertaking, which is why a healthy dose of caution is necessary.

Much is at stake because the picture is admittedly bleak: a prolonged housing slump stranding millions of owners with negative equity, inhibiting family choices about employment, marriage or divorce, whether to have children, how to care for ageing parents; the retraining of unemployed construction workers; deferred maintenance especially of rental properties; continued banking balance-sheet fragility; unaffordable housing for millions in cities where there are jobs for them; and a banking sector adverse to lending. The number of households in inadequate housing in 2025 in developed countries could reach thirty-two million, reversing recent gains (McKinsey, 2014). Municipalities will be hard-pressed to maintain the current level of property taxes in real terms, leading to difficult decisions about which services to continue, which to cut, and which to provide for a fee. And housing prices will remain high in the large, global cities such as Paris, London, and New York, reflecting demand from foreigners seeking financial and political diversification and from a small number of high-end, competitive professional sectors, and the sheer size of their labor markets. The tensions between regions characterized by falling, stagnant, or rising property markets will weigh on national governments when considering interest rates, fiscal policy, and visas for non-citizens. Can this policy mess be untangled?

The middle class is critical to the political economy of reform in a public culture that increasingly facilitates and promotes public participation, and is suspicious if not intolerant of top-down decisions taken without public consultation. Building a constituency for reform is critical to the success of any reform strategy, and perhaps more so for structural reforms which affect each household's economic opportunities. Parliamentary democracy, the expansion of the suffrage and active participation in public affairs have been associated with the growth of a middle class with a high level of social capital, a commitment to education, and a willingness to adopt innovations. But its optimism has been undermined, evident in indicators of declining trust in government across a variety of countries with different growth rates over the past two decades. Trends that are the frequent subject of columnists today reflect concerns that were already manifest twenty years before: the slow growth of the earnings of male workers; the likelihood for many that their children will do less well; and trends showing that housing and a college education, those two key features of middle-class families in the postwar era, may be less likely to repay the investment they absorb.

Why bring up the issue of the middle-class squeeze? Without middle-class support, the politics for reform in the housing sector remain elusive at best. The insecurity of the middle class shifts the politics of reform away from rebuilding economic fundamentals and toward reassurance of existing measures of social protection. Any package of reforms in favor of markets and consumer choice, combining reforms of housing finance and taxation, tenure contracts and rent regulations, land-use and zoning rules and objectives, environmental policies and the modernization and extension of infrastructure and transportation services, will have to persuade the middle class that the future can be better and safer.

The challenge – perhaps in housing more than in anything else – lies in finding ways that blend a liberal approach to economic change with the social and environmental concerns of people in the places where they live. How and where – and for whom – new housing is built will shape the next phase of urban development. Strategic spatial planning becomes critical – not restrictive, predictive planning which freezes the status quo, but a creative exercise to identify the assets of places and to enhance their potential. As a form of strategic insight, it helps give policy-makers and the public a range of options and some insight into the consequences that could follow. Its task is to exert influence by framing ways of translating intentions into reality, mobilizing many actors, leveraging investment. It can clarify the problems of policy coherence, the obstacles to implementation, inherited professional specializations, the lack of multi-year and multi-sectoral budgets, the different timeframes of public and private sector decision-makers. Perhaps it can contribute to solutions that transcend them (OECD, 2006: 135–6).

Housing is linked to three of the most important issues facing government and society: how to accommodate an ageing and changing population with its specific needs, inclusively; how to promote green growth when construction, as an activity, is energy-intensive, and when the built housing stock and its relationship to transport and land use are responsible for significant recurring impacts on the use of energy and resources; and how to reduce the risks of physical and social disasters. Policies and strategies that mobilize private investment in relation to one or more of these objectives will help restore housing to a sustainable path by working with long-term trends. Structural, fiscal, and regulatory reforms aligned with these policy objectives may be more likely to attract political support than reforms grounded in macro-economic theory which are too remote from the preoccupations and interests of people in the cities where they live.

Ageing, from the macro-economic perspective, is a question of how to provide quality housing to people on fixed incomes whose needs for social and medical services increase over time. The crisis has brought back fear of a return to the time when the elderly fall back into poverty, or at least to a lower standard of living. Independence and self-reliance for the elderly will be as important to people in the middle class aged twenty-five to fifty-five as to their parents; the alternative, the multi-generational household, has already returned due to the circumstances facing young people (delayed marriage, unemployment, etc.); it could again be a pattern that marks advancing years.

The challenges for housing an ageing population include: adapting dwelling units so that people can stay in them even as their physical and mental conditions alter; maintaining contact at the local level and across distances, including the use of telecommunications and video; convenient and accessible transport for people; and arranging housing to promote social interaction including across generations. Local cultural and socio-economic circumstances will dictate particular solutions, but innovative methods to renovate housing (or even to build housing so that it is suitable to people as they age), and of the financing to cover the costs, will bear international, cross-cultural comparison (OECD, 1992, 2003).

Green growth is one of those elusive terms that means different things to different people. In one sense it is nothing new: a conservative use of resources is always to be preferred to waste. What then is distinctive about green growth? First, that the parameters and targets can and will be measured, with indicators that can be disaggregated down to the level of the individual household and aggregated upwards to large metropolitan areas. Individual efforts will be necessary to achieve collective results. In terms of housing, this will call for extensive renovations to the existing stock, designs and technologies for new buildings which in turn will need renovation over time to remain state-of-the-art, monitored construction and waste treatment operations, integrated transport-housing strategies, and much more.

The transition from established city-building practices to new standards and procedures will itself generate economic activity. Green growth will affect public procurement, trade in urban goods and services, and employment, of course positively in the eyes of those who promote it. Because different parts of a metropolitan area call for different degrees of change, and because the costs and benefits of change vary accordingly, investments for green growth will have implications for the perceived value of individual properties and neighborhoods. New governance arrangements for green growth management will be needed as well. And existing tax arrangements affecting housing and public service investment will need to be re-examined (Corfee-Morlot et al., 2009; and Kamal-Chaoui et al., 2009).

This is a huge agenda. In 2010, the OECD's third Urban Roundtable of Mayors and Ministers focused on cities and green growth. Nations cannot reduce environmental costs and impacts except by tackling them at the urban level, a challenge that can be met only if national policies and price signals can be combined with different sectoral funding streams and financial instruments that help cities adjust. Energy, transport, public procurement, jobs in the environmental sector, dominate the agenda. Interaction between experts, officials, stakeholders, and the public, to understand what is at stake, and to develop a medium-term strategy that might survive electoral and economic shocks and cycles; capacity-building to support adaptation at local and regional scale; and a framework to help cities assess progress over time as well as across locations, critical for cross-sectoral co-ordination: all these matter. But the closest the OECD report on cities and climate change (2010) came to discussing housing was in the reference to density and spatial form, whether in compact cities where development is concentrated in and radiates from an urban core, or in polycentric city-regions.[1] A separate report on compact cities however went into the details about measuring densification and housing affordability, regulatory tools for greenfield sites and for better use of existing, built-up areas, and how high-quality urban design can improve the acceptability of higher density (OECD, 2012).

Risk, the third challenge, is closer to the management of public goods and private rights. The emergence of the gated community or enclave, and the spread of passive tele-surveillance technologies, are symptomatic of the demand for security, but also of its political and social costs. At the very least, they speak of the felt need to identify with a place, and to live in a place with an identity. Anything that threatens this is perceived as a threat to the community, and weakens trust in government.

People expect to be protected against known risks with catastrophic potential, and to be assisted should a catastrophe occur. Millions of people live in areas where they are exposed to natural disasters: redevelopment to sustain urban life in these city-regions could be an enormous opportunity for the long term. Then there are the phenomena of rising urban heat, water shortages, air pollution, trends that are intimately linked to the shape and structure of individual cities. Density, largely a matter of housing, is a key variable: higher density alleviates many of the negative consequences of large settlements. States possess legal powers that allow governments to prevent construction in flood plains or in zones prone to devastating fires, to force relocations under certain conditions, and to suspend the operation of certain rules and obligations during an emergency, and impose others. But their ability to protect people against the loss of a house in an economic storm which washed away equity and left a deep residue of debt is limited.

We know that people are notoriously poor judges of the risks to which they are actually exposed; that emergency services often prove to be chronically deficient when asked to perform; that governments at all levels are ill-prepared to reconstruct a territory that has been badly damaged or destroyed in a catastrophe; that governments are reluctant, to say the least, to re-shape the settlement pattern of a region in the light of new evidence that the risks of a disaster are far greater than had previously been believed; and that popular enthusiasm to do things differently, which is so strong in the immediate after-effects of a crisis, abates quickly. Housing economics do not yet price in the level of risk to which owners are exposed, depending on the frequency of a flood, and whether it is linked to other environmental handicaps. Climate change could alter the exposure of property and increase the likelihood that more than one disaster could occur at the same time (Chen et al., 2011). Providing a reasonable level of protection against social disorder and environmental disaster was the responsibility of the medieval commune; why not of the modern metropolis?

These three imperatives – housing for an ageing population, green growth, and protection against disasters – imply changes in the fabric, scale, and complexity of cities from the level of the individual neighborhood to that of the metropolitan region. Putting them together into an intelligent urban housing strategy will mark a break with the market-based macro-economic policies of the past which put more emphasis on housing starts as a leading indicator, and treated housing as a branch of finance: these have signally failed to cope either with the unmet demand for middle-class and low-income housing in cities where housing costs are well above national averages and affordability norms, or to improve the prospects for growth in cities which are highly affordable because their economic outlook is not bright.

Housing policy reform is a governance challenge, operating on all levels of government and across sectors. Critical to the making of the crisis, housing is emblematic of the kind of "blind spot" when policy-makers focus on a topic from a narrow, and in this case macro-economic, perspective. Since the early 2000s, reports and news articles have been tracking the upward trend in house prices, identifying the early symptoms of an asset bubble and outlining possible scenarios that might follow from actions taken by central banks and governments. Policy- makers knew then what to do: there was no lack of information about packages of short- and long-term policy measures to bring housing supply and demand into better balance – and of the risks and costs of not doing so. Yet little was done: not only was it easy to procrastinate; it was also hard to see how reforms could be translated into political gains. The only remaining option then was to wait to act until a crisis in the hope that the crisis would make reform easier; instead reform has become more difficult.

Inertia has become a substitute for policy when difficult decisions with long-term consequences are needed. Yet few decisions can have greater consequences for the organization of cities and regions than what kind of housing should be built, and where. Simplistic measures to relax land-use permits or provide subsidies for down payments reflect short-term imperatives, overlook the lessons of past errors and lack a vision of the future our cities and regions, making the challenges of ageing, risk reduction, and green growth more, not less, difficult. Having mis-labeled the problem of housing policy as a matter of finance and monetary policy because banks failed, governments have avoided micro-economic reforms to redirect housing policy away from twentieth-century goals and toward twenty-first century policy objectives.

A shorter version of this chapter appeared in Town and Country Planning, *March 2012: 156–60.*

Note

1 This publication includes a lot of the material in the 2009 report edited by Kamal-Chaoui, et al. On traditional and innovative governance tools, with an

emphasis on rebuilding cities and their housing stock, see Jeroen van der Heijden, *Governance for Urban Sustainability and Resilience: Responding to Climate Change and the Relevance of the Built Environment* (Cheltenham: Edward Elgar, 2014).

References

André, Christophe (2010), "A bird's eye view of OECD housing markets," OECD Economics Department Working Paper no. 746, 28 January, p. 10.

Andrews, Dan, Aida Caldera Sánchez and Åsa Johansson (2011), "Housing markets and structural policies in OECD countries," OECD Economics Department Working Paper no. 836, 25 January.

Chen, Yu, Gwilym Pryce and Danny Mackay (2011), "Flood risk, climate change and housing economics: the four fallacies of extrapolation," University of Glasgow: Adam Smith Research Foundation Working Papers.

Corfee-Morlot, Jan, Lamia Kamal-Chaoui, Michael G. Donovan, Ian Chochran, Alexis Robert and Pierre-Jonathan Teasdale (2009), "Cities, climate change and multilevel governance," OECD Environmental Working Paper no. 14.

The Economist (2003a), "Close to bursting; house of cards," 31 May;

The Economist (2003b) "Shaky foundations: the higher house prices climb, the more they are likely to fall," 29 November.

The Economist (2005), "After the fall: soaring house prices have given a huge boost to the world economy. What happens when they drop," 18 June.

The Economist (2007), "Cracks in the façade: America's riskiest mortgages are crumbling. How far will the damage spread?" 24 March.

The Economist (2009), "Home ownership," Briefing, 18 April.

Financial Times (2012), Lex column, "US house prices," 3 January.

Financial Times (2006), Martin Wolf, "Dangers of great housing market delusion," 17 April.

Glaeser, Edward L., Joseph Gyourko and Raven E. Saks (2005), "Why have housing prices gone up?" NBER Working Paper no. 11129.

Kamal-Chaoui, Lamia and Alexis Robert (eds) (2009), "Competititve cities and climate change," OECD Regional Development Working Paper no. 2.

Kelly, Jane-Frances (2011), *The Housing We'd Choose* (Melbourne: Grattan Institute).

Klineberg, Eric (2013), *Going Solo: The Extraordinary Rise and Surprising Appeal of Living Alone* (New York: Penguin).

Kramer, Steven Philip (2014), *The Other Population Crisis: What Governments Can Do About Falling Birth Rates* (Washington DC: Woodrow Wilson Center Press, and Baltimore: Johns Hopkins University Press).

Le Monde (1995), "Pres de six millions de personnes vivent seules, selon l'Insée," 20 April.

Le Monde (2010a), "La fôret ne gagne plus la France," 9 February.

Le Monde (2010b), "L'Insée dessine la France de 2040 et la répartition de ses 73 millions d'habitants," 9 December.

Le Monde (2010c), "En 2050, un français sur trois aura plus de 60 ans, estime l'Insée," 28 October.

Le Monde (2011), Gregoire Allix, "Les banlieues champignons prospèrent en France," 5 July.

McDonald, Robert I., Richard T. Forman and Peter Kareiva (2010), "Open space loss and land inequality in United States' cities, 1990–2000," *PLoS One*, 5:3: e9509 DOI:10.1371/journal.pone.0009509.

McKinsey Global Institute, (2014), "A Blueprint for Addressing the Global Affordable Housing Challenge."

Mian, Atif and Amir Sufi (2014), *House of Debt: How They (and You) Caused the Great Recession, and How We Can Prevent It from Happening Again* (Chicago: University of Chicago Press).

Newton, Peter W. (2011), "Beyond greenfield and brownfield: the challenge of regenerating Australia's greyfield suburbs," *Built Environment*, 36:1: 81–104.

OECD (1992), *Urban Policies for Ageing Populations* (Paris: OECD). ISBN: 92-64-13758-0.

OECD (2003), *Ageing, Housing and Urban Development* (Paris: OECD). DOI: 10.1787/9789264176102-en.

OECD (2006), *Competitive Cities in the Global Economy* (Paris: OECD). DOI:10.1787/9789264027091-en.

OECD (2007), *OECD Economic Surveys: United States 2007* (Paris: OECD); on household debt, pp. 75–96. DOI: 10.1787/eco_surveys-usa-2007-6-en.

OECD (2008), OECD Competition Committee, Roundtable no. 86 on "Land use restrictions as barriers to entry," and no. 87 on "Competition in the construction industry." Reprinted in *OECD Journal: Competition Law and Policy*, 1–2:7–73 and 153–71 respectively. DOI: 10.1787/clp-10-5kmhbhp87tbv.

OECD (2010), *Cities and Climate Change* (Paris: OECD). DOI: org/10.1787/9789264091375-en.

OECD (2011), *Economic Policy Reforms: Going for Growth* (Paris: OECD). DOI: 10.1787/growth-2011-en.

OECD (2012), *Compact City Policies: A Comparative Assessment* (Paris: OECD), OECD Green Growth Studies. DOI: org/10.1787/9789264167865-en.

Siedentop, Stefan and Stefan Fina (2010), "Urban sprawl beyond growth: the effect of demographic change on infrastructure costs," *Flux*, 79–80 (January–June): 90–100.

3

Infrastructure and innovation: new limits to growth

Infrastructure investment and innovation come up repeatedly in discussions of urban and economic growth. To state the obvious, infrastructure is concentrated in cities, and innovation is an urban activity *par excellence*. Less well known are (1) the gap between the funding needed to maintain and modernize infrastructures and the sums invested and (2) what the European Commission referred to as an "innovation emergency" in 2011: these new limits to growth increase the costs of congestion, add to the problems of waste management and water, lower productivity and job creation, compromise the diffusion of new technologies, and retard the adjustment to climate change. Editorialists remind us that it has never been cheaper for governments to borrow and that many corporations have record cash reserves. Missing are more projects to make cities better, safer, and more productive.

The infrastructure deficit

The size of the economic stimulus packages in OECD member countries averaged 2.5 per cent of GDP; in Australia, Canada, Korea, New Zealand, and the United States, the fiscal stimulus exceeded 4 per cent. Grants earmarked for capital investment amounted to more than 70 per cent of stimulus spending in Korea and Spain, 56 per cent in Australia, 27 per cent in France and 26 per cent in Germany. Looking for ways to get money into the economy quickly, governments released billions for infrastructure projects, some of which had been suspended in the crisis of 2008. Not much happened. Yes, there were road works; some projects were fast-tracked. But tellingly, government deadlines to spend the money by the end of 2009 were extended, in some cases to 2010 or 2011. But the headline on the front page in May 2012 was sobering: "Finance for big projects cut as banks are squeezed. Money for airports and hospitals down a third. Hope of infrastructure boost for economy hit" (*Financial Times*, 2012a).

Should governments spend more? In a survey of the literature, the OECD concluded that it is hard to tell whether the direction of causality runs from public infrastructure investment to growth or from growth to investment (OECD, 1998), the kind of conclusion that Treasury officials, looking to turn down budget requests, would welcome. In 2008 the OECD Economics Directorate prepared a study of infrastructure investment. But if policy-makers had been interested to see what impact more investment during the crisis would have on growth, they would have learned only how difficult forecasting is. Yes, there would be an impact on output because infrastructure investment would lift employment directly and increase the demand for materials. In addition, infrastructure affects labor markets, competition, the diffusion of technology, access to markets, and environmental costs, among other variables. "While infrastructure can have growth-enhancing effects, the relationship has been difficult to establish empirically," the OECD noted, commenting that the lack of research on this important topic is "somewhat surprising" (OECD 2008).

That there has been a significant deficit in infrastructure investment has been known for years. If governments believed that the private sector needed only an infusion of funds and a relaxation of credit to boost investment in infrastructure, they were sadly mistaken. Financial models were compromised because the crisis itself altered long-term economic forecasts: the rate of return on major investments depends on projections about how the urban economy in 2025 or 2050 might perform, a matter of conjecture and imponderables. The old trend lines no longer apply. What could be the cost of energy? The rate of taxation? Interest rates? How will urban economies and governments generate the revenue to repay loans or provide the fees necessary to make today's investments worthwhile in fifteen or thirty years? Only governments can adopt long-term strategic frameworks, reducing the level of uncertainty.

The crisis occurred at a time when the private sector needed more than money: long-term plans, a vision of the future of cities and of their connections in a global economy, guidance about environmental issues ranging from energy and water to transport, and confidence to solve problems that come between project proposals and their realization. We do not know whether urban development would have continued on previous lines if there had been no global financial crisis in 2008. We know however that the crisis has brought to light deep-seated problems which had been tolerated as "business as usual," that evidence of infrastructure needs had not provoked a major policy reassessment, and that the future of cities depends in part on whether this reassessment can now be launched. And this calls for more and better planning, both strategic and project-based.

Already there was concern about an investment gap for urban infrastructure in the United States in the 1980s when the economist Pat Choate (later, Ross Perot's running mate in the Reform Party in the 1996 Presidential election) identified a range of problems from wastewater treatment plants running at full capacity, to the number of bridges in New York City that must be repaired, and port expansion for imports and exports. Fragmented decision-making, inadequate information, no monitoring system of projects already approved, disorganized capital budgeting, high transaction costs among jurisdictions to determine who pays for what and when, no national inventory of public facilities and the capital stock of fixed assets all combined to make an estimate of current and projected capital needs difficult to set, let alone any estimate of the costs of not meeting those needs, or of the benefits that would follow if those needs were met. The evidence of infrastructure needs remained ad-hoc and episodic, in part, one assumes, because decision-makers were unprepared to deal with the consequences of a national assessment which would generate pressures for a national capital budget and other instruments for sound strategic planning (Choate and Walter 1983).

Some Republicans in the House of Representatives known as the House Wednesday Group recognized the bi-partisan nature of the issue, recommending a federal capital budget as well as a mix of privatization and regulatory reform to reduce delays and achieve managerial efficiency – goals of sound public administration in the days of Herbert Hoover before his legacy was overtaken by the New Deal. Estimates of as much as $315 billion for road repairs, $47.6 billion for bridges (nearly half the US stock was classified as obsolete or deficient), $229 billion for sewerage and water mains, and $50 billion for repairs to public transport systems far exceeded the $33 billion that the Reagan administration was prepared to propose. And these sums would not expand capacity ($130 billion would be needed to complete the Interstate Highway System, 10 per cent of which needed immediate resurfacing) or facilitate the use of new technologies! (*The Economist*, 1982).

The costs of the Reagan era were clear for many to see. *The Wall Street Journal*, not noted for its support for big government, published an op-ed piece by David Alan Aschauer, an economist at the Federal Reserve Bank of Chicago, arguing that an increase in public investment was necessary to lift profit rates and private investment, not to mention productivity (*Wall Street Journal*, 1990a). Not long thereafter, the same paper returned to Aschauer's analysis on its front page to highlight the link between infrastructure and productivity, labeling the former "the third deficit," after trade and the budget (*Wall Street Journal*, 1990b). The newspaper cited data from Aschauer, who made a correlation between the annual growth of productivity in the US which was below that of the UK, France, Germany and Japan, and the lower American level of non-military public investment. The Bush administration's first budget proposed to spend only 3.6 per cent on infrastructure, down from 5.3 per cent in the final year of the Carter administration, in 1979, ten years earlier. Meanwhile states and cities found themselves increasingly unable to make up the difference, faced by rising demands in their own jurisdictions and fiscal limits on what they could borrow and spend. By 1998 the City of New York estimated the cost of keeping its schools, sewers, roads and subways in good repair for ten years at $92 billion, of which more than a quarter, $28.43 billion, would be for the public schools. When budgets were allocated, however, the funding for bridges and roads reached over 65 per cent of need, but public school buildings, barely 45 per cent (*The Economist*, 1998; *New York Times*, 1998). Such figures are open to criticism: Were they inflated as a way of lifting the floor in budget discussions? Were deals implied with the city's construction workers and firms? How transparent would public procurements be? But the visible evidence of unsafe schools and obsolete public transport equipment could not be overlooked.

Financing constraints were imposed by political imperatives having more to do with a dramatic change in federal–state relations in an effort by Reagan to revert to the status quo before the Roosevelt era. If the objective was to limit the burden on the national budget, it was doomed from the start given the expansion of federal regulation and of public policy objectives. (Unfunded mandates had something of the same effect when introduced in the 1990s: the federal government imposed costly requirements on sub-national authorities without allocating the resources needed for compliance, and this when the national government could run a deficit but cities and states had to balance their budgets.) Locally financed infrastructure seemed simpler eighty years before when the goal was to supply most homes with electricity, running water, and sewer connections, when roads had to be paved for the first time, when streetcar networks provided public transport connecting suburbs and city centers. What would Reagan, the former Governor of California, have responded to business leaders in that state who called for $90 billion to be spent over the years 1998–2008 on roads, education, and public services, to cope with an increase in the state's population in the past twenty years and the challenges of future growth? A state which had once led the United States in per capita infrastructure spending ranked twenty-sixth in 1998 (*Financial Times*, 1998).

Built to last, many infrastructure systems continued to function without much regular maintenance, but not indefinitely. Bridge failures are spectacular, and potentially fatal; other systems are more easily ignored, literally "out of sight." Manchester's sewage system of 2,790 miles, most of it built before 1850, had an average of three collapses a day by 1980. Managed by regional water authorities, sewer systems ranked lower than reservoirs, a classic problem when a regulatory authority must meet many different policy objectives. Under-investment meant that the costs of maintenance and renewal of some 1,200 miles must be stretched over many years: by the time the current backlog is reduced, a new list of projects will have taken its place. Meanwhile costs will have risen: the estimate in 1980 to replace 1,200 miles at a cost of £1.2 million per mile would call for a budget of £1.4 billion; but spread over twenty years the cost per mile at the end will inevitably be higher than at the beginning of the process (*The Economist*, 1980).

By the time better methods for mixed public and private financing and better regulation were available in the 1990s, the problems had grown in scale and urgency. The great Chicago leak of 1992 was an example of the kind of problem which, buried literally under the city, could be overlooked only for so long. Without maps of many individual subterranean systems and networks, comprehensive maps could not be composed. Anyone who had to dig or build had to make the rounds of the different agencies and companies that possessed maps of their own. In the pre-digital era, these complexities made it virtually impossible to plan to reconstruct the subterranean infrastructure of a modern city comprehensively, water, sewers, gas, power, transport, etc., unless of course a district has been destroyed.

Privatization and, with it, diminished direct provision of public services by government called for a proper regulatory framework with new sets of rules and new agencies. Governments needed time for proper sequencing so that the agencies began to function before they assumed the full range of oversight responsibility. This was not always the case, nor has it always been possible to recruit competent staff without hiring people who had been working in the sector affected; information asymmetries can be a major problem. Consumer benefits in the form of low rates are often more attractive politically than a tariff structure that encourages investment. The rapid increase in the number of independent regulatory agencies in the 1990s nevertheless changed the landscape for infrastructures at a time when port expansion to accommodate container traffic was an imperative, major new airports were needed to cope with the growth of traffic (itself a response to deregulation), energy demand increased above forecasts, and a new discourse about competitiveness and livability in the context of globalization made comparisons between cities politically salient (OECD, 2009). But when deregulation appears as a factor – and often a decisive one – in an infrastructure crisis (blackouts and power shortages, inadequate maintenance of a railroad or a bridge, etc.), market-oriented reforms are compromised for the future because their social acceptability has been badly damaged in public opinion.

The view that nothing much can be done to improve things seems to have taken hold in some parts of the developed world. Unable to determine when Americans developed a sense of "fatalism about the declining quality of their infrastructure" when their country had been so "dazzlingly futuristic" in the 1950s, Edward Luce remarked simply that Americans "have adapted around" an infrastructure which has shown its age (*Financial Times*, 2012b). Even if there is massive public pressure to improve public facilities and utilities, change will take years to effect. Meanwhile Americans, who may assume that their country is still ahead, "are unaware of how far behind the rest of the world their country has fallen" in air transport, electricity supply, and most other categories of infrastructure that are factored into the World Economic Forum's competitiveness report. The American Dream which had been built for two hundred years on mobility and communications had become a daily nightmare for millions.

The 1990s, as it happened, was a time of urban change in Europe far more than in the United States. Cities in Central and Eastern Europe absorbed considerable investment in infrastructure, property development especially for retail facilities and industrial plants, and housing. The modernization of a huge stock of postwar, prefabricated multi-storey housing remains a major burden both in terms of cost, and urban redesign. But drawing on lower rents and labor costs as factors to enhance investment, cities such as Warsaw and Leipzig developed new vocations. Europe's changes have been uneven. Rural hinterlands – think of Brandenburg and Mecklenberg-Vorpommern – are no longer inter-dependent on a major metropolitan center, such as Berlin. Cities and regions have declined in eastern Germany, western Poland, eastern Czech Republic, northern France, and northern England, notwithstanding upgraded infrastructures and other public investments or subsidies to address the fortunes of declining industrial and metallurgical districts, and the legacy of decades of environmental pollution. Nevertheless, massive infrastructure investment, especially in and around transport networks in Western and Central Europe, helped to leverage investment in residential and commercial property during the 1990s and after.

It is worth remembering that, in the early 1990s, politics trumped economics, not in the sense that projects were funded which were justified only in terms of electoral calculations or cost-benefit analysis, but in the sense that infrastructure investment was part of a political project, the creation of a new Europe whose borders had changed, whose people would enjoy a new identity and new opportunities. Just as at the end of both World Wars when leaders wanted to redeem sacrifice with a new instauration of social welfare and economic growth, the post-Cold War era redeemed the promises made during the long decades of division and enmity, to reunify the continent by expanding the political and institutional frameworks created in the 1950s and 1960s. Stabilizing democracy often meant then – as it does now – subordinating the economy to politics.

And it happened that there was an economic return on this investment. Chancellor Kohl's decision to convert East German Marks at parity to the Deutschmark gave a spending boost to former DDR citizens. Economists criticized this measure then as making East German labor uncompetitive, given the lower level of skills and productivity after decades of communism. In hindsight, the unification of Germany was well-tempered by several things: the ability to change the education of younger East Germans while they could benefit from greater labor mobility; the geographical proximity between East and West which allowed for a rapid restructuring of productive capacity as firms moved onto high-grade greenfield sites in or on the periphery of cities with an old tradition of trade and manufacturing; and the general economic trend, which carried demand upwards. The cost of German unification inevitably involved some over-spending; no one could know in advance how much needed to be spent, where and on which programs for education, environmental remediation, reforms of the housing sector, or modernization of public administration. But with hindsight, it is possible to argue that, had this investment not been made then, the strength of the economy of Germany and of several of its neighbors, both east and west, would not be as great as it now appears to be. Europe's more competitive economies in the second decade of the twenty-first century are precisely those with the best cross-border and internal infrastructure networks. Cost-benefit analysis to evaluate projects and their financing is highly imperfect. What may look like a sound investment may turn out to be too expensive to operate or upgrade; what may look Pharaonic may turn out to have been far-sighted.

What is a good infrastructure for cities worth? The question is intriguing and absurd at the same time; historical evidence can be used to justify almost any decision. Replacement cost is an accounting fiction. The National Water Council (UK) reported in 1977 that Britain's 350,000 miles of sewers and water mains would cost £28 billion to replace at 1975 prices; that sum today could be more than ten times greater. Without its water supply, New York would be the functional equivalent of Lagos; without its sewer system, London would resemble Calcutta. A US National Council on Public Works put a value of $1 trillion in 1988 on the basic parts of the American national infrastructure (but not including power and communications) (*Wall Street Journal*, 1988). Economist John Kay imagined what would happen if someone today proposed the sewer network built in London by Bazalgette 150 years ago: Treasury assessments of costs and benefits, environmental impact studies, citizen challenges would have added costly delays and reduced the scale of the project. Opportunity costs are impossible to calculate because, without its modern infrastructure, London would not have ridden astride a global empire, or transformed itself in the era of decolonization into a global financial capital. The question of the sewers in 2013 was not just a matter of their remarkable age: the surplus capacity built into the system had reached its limit, and massive new works are now necessary. In the end, however, Kay argued that the issue is not so much value for money as "whether we as a generation leave a better city, or a better environment, than we found" (*Financial Times*, 2013).

Will innovations in information technology reduce the need to update and expand physical infrastructure networks? The hope today is that digital technology, applied to all aspects of urban living and management, will somehow transform the old into the new, capturing the benefits of the digital age to solve the problems of cities. Open data, transparency: the ubiquity of data assumes that we, the people who are generating all this information, will be able to control our lives better with the tools that data can capture. Perhaps information technology will help design policies which are more socially acceptable, drawing citizens and elected officials closer together. But this evokes a wave of the magic wand, a pretentious and simplistic hope that technology will solve a socio-political or environmental problem at little or no political cost: in fact the use of big data by city governments will call for new investment and capacity-building, which is why partnerships between cities and the private sector are so attractive. History teaches that there will be unintended consequences from innovations, but it cannot predict whether they will be for good or for bad. We are still learning how to interpret and assess the impact of the introduction of printing and the growth of publishing in the pre-digital era! The insight of Victor Hugo in *Notre-Dame de Paris* when he put the famous phrase *Ceci tuera cela* ("this will kill that") into the mouth of Frolo as he evoked the impact of the printed book on architecture is still relevant: the biggest impact of technology is on culture and values, systems of authority, and democratic participation.

The scale of infrastructure needs has been known for decades. Public spending on infrastructure investment had been falling in the United States, Japan, and many (but not all) European countries since 1970. In the 1990s, analysts diagnosed a triad of issues which remain familiar: rising congestion; regulatory delays on projects; growing public indebtedness. How to break this triangle? The OECD recommended governments to revise budgeting for value-for-money and better capital spending programs and to revise financial regulations affecting what governments can and cannot spend, to increase the involvement of the private sector to achieve greater efficiency in construction and operations, and to change demand and make existing systems function more efficiently with a mix of privatization for efficiency, competition, regulation (on issues such as pricing and risk sharing), and access. Regulatory delays related to planning were caused not only by the complexity of projects but also by the procedures stipulated in the rules themselves, the proliferation of agencies with jurisdiction, and the lack of cross-sectoral and cross-border co-ordination.

The OECD ended the 1990s with a focus on policy-making and governance, highlighting the need to integrate transport and other related policies and to present packages of measures in a coherent way: adopt long-term policies for effective decision-making across economic and electoral cycles; adjust infrastructures in design such that they are more flexible and hence more sustainable; co-ordinate institutions at the level of agglomerations; take better account of indirect economic effects; and leave planning risks to the public sector (meaning that the private sector takes commitments after consultations have been concluded and approval granted). Taken together, this set of recommendations is a tall order. Most countries however lack an inventory of infrastructures: broad objectives about mobility, connectedness, and competitiveness are still tackled sector by sector, and on the basis of individual cities and regions, often with one eye on the next election. Since the introduction of networked utilities in the period 1880–1920, control over space has become a matter of regulation by government, distributed across the agencies and departments in charge of different sectors and districts. Unfortunately, sound analysis and bold plans are usually not enough to convince political leaders to change decision-making (OECD 2000; OECD and ECMT, 1995).

When infrastructure problems get worse, the matter becomes political. Attitudes matter: those who pay the costs of outmoded and inefficient infrastructure in rich and poor countries alike are dispersed and disorganized; the solutions are in the hands of government officials and politicians who rarely find their future in office threatened by protests when people "can't take it any more," as happened in June 2013 in Brazil when the government was shaken by an uprising sparked by a small increase in the bus fare in São Paulo at a time when huge sums were being spent to finish several sports facilities in time to be used when Brazil hosted the World Cup in 2014.

Things are worse now

The entire urban fabric and the systems sustaining it must be rebuilt, and at an accelerated rate. In a business-as-usual scenario, cities are rebuilt at the rate of 1–2 per cent per year; this is clearly inadequate not only to renew and modernize urban infrastructures, but also to retrofit the existing building stock to adapt to climate change objectives. This is a historic opportunity because different infrastructure networks, each with its own useful life-cycle, have reached their limits at the same time. Infrastructures such as super-highways built twenty-five to thirty years ago are at the end of one useful life-cycle at the same time as older systems for rapid transit built seventy to a hundred years ago and the first major water and sewer networks of the mid-nineteenth century. This convergence of "use-by" dates in all the major infrastructure systems for metropolitan life is absolutely unprecedented.

Estimates of future infrastructure investment generate staggering figures in the *tens of trillions*. It takes a while for figures of this scale to sink in. This investment is essential to renew and modernize cities and regions in OECD countries where population growth is modest at best, as well as to build and develop cities and regions in emerging countries where population growth is largely concentrated.

In 2006, the OECD released a report on *Infrastructure to 2030: Telecommunications, Land Transport, Water and Electricity*. The OECD calculated that, by 2030, global investment in these sectors could reach $71 trillion, or 3.5 per cent of global GDP, with OECD countries absorbing roughly two-thirds of the investment, and the BRICS (Brazil, Russia, India, China, South Africa) about 20 per cent. Leaving telecommunications to one side at about $650 billion yearly to 2020 and then falling to $170 billion yearly, the greatest investment in public network utilities would go toward maintaining and repairing water systems, rising from $770 billion yearly to over $1 trillion by 2025; the second largest portfolio would be for power generation, then for roads, and in fourth position railroads (OECD, 2006: 24–30). Using a somewhat different methodology, a few years later McKinsey came up with a similar number: $57 trillion for global infrastructure investment between 2013 and 2030 just to keep up with the projected growth in global GDP. To put this figure in perspective, McKinsey pointed out that, over the past eighteen years, $36 trillion had been spent on infrastructure investment; this level has to increase some 60 per cent and might then still not be enough. These figures do not take account of further change to cope with global warming, forecasts of more destructive storms, etc., or an increase in the rate of growth in emerging economies (McKinsey, 2013).

Similar figures can be compiled for countries. The American Society of Civil Engineers produced a five-year investment bill, showing a gap between actual spending of $903 billion and estimated needs of $2.12 trillion, with significant shortfalls for infrastructure related to drinking and waste water, hazardous and solid waste, transit, and roads and bridges. Only $71.76 billion of the $903 billion committed would come from the American Recover and Reinvestment Act; obviously without this extraordinary measure the situation would be even worse (ASCE, 2009). Many factors and variables go into the detailed tables that fill sectoral chapters, and support an analysis of pricing, regulation, drivers of demand, the governance of financing, and policy. The costs of doing nothing however do not get factored into the cost-benefit analysis: "The American Society of Civil Engineers estimated in 2009 that 36 per cent of America's major urban highways are congested, costing $78.2 billion each year in wasted time and fuel costs" (*The Economist*, 2011). This eats into productivity and reduces the time people have for other things, including civic activities.

The accuracy of these estimates is not what matters: it is the order of magnitude that must be grasped. In effect, the value of cities as physical assets – hypothetically, what it would cost to replace a city if it were destroyed – has to be invested to assure their existence. The average annual renewal rate of 1–2 per cent, which nonetheless amounts to between 100 and 200 per cent over a century, is too slow, especially if climate change mitigation is considered. Instead, the stored wealth represented by cities must be reinvested on an accelerated schedule. Without these investments, the capital stock of cities, on which both economy and society rest, depreciates. Without an adequate level of investment, is there disinvestment?

To return to the question posed at the beginning of the chapter: given the presumed demand for infrastructure investment, why did the stimulus packages fail to deliver a boost to infrastructure investment? Surprisingly little analysis has been devoted to this question. Two answers are glaringly evident. First, the drawers where projects lie dormant in government offices, consultancies, and engineering and planning firms, waiting for the right opportunity to be approved, were far from full, and those ready to go were often for the very short term. And second, the approval of projects to go forward is usually subject to time-consuming regulatory procedures which in most countries have not been revised to make them more efficient while protecting the public interest. In other words, business as usual, even during a crisis.

What is the link between these two factors? The control of spending by treasury and finance departments. In practice, the macro-economic analysis applied to spending decisions is grounded in long-term trends of infrastructure investment as a share of capital endowment. Treasury officials are alert to the risk that politicians and departments, eager to build programs that must be financed over many years, will promote costly projects of limited economic and social benefit that create an infrastructure surplus of sorts. As a result, and in the absence of a capital budget that takes depreciation and modernization into account, maintenance is funded out of operating budgets, and investment in capital plans is rationed, reducing the opportunities to structure projects efficiently. Infrastructure projects therefore get funded in relation to macro-economic trends and concerns about borrowing limits, interest rates and currency exchange rates – and not in terms of how infrastructure contributes to better productivity in cities and metropolitan regions. Departments of finance have not had the responsibility to look after renewal and modernization of the totality of infrastructure networks and systems as they age. Sectoral departments and, increasingly, sub-national authorities at state or regional level which cannot evade that responsibility resort to more complex and mixed forms of financing projects to alleviate the pressures of congestion, limited power generation and transmission, bottlenecks in ports and airports, capacity limits for waste management, and overburdened water and sewer systems which remain the daily handicap of businesses and the source of frustration to households. The figures of time wasted, of opportunities lost, are simply not added in to the Treasury equation – even though they should have an impact on total factor productivity.

Infrastructure investment could be greater if there were a compelling and bold vision of the city of the future. The critical role for government in this strategic effort has been eclipsed by the focus on the private sector as an agent of change, but government controls many key variables from regulations on public procurement and the environment, to energy policy and the price of power, access to water, and land-use and transport planning which matter vitally to firms that want to invest in the future of cities. And government must take the lead in consultations with the public at large, to build consensus for and social acceptability of long-term, transformational initiatives. Place-based development around the city of the future would revive something that existed and performed reasonably well for decades, called planning. The sources for it go back to the pre-1914 period when electricity, railroads, steamships, and telecommunications emboldened engineers, architects, planners, investors and politicians to embrace a program to transform cities and, later, rural regions. The interwar depression reduced what could be accomplished without collapsing the program itself, which supported postwar reconstruction with a cadre of professionals and a catalogue of designs and concepts shaped by developments under way earlier in the century. Bold, visionary plans to transform and remake the spatial structure of metropolitan regions lost their political appeal at the end of the post–1945 wave of planning and spending. In the Reagan–Thatcher period of the 1980s, the withdrawal of the state from the direct construction and management of many infrastructure systems limited debate or discussion about the future of cities. If the private sector is driving change, so their logic went, then how can planning, in the hands of government, anticipate changes in growth and provide solutions five, let alone twenty-five, years or more in the future? Planning disasters and mistakes – often sanctioned by governments – became the argument of choice of politicians against planning. Not surprisingly, the capacity to manage large-scale, complex projects has contracted: people with the right skills and experience, including the capacity to work across cultures, are in short supply. The fall of communism further discredited planning as an instrument of resource allocation, a symbol of command-and-control regulation and a model of a failed interventionist state. Starved of resources and funding, the capacity for planning was eroded; time will be needed to rebuild this capacity which is critical to assess underlying strengths and weaknesses, manage risks, handle complex policy issues, and carry multi-level and cross-sectoral programs through to completion. Now the situation may be starting to reverse because governments see that innovative technologies could combine an urban transformation with the development and expansion of new markets for those very technologies: it may not be the right place to start but at least it is a start.

The regulatory process of infrastructure project approval and management – which cuts across many jurisdictions and sectors – has not been reformed since the start of the crisis in 2008. Regulatory barriers that impose time-consuming procedures at different levels of government and in different sectoral ministries play into the hands of those in government who want to control the flow of funds more tightly. Under the circumstances, cross-sectoral and cross-jurisdictional projects in transportation, water supply, waste management, health, and environment remain very difficult to design: transaction costs are high, and the chances of funding approval low. Initiatives by the World Bank and the G20 to promote more infrastructure investment seem to focus on improving financing and controlling the design of projects to make them more attractive to investors. The governance and regulatory barriers to better infrastructure projects, as well as strategies for the future of cities, do not appear to get the attention they deserve.

It is impossible to say whether the unspent funds allocated for infrastructure made a difference to the course of the crisis: had more money been invested earlier, the crisis might not have ended sooner. But the question is worth asking because the failure to spend and invest highlights the high degree of medium-term uncertainty felt in the private sector about the future model of urban economies. Each sector manages a separate part of what is, in the end, a complex and inter-related structure operating across territories and jurisdictions – as everyone realizes when a power failure in Ohio causes a black-out in New York City. Of course how projects are financed matters, but this issue should not stand in the way of projects that have the potential to deliver benefits beyond the short-term effects on construction. The IMF "World Economic Outlook," released in the midst of a recurring debate about government debt levels and austerity in 2014, contained evidence that additional public investment is positive, generating additional private investment; the scale of the impact may be affected by whether the investment is made through borrowing, taxes, or spending cuts elsewhere, but financing does not affect the net positive gain (*The Economist*, 2014).

We are back to basics: *to know better what projects will lift productivity in cities and help cities and regions make better use of their assets*. Even with better data, this will take some educated guesses and calculated risks because people use city space in ways that planners and designers cannot predict. Maintaining and upgrading the existing infrastructure is just as important to this objective as big projects to transform cities and, indeed, metropolitan regions. This is a matter not of "either/or," but of "both/and." If there is no future for a city – no vision of how things could be better tomorrow – why would government or the private sector spend money on the betterment of existing public goods? But if a focus on "smarter and greener" or on ten-year mega-projects

Infrastructure and innovation

takes the place of getting all the little things done, the connections within cities, which after all are what infrastructures are supposed to deliver, will deteriorate. The first step people take when leaving a high-speed train is on a city pavement.

To sharpen the argument: either the scale of urban development and renewal must be cut back to reflect the pace and scale of infrastructure investment, or the model for that investment needs to be revised to reflect the needs of cities and their potential to generate wealth. We are at the core of what is at stake when trust in government is so low: in ten or twenty years, people will want to know why more was not done now; those in power then who will have to struggle with the problems they inherit will only be able to blame their predecessors.

Innovation and the needs of cities and regions

Since the beginning of the Industrial Revolution, innovation has fed the imagination, inspiring people to conceive of cities and landscapes adapted to and transformed by new systems of communication, transport, environmental management, and construction. Visions of the city of the future embody technologies, whether for controlling rivers and streets, for railroads or automobiles, or for gas and electricity in every home or place of business. If technological innovation is key, then studies of long cycles of innovation place us toward the end of one period but not yet far enough into its successor.

There is a clear relationship between infrastructure systems and innovation. Not only can electricity be seen as a technological and scientific breakthrough; the means to generate, distribute, and sell electricity were also a major innovation (see Chapter 9); other networks, such as water systems, are heavy users of electricity; new firms emerged to offer goods and services based on the work that electricity could provide. This is an example of what Peter Hall referred to as "*a chain of innovation* – social, organizational and institutional – which affects the rate of diffusion of what is not a single new thing, but a new technological system" (Hall, 1998). New technologies, of which Information Technology (IT) is perhaps the most visible in the public eye today, are expected to have major implications for the shape and management of cities in the future. The challenge is to think of how things could be different, and better.

We might just be at the bottom of the trough, at the point in time when the benefits of the past wave or waves of innovation have mutated into new barriers to growth – or, in other words, opportunities for a fresh wave of problem-solving innovations. Many of the technologies applied to and concentrated in cities, sustaining the growth of markets, enabling billions of people – even in poverty – to enjoy the absence of hunger – are in fact decades old: telephony, elevators, rapid rail transport, automobiles and aeroplanes, container ships powered by fuel, vaccines, property insurance, refrigerators for food storage, electric power, the list lengthens. This does not mean that they are past their "use-by" date, only that another wave of innovations may be overdue. The last major wave of innovations, in the era 1880–1920, took place at a time of social and geo-political conflict within the cockpit of western civilization; the same era however was also marked by a strong progressive impulse, something which today seems oddly missing.

There is serious reason for concern: the rate of innovation for cities probably peaked decades ago, partly explaining a decline in multifactor productivity, reducing the benefits of agglomeration since the mid-1970s. Some might rush to the conclusion that regulation and state intervention are part of the problem, stipulating through health and safety rules how (or how not) to do certain things, restraining market entry, slowing down the diffusion of innovation; others argue that a proper role for regulation and public policy is necessary to sustain the preconditions for innovation and for their application through social organization. How to get there is a problem of political culture (Gordon, 2012).

Whether there have been fewer radically new breakthroughs recently, and if so why, are a matter of controversy but the need for a transformational burst of innovations is not. Innovations are critical to foster the transformation of oil-dependent, high-energy-consuming, carbon-producing cities. Some innovations will take the form of policies, regulations, and changes of behavior; others in instruments, devices, and the like; others will take the form of new systems that connect things or allow people to control their environment differently. And then there must be scope to incorporate what does not yet exist into the shape and form of cities and into the daily lives of those who live in them. Yes, solutions will bring new problems, but these too can generate solutions – the virtuous cycle is a protean element but one which puts a premium on the adaptive capacity of cities.

Innovation speaks to the capacity of urban economies to renew themselves and the institutions they need. In one sense it does not matter that, in a particular domain, one city may lead, and others follow: what matters is the pattern of diffusion. For this reason, urban innovation is a form of mixed public good: cities that lead may hold an advantage, but they cannot exclude others from adopting what works, a point which does not get enough attention in discussions of urban as against national development or the rise and fall of sectors. Cities are where innovation happens; cities need innovation; cities are where innovations are incorporated into daily life.

It sounds so simple. If cities are where innovation happens, then the level of urbanization in the world today is promise of further innovations in the future: more cities, more innovation. This future however cannot be taken for granted. Our knowledge about innovation as an urban function is still very limited, based largely on recent and retrospective case studies. Even the few studies in the history of science and technology that try to reconstruct the conditions favorable to creativity and innovation in, say, seventeenth-century London, or early twentieth-century Berlin or New York, result in highly contingent, contextual patterns within which small communities of scientists and inventors collaborated.

There are few topics which should be more exciting to study than to try to uncover the secret of creativity, perhaps the defining nature of humankind in society. The fact remains that creativity is not reducible to a formula. Consider that innovation, as a social and economic activity, is so uneven spatially: Why are some cities at the leading edge of innovation? If a city has the potential to support more innovation, what does it take to realize that potential? If innovation depends so much on the knowledge and imagination of people, in a world of mobility how can a city retain – or increase – its capacity to support innovation? If urban problems generate problem-solving innovations, why are some problems the subject of innovation, and not others? How can innovations to improve cities become part of the market economy, generating jobs and nurturing firms?

Another set of questions, also extending into a multi-year research agenda, looks at the disruptive nature of innovation. The most productive innovations may come from cross-sectoral efforts, but the natural pathway in bureaucracies and disciplines is to become more specialized. How are connections made between innovations in one domain and opportunities to draw on those innovations in another? Does innovation in the growing cultural sector call for different models of urban development than, say, innovation in manufacturing? What are the pathways for diffusion of innovations, and what barriers arrest or retard this process? Can better urban management and a higher level of investment in the infrastructures that connect cities and enhance inclusion within them contribute to an urban environment that is conducive to innovation?

The place to look for some answers is between the covers of *Cities in Civilization: Culture, Innovation and Urban Order* (1998) by the late Peter Hall. For Hall, the golden age of a city, the moments which earn it a place in history, is when it is bursting with creative energy. It usually lasts but briefly, whether measured as a burst of artistic development in Renaissance Florence, or of technological innovation in late nineteenth-century New York, or of new institutions for social welfare in seventeenth-century Amsterdam. Comparisons abound between Manchester, Glasgow, and Detroit, between New York and Los Angeles, between Tokyo and Silicon Valley, between Berlin and Paris, with some of the same cities featured in more than one section on culture, commercial and industrial innovation, and infrastructure and planning as structural elements. Very, very few cities become leaders in more than one field at once: Paris in art, commerce, and a model of urban order in the mid-nineteenth century, and New York in the same fields in the 1920s, are the exceptions. Innovation may also erupt in unlikely places, or places that look unpromising until their economic and social makeup is dissected: Memphis for recorded rock and roll, Los Angeles for cinema production, Detroit and the mass-produced automobile. Such cities are not necessarily the places of the first inventions, but of a process or system to exploit inventions and enlarge the scale of production. Can more be said than that new industries will emerge "in a special kind of city, a city in economic and social flux, a city with large numbers of new and young arrivals, mixing and merging into a new kind of society"? (Hall, 1998: 607). These preconditions are not the outcome of any deliberate plan, but the result of many changes and factors, each with its own logic and degree of unpredictability that somehow cohere in one place, at a time when certain individuals seize the opportunity at hand.

The preconditions that "either enjoin urban innovation, or at least powerfully encourage it ... never actually guarantee, inexorably, that it will happen: urban innovation is not the monopoly of one kind of place, even at the same period of capitalist evolution, let alone different eras" (Hall, 1998: 939). Some of the factors favoring innovation are latent in culture, but also reversible, meaning that they could erode as well as strengthen. Hall's list included:

> A pervasive ideology of scientific and technological progress; a high level of both general and technological education; a general feeling of commercial confidence in the future; an ability to develop large-scale, coherent, technological capacities, with supporting standards and regulatory policies; integrated corporate structures where needed; a capacity to develop and to diffuse new technologies; a high level of industrial and commercial investment; and access to long-term risk capital. (Hall, 1998; 282)

Even without being able to measure these variables and compare countries, it is clear that no country has all these attributes, distributed across all locations and social groups. Even Israel, which invests more in research and development as a percentage of GDP than any other OECD country (4.25 per cent in 2010, a fairly consistent level since 2000), has noticeable domestic socio-spatial disparities and irregularities, exposing the north and the south in this small country, as well as the local Arab and ultra-orthodox Jewish populations, to forms of marginalization in this regard.

There are theoretical frameworks about the rise and decline of cultures, about the role of money and power, about the rise of new industries and their decline, and about the influence of ideas as agents of change, but these are too abstract; in Hall's words, many theoreticians "are deliberately, rather infuriatingly a-spatial: they are entirely uninterested in the question of what happens where, and why" (Hall, 1998: 14).

Hall admitted that "the generation of successful innovative milieu still presents a considerable degree of mystery" (Hall, 1998: 498). Nevertheless, teasing threads out of many tapestries woven by other scholars, Hall arrives at a picture of a "creative milieu" where it is easier to make connections, between people, between skills and techniques, between those who create and those who recognize and exploit its value: a measure of freedom from constraint and over-regulation, a degree of tension from the presence of new minorities, a many-sided environment concentrating many different activities and skills which allows people to borrow from one another to make something new, all are to be found in cities at the junction between cultures, markets, power systems. There is a greater degree of instability in such places, if only for a limited period of time, provoking a willingness on the part of some to turn against routine.

Two facts emerge from another study of Hall's on the geography of innovation in information technology in the age of electricity, going forward from the invention of the telegraph: first, innovation shows considerable inertia; and second, a very old industrial region such as Boston can remain innovative if it maintains an innovation milieu balanced between fundamental research and commercial exploitation (Hall and Preston, 1988). Such patterns raise questions about the role of state or public institutions and policies to direct research, about the initiative of individual cities or city-regions to attract or retain organizations employing above-average numbers of researchers, and about the share of private-sector investment in innovation.

To be sure, there is a pattern of continuity, at least in the short term, in the centers for research and development. The OECD 2011 edition of *Regions at a Glance* shows that small countries as well as large can support innovations which lead to patents, but the process may not be the same: in the United Kingdom, the Netherlands, and Korea, a single region is the top performer, whereas in Japan, Germany, France, the United States, and Switzerland, more regions are the sources of patents. But even in Japan, Germany, and the United States, patterns of spatial concentration show the importance of local networks: around 40 per cent of the collaboration between non-business and business actors takes place in the same region and 40 per cent among regions in the same country. In Estonia, Turkey, the Slovak Republic, and Finland, international exchanges dominate business and non-business collaborations. No matter whether the level of investment in research and development in a given country is high or low, the pattern is usually for concentration: in 2007, around one-third of total R&D expenditure in OECD countries (on average, 2.3 per cent of GDP) was performed in just 10 per cent of regions.

It is just as difficult to predict when or where a burst of innovation will occur as it is to anticipate what shape innovation will take. But wherever or whenever, innovation captures three key attributes of cities, attributes which changes in technology and design only appear to reinforce because they speak to a deeper social need which cities help to fulfill: specialization, agglomeration effects, and person-to-person (face-to-face) contact. These are, in many ways, inter-dependent. Specialization is possible when there is sufficient density to support a larger labor market and trading connections with other places, to assure demand for specialized products and skills. Specialized skills may be needed by many firms which they cannot afford to supply themselves. And they are a social phenomenon: the acquisition and perfection of specialized skills, historically, has been a corporate affair, engaging individuals whose knowledge is their own as much as their employers. "Localised knowledge spillovers (due to inter-firm linkages, a versatile labour pool, strong innovation related infrastructures, etc.) can be a tangible source of productivity gain for firms and can constitute a persuasive argument against relocation of in favour of investment" (Hall and Preston, 1988: 12). Proximity matters: when research led by Edison and Bell Telephone in telephony and electronics moved from New York to New Jersey, it was to locations directly connected to Washington and New York by efficient rail service.

The ability of people to share information and change jobs is crucial to trust-based relationships. Alfred Marshall (1890) described the importance of local labor markets based on the close proximity of firms and a concentration of labor: density enabled firms to find the people they needed with the right skills and the capacity to learn and innovate on the job; workers were better assured of stable employment when they could find work more easily. Geographer Jean Gottmann, whose pioneering and still definitive study of megalopolis showed how information networks had functioned in the northeastern region of the United States since the early Republic, would say that half the phone calls are to ask someone to meet for lunch (Gottmann, 1961). When I asked a senior professor of physics at the University of Warsaw what would make a difference to lift research in Poland, without hesitation he replied "infrastructure" – although major university cities are not far apart when measured in kilometers, travel time by rail or by road makes collaboration, joint seminars, etc., impossible. There are places in Tokyo, Seoul, and Los Angeles where trend-spotters observe the style and behavior of adolescents and young adults. Sprawling these cities may be, but the places where new things happen and can be seen to be happening are not in the suburbs, or in districts of uniform, secluded high-rise apartment blocks, but at the raucous junctions of Shibuya, or in the Myeong-dong market district where night markets follow daytime retailing. But other things matter as well, such as easy and efficient inter-city travel, and congenial and accessible places to meet and interact in social settings.

America still dominates research and innovation, an example of momentum: a lead can be maintained even as other countries catch up. Much of the attention today is on the potential of emerging economies, and in particular India and China among the large ones, and Singapore and Hong Kong among the small. What about Europe, which led in innovation until the twentieth century?

During the past two decades, the rate of growth in the percentage of researchers in the labor force has been greater in Europe than in the US. In Finland, Germany, Denmark, and Portugal the number of researchers per ten thousand in the labor force increased by a factor of three since 1990; significant but smaller increases, in per cent, were made in France, Ireland, Sweden, and the United Kingdom. OECD statistics gleaned from annual yearbooks show that the level of researchers in the labor force in the United States grew at a slower rate, and is now below the best-performing EU countries, as well as Japan and New Zealand.

The growth in the stock of researchers in the labor force of many European countries together with the presence of so many European cities in the top rankings of livable cities, demonstrate adaptive evolution, often against considerable odds, and an investment in the components of growth. The major challenge for growth in Europe is to link investment in infrastructure and urban development, taking advantage of Europe's dense, livable city centers and urban networks, with the potential to lift the productivity of Europe's growing stock of researchers and knowledge workers. Clusters are one model at the local or regional scale; their corollary concerns connectivity in sectors where people work in teams, and where teams are often in different locations separated by greater distances. If urban livability matters to innovation, then Europe's cities are an asset to help make its workforce of researchers more productive, and more stable. The attention paid to the creative class highlights the urban features which attract such people (Florida, 2012). In many European cities the university precinct is being built afresh, often in the city center or linked to it by efficient modern transport such as a streetcar network (Leipzig, Lausanne, Grenoble, but also Paris and Berlin, and soon Glasgow). This is in contrast with the United States, where university precincts tend to be enclaves when in metropolitan cities, or on greenfield sites. Why might city–university relations matter? Researchers whose work is close to the city center in Europe may also live close to the city center, making daily life for young families, for double-income couples, and for single people easier to organize. With more places to meet – galleries, museums, coffee shops, stores, sports facilities – people with overlapping interests may do just that, meet, as often by chance as by design. In other words, the design and management of the city center becomes an ingredient in innovation by creating some of the intangible but material circumstances that favor intense creative work, cross-fertilization, and stimulation. From this perspective the case of London, where housing costs far outstrip the salaries of professors, becomes a problem: only better transport connections connecting London to a vast hinterland beyond the green belt can compensate.

There are good stories to tell against the backdrop of slow or no growth since 2008. But there is what to worry about. Innovation depends not only on people with the education and skill to generate innovations; it also depends on how well people can learn as adults, a set of proficiencies which is at its peak when people are around thirty, with years in the workforce ahead of them. The OECD's study of adult skills revealed that in some countries (US, UK) younger generations are not much better prepared than those who are retiring; that many firms are not employing people appropriately for the skills they have; and that people whose skills are already weak are less likely to improve their skills through adult education and training (OECD, 2013). Well might Peter Hall have ended his magisterial study of *Cities in Civilization* with a challenge: whether technology in urban contexts will contribute to a more inclusive and productive society and economy (Hall, 1998: 986; Brickwell, 1991).

Adapting cities for sustainable growth and development

A common thread to both innovation and infrastructure is the need to introduce changes in cities as they already are: if change is not possible, then neither is innovation. The OECD has long affirmed that adaptability is perhaps the major challenge facing countries; a study of *Globalisation and Regional Economies* concluded that "perhaps the most important role for regional strategies is to favour adaptation to change" (OECD, 2007: 16). Adapting the city of today must focus on two problems. The first is the challenge to transform existing cities and cities being built in the years to come to the energy, water, and other environmental constraints which can already be anticipated. This means bringing researchers, government, and the private sector closer together. The second is to make change socially and politically acceptable in the face of popular resistance, when people are skeptical that the future they don't know will be better than the present. Taken together, this is an agenda for innovation and for infrastructure for a generation.

It is difficult to measure how adaptable modern cities are, but the evidence from the development industry or those in charge of major public works projects is that changing the urban fabric is complicated and time-consuming, and time costs money. The modern infrastructure system of utility networks and services was itself an innovation when it was created in the period 1880–1920. Its evolution – a matter of engineering and technology, combined with bureaucratic corporations and state agencies together with novel forms of finance and control – helped make the rise of living standards in the twentieth century possible. But it also generated a form of economic regulation based on sectors which took over control of space: what goes where is a matter of who decides. Network infrastructures have a tendency to fix land use patterns and set capacity limits. More important, the management of infrastructures by different public and private offices and agencies can slow down and complicate the task of finding out what can be done with any given building or plot of land. Power – market power – flows toward those who make a successful business of mastering the system. It is no surprise that the field of activity known as property development took off only after World War Two. Thus, there is a degree of permanency literally built in to infrastructures, not only in their capital-intensive physical forms, but in the degree to which they make changes in land use more costly and difficult.

Academic experts have long paid attention to the building cycle as a function of the rate at which land uses change and buildings age. In one of the few studies that exist, Larry Bourne, writing about Toronto, noted that the physical and economic life spans of buildings are not the same: "The result is that with the passing of time the character and distribution of the building stock of a city become increasingly out-of-phase with the demands of physical space. It is this *conflict between fixed real estate resources and highly mobile social and economic demands* which underlies many of the basic maladjustments in the spatial structure of modern cities" (Bourne, 1967: 2–3, italics in original). This is a systemic, structural problem, as much in evidence in postwar American suburbs as in the new middle-class districts of Chinese cities. It is another thing to design newer places to adapt better over decades, even centuries.

Cycles of obsolescence and renewal have to take better account of the difficult and costly effort to adapt buildings and entire districts that were built well enough to last for decades to changes which have intervened at a faster rate. The costs of renewal or rehabilitation may exceed the economic potential of renovation; greater mobility makes it easier for people to move away from older areas and settle on greenfield sites, further reducing the incentive to rebuild. That there are countervailing trends of regeneration and gentrification only calls attention to the higher stock of amenities and assets – and potential for property appreciation – in places where this phenomenon occurs.

Crises highlight problems which reveal fundamental deficiencies in conventional policy and practice:

- Hurricane Sandy raised questions about the pattern of development in New York and New Jersey, a single economic region with very different governance systems and strategic objectives. People in other coastal regions in the world exposed to similar threats must be wondering what their fate might be.
- The tsunami which devastated Fukushima with global repercussions on the nuclear power industry exposed significant shortcomings domestically: other Japanese cities and regions lacked the funds or the regulatory flexibility to compensate for the collapse of that region's economy by welcoming displaced households and firms. Having decided to end its use of nuclear power, Germany is struggling to make up the gap without adding to global warming.
- Housing, convention centers, airports, museums, business parks and sports facilities in Athens, Lisbon, Madrid, Valencia, Las Vegas, Phoenix now appear to have rested only on the premise that prices always rise. And they are difficult to adapt to other uses. When the market recovers, will the same vicious cycle repeat itself?
- The mis-alignment between national financial regulation and local regulation of land use, housing and construction contributed to the

crisis in Spain, Iceland, Ireland, Greece, the United Kingdom, and the United States, and could be a factor in China.

These are not minor problems, nor are they self-correcting except over many years and at considerable social and financial cost. They reflect the shortcomings of policy interventions which treat space as a dependent variable, and the cumulative effect of incremental decisions, often in the absence of a strategic planning framework. Public policy and administration tend to separate the physical and social aspects of cities which instead need to be connected. A policy for cities should make it easier to see how the different aspects of cities are inter-related, challenging modes of governance based on administrative or legal boundaries or sectoral silos. It is this nexus which needs to be tackled to improve the adaptability of cities.

The risks of change can be managed better. There is a need to build the innovation competences of leaders at the local level, and to build as well their appetite for risk. Leaders are more willing to try something new if they can see it at work, meaning that identifying and documenting urban innovations is as important as it is likely to be neglected. Every good practice started as an experiment. Consider an idea in a 1968 report "Building the American city" from the (US) National Commission on Urban Problems, and this in a year of urban riots and student unrest. The authors of the report recognized the need for new approaches:

> What we need most of all is working capital for *ideas*; that is, for *design* ... "Design" as used here does not just mean building design. It means social, legal and financial design. It means creative thinking in all fields. Money must be made available for all these functions ... A start might be made by establishing a *design development bank*. There are development banks of all kinds for international development. It seems sound to apply this principle to design. (Konvitz, 1985: 193, note 14).

Some problems that cry out for innovations in public health, the environment, building safety, energy, transportation, water and waste management are linked to risks to cities. "So a very important part of living, and the creativity that comes out of it, has consisted in finding solutions to the city's own problems of order and organization," wrote Peter Hall (1998: 6), echoing Jane Jacobs, who decades before had written that "life in cities ... generates problems, which become the stimulus of invention, innovation, improvisation" (Jacobs, 1969: 105). Innovation depends on both the free exercise of imagination and intelligence to challenge conventional wisdom and established practices championed by the risk-taking role of the private sector, and on public investment in the capacity of government to reform regulations, set new priorities, and implement policy changes: precisely the kind of symbiotic relationship praised by Jacobs in *Systems of Survival* (1992).

Innovation implies that things can be different and better; in other words, beyond curiosity, innovation is a *critical* undertaking, in some way a rejection of the status quo as good enough. It is also critical in another, more common sense, that of being decisive to the solution of many problems. "The usefulness of cities is that they supply contexts in which those inputs – insights and adaptations – can be injected into everyday life" (Jacobs, 1984: 193). Incorporating innovation into everyday life is itself one of the drivers of urban change – and it also shows how rigid, how costly to modify, how resistant to change many of the not-so-old areas of modern cities can be. There are two challenges for government: First, the process of adjustment can put too much of the burden of coping with change on those least able, economically and culturally, to benefit from or find new opportunities in this dynamic process. And second, priority-setting, regulatory reform, and capacity-building at all levels of government are needed to generate the plans and execute the projects that can mobilize infrastructure investment and make best use of innovation.

Fifty years ago, in *The City in History*, Lewis Mumford wrote that "One cannot bring about the renewal of the city by replacing old structures with new buildings that only confirm the obsolete pattern of city growth and that rest solely on the equally obsolete ideological foundations of 'mechanical progress'" (Mumford, 1961: 554). The adaptation of cities as they exist to the changes in energy use and in carbon needed to cope with climate change must begin by assessing the factors that make cities as they have been built so difficult, costly, and time-consuming to change. Changing normative practices that are embedded in professions, policies, and administrative practices, like ending subsidies, is very hard indeed. The process of un-learning, of changing behavior that is counterproductive into a virtuous cycle, is itself a learned art.

References

American Society of Civil Engineers (ASCE) (2009), *Report Card for American Infrastructure* (Reston, VA: ASCE).

Bourne, Larry S. (1967), "Private redevelopment of the central city: spatial process of structural change in the city of Toronto," Research Paper no. 112, Department of Geography (Chicago: University of Chicago).

Brickwell, Ditha (1991), "Research and technology development for cities," *Ekistics*, 350 (September–October): 324–9.

Choate, Pat and Susan M. Walter (1983), *America in Ruins: The Decaying Infrastructure* (Durham, NC: Duke University Press).
The Economist (1980), "Sewers, clogged," 23 August.
The Economist (1982), "All cracking up: roads, bridges, pipes, trains," 4 December.
The Economist (1998), "New York's infrastructure," 29 August.
The Economist (2011), "The efficiency conundrum," 19 November.
The Economist (2014), "Public investments in infrastructure do the most good at times like the present," 4 October.
Financial Times (1998), "California told to spend more on infrastructure," 24 August.
Financial Times (2012a), Robin Wigglesworth and Daniel Dombey, "Finance for big projects cut as banks are squeezed," 3 May.
Financial Times (2012b), Edward Luce, "Why Congress should care About elderly infrastructure," 26 November.
Financial Times (2013), John Kay, "The lesson of Victorian London's rise from sewer to spectacle," 16 January.
Florida, Richard (2012), *The Rise of the Creative Class Revisited* (New York: Basic Books).
Gordon, Robert (2012), "Is U.S. economic growth over? Faltering innovation confronts the six headwinds," NBER Working Paper, no. 18315 (Cambridge, MA: NBER).
Gottmann, Jean (1961), *Megalopolis: The Urbanized Northeastern Seaboard of the United States* (New York: Twentieth Century Fund).
Hall, Peter (1998), *Cities in Civilization: Culture, Innovation and Urban Order* (London: Weidenfeld and Nicolson).
Hall, Peter and Paschal Preston (1988), *The Carrier Wave: New Information Technology and the Geography of Innovation, 1846–2003* (London: Unwin Hyman).
Jacobs, Jane (1969), *The Economy of Cities* (New York: Random House).
Jacobs, Jane (1984), *Cities and the Wealth of Nations: Principles of Economic Life* (New York: Vintage).
Jacobs, Jane (1992), *Systems of Survival: A Dialogue on the Moral Foundations of Commerce and Politics* (New York: Random House).
Konvitz, Josef, *The Urban Millennium: The City-building Process from the Early Middle Ages to the Present* (Carbondale, IL: Southern Illinois University Press).
McKinsey Global Institute (2013), "Infrastructure productivity: how to save $1 trillion a year," January.
Marshall, Alfred (1890), *Principles of Economics* (London and New York: Macmillan).
Mumford, Lewis (1961), *The City in History: Its Origins, Its Transformations and Its Prospects* (New York: Harcourt, Brace and World).
New York Times (1998), John Sullivan, "Study puts high price on fixing a crumbling city," 8 August 1998.

OECD (1991), *Urban Infrastructure: Finance and Management* (Paris: OECD). ISBN: 92-94-17120-7.
OECD (1998), "Public investment activity: an overview," Paper for Working Party no. 1 on Macroeconomic and Structural Policy Analysis, paras 4 and 5.
OECD (2000), *Integrating Transport in the City: Reconciling the Economic, Social and Environmental Dimensions* (Paris: OECD), ISBN: 92-64-17120-7.
OECD (2006), *Infrastructure to 2030: Telecommunications, Land Transport, Water and Electricity* (Paris: OECD). DOI: 10.1787/9789264023994-3-en.
OECD (2007), *Globalisation and Regional Economies: Can OECD Regions Compete in Global Industries?* (Paris: OECD), DOI: 10.1787/9789264037809-en.
OECD (2008), "Infrastructure investment: links to growth and the role of public policies," Paper for Working Party no. 1 on Macroeconomic and Structural Policy Analysis, para. 20.
OECD (2009), "Infrastructure services: lessons from 30 years of reform in OECD countries," chapter 5, pp. 189–228. In *China: Defining the Boundary between the Market and the State* (Paris: OECD), OECD Reviews of Regulatory Reform, chapter drafted by Reza Lahidji. DOI: 10.1787/9789264059429-en.
OECD (2011), *Regions at a Glance* (Paris: OECD), section 14, on research and development expenditure in regions, pp. 62–3. DOI: org/10/1787/reg_glance-2011-en.
OECD (2013), *OECD Skills Outlook 2013: First Results for the Survey of Adult Skills*. DOI: org/10.1787/9789264204256-en.
OECD and ECMT (1995), *Urban Travel and Sustainable Development* (Paris: OECD) ISBN: 92-64-14370-X.
Wall Street Journal 1988), "Infrastructure repair needs more than money," 29 March.
Wall Street Journal (1990a), David Alan Aschauer, "Public spending for private profit," 15 March.
Wall Street Journal (1990b), Alfred Malabre, Jr, "Economic roadblock: infrastructure neglect," 30 July.

4

Managing space better: the problem of shrinking cities and economies

Countries have no alternative but to look to their cities to find new sources of growth. It is not the amount of land that makes a society rich, but what it does with it to generate and enhance productivity. More than half of the fourteen "big hub" regions which are disproportionately responsible for GDP growth in the OECD are in the United States, and the rest are in Japan, France, the United Kingdom, Italy, as one would expect. These "big hubs" however cannot carry an economy forward on their own: many of the fastest growing regions are second-tier cities and regions of intermediate density, neither rural nor metropolitan: policies need to help these places improve performance, too. And not all large urban regions contribute to aggregate growth. There is, after all, no such thing as an average region (OECD, 2011a: 39).

This chapter takes a look at "spatial sociology" (a phrase attributed to Buckminster Fuller by Peter Drucker in personal correspondence with the author). Drucker believed that "to link demographic structure in geographic space to ideology and economics" is of vital importance. He "dreamed of a study of the relationship between the depopulation of the cities of the Western Roman Empire and the decline of Rome," putting forth as a hypothesis that "Gibbon had seriously missed the depopulation of the Western cities – and not only Rome itself though it declined the most – as a major factor in the disintegration of the Empire." Peter Drucker asked whether we can "yet develop concepts to distinguish between productive urbanization, i.e. urbanization that creates centers of artistic, spiritual, philosophical and economic creativity as did the European urbanization of the 19th century (Vienna may have been the best example but so was Budapest) – not to mention Paris between Balzac's birth and his death – and what I would call 'sterile' urbanization, i.e. the favelas of Latin America or the horror cities of Sub-Sahara Africa?" He added: "And where does Los Angeles fit? I consider Hollywood a favela."

This is not just a matter of elite versus popular culture, as might at first appear to be the case, but about the capacity of cities to promote wealth creation and not just mere consumption to sustain demand. This involves transforming the gains of trade, innovation, productivity into more permanent value, whether in the form of institutions and practices that help people live longer and make better use of their talents and capacity to learn, or to create public goods that serve both commerce and culture.

As Peter Hall wrote, "The central question, now, is precisely how and why city life renews itself" (Hall, 1998: 23). The process is anything but uniform. The assets that enhance the power of attraction of individual cities are often immaterial, and even more often immovable. It takes intelligence and the skill to make best use of these endowments, and in particular to exploit assets which are under-utilized. As Jane Jacobs wrote, "The basic idea is to use whatever commercial strengths and resources a locality already has, but that it has been neglecting, wasting or overlooking" (Jacobs, 1992: 172). These issues go to the crux of the problem of how cities will function in a low-growth economy.

To understand the importance of locally specific assets, this chapter begins with a look at two stellar examples of contraction, Detroit and Greece; a second part covers OECD studies from the 1990s about urban decline and regeneration. Detroit and Greece provide a ready-made case study to assess how four dimensions of specific urban or territorial advantage – economic diversification; agglomeration effects based on making best use of land, housing, education; borders and international links as an endowment; and public goods and governance – can be squandered. As often, extreme cases reveal wider trends. Detroit is a metropolitan region bigger than some countries or states, and Greece a mid-size European country with two major cities. Both are limited in their capacity for self-generating growth by local circumstances and poor governance. The recovery of the American economy depends on how badly performing cities cope with their problems just as the recovery of Greece depends on whether its best-performing city, Athens, makes better use of its opportunities. The links between major cities and nations work in both directions.

The fate of both Detroit and Greece has international ramifications. Detroit filed a plan for bankruptcy, which was approved on 7 November 2014; the level of public debt in Greece at 140 per cent of GDP is likely to rise and may become unsustainable if a recovery takes longer than expected. For Greece and for Detroit, this is the post-crisis crisis: they may remain permanently afflicted even when other cities and countries return to growth. The restructuring of debt for failing economies is based on the assumption that a recovery will be under way before refinancing becomes a pressing issue. If however the level of growth necessary to repay loans is too low, or if deflation takes hold which makes the repayment of debt more costly, or if there is public, political resistance, another debt crisis – perhaps with greater political costs than what we have seen in 2011–13 – cannot be postponed. Without signs of recovery, longer-term projects and investment will be hostages to fortune; but without them, any recovery will depend entirely on exogenous forces.

People want to know what the prospects of a recovery in Greece and Detroit are: How much change for the better can be expected in the short term? Will they ever be able to grow on their own? Can their problems be contained? Answers which appear in the media are often based on extrapolations from history and insights from economic theory. Wolfgang Münchau, writing in the *Financial Times* (2013a), told readers that he had he never seen a city as empty as Detroit, which will decline to "a permanently lower level." The question he asked is whether Greece faces "nonreversible long-term economic decline" like Detroit. What can a city or a country do if people leave in search of opportunity, if transfer payments are not sufficient to cover the huge costs of modern public services, or if falling wages fail to increase employment? Some cities, and indeed some countries, may just shrink. But this is not necessarily the natural order of things, as if some kind of Darwinian (or Schumpeterian) process decreed that some must disappear so that others can flourish. It is all too easy to give in to *schadenfreude*, that is, to look at Detroit or Greece and be grateful that one does not live there.

Governance is a bigger challenge than budgets and the level of demand. To manage the decline of a city or a country is very different from the restructuring of a corporation in the private sector, which can cut loss-making lines or units without consulting customers. To argue that public sector reforms must wait until the budget is stabilized and a recovery has begun simply postpones both reforms and recovery. Until public sector reforms are initiated, the effects of better macro-economic and monetary policy will be attenuated; local entrepreneurship will remain low; and the exploitation of immovable local assets will be compromised. Unfortunately, governance reforms take time, and generate significant constitutional and political debates of their own.

Detroit

The statistics for Detroit are appalling. The city's population fell 25 per cent from tenth to eighteenth in the United States between 2000 and 2010, to reach 713,777; it had been home to 1.8 million in 1950.

Vulnerable and poor, people in Wayne County, which includes Detroit, have a life expectancy three years below the state average (72.4 instead of 75.7 years), and six years below that of middle-class people living in neighboring Oakland and Washtenaw Counties. The fact that 25 per cent of births in Detroit are to mothers under the age of twenty speaks to the social reproduction of a syndrome that becomes more difficult to break, the longer it lasts. Of Detroit youth aged sixteen to nineteen in the labor force, sixty per cent are unemployed, as are 40 per cent of young Detroiters aged twenty to twenty-four. In twenty-five metropolitan areas in the United States, in 2012, 17 per cent of those aged sixteen to twenty-four were neither in school nor working; Detroit had the third highest rate of youth disconnection. Migration, which macroeconomists favor as a mechanism of adjustment, is no solution for the unemployed in Detroit who are unqualified for jobs elsewhere (Burd-Sharps and Lewis, 2013).

That Detroit and the automobile industry are associated in the public mind calls attention to the city's major economic weakness. The mix of trades and skills and resources that came together in Detroit to make the mass manufacturing of automobiles possible more than a century ago disappeared years ago, compromising the renewal of the city's economic base. It is difficult to see what other new product or service could be invented there now. Every time there has been a recession in the car industry, the cry to diversify would go out, only to be lost in the noise of the factory once the production of cars resumed. But this is only part of the story. The decentralization of the car industry accelerated in South East Michigan in the 1940s, widening the gap between where people lived and where they worked. The success of the car industry in the United States today depends in part on the territorial diversification of research and manufacturing: vast complexes, often on previously undeveloped or greenfield sites, support the windowless plants and huge logistical facilities for domestic and foreign firms and their suppliers, linked by the interstate highway system built in the 1950s, one of the most powerful agents of decentralization of the late twentieth century. The revival of the American car industry will benefit Michigan, but it owes little to Detroit.

Managing decline is one of the least attractive options for a politician. This means, by and large, dealing with the city or country – Detroit or Greece – as it is. When a city or country is growing, the cost of investment to expand infrastructure can be recouped in the future. But how can decline be managed, given that its fixed infrastructure and level of services involve capital and maintenance costs that cannot be covered by annual budgets? During the debt crisis of New York City in 1976,

Roger B. Starr developed the idea of planned shrinkage (Starr, 1976, 1985). Basically the idea was to husband public resources through a process of relocation. Planned shrinkage would mean cutting off services to certain areas with few jobs or households, with the result that efficiency and quality would remain higher in more viable areas than otherwise. But even in the pre-Reagan era, this smacked too much of state control, inhibiting individual choice. The alternatives became the enclave, an area effectively insulated from municipal jurisdiction and oversight, or semi-privatized entities which take over some municipal services and levy charges on terms negotiated with municipalities: often celebrated as examples of the power of competition and of the superiority of private over public-sector methods, both are desperate measures taken when public-sector reform is hopeless. A bankrupt municipality – bankrupt financially, to be sure, but also of ideas – is in a weak position when powerful corporations and investors with deep pockets sit across the table, offering to transform blighted areas into new zones of activity which they want to control. The city needs tax revenues, either from sales taxes or property taxes; developers however are used to receiving rebates and being granted incentives to take risks in places like Detroit.

Shrinking is not an exclusively urban phenomenon. The "hollowing out" of the Great Plains of the US has been under way for two decades; indeed two-fifths of all counties in the US are shrinking. Parts of the Great Plains are more sparsely inhabited today than when the federal government opened them for settlement in the late nineteenth century! (*The Economist*, 2008). As a result, schools must be consolidated; people have to go further for basic services such as pharmacies. OECD data show that "most regions experiencing sustained net out-migration also display other indicators of economic distress" including higher shares of employment in agriculture and lower productivity in that sector, very low public sector productivity, higher unemployment rates, and lower GDP per capita. "This reinforces the idea that regions may struggle to improve local labor conditions and productivity if those leaving are the most talented, educated and entrepreneurial" (OECD, 2011b: 50).[1] In a vicious circle, abandonment – desertification – leads to "human erosion," to use a phrase coined by Dorothea Lange and Paul S. Taylor (1940), illustrating Lange's iconic picture of a migrant mother in Nopomo, California.

Because Detroit looks exceptional, it is easy to fall into the trap of believing that it is atypical. One reason to take Detroit seriously is because shrinking cities, as a category, although comparatively few in number now, could be more numerous in the future. UN-Habitat estimates that between 1990 and 2000, eighty-six Asian cities lost 9.7 million inhabitants, another fifty in China lost 6.8 million. In developed countries, 40 per cent of all cities (20 per cent in North America, 25 per cent in Japan, but 50 per cent in Europe) lost population, a trend which is not all negative if the net result is more compact cities (*Le Monde*, 2008).

Nevertheless, Detroit, whose population has fallen by nearly half since 1950, has become the epic, iconic example of abandonment and re-concentration. In the heart of its downtown stood Hudson's, America's second largest department store, after Macy's, and, like Macy's, associated with an annual Thanksgiving Day parade that entertained millions and marked the start of the Christmas shopping season. On 24 October 1998, it was demolished in twenty-seven seconds with a charge of 2,728 pounds of explosives, the largest inhabited structure, 2.2 million square feet, yet demolished. Between 1970 and 2000, more than 161,000 dwellings, one-third of the city's occupied housing stock, were lost – more than the total stock of the city of Cincinnati, Ohio. Transforming a chaotic and random process into something akin to planned shrinkage, the City of Detroit plans to accelerate demolition and simultaneously reorganize what's left into something more coherent and manageable. Some have even conceived how the remaining cityscape could become a theme park, attracting visitors to see a radically different version of Disney's Tomorrowland (Bayles, 2006). Nothing on such a scale has happened since the Barbarians turned Rome into a provincial city. The magnificent photographs taken by Yves Marchand and Romain Meffre (2010) show not only empty lots, vacant streets, and uninhabited structures, but also interiors of auditoriums, schools, office buildings, and houses which appear to have been abandoned without any preparation, as if some 800,000 people simply vanished, taking nothing with them. Their book has become a collector's item, perhaps not so much for people who knew Detroit as it once was and who have seen how little government did to arrest or cope with its decline, as for people for whom this had been unimaginable until it was made visible.

It is too easy to fall into the trap of blaming the city's crisis on politicians, transport engineers, the domestic automobile manufacturers and American racism for the syndrome of out-migration, failing schools, high rates of crime, crumbling infrastructure, highways which divided neighborhoods but made commuting to suburbs easy, and collapsing business models. This list is actually not long enough. Government helped: in Michigan a combination of weak regional government and weak state laws facilitated the conversion of rural land to urban uses. A construction and development industry ready to roll out suburban strip malls and shopping centers along six-lane highways giving access to endless tracts of suburban, low-density housing found common interest with state politicians all too willing to do deals with Detroit leaders to carve out spheres of influence which limited the scope for state or federal initiatives.

The recent history of Greektown as part of the non-basic economy becomes illustrative. Listed on the National Register of Historic Places in 1982, Greektown is a non-residential district in downtown Detroit with excellent road and public transport connections. Greeks moved into the area when it was still residential, replacing many German families who moved to other, newer parts of the city in the early twentieth century. When Greek families in turn sought newer and better housing elsewhere, they left behind businesses they had established, many serving the minority community as coffee shops, stores, and restaurants. The same process in many cities around the world has given Paris, London, Chicago, Melbourne, Montreal distinctive minority neighborhoods with an identity strong enough to survive changes in consumer preferences and planning ideologies. As Detroit declined, Greektown remained one of the few areas with a strong link to a past and a human scale. But the city's decline also changed the economic dynamics. Since 2008, the New Hellas restaurant (established in 1901), the Laikon, the Cyprus Taverna, and the Olympia have closed: families do not want to stay in this line of work, and health and safety laws add to the costs of restaurant operation when margins are small. Many restaurants with Greek names (The New Parthenon, Golden Fleece, Pegasus Taverna) serve Greek food but few are owned and managed by Greeks. The hub of Greektown is a casino, a product of postwar postmodernism based on exaggerated imitation, creating in the process a newly authentic space for consumer culture. The underlying value of the land near the center of Detroit helped Greektown survive. But its capacity to attract people with disposable income makes the businesses in Greektown very dependent on changes in household income and wealth and consumer spending elsewhere. There are projects for investment, including new transit systems connecting downtown and New Centre, but, without the commitment of corporate executives and investors who have long-time ties to Detroit, it is not clear how much of this would happen. This is not a sustainable model for urban regeneration. Regulatory complexity and "red tape" hold back investment, stifle entrepreneurship, and cause undue delay to worthwhile ventures. In dynamic, growing cities, people continue to invest despite administrative complexity, delay and even corruption; in declining cities, these become a barrier to investment, a major factor in the loss of confidence.

To complete the picture, Detroit has not made best use of its endowed asset as a border city. Detroit faces the city of Windsor in the Province of Ontario, to its south. (Due to the course of the Detroit River the city of Detroit actually lies to the north of its neighbor.) America's largest border city with Canada, Detroit is responsible for a significant share of the trade in manufactured goods between the two countries. Before 2001, when crossing was a more casual affair, people went from one country to the other to buy things that were otherwise not available locally, to have lunch or dinner, to meet friends and family, to attend a sports game or concert. Cars still dominate the traffic through the tunnel under the river which connects the two city centers; the 7,500-foot-long Ambassador Bridge further to the south is heavily used by ten thousand or more trucks each workday. The Ambassador Bridge, which carries more than 25 per cent of all merchandise trade between the United States and Canada, however is privately owned, perhaps uniquely for such a strategic location. Built between 1927 and 1929, the Bridge is owned by Manuel Moroun through the Detroit International Bridge Company in the United States (and the Canadian Transit Company in Canada). Not surprisingly, the absence of competition adds to the costs of business and exposes a key international link to added risk due to the lack of any alternative for heavy freight. The Province of Ontario and American jurisdictions are willing to build and share ownership of a new bridge (the New International Trade Crossing) in another location, a move contested in the courts by Moroun who took the unusual step to promote a referendum on the 2012 state ballot which would have precluded the construction of a new bridge without the consent of the people of Detroit. This proposition was defeated, massively, by the Michigan electorate. When the Department of State issued a permit to the State of Michigan for the new crossing in April 2013, Moroun filed a lawsuit to block it. It may be several more years before the bridge is built and open to traffic: aside from the sheer scale of the project and the likelihood of engineering difficulties, delays are likely to arise from the problem of land acquisition; as of 2014 the United States had yet to authorize the funds needed to build a new customs plaza.

The bridge episode illustrates the considerable uncertainty that surrounds major infrastructure projects to exploit Detroit's favorable geographic position in the global economy. Long delays to reach decisions over needed infrastructure projects have plagued the United States since the 1970s, compromising its competitiveness. A major project of this kind has a transforming, dynamic effect, making possible other changes which had not been considered feasible before. And that's just what Detroit needs. In better times, Detroit could grow and prosper even if

Managing space better   111

Greektown did not; now Detroit needs Greektown and places like it. What happens to Greektown can help us understand what a recovery of Detroit would take, and why it may not happen. The lessons do not stop at the shores of the Detroit River, either. The distance from Detroit to Athens, Greece, is 5,229 miles or 8,416 kilometers. They are remote in age as well: young as is Detroit, so Athens is old. But what counts today is their contemporary experience. The Greektown story has some uncanny similarities with the unwinding of the economy in Greece itself.

Greece

Athens may have high unemployment, but the prospects for many are worse in rural and remote areas. Regenerating tourism, agriculture, even light manufacturing in non-metropolitan regions will not generate a Greek recovery; only Athens and Thessaloniki can support growth based on higher value-added and higher productivity on a sufficient scale. Greece needs Athens more than the State of Michigan needs Detroit. But the electoral dynamics in Greece as in Michigan tend to be weighted more toward non-metropolitan constituencies and interests.

Greece waited impatiently until 2004 to host the Olympic Games in Athens. What an opportunity to set a vision for Athens for 2020! The lesson of the Barcelona Games of 1992 is precisely the importance of a medium-term strategy for development along a timeline which begins before a proposal for the Games is made and ends well after the event. For Greece, hosting the Games was the objective, the realization of a dream, not a part of a longer-term vision. The time to fashion a vision was during the years of rapid growth, when Europe and the economy seemed likely to lift Greece for years to come, but the opportunity came and went. Complacency was misplaced. Now in the deepest, longest recession of any EU country, when the future looks bleak, vision-building seems a luxury. But without a vision, the future in Greece, as in Detroit, is a record of what might have been, a bitter legacy.

Detroit is making some effort to clear its land of abandoned houses; Greece is only now able to use a cadaster to record property ownership and assess taxes. Without a cadaster, people built without regard for zoning, building codes, and planning in the expectation that eventually the claim of usage and the cost of demolition would be converted by the authorities into rights. Greece has too many jurisdictions with a hand in planning and building criteria, but also depends on "command and control" regulation which tends to inhibit adjustment to changing economic and social circumstances. Regulatory uncertainty, corruption, and an unusually high percentage of very small firms in Greece deter inward investment and depress the take-up of innovations.

This pattern, sanctioned by time and a heritage of self-building, helps to explain why there has been so little in the way of co-ordinated land-use planning to cover the peri-urban zone where city meets forest, where towns face the sea: natural environmental assets have been too easily squandered, and land has been exposed unnecessarily to devastating disasters, including massive fires. The fires of 2007 have not been forgotten: three consecutive heat waves of over 40°C and severe drought; three thousand fires, including three hundred at one time; the destruction of 270,000 hectares of forests, olive groves, and farmland, equal to 2 per cent of the total area of Greece. These things do happen elsewhere, but the gap in Greece between formal rules and effective implementation is perhaps wider than almost anywhere in Europe. The mapping of forests was supposed to have been completed in 2009, to complement a map of coastal zones. These instruments would have supported better land-use management, but, without resources to compensate owners whose property impedes a strategic redevelopment or risk reduction, they can have an impact only at some distant time in the future. The fact that a cadaster has been a low priority for so long – Greece is the only European country without one – implies a deliberate intent to keep land ownership opaque, and land tax low.

Spatial planning and regulation are typical of issues which people exploit to advance private over public interests. Resistance to reform therefore expresses the concerns of stakeholders who may lose what leverage they have if procedures are simplified and more transparent. Environmental protection can be a pretext to protect private property rights; well-meaning arguments that more studies are needed, more hearings must be held, more procedures completed give the appearance of respect for process but only delay decisions. Greece needs a framework for land use which is dynamic, leading to more investment, better energy use, reduced risk, and better protection of heritage. This calls for more emphasis on a mix of what needs to be preserved and what changed in rural and urban areas, ways to make and revise spatial and land-use plans in less time, better inspection and enforcement, and, above all, greater cross-sectoral regulatory and policy coherence (Giannakourou and Balla, 2012).

Athens, the largest city in Greece, also has the country's largest population of university students. This should be a major asset attracting employers and reinforcing any strategy to lift entrepreneurship and promote new business start-ups. But surveys of higher education in Greece point out how poorly equipped students are for employment:

because universities do not offer top-quality education in the fields most in demand, engineers and medical practitioners, among others, study abroad and often stay abroad. In a job-starved economy, what is the incentive to improve higher education in Greece if it is easier for graduates to leave than for foreign firms to establish themselves in Greece, to employ them? If education is not reformed, what will happen as more people, and especially younger people, fall into poverty, facing lower lifetime income even when a recovery comes?

The crisis has increased unemployment dramatically in Greece, even among categories whose level of education, while not a guarantee of employment, is usually enough to limit the risks of unemployment. The unemployment rate in Greece at 24.2 per cent in 2013 was more than three times the OECD average; that for youth was a record-breaking 55.3 per cent, compared to an OECD average of 16.2 per cent already considered unacceptably high. Not surprisingly, long-term unemployment is the fate of nearly 15 per cent of the Greek population – and this in a country with a high degree of informality (representing an average of 27 per cent of GDP between 1999 and 2007). The economy was able to employ a lot of unskilled workers in 2009: only 10 per cent of those who had not finished primary school or who had no schooling were unemployed then. No one is surprised to learn that 40 per cent in that category are unemployed in the depth of the crisis, but what about the 30 per cent rate of unemployment in 2013 among those who completed secondary school, or the figure of 15 per cent of those with postgraduate education (a level twice as high as in 2009)? The social impact of the crisis put pressure on families and on public services; neither has adequate capacity to help people absorb these shocks and prepare for a recovery (OECD, 2013: figures 2.12 and 2.13).

Greece appears as a country on the periphery of Europe only in relation to the central regions between the North Sea and the Alps. "Periphery" is sometimes a code word for "marginal," but some of the richest regions in Europe are on the geographic periphery, in Scandinavia. To call the Mediterranean "peripheral" also seems strange when for centuries it was the center of European civilization. In the twentieth century however southern Spain, southern Italy, and Greece were characterized by under-development. The port cities around the Mediterranean are no longer connected to one another, stimulating development. For much of the period after 1990, Greece held a unique position within Europe as the only EU country whose immediate neighbors were Turkey and the formerly communist countries of the Balkans. But the modernization of transport routes which improved access to the rest of the Continent also exposed Greece to foreign competition for which its firms are unprepared. Globalization and the expansion of the European Union enhanced the potential for Greece to position its service sector as a base accessible to its contiguous hinterland to the north, and across the Mediterranean, to the Levant and to North Africa. China has entered Greece as a major investor: at $5.5 billion, a portfolio not much smaller than the $5.9 billion invested in Germany, but far less diversified: in Greece China has concentrated on the transport sector, upgrading the container terminal in Piraeus, and participating with Greek and Gulf investors in the redevelopment of the old Athens airport (*Financial Times*, 2014). But the spillovers from freight logistics into the rest of the Greek economy will meet the same regulatory barriers that domestic governments under pressure from the IMF and the European Union have found difficult to dismantle: Greece still needs to liberalize its professions and modernize its codes for building and planning in its key urban centers of Thessaloniki and Athens if it is to attract investment and support the growth of firms which could serve the economies around the eastern Mediterranean. Nothing like this happened; in the meantime other countries increased their domestic capacity to serve a wider regional economy.

As a country, Greece cannot just shrink or disappear. In 1948, the fear of an invasion of Greece (or communist coup) helped bring about the creation of the North Atlantic Treaty Organization (NATO). The days when its weakness could have provoked a rival power to invade it – as happened often enough in its history – are over. We can measure how much the world community has advanced thanks to the creation of the European Union. Geo-political tensions now lie along a north–south fault line just to the east of Poland and extending south to Turkey, Egypt, Kenya and Somalia. The entire western world was struggling to learn how to manage this new frontier when Ukraine dominated the news in the spring and summer of 2014. This fault line is itself centuries old; what is new is the fact that the threats to the West appear limited to a lower level of incipient violence in the form of terrorism, illegal migration, and organized crime, rather than invasion by armies. And in this respect, the lack of hope for the Greek economy poses a threat, exposing younger people to other, less legitimate, callings. Things could indeed be worse.

Were Greece to leave the euro, its geographic position would make it vulnerable to an expansion of illegal economic activities already present in Africa and the eastern Mediterranean. Economists who consider the strains between surplus and deficit countries in the Eurozone to be unsustainable advocate a Greek withdrawal from the Eurozone (Grexit) because Greece could then devalue – as if the Greek economy produces so many goods and services for which there is a market if only they cost less. Indeed, with a floating Greek currency, the price of imported goods would rise, depressing real incomes. Grexit ignores the demoralizing consequences of an action which would imply that years of sacrifice and commitment within the EU have been in vain. Imagine the scenario: the Euro remains in circulation because it is the only currency with which people are familiar; counterfeit Euro notes enter Greece and circulate in parallel with a newly issued drachma, in which people lack confidence. As the Greek economy fails to stabilize and as inflation skyrockets, organized crime penetrates Greece with offers of employment and bribes to officials, taking advantage of the huge coastline and mountainous land borders of the country. To protect themselves, other countries would have to close the Schengen borders not only of Greece but between the Balkans and other EU countries, and NATO would have to intensify patrols in the Aegean and Adriatic. Fanciful? Look at what happened in recent decades to Mexico, crossed by supply routes in the drug traffic between Central America and markets in the United States: does the figure of sixty thousand dead in drug wars and the impression of passivity or corruption in local police and judiciary have to be strictly accurate to generate a nightmare scenario of an endemic civil war in an EU member state?

Things cut both ways. International borders should be an advantage. But for Detroit and Greece, geography has turned into a handicap: the mix of core industries and services is too limited and relies too much on incomes and investment from elsewhere; the match between jobs and skills is poor; land use, housing, and planning already pose significant handicaps, not to mention added regulatory costs. The comparative advantages provided by physical and political geography have been squandered.

Toward the future – but what future?

Both Greece and Detroit possess assets on which to build a new economy open to innovation and entrepreneurship, but are constrained in their ability to use them. Both seem unable to reform except under outside pressure, but are unable to grow without reform. Still fighting over who is to blame for what, politicians appeal for support by promising what cannot be delivered. In such an atmosphere, can a government that is likely to implement bold reforms get elected?

The list of shortcomings in public administration covers some things both Greece and Detroit share, and some things that are specific to each. They both face well-organized and determined labor unions;

over-staffing and insufficient flexibility to reallocate resources; massive pension and welfare liabilities; legal restrictions on terminating employment; a culture of clientelism and regulatory capture; and a legacy of endemic corruption (OECD, 2011c). Rebuilding the public sector so that Detroit and Greece have the capacity to repair years of damage and prepare for a better future, and can cope with crises when they occur, will itself take time. A generation may be needed to change an administrative culture from one of denial and passivity, to one which is proactive and puts the public interest first. Before the transformation is complete, however, further debt rescheduling and budget cuts may be unavoidable (*Financial Times*, 2013b). Both Detroit and Greece show the limits of large, autonomous, semi-independent jurisdictions – Detroit was once the tenth largest city in the United States; Greece is still a mid-size member of the European Union – to solve their own problems. Institutional design matters but so does political culture, or to use the Greek word *nous*, or understanding. No wonder that governance appears on international comparative bench-markings of both competitiveness and livability.

All good memos provide decision-makers with at least three options. Here are four:

- Scenario A: Enlightened leadership. Critical decisions are taken by officials and executives who act as stewards, confident of public support domestically and from international organizations.
- Scenario B: Greece remains in debt at an unsustainable level, and Detroit, although out of bankruptcy, remains under close supervision; neither is able to guide its destiny. In order to prevent contagion, other governments and lenders continue to provide extraordinary additional funding measures. Eventually, Greece and Detroit prepare to return to the markets for debt financing.
- Scenario C: Anemia – but not yet amnesia. Reforms are launched but meet with delay and reform fatigue; a long-term cycle of erratic economic and social trends, cumulatively reinforcing the negatives.
- Scenario D: The equivalent of a coup. What if the city of Detroit were dissolved, its territory redistributed among other jurisdictions, and a new river-front and border city were created within the shrunken space of the previous city? What if a new federal structure of Europe were created within which economic and social policy would be carried out, not by an unelected Secretariat, but by an elected government to which member countries had transferred some of their sovereignty?

Scenario A appears unlikely unless there is a dramatic change in the body politic. Some combination of B and C, which already describe the state of affairs at the end of 2014, appears probable. An end to the crisis would only make the debt of Detroit and Greece easier to manage but they would remain stuck with problems that growth by itself cannot solve. Scenario D is probably a leap too far for now.

What follows is not a blind defense of the status quo. Deserted villages were a phenomenon in Europe after the Black Death of 1648; small towns vanished in the United States in the 1930s – by the 1970s, there was nothing left of Roosevelt, New Jersey, but an abandoned gas station. Shrinking cities face some problems that in certain respects are the mirror image of growing cities: adjusting the provision of public services to the fiscal base and to population needs and demands; maintaining the skilled employees needed for health care, policing, social services. Some are distinctive: providing good-quality education to young people who are likely to leave in search of better opportunities. Remedies such as tax breaks and subsidies, or enterprise zones, all of which are distortive, are easy and popular to introduce, and keep government from getting overly involved to help reorient local development strategies. But on balance, shrinking cities are simply a special case of cities in general in the post-crisis environment.

It has been an easy excuse for hard thinking to put shrinking cities – those losing jobs and people – and growing cities – those attracting jobs and people – into separate categories. This is a false dichotomy: cities, whether growing or declining, follow similar dynamics in a broader policy and economic environment. Some shrinking cities can find a new equilibrium, with rising living standards and economic opportunities. Some growing cities generate unmanageable problems of housing markets, congestion, and areas of deprivation. Just as it is difficult to turn the dynamics of shrinkage into a success story, so it is to keep a growing city – which Detroit once was – from imploding. Both are at risk of market and policy failures.

In 1986, *The Economist* published a survey on "The Anatomy of Cities" focused on how nine cities had adjusted to structural change as the service sector outpaced manufacturing in the western world as the engine of growth. The final section, devoted to civic government, was tellingly entitled "how cities can help themselves." Recognizing that there is no formula, "no rigid blueprint," the newspaper recommended "education, further education, entertainment and culture. These things will bring in the human capital: ring-roads, multi-storey car-parks and echoing plazas will not" (*The Economist*, 1986). It is always good to have evidence that what seemed intuitively to be true is in fact close to reality. Recent research notes that a 10 per cent increase in the share of university-educated workers in a city raises the productivity of other workers in that city by 3–4 per cent (OECD, 2014: 51–2).

Urban regeneration in the 1990s: OECD studies on distressed urban areas and urban regeneration

The period 1990–2008 was shaped by two trends or forces. A form of neo-classical liberalism which is often referred to as the Reagan–Thatcher ideology in favor of markets helped to deregulate the financial sector, increasing the flow of funds for (expensive) mega-projects and tall buildings often sited in the centers of historic cities in Europe, Japan, and North America but also creating new centers in Singapore, Hong Kong, Shanghai, and the Sunbelt states of North America where service-sector firms captured the flows of funds for trade and investment, and for privatized or deregulated network utilities. The fluid, intangible, even immaterial nature of finance provoked a reaction, placing greater emphasis on the social and cultural values associated with places and their differences which highlighted social disparities, exclusion, and the loss of identity. Was this just another trade-off associated with growth? "Why not simply let community groups, 'do-gooders' and the 'morally minded' pick up the pieces of economic decline and social degradation?" Ash Amin and Stephen Graham answered their own question, affirming that social cohesion is an economic asset: "a sense of place and belonging taps into hidden potential and the sources of social confidence that lie at the core of risk-taking entrepreneurial activity." This assumes of course that the there is a quantum of social capital and territorial identity that can be put to good use (Amin and Graham, 1997: 426). Debates today about widening disparities and the emphasis on inclusion amplify these concerns.

In a nutshell, the question is about the link between firms and territories. If more places offered roughly comparable facilities and policy packages, why would a business come? Stay? Leave? People want to know where the jobs of tomorrow will be, and what regime of public spending is appropriate to a post-industrial, knowledge-based society. A growing literature on clusters, innovation, social enterprise, and migration highlights the shortcomings of traditional industrial policy supported by subsidies and fiscal incentives, and calls instead for a new paradigm which would make better use of specific local assets. But place-based economic and social policy remains compromised by the inability of micro-economics to predict outcomes and by the overwhelming impact of mainstream sectoral budgets and programs. What would it take to make a place-based paradigm operational in political and policy terms?

Wars often end with a sharp economic decline, even a depression, as soldiers are demobilized, factories reconverted to peacetime production, and governments stop borrowing and spending. This was the pattern after 1815, 1918, and 1945. The end of the Cold War was followed by a recession, not so much due to the fall of the Iron Curtain as to the coincidentally high rate of borrowing and subsequent asset bubble, especially in housing markets in the United States, United Kingdom, Ireland, Sweden, Finland, Australia, and Japan. The subsequent fall–out was attenuated because the fall of communist regimes in Central and Eastern Europe also opened opportunities for investment, productivity increases, trade, and rising productivity. It was far easier for Prague, Budapest, and Krakow to look to their futures, retaining their historic cores while modernizing districts built under communism, than it was for many old industrial cities such as Glasgow, Turin, and Essen where the phrase "hollowing out" captured the loss of manufacturing. Concerns about a new urban underclass resurrected fears familiar to readers of nineteenth-century novels by Dickens and Hugo. It would indeed have been ironic and tragic if the end of the Cold War made life in cities less tolerable.

Distressed urban areas can be found in growing and declining cities alike. They raise basic questions about when, how, and why governments should intervene in the economic and social transformation of cities. This is not just about poverty or access to opportunities, problems which could be otherwise addressed through redistributive measures or by waiting for the normal operations of labor markets to work. The people who live in distressed urban areas suffer from the effects of multiple deprivation which are spatially concentrated. When the OECD study was carried out between 1994 and 1996, a survey of ten countries representing close to half the population of the OECD showed that the proportion of the population of major urban areas living in distressed areas ranged from 7 to 25 per cent. These are not slums sunk in poverty: many who live in distressed areas are employed and enjoy average incomes. Whether such areas are inner-city or suburban does not affect the fundamental processes by which they deteriorated, the outcome of complex interactions between economic, social and spatial factors, and the unanticipated outcomes of certain public policies (Conway and Konvitz, 2000; OECD, 1998: 11).

The OECD report on distressed urban areas described the downward spiral, a dynamic process of concentration and change at neighborhood level:

- Local residents have difficulty obtaining educational or vocational qualifications as a result of poorer educational facilities and fewer role models.

- Low-skill workers become spatially isolated from jobs.
- Local enterprises move away from the area.
- The population is younger than average, with higher concentrations of single parents.
- High crime rates and vandalism inhibit local employment opportunities.
- Low rents or public housing attract the least-well-equipped migrants from other cities, rural areas or other countries.
- The informal economy is large.
- Address effects, or a form of discrimination based on place of residence, discourage employers from hiring local residents, and banks from offering credit to people who would establish local businesses.

In a distressed area, the conditions are favorable for the social reproduction of a spiral of decline based on low expectations, or, worse, hopelessness: "everyone would leave if they could" (OECD, 1998: 58). Distressed urban areas demand cross-sectoral and multi-level policy co-ordination. In these neighborhoods, the prevalence of one negative characteristic produces prevalence of another. In other words, when social problems are concentrated they will tend to aggravate. No wonder that social scientists and policy specialists – and the media – resort to terms such as alienation to project a sense of a deep-rooted syndrome that would be difficult to overcome. It is important to note the central role of *perception* as well as *objective fact* in influencing the decisions made by local residents and businessmen, government, and other public and private sector actors. There is a need for a set of qualitative and quantitative indicators for an early warning system, but, given the variation across countries in what is measured and at what level, progress on such a set is likely to be very uneven. Related to perception is the challenge of effective communication to build public support and understanding (Conway and Konvitz, 2000: 768–9).

The basic model stresses the interaction between individuals who have a choice about where to live, work, and invest, and those whose choices are more circumscribed. Ideally, distressed urban areas should be improved to the point that people can leave if they want to, but chose to stay. Policy should help local economies survive in the face of competition, but also facilitate global flows of finance, goods, and services which thrive on competition. There needs to be a balance between the cohesion within a neighborhood and the connectedness of neighborhoods to wider economic and social contexts. This is not unlike other trade-offs between equity and growth at larger spatial scales. Mobility helps people to come and go, but also generates environmental costs. What may be good at one scale may not be good at another: is it more important to connect disadvantaged localities and regions to corridors of growth, or to connect leading regions with each other? If it costs more to deliver services to disadvantaged communities – or regions – should they be compensated through transfer payments, or given a "free ride" (Spiekermann and Wegener, 2008)?

Evidence of the high costs to residents, to businesses, and to society as a whole associated with the persistence and growth of distressed urban areas has not been enough to redirect policy. The life chances of people living in distressed urban areas are significantly different from those of individuals with the same socio-economic characteristics living elsewhere. If ever there was needed a clear example of how cost-benefit analysis breaks down in practice, this is it. The emergence of distressed urban areas cannot be dismissed with the argument that they are the inevitable accompaniment of growth and change. There is nothing inevitable about such areas. Before shifting resources, decision-makers should ask how much more needed to be spent, to be set against the long-term savings to the treasury from properties of rising value, reduced security costs, fewer people receiving long-term social benefits, more people working, and more businesses in the formal economy.

But first policy-makers have to see that there is a problem. In respect of distressed urban areas, the OECD study showed that:

- People have difficulty finding common terms when discussing similar phenomena that in some places are inner-city, and in others suburban.
- The growth of the informal economy, which involves legal activities that are not declared or registered, and health and housing issues, receive insufficient attention.
- The need to show short-term results and competing priorities compromise programs that stand a chance of making a difference.
- Large-scale projects and strategies are often poorly integrated into city-wide contexts.
- There is little interest in either early-warning systems or preventive measures.

The problems of problem areas cannot be solved by policies and programs that focus on these areas alone. To succeed, urban policy should take a comprehensive approach to cities, so that preventive measures can reduce the incidence of distressed areas in the future, and so that remedial measures can integrate the distressed areas which already exist into the social, economic, and physical fabric of the city. All parts of cities and metropolitan regions are inter-dependent and inter-related. It is not so much a matter of exceptional measures as of taking the normal activities, roles, and responsibilities of government in cities – education, infrastructure, health, policing, welfare, etc. – and applying them more effectively, taking better account of the factors that generate and perpetuate distressed urban areas (OECD, 1998: 118–19). The seven guiding principles that emerged from this unique, cross-country OECD study recommend governments to:

- avoid stigmatizing particular areas.
- develop a transparent system for identifying areas of need.
- act early enough and take preventive measures.
- adapt the strategy to the diversity and complexity of the local context.
- make urban regeneration policies more comprehensible to local actors and to the population.
- actively monitor and evaluate policies.
- adapt the strategy to the diversity and complexity of the local context.

To tackle multiple problems in a comprehensive way calls for space-based sectoral co-ordination, holistic in its methods. How is this to be accomplished? The exceptional scale of distress could justify exceptional measures, but, by the same token, those measures risk being stigmatized just like the problem areas to which they were being applied. Could an integrative spatial approach be mainstreamed, or in other words made operational when addressing not just distressed urban areas, but a wide range of urban development problems, both in communities in decline and expanding communities?

Integrated spatial planning was taken up by the OECD in the Ecological City project as a follow-up to the UN summit of 1992 in Rio on sustainable development. In brief, the objective was to use space at the scale of a neighborhood, a district, or an entire city as the operative unit to bring different policy interventions together, to see how their combined effect and interaction could achieve more coherent, effective and efficient results. Using the active voice, an "ecological city strives to become better at finding and implementing solutions to environmental problems." Because the quality of the environment is shaped by diverse activities stretching from consumer food patterns to daily transport, the heating and cooling of buildings, water use and waste management, to mention only a few, incorporating environmental considerations into decision-making in public and private sectors alike is a major challenge. An ecological city therefore is not necessarily a city with only a few environmental problems; rather the term applies to jurisdictions where decision-making and budgetary priorities incorporate environmental considerations (OECD, 1996: 11).

A transition between managing space based on sectoral administrative control, as things are, and cross-sectoral co-operation, as they could be, calls for a long-range vision, and a plan to sustain the implementation of a new mode of work until it is tested, improved, and normalized. Skeptics can always argue that the status quo is good enough, that the unpredictable nature of urban change and of the evolution of the environment compromise planning, and that cross-sectoral co-ordination is too costly and time-consuming. To help test innovation, the OECD Ecological City report advocated "sustainability performance areas" (OECD, 1996: 130–1). The first step would begin with a local community environmental audit (where we are) and the development of an environmental plan (where people want to go, what to change, what to maintain). Then the local or regional government would evaluate the community plan in relation to wider metropolitan goals. The third step would be taken when a Sustainability Performance Area is declared with an integrated administrative structure and an authority to adjust regulations and fiscal measures linked to the implementation of the local area plan for a limited period of three to five years, but longer than one economic and electoral cycle. This would permit selective reform of normative policy instruments to test the market for transformation and investment at district-level scale, thereby reducing the risks and uncertainty associated with the introduction of new priorities.

The problem, as always, is not to design a new city, but to rebuild the city that exists. Environmental issues often linked to previous phases of development were the focus of the Urban Renaissance Studies carried out by OECD in 1999–2002 on a small geographical area at a city center where regeneration efforts had been made over the past decade. The focus on centers was deliberate because this was where many unused or under-valued assets could be found. The term "renaissance" is increasingly cited in the media to refer to older cities experiencing an economic recovery. It should also call attention to the will and imagination of people: the rebirth of confidence matters perhaps even more than the physical renewal it engenders. Nothing will happen when people have a fatalistic attitude that sees change in cities as largely negative, and cities as the victims of circumstances over which they have no control. The resources to address urban problems are not only material; they include elements of social capital, flexible and visionary institutions, and the creative, imaginative work of people in both the public and the private sectors. There is enormous potential for architecture, planning, the design arts, engineering, and social and environmental sciences to guide urban development, not just to create profitable property markets, but to create a design dividend, better uses of space for living and working, generating returns over many years. People believe what they see.

Krakow, Glasgow, Belfast, Kitakyushu, Canberra, Berlin all faced a period of profound structural change which also implied a change in the way in which the city center is developed and managed.

- In Krakow, a city transformed under communism when thousands of peasants were brought in to work at the Nova Huta steel works as part of the effort to erode the bourgeois character of a city which had great historical associations for Polish nationalism, the challenge was to restore and manage the city's center, where its famous university was headquartered. The context for action was also related to the creation of new regional administrative units in Poland as part of the process of preparing for EU accession.
- Glasgow's waterfront on the Clyde, adjacent to its historic Merchant City and vibrant retail district, now the second-largest in the UK, was ready for redevelopment. After three centuries of shipping and shipbuilding, would the regenerated riverfront remain a separate district, or could it contribute to a broader redevelopment of Glasgow?
- Kitakyushu, one of the first cities in Japan to be open to foreigners in the nineteenth century, had once been far better known than Fukuoka, not more than an hour away. But Fukuoka's growth on the basis of the service economy in recent decades mirrored Kitakyushu's decline as a manufacturing center. Innovation in manufacturing ceramics, together with a strong international center for training in development assistance, indicated how Kitakyushu could renew its historic roots while regaining momentum. Given Japan's ageing society, what would this imply for the redevelopment of an older urban core?
- The release by the Australian Navy of undeveloped inner-city lands known as Jerrabomberra sparked a reassessment of Canberra, largely a postwar, car-based city and Australia's federal capital, which had become dependent on the public sector. The downsizing of federal employment put pressure on the private sector to create jobs, but the city's commercial center, Civic, was in serious need of redevelopment if it were to serve as a platform for the growth of a high-tech service sector. Canberra's two universities had the potential to contribute research and lift the international profile of both the city and the nation.
- And Berlin, the most famous reunited city in recent decades after Jerusalem, faced the withdrawal of subsidies for manufacturing jobs and the need to create a fabric supporting activity in districts which on either side of the wall had accumulated environmental and

housing problems. With an infrastructure for a city with a million more people than were living in Berlin in the 1990s, the city had enormous potential. About one-third of the population living in Berlin by the end of the 1990s would be newcomers.

In each of these cases, land management focused on brownfields, areas subject to contamination from previous industrial uses which had to be remediated before they could be converted to new uses. This may sound banal, fully within the routine of normal administration. But in every case, the problems posed by small areas could not be treated as a purely local matter, and instead led to the need for a strategic plan taking long-term economic and social change into account.

Belfast tells the story best, and maybe has the best story to tell. The growth of Belfast accelerated in the second half of the nineteenth century as textile manufacturing, engineering, and shipbuilding expanded (Harland and Wolf built *Titanic* in Belfast). This export-reliant economy suffered badly during the global depression of the 1930s, exacerbating sectarian rivalry between Catholic and Protestant communities. Things did not improve after 1945: in the 1970s a hundred thousand people left the city, whose population fell to around 280,000 by the end of the twentieth century. On the one hand, the level of participation in higher education stood at 40 per cent in Belfast, but on the other, one in five people in employment had no formal qualifications, a handicap which rises to one in three among the unemployed. A historic turning came with the Belfast Agreement of 10 April 1998, which all but ended the civil disturbances known as the Troubles, and created the Northern Ireland Assembly, and the Regional Strategic Framework Document and Strategy. These changes came toward the end of ten years of investment and initiative by the Laganside Corporation, a public agency responsible for redevelopment in the city center which created a new economic space first by tackling the environmental problems of the heavily polluted River Lagan, and then by creating residential, civic, and commercial properties along the riverbank. The successful redevelopment of lands adjacent to the River Lagan was dependent upon the successful environmental management of the river itself, beginning with the construction of a weir to prevent or minimize flood risk to the central part of Belfast City. This sequence was an important element in Laganside's overall strategy. Previously, the city had turned away from the river; regeneration along the Lagan created an opportunity to integrate this part of the city, which was largely neutral in terms of sectarian politics, into the rest of Belfast where communities often remain isolated in different parts. It is important to note that the Laganside initiative – a catalyst for change – began before there was a resolution of the outstanding political issues which affected inward investment, and led to the creation of places of economic and social value which were qualitatively different, in political terms, from other precincts.

This is a rare example of success for the kind of vision which characterized the original Italian Renaissance, to put the moral welfare of society and the survival of the polity first. The economy of Belfast diversified: a total of £720 million of investment and ten thousand new jobs had been achieved by 2000. Following the OECD recommendations, a Regeneration Committee was formed in 1999 which included Belfast City Council and other key stakeholders to enhance partnership in the city and to ensure a more strategic approach to city-wide regeneration, including greater attention to disadvantaged communities. It is worth emphasizing that the somewhat technocratic method of Laganside which enjoyed jurisdiction over a designated area and had the means to assemble sites into marketable development opportunities was successful in a city with some seven hundred civic and neighborhood organizations where everyone was preoccupied by the concerns of small groups but without a perspective on the community as a whole. In the mid-1990s Laganside developed the post of Community Officer, to work with social partners and community groups, to ensure that this revitalized part of the city achieves broader objectives. Partnership to maximize potential while reducing risk with the private sector was, if anything, easier.

Rebuilding economies after structural change calls for a flexible public sector:

- a strategic framework that targets the parts of the city which are its key assets, and identifies threats to their development.
- emphasis on environmental benefits in a sequential logic leading to economic and social outcomes.
- good-quality design and the capacity to carry projects through to completion, including adequate financing.
- public participation and public–private partnerships to build a vision for the future.
- social inclusion to diversify the economy, mirrored by a more diverse society.
- a dynamic and creative public sector as a force for change.

The OECD urban renaissance studies focused on difficult urban regeneration projects, often initiated when there were few comparators, no set of good practices, high hopes but few predictors of success. After developments in Bilbao, Manchester (Salford Quays), Turin (Lingotto complex), Newcastle–Gateshead, Canary Wharf among others had generated visible results, *The Economist* could take a forward–looking view of urban regeneration linked to brownfield redevelopment because both the public and private sectors could see a way forward, once imagination married with need. Regeneration on brownfield sites involves huge regulatory issues related to health and the environment. Not usually a newspaper which finds much in red tape to recommend it, *The Economist* said that it "does have its uses. It certainly focuses minds, identifying the different actors and their relations, establishing frameworks for co-ordination, setting priorities and aims, and establishing programs for meeting those objectives" (*The Economist*, 2005).

Clearly the things that worked in Belfast, Glasgow, Berlin and Kitakyushu can work in cities that are growing as well as in cities coping with huge structural problems. This conclusion only reinforces the impression that a distinction between shrinking and growing cities is misleading: the distinction is between cities where problems are tackled sensibly and often creatively, and where they are not. To answer some questions which arise out of the story so far:

- Must cities have a center? Yes. It may not be sufficient to create a strong identity around which people can organize and plan, but without a center this is even less likely to happen.
- Why are some communities more resilient, or more fragile, than others? Being connected to a wider region or network of communities makes a positive difference; being isolated, disconnected, is a strong handicap.
- Does it take a major shock to get political and social leaders to tackle the problems of urban distress? Often, but there are many examples when a major shock does not lead to action; instead, leaders evade change, prevaricate.
- What is the optimal level or unit for intervention? All areas, or a selected few? We still do not know.
- How much needs to be spent? We do not know either. If too little is spent, much of it will be wasted because not sufficiently effective. It may be necessary to spend too much to get results. Finding the right level through incremental increases however may only generate rent–seeking; spending too much too fast may overwhelm the capacity of institutions to make best use of the funds.

There is one over-arching question: given what was learned in the 1990s about the causes of urban distress and the factors that promote regeneration, why are there such egregious examples as Detroit and Greece in the second decade of the twenty-first century? Why is it sometimes so difficult to use the knowledge we have? In her assessment of why some societies fail to break out of a "vicious spiral," Jane Jacobs focused on "cultural failures to teach and learn" (Jacobs, 2004: 158). There are already lessons to be learned from Greece and Detroit; it is too soon to tell whether these lessons are absorbed.

Good practices? Or paradigm shift?

What is the difference between a Belfast or Glasgow, and a Detroit? Between Portugal or Ireland on the one hand, both of which suffered severe recessions in the crash, and Greece on the other? The lessons drawn out of the OECD studies on distressed urban areas, or from the Urban Renaissance case studies, highlight two essential variables: the ability of national government to encourage and support local initiatives; and a willingness to innovate and improvise, which can happen only when leaders in the public, private and civic sectors are willing to take risks. Admittedly, the situations they faced were often fairly extreme, as the case studies reveal: inexorable fiscal pressures (Canberra), severe structural adjustment to changing markets (Berlin, Kitakyushu, Glasgow), radical institutional change (Krakow); a combination of sectoral conflict and de-industrialization (Belfast). Early success built confidence; good practices led to knowledge exchange; a willingness to break with the past encouraged people to be visionary and optimistic. In the 1990s, at a time when the economy was expanding, it was reasonable to expect that places with untapped and under-developed assets would grow faster if it were easier to unlock their potential: this is the strategy of convergence by which government intervention in lagging cities and regions has long been justified.

There are sound reasons for arguing that the things that make a difference in places like Berlin and Belfast can be generalized. The value of theory goes beyond predicting outcomes in a field as complex as urban development, in which evaluation must take account of many variables including spillover effects which leap across boundaries, and time frames which can extend over decades. Theory confers intellectual authority, enabling politicians to assert that policy is grounded in reason, deflecting charges of political expediency, electoral considerations or ideological orientation. Ideas do matter, as well as sufficient data to back them up.

The OECD work on urban regeneration in the 1990s was carried out before the Organisation's territorial database was being constructed and before a conceptual framework for territorial development policy had been drafted, let alone endorsed. Largely empirical, OECD reports and case studies – driven by problem-specific agendas set by governments uncertain how to proceed when confronted by fast-changing economic and social conditions – analysed practices which had been demonstrated to be effective, but without being able to compare places which had made such efforts against places which had not. Good practices can be documented and codified, but an evolving textbook of good practices is no substitute for theory. Because so many studies had been completed by the end of the 1990s, and in order to make the transition within the OECD from a hybrid committee structure serving experts on rural, urban, and regional policy to a higher-level Territorial Development Policy Committee, an effort was made to articulate the purposes, risks, and opportunities of a more coherent approach to sub-national development. Given the disparities within societies and economies, what are the economic benefits of greater cohesion? How can all regions, given their different levels of development, contribute to growth? In a world of mobility, why does space matter?

Territorial development is several things:

- a national objective to achieve better balance among regions, and enhance productivity
- a policy objective with explicit territorial dimensions such as reducing long-term unemployment, mitigating climate change, building affordable housing
- a policy objective with implicit territorial dimensions such as improving the quality of education, promoting foreign direct investment, fostering the information society, enhancing disaster preparedness
- a local or regional objective with national implications such as relieving congestion, integrating minorities, expanding higher education and research, developing tourism, reducing environmental risks

Territorial development policy as advanced by the OECD did not seek to eliminate disparities but to reduce the barriers to development that may be linked to them. Uniform policies which treat all areas equally have been subject to several criticisms: a level of infrastructure and public services either too high or too low; financial transfers to regions without real economic justification or capacity to make best use of them; short-term but costly incentives to attract corporate investment. Because prosperous and fast-growing areas and lagging regions alike face barriers – but of different kinds – it becomes important to identify the factors in each that are conducive to development, and to implement policy with appropriate tools of governance to leverage partnerships and enhance accountability at the local or regional level. This is what lies behind the notion that each territory has a stock of "territorial capital ... which enables it to develop activities that will be more profitable than if they were located elsewhere ... leading to higher overall profitability" (OECD, 2001: 16).

The argument about whether growth increases disparities was important twenty years ago and remains so under the impact of the crisis and of quantitative easing, and following the publication of studies such as Thomas Piketty's *Capital au XXIe siècle*. Regions which can be classified as "worst-performing" contribute almost nothing to aggregate growth. No wonder the OECD, looking for new sources of growth after two years of recession, argued that, if such regions began to grow, the results aggregated at national level could be considerable (OECD, 2011b 44). During this 2008-and-after crisis, however, a place-based approach combines a "help-yourself, self-reliance" morality for endogenous development with a concerted effort to cap national expenditure and debt. The problem as always is timing: until cities and regions perform better they cannot increase their revenues and national governments cannot collect more taxes, but, without additional resources, the valorization of specific local assets will take longer.

Territorial development policy has problems of its own: national institutions do not possess enough knowledge to know what is best for particular places, and lack the capacity to generate local consensus and trust; local initiatives could lead to rent-seeking and anti-competitive actions; electoral calculations distort decisions; there are significant data gaps at the sub-national level as well as insufficient capacity to make better use of data; the people on the ground who may know best what needs to be done may not be able to develop a coherent strategy or have the capacity to carry it out. Vertical as well as horizontal co-ordination are necessary. The promise of territorial development runs up against the challenge of overcoming the limits of sectoral policy which often leads to trade-offs or to negative externalities (as when the construction of a highway to by-pass the historic center of a town leads to problems of water management). On the other hand, arguments in favor of the new territorial development policy were grounded in analyses of the failures of traditional policies, and of future risks to national welfare in the absence of efforts to make better use of local assets; no one believed that a transition to a new framework would be easy.

The policy shift to territorial development shows that both leading and lagging cities and regions can apply and benefit from a place-based approach to economic development. But this does not mean that *all* cities and regions can do so.

Looking back on Greece and Detroit from the perspective of the first decade in the post-Cold War period, it is clear that they did not meet institutional preconditions to the successful implementation of a territorial development strategy. OECD reports are full of tables, analyses, and guidelines about what governments at local, regional and national level are or should be doing to provide a framework for territorial development based on better use of specific local assets and opportunities. There is nothing fatalistic or predetermined about this: some cities, some countries, have taken measures to turn a bad situation around, or to prevent one from getting worse. But others have not. The institutional failures that contributed to the crisis in Greece and in Detroit began well before 2008; and, had the crisis not occurred, they might well have been tolerated for many more years. Detroit and Greece and places like them squandered credits and investments, and became dependent upon the good will of lenders and funders to extend repayment periods. Bankruptcy negotiations, and agreements to renegotiate the repayment of loans contain conditionality, that is, specific steps that the authorities must carry out as part of the deal. Conditionality assumes that the government receiving support has adequate legal and institutional capacity to uphold and implement the terms to which it has agreed. To question whether this capacity is sufficient is not permissible in public.

It is one thing to press governments to take responsible steps when small problems which risk getting out of hand can still be corrected or contained. It is another to impose reforms when they fail to do so. Greece, the home of democracy, and Detroit, once the arsenal of democracy, can be stabilized only by accepting a level of dependency for years to come. On the one hand, this is resented by those who have to pay for what look like the mistakes of others. If the people elect and then re-elect incompetent, dysfunctional governments, perhaps, so the thinking goes, they have only themselves to blame. On the other, because the cost of bad loans and debts, depressed land values, subsidies, lower incomes, higher welfare budgets in Greece and Detroit is very small in the large economies of the European Union and the United States, it may be better to extend credits and delay the repayment of debts in the hope that their problems can be contained. To do so however raises an unconventional version of moral hazard, a term applied to financial transactions when there is a mismatch in the risks assumed by a borrower and a creditor, to the latter's disadvantage: if more assistance is given to Greece and Detroit or to places like them, even with some strings tied tight, would other jurisdictions postpone needed reforms, knowing that in the end a lifeline will be thrown to them? There may be no good choice.

Note

1 See especially Fabrizio Barca, "Alternative approaches to development policy: intersections and divergences," pp. 215–25, and the trenchant criticism of spatially blind and space-neutral approaches at the central level by Philip McCann and Andrès Rodriguez-Pose: "Why and when development policy should be place-based," pp. 203–13. The conceptual challenges of using geography as an analytical framework in a society and economy organized principally on the basis of time are addressed by Robert A. Dodgshon, in *Society in Time and Space: A Geographical Perspective on Change* (Cambridge: Cambridge University Press, 1998).

References

Amin, Ash and Stephen Graham (1997), "The ordinary city," *Transactions Institute of British Geographers*, New Series 22: 411–29.
Bayles, Jeff (2006), "Disappeared Detroit," *Lost Magazine*, 2 January; reprinted from Jeff Bayles, *Rubble* (New York: Random House).
Burd-Sharps, Sarah and Kristen Lewis (2013), "One in seven: ranking youth disconnection in the 25 largest metro areas," Measure of America of the Social Science Research Council. (Brooklyn, NY: SSRC), www.measureofamerica.org.
Conway, Maureen and Josef Konvitz (2000), "Meeting the challenge of distressed urban areas," *Urban Studies,* 37: 4 749–74.
Drucker, Peter, personal letter to the author dated 18 November 2001.
Duranton, G. and D. Puga (2004), "Micro-foundations of urban agglomeration economies," in J. Henderson and J. Thisse (eds), *Handbook of Regional and Urban Economics* (Amsterdam: Elsevier), vol. 4: 2063–117, reprinting their NBER Working Paper no. 9931, September 2003.
The Economist (1986), "The anatomy of cities," 20 December.
The Economist (2005), "Urban regeneration," 2 April.
The Economist (2008), "The Great Plains drain," 29 January.
Financial Times (2013a), Wolfgang Münchau, "Lessons for Greece from down-and-out Detroit," 2 September.
Financial Times (2013b), Felix Rohatyn, "US cities have a choice: pull together or go bust," 24 April.
Financial Times (2014), "Greeks welcome Beijing bearing gifts," 7 October.
Giannakourou, Georgia and Evangelia Balla (2012), "'Privatizing' urban planning in Greece? Current trends and future prospects," presentation to an International Conference of Experts on Planning Law, Lisbon, October.
Hall, Peter (1998), *Cities in Civilization: Culture, Innovation and Urban Order* (London: Weidenfeld and Nicolson).

Jacobs, Jane (1992), *Systems of Survival: A Dialogue on the Moral Foundations of Commerce and Politics* (New York: Random House).
Jacobs, Jane (2004), *Dark Age Ahead* (New York: Random House).
Lange, Dorothea and Paul S. Taylor (1940), *An American Exodus: A Record of Human Erosion* (New York: Raynal and Hitchcock).
Le Monde (2008), "L'urbanisation ne gagne pas toutes les villes," 21 November.
Marchand, Yves and Romain Meffre (2010), *Detroit, vestiges du rêve américain* (Göttingen: Steidl).
OECD (1996), *Innovative Policies for Sustainable Urban Development: The Ecological City* (Paris: OECD). ISBN: 92-94-15915-5.
OECD (1998), *Integrating Distressed Urban Areas* (Paris: OECD). ISBN: 92-64-16-62-0.
OECD (2001), *OECD Territorial Outlook*. (Paris: OECD) ISBN: 92-64-18602-6.
OECD (2003), "Synthesis report, urban renaissance studies," GOV/TDPC (2003)10, prepared for the 9th session of the Territorial Development Policy Committee; unpublished.
OECD (2011a), *Regions at a Glance* (Paris: OECD). DOI: org/10/1787/reg_glance-2011-en.
OECD (2011b), *OECD Regional Outlook: Building Resilient Regions for Stronger Economies* (Paris: OECD). DOI. org/10.1787/9789264120983-en.
OECD (2011c), *Greece: Review of Central Administration* (Paris: OECD). DOI: org/10/1787/9789264102880-en.
OECD (2012), *Better Regulation in Europe: Greece* (Paris: OECD), DOI: org/10.1787/9789264179288.
OECD (2013), *Economic Survey of Greece* (Paris: OECD). DOI: 10.1787/eco_surveys-grc-2013-en.
OECD (2014), *OECD Regional Outlook: Regions and Cities: Where Policies and People Meet* (Paris: OECD) DOI: 10.1787/9789264-201415-en.
Piketty, Thomas (2013), *Capital au XXIe siècle* (Paris: Editions du Seuil).
Spiekermann, Klaus and Michael Wegener (2008), "The shrinking continent: accessibility, competitiveness and cohesion," in A. Faludi (ed.), *European Spatial Research and Planning* (Cambridge MA: Lincoln Institute of Land Policy), pp. 115–40.
Starr, Roger (1976), in the *New York Times Magazine*, 14 November.
Starr, Roger (1985), *The Rise and Fall of New York City* (New York: Basic Books).

5

Jobs to people: livability, governance, and strategic planning

Policies and markets

People to jobs? Or jobs to people? Changing the sequence is not just a word game because the implications for policy at every level are significant. In the nineteenth and twentieth centuries, urban economies attracted people to jobs when surplus labor shifted from agriculture to manufacturing, and when firms or sectors in decline in one region – mining, textiles – were succeeded by firms or sectors in expansion elsewhere – oil production, aviation. This is still going on, but in the service economy things work a bit differently. The trend to attract jobs to the places where people want to live and work elevates the livability of cities as a driver of their competitiveness. The people-to-jobs logic leads to patterns of housing and building that are more alike, wherever they are; the jobs-to-people logic pays greater value on the things that make places different. Moreover, both logics may be at work simultaneously, often in different regions but also in different parts of the same metropolitan area.

In the people-to-jobs economy, production for export led to the classification of jobs into basic and non-basic. The city was conceived to be non-self-sustaining. The jobs which earned the money for the urban economy to pay for its imports were *basic*, largely manufacturing; the rest were *non–basic* (Alexander, 1954). The non-basic – or service sector – dominates today. This sector was once classified as "non-tradable" on the grounds that people in one city do not go to another to get a haircut or get a pair of shoes repaired, or even to get a bank loan. But do these distinctions make sense in an age of franchised hairdressers, tourist medical care abroad, cross-border lending, the electronic editing of texts, or when it is possible to send shoes by express mail from one city to another for custom repairs? The non-local dimensions of many supposedly non-basic sectors such as culture, tourism, education, business-to-business services in finance, accountancy, and law weigh heavily upon the balance sheet.

The binary distinction between basic and non-basic has implications for what goes where in cities, and therefore for investment in urban design and infrastructure. Economists have been able to study agglomeration effects at city scale, but analyses at the smaller spatial scale of districts within cities where decisions have to be made about public and private investments for transport, housing, public facilities, retailing, parks, etc., are very difficult to carry out. Yet it is at this smaller scale that much of the place-based, non-basic economy takes place (Konvitz, 2001). The basic economy needs transport above all, as well as space for manufacturing and warehousing, and support from services such as banking which contribute to the efficiency of manufacturing and trade; everything else is secondary. Today, manufacturing, distribution, transportation, logistics, and back-office activities are more likely to be located outside the city core on redeveloped sites or on greenfield land where very large surfaces can be built at lower cost. The non-basic economy (now the new basic in many ways) is more likely to grow in older areas; the old basic, in outer-edge or semi-urban areas. The basic – non-basic model of the urban economy still influences foreign direct investment and import substitution strategies. Urban statistics and their application in everything from advice to firms seeking cities in which to locate, to government offices evaluating the future demand for elementary schools or comprehensive hospitals, are still catching up with these profound changes.

To be sure, manufacturing is not dead in OECD countries; in Mexico and Germany, high-income and low-income countries, manufacturing helped keep their economies out of the deep recession that has characterized Italy, France, Spain, and the United Kingdom since 2007, countries where manufacturing declined. High-tech manufacturing in California and Texas, aircraft production, armaments, oil-related manufacturing in many states, and a restructured automotive industry have renewed the economic base of the United States. (San Jose and Los Angeles–Long Beach have levels of manufacturing employment that rival Boston, Philadelphia, and Chicago which grew during the Industrial Revolution.) Averages being what they are, some cities generate a high percentage of trade in the basic economy relative to their GDP, others a smaller percentage. Much is done at state and local levels to keep up the growth of manufacturing: changes in state regulations and taxes and improvements in transport connections are often mentioned in lists of good practices, but shortages of skilled workers, high housing costs, red tape for small businesses and start-ups are prominent in lists of problems in the non-basic economy that government does not seem to be good at remediating. Some cities – New York, for example – can survive the loss of manufacturing; others – Trenton, Albany, Lansing, all state capitals – would be hard pressed to do so.

The distinction between basic and non-basic aspects of the urban economy has huge implications for those who have to select among infrastructure investments by trying to assess a cost-benefit analysis, the rate of return, or what the competition is doing elsewhere. One approach is to provide enough transport options to let firms locate where it makes best sense for them. The expansion of regional transport in Greater Paris which depends on some government tax measures as well as infrastructure investment creates a vast labor market which lifts productivity, enabling firms to increase profits and employees to enjoy higher salaries. The surplus wealth generated in Paris through the greater productivity of the people working there is captured in local expenditure and in personal and corporate income tax and in a special levy on larger firms that benefit from such a vast labor market. A city's capacity to service debts depends on its ability to tax, something more likely to be determined nationally or regionally, with little regard to the makeup of its economy. A recent political debate in France over raising the tax on hotel rooms demonstrated this: the City of Paris wanted the tax increase but the national government did not, concerned that the tax would send the wrong signal that France discourages tourism. Value-added tax at least has the advantage that what can be taxed in local transactions and in the service sector is little different from what can be taxed on traded goods. A city that produces a lot for export is not necessarily running a surplus in its public budget if its expenditures are greater than its tax revenues. This is why national or regional governments collect (and redistribute) taxes on sales, and local authorities on immovables such as real estate, and why taxes collected over a larger area are redistributed to local governments. When there are year-on-year increases in the economy this is not a problem, but it is if the economy declines, or has entered a long low-growth phase: fiscal equalizers or surplus investment funds will work for only a short term.

The new global market in urban goods and services shows how the binary basic–non-basic has broken down. Heretofore, many public procurement policies had created mini-markets for the goods and services purchased by and consumed in local jurisdictions. National restrictions on locally produced content for public procurement, still significant in the United States and some other jurisdictions, effectively closed the market for imported goods and services to build and maintain cities. When shipping costs were high and delivery times were long, it seemed logical that urban goods such as parking meters or street lights, and urban services used by environmental or financial departments, provide local manufacturers and firms with regular business. But once the protection of such markets was undermined, local governments found that their needs could also be met by firms which could be far away. Urban goods and services have become tradable in international commerce, limited however by requirements to hire locally certified professionals, by unique technical standards, by local content measures or other restrictions on public procurement – barriers which are anything but uniform from one country to another. Still, new multi-national businesses took off to run public services on a contractual basis; suppliers of traffic lights in Sweden do business in Mexico, and the Paris airport authority designs and builds airports in South East Asia. Public services, too, are increasingly a tradable sector, again blurring the distinction between basic and non-basic: people travel for health care; universities attract non-local students and "export" courses and research; environmental services are part of the green economy. National statistics do not track this form of cross-border business uniformly. When an Austrian architect has a contract in, say, Poland, should this be credited to Austria as earned income, or as an export?

Culture – why trade, production, and consumption are so hard to separate

Culture is an excellent example of the extent to which the distinction between the basic and non-basic sectors of the urban economy has evolved. Culture, like sport, is often considered extraneous, useful for public relations and social welfare but for little else. It is therefore detached from the economic portfolio of local mayors or national government ministers, as a kind of preserve for amateurs and boosters. When looked at statistically, however, this portfolio should be linked to enterprise and to innovation, to IT and tourism. It is a mistake to think that cultural industries are for leisure, a sterilized form of production that ends up as consumption. Broadly defined as a creative sector, culture includes architecture, video and film, music and the performing arts, publishing, software and electronic publishing, radio and television, design and designer fashion, as well as heritage, ballet, opera, and museums, the more familiar categories. The cultural sector is more likely to increase employment, including volunteer and part-time work with higher levels of workforce participation by women and minorities, and to generate new small and medium-sized enterprises. There are distinctions between high and popular culture, professional and amateur production, the trendy and the tasteful, as to be expected in a sector attracting some people who want to work within the mainstream, and others who want to create something new. There is a growing international trade in the goods and services of this sector, albeit regulated by national restrictions on, for example, art, or intellectual property rights. As a sector least dependent on natural resources, culture comes closest to a dematerialized unit of account whose value is based on higher-order categories such as pleasure, information, or knowledge which are incorporated into the very being of the consumer.

Culture and the creative sector are generators of growth. Today, the cultural sector is at the leading edge of the blend between technological innovation and new uses of information, mixed media, and a better balance between work and leisure. An initial effort by OECD statisticians to estimate the contribution of cultural industries to GDP for five countries, Australia in 1998–99, Canada and the US in 2002, and France and the UK in 2003, ranged from a low of 2.8 in France to a high of 5.8 per cent in the UK, with the other countries between 3.1 and 3.5 per cent. Even with all the attendant qualifications concerning what is being counted, these are serious and respectable numbers (OECD, 2006). On the one hand, there is evidence that the cultural monuments built in the past – whether churches in Rome and palaces in Florence or the Eiffel Tower and London Bridge – are worth millions in today's economy; on the other, the high cost of erecting their equivalent today generates debates about whether the money could be better spent on other things, raising the question what cultural monuments and institutions are being created today that will appreciate to such an extent in the future, extending perhaps over centuries. By dithering and delaying, the municipal council of Boulogne–Billancourt lost the chance to anchor a major redevelopment of the former Renault car factory on an island in the Seine when François Pinault decided instead to install his collection in the Dogana in Venice, renovated for that purpose. The redevelopment of the Renault site has taken years longer, compromising the opportunity to create a "river of culture" along the Seine from Boulogne to the Louvre. Bernard Arnault, Pinault's rival in the world of retail and luxury goods, opted to house his contemporary art collection in a museum designed by Frank Gehry, Fondation Louis-Vuitton, in Paris's Bois de Boulogne; legal challenges to the zoning were dispatched quickly, and the museum opened in October 2014.

Cultural industries – which are heavily concentrated in cities – contribute to growth. When we speak of an urban renaissance today, it is rather to rebuild the productive basis of an urban economy and lift its social and human capital, promoting innovation. This process takes two forms. One approach helps to define a city and its place in a world of cities, valorizing assets and strengthening a sense of identity.

As manufacturing in Hong Kong declined and its financial and service sectors have grown, it has had to follow Singapore's example to build up its cultural sector with new facilities, schools, and festivals. The creative industries play a key role in the branding of cities, a matter of defining and shaping an identity for residents and in world opinion. Culture goes a long way toward compensating for such handicaps as high cost (New York and London), or distance (Melbourne). Cities that have their own lifestyle, food-ways, dialects enjoy (or suffer from) a degree of distinctiveness that by definition must be experienced locally and cannot be exported or transplanted: Scouse, Geordie, Brummie, the Patter, the rapid verbal comedy of Berlin or the repartee of New Yorkers. There are dozens of novels set in Glasgow or in Stockholm: why do some cities give rise to a literary school or art movement and not others? The other contribution of culture is as a spark for innovation. Exposure to any of the creative arts at a high level of excellence demonstrates the power of imagination, hopefully inspiring people to be more creative. If innovation is indeed critical to the search for new sources of growth, and if urban problems are to generate job-creating innovations, then the creative industries provide the foundation on which much else will be built.

What happens when governments look to cut their budgets? Reductions testify to the impact of the crisis. More sensitive to shifting ideological positions, a euphemism for the cultural wars between liberals and conservatives, nationalists and cosmopolitans which often have racial and religious undertones, governments are quick to sacrifice the allocations of culture ministries to the deity of austerity. How small the cultural budget is in relation to the overall national budget, or even more, the national debt! There is no such thing as too much culture, making it difficult for an economist to measure the point at which demand is satisfied, or whether the money could be better spent on something else.

And so what, might an economist say, noting that the number of tourists visiting the main Madrid museums, the Prado, the Queen Sofia and the Thyssen-Bornemisza, set records during the crisis? Would more spending by government lead to over-investment? The Prado attracted 2.3 million visitors in 2013; the Queen Sofia, which includes Picasso's *Guernica* in its collections, attracted 3.1 million visitors, a figure boosted by the Dali exhibition previously at the Pompidou in Paris which drew over 700,000. In France in 2013, more than 24 million visitors entered thirty-five museums under the Ministry of Culture. Smaller museums benefited as well as the largest: nearly 9.4 million people came to the Louvre, which seems to have no limit to its growth (500 per cent since the Pyramid was opened nearly three decades ago), 6.5 million to the Château de Versailles, 3.75 million and 3.5 million respectively to the Centre Pompidou and to the Musée d'Orsay (*The Art Newspaper*, 2014). Young people aged eighteen to twenty-five enter free; between 2009 and 2011, their numbers doubled. People travel within France too: 1.3 million went to Mont St Michel, and since 2010, 1.2 million to the Centre Pompidou in Metz. The services that attract and retain tourists, whether at airports or museums or in hotels and restaurants, or the range of luxury goods in shops, have little to do with daily life for residents who care about neighborhood policing, garbage collection, and access to pre-school education. It does no good to point out that the city's tax revenues are greater because more tourists come. The issue is not whether to grant subventions to or underwrite the arts, nor what the consequences of government funding for freedom of expression the creative arts might be. The primary questions instead should be whether the stock of public goods is sufficient, whether it is being increased to meet the needs of future generations, and whether the existing stock is adequately valorized and made accessible.

And this has implications for the use and design of urban space. In traditional forms of urban planning, the Paris Opera and New York's Metropolitan Museum of Art, as well as the Sydney Opera House, were located in prestige locations of high symbolic value, and, for the same reason, isolated from their immediate urban surroundings. Great buildings can also change the value of a site. Charles Rennie Mackintosh's Glasgow School of Art (1908), arguably one of the most inventive, precedent-setting, path-finding structures of its decade anywhere, was erected on a hillcrest above the city's main commercial thoroughfare, Sauchiehall Street, its magnificent, well-articulated back being the most significant part visible from below. By the 1990s, Mackintosh design had replaced the Gorbals, once one of the most decayed and dangerous districts in any European city, as Glasgow's defining image. Paris has deliberately created a new district for the study and performance of music at the Porte de Pantin in the hope of enlarging the audience. Not only does space have a cultural value, which is why important heritage sites include parks and vistas as well as buildings and their immediate surroundings. Urban space is highly consequential as a variable in the production and consumption of cultural goods and services. Space for recording studios in Melbourne or Glasgow and for film-making in Berlin and Paris, studios for artists, housing for musicians and technicians, places for writers to meet and for architects to work in teams – not to mention galleries, showrooms, storerooms, etc., all familiar from the history of seventeenth-century Amsterdam, Paris in the 1880s, or New York in the 1940s – show how new technologies and activities are absorbed into a dense urban environment when low costs create prestige value out of old tenements or factories that are no longer suitable for other uses. Propinquity, proximity are as important in Stockholm as in Seoul or Berlin, even if their cultural districts are very dissimilar. Sound urban management must be sensitive to the property market, to the services that workers in this sector, often with low or unstable incomes and young families, may require, and to the need for adaptive re-use or redevelopment of districts which fortune or fate has situated close to the city center.

Culture defines how we live and work in cities. The superficial similarity of hotels, airports, convention centers, shopping malls, and skyscrapers around the world tells us little about how local lifestyles and cultures fit within the global economy and indeed support it. In the global economy we all have two cultures, a global consumer culture and a local community culture. Each of us participates in a mass consumer culture based around new products, designs, and services which are available worldwide with minimal lags. Because producers can also meet local market requirements and adjust production to changing demand quickly, the rate of change within this mass consumer culture is rapid and continual; it also generates virtual communities of people who share similar preferences wherever they live, be it Prada bags, skiing, or East European films. Each of us also has a local community at the neighborhood scale, where the rate of change is slow and irregular. We recognize our neighborhood's boundaries by many clues, including distinctive sounds, even accents, as well as the look and feel of streets and buildings, changes in density, and odors. We know when we are coming closer to home. Most people may have many global consumer cultures, but only one local community.

A third global culture is made up of people in growing numbers who participate in a profession with internationally recognized and uniform norms and standards. Deck officers on freighters and pilots of commercial aircraft, architects, accountants, bankers, medical researchers are members of a knowledge-based community of professionals who meet the same standards, and share information along formal and tacit networks in a global labor market, raising questions about taxation of income as well as licensing and residency requirements, schools for children, and pension funds.

The new global elite are people with the ability to understand and communicate in different cultures, in different places, at the same time. They know how to relate to co-workers in ways that recognize their local cultures, languages, history, outlooks. In other words they can feel at home in more than one country, in more than one neighborhood, with more than one set of colleagues. Cosmopolitan living and working represent a new form of the Enlightenment ideal of a culture which transcends borders. They do so however not by annihilating differences but by finding value in them, the true basis for tolerance. "Cosmopolitan", once a term of hate used by fascists and communists alike who attacked footloose, international capitalists, of whom the bourgeois Jew was the archetype, may be recovering its original meaning when it represented a noble ideal. Its revival however may be short-lived. Economic shocks and financial panics tend to reinforce populist nationalism. Resistance to change is unlikely to take the form of another anti-urban romantic revival of the rural pastoral, last promoted by fascists in the 1930s, but, as the skylines of London and New York are shaped by the investments of foreigners, one wonders whether those who cannot afford to live in their shadow will fight back, and, if so, when and how. Scapegoats can always be found, which is why debates on immigration are so troubling. Given the links between immigration, culture, and entrepreneurship, if integrating immigrants into cities becomes a lost art, we will all be poorer.

Livability versus competitiveness, and why competitive cities aren't more livable

Rankings yearly of the most livable or competitive cities in the world provoke debates about what people need, like, and want. It is easy to dismiss these exercises by journalists and consultancies which promote the commodification of cities through branding and image-building when the emphasis should be on infrastructure and economic strength, the environment, health care, education, stability, and infrastructure reflecting long-term investments and trends. Annual rankings of this kind could even do harm if decision-makers think that success can be achieved through a formula. If however they help people assess shortcomings and under-valued assets and develop projects for the future, they serve a purpose.

The interest of a firm is in attracting people who can bring in the latest or most relevant skill, or information. As Alfred Marshall pointed out over a century ago, the urban labor market and its fluidity, which valorize the tacit knowledge acquired by workers and enable them to move from one job to another, contribute to growth in productivity. Firms that succeed want to be in places where people can easily acquire and share knowledge. This is what makes clusters so successful in research, high tech, design, health care, finance, or the manufacturing of ceramics. Both livable and competitive cities can operate in a Marshallian logic.

The sheer scale of cities today poses challenges. Australia, a country which has yet to reach its potential for higher value-added research and development, highlights the spatial mis-match between where people live and work which is widening geographically in terms of distance, travel times, and housing costs, and economically in terms of income inequality. The two together are often mutually reinforcing. This is why a 2013 study from Melbourne's Grattan Institute, "Productive Cities: Opportunity in a Changing Economy," is so relevant. Produced at a time of growing concern that transport and land use patterns to accommodate a growing population are likely to exacerbate problems that already exist, the report focuses on the basic advantage of agglomerations for a better alignment between the skills of workers and the needs of firms. Policy-makers need to see that "increasingly congested transport systems are holding back productivity by making it harder to get the best match between the skills of a worker and the demands of a job" (Grattan, 2013: 43). The Grattan Report concludes with recommendations to increase housing capacity in areas closer to city centers, and to improve the "organization, operation and networking of public transport systems" (Grattan, 2013: 40, 42). Melbourne remains one of the world's most livable cities, but for how long?

There is no simple formula by which a city can be classified as livable or competitive. Each term embodies a package of attributes, illustrated by particular examples. Munich or London are both vibrant; their advocates celebrate the same things, spontaneity, tolerance, and the visible and intangible attributes that make each city distinctive. But the categories are not interchangeable: Munich is a livable city, whereas London's game is competitiveness. These are two economic logics at work, with significant implications for private and public investment.

Livability is a fine-grained composite. Tyler Brulé, writing "The city of your dreams" in the *Financial Times* (2009a), introduced three criteria for the 2009 *Monocle* rankings: the independence of a city's retail and restaurant scene, the ease with which small business owners can start up operations, and planned infrastructure improvements. The first and second criteria relate to endogenous development, a place-based approach focusing on goods and services that are locally generated and consumed (the non-basic component of the urban economy). Why do planned infrastructure improvements matter? Writing about "Why easy living can be so hard" (*Financial Times*, 2011), Brulé, continuing on this theme, wrote, "More broadly, we considered the way in which locals and visitors are able to navigate and use everything from public parks to the local property market." It is all about the urban experience. "Places with the best quality of life are those with the fewest daily obstructions, *allowing residents to be both productive and free of unnecessary stress*" (emphasis added). From this perspective, livability focuses attention on the urban milieu, the dense network of newer and older buildings that form districts characterized by successive waves of adaptive reuse. Design matters: Brulé writes about road width, building facades, even street lighting. Livability enhances conditions that favor spontaneous interaction among people and firms, supporting the fabric of specialized knowledge and commercial structures associated with clusters, collective learning, informal co-ordination, sharing of information, a strong sense of identity – the ingredients of the innovative milieu. Suggesting that people with shared identities and friendships are happier, researchers suggest that principles of social interaction should influence design and governance at the urban level (Helliwell et al., 2014: 24).

Competitiveness is based on bold, solid features, which may be why skyscrapers and trophy buildings by star architects seem fitting image-making objects. The advocates of competitiveness appear to focus on " core" cities where firms and organizations with global influence have their headquarters (*Financial Times*, 2009b). Competitive cities are popularly depicted as bigger and more vibrant, places with more variety – the urban experience matters – but also more extremes. This is another way of saying that, in competitive cities, people put up with more negative externalities such as smaller or less affordable housing, traffic congestion, noise, air pollution, and mediocre public services (or worse, insecurity) to enjoy greater opportunities and mobility, more freedom from conformist pressures. In the final analysis, advocates of competitive cities – New York, for example – defend, even celebrate, the stress that living in them induces.

It is a mistake to assume that livable cities are smaller than competitive cities: in the 2013 Monocle quality of life rankings of livable cities, Tokyo is fourth, and Paris fourteenth on a list that ranks Copenhagen first and Düsseldorf twenty-fifth, and includes several cities in the range of four to eight million inhabitants. The 2014 list was not much different: Tokyo moved up to second place, after Copenhagen; Paris fell four rungs to eighteenth.

Is there really a difference between livability and competitiveness as urban parameters? Yes. Competitive cities are, as the term implies, competing against each other; livable cities – notwithstanding the rankings and benchmarking–are not. Livability and competitiveness refer not only to different models of the urban economy, or to two different types and levels of stress in daily life, but to two different ways of achieving better resource allocation of labor and capital.

Competitiveness correlates more strongly than livability with the basic component of urban economies, the firms and sectors which generate exports needed to pay for the goods and services used in cities. The competition is to attract mobile firms, which often means inducing firms already implanted to stay, and mobile talent. If the financial sectors in New York served only the United States, and in London only the United Kingdom, these two cities would not be in competition. The problem for New York and London, which compete globally, is that their ability to attract and retain business in financial services depends in part on the regulatory frameworks (and immigration rules) set by national governments and international agencies: these, as much as tax breaks on property or other inducements, are critical tools for those cities' development strategies.

To the extent that livable cities are grounded in place-based development that attracts and retains people, they are not in direct competition for the same jobs: Munich and Zürich, Copenhagen and Stockholm may compete to be high on a ranking of livable cities, but their key sectors are not likely to move from one to the other as a result. It is striking how many cities on the most-livable list are in small and medium-size economies, and are often excentric geographically, more remote from the main corridors of traffic and power. Their firms and sectors are more deeply embedded in a local milieu, or territory. This is even true for Sydney and Melbourne, whose sectoral composition and international roles are quite different. In this sense livability gives some cities a higher profile globally than the size of their economy or the control exercised by firms headquartered in them would suggest. As long as such cities continue to attract and retain a better-educated population more likely to be employed in firms and sectors that call for specialized skills, these cities can function as hubs or service centers. It may just be the case that non-basic trumps basic: many smaller and intermediate-sized countries (under twenty million) with very high GDP depend on the attractiveness of cities that rank high on livability (Tel Aviv, Copenhagen) to sustain national competitive advantages in services and the knowledge economy.

The differences between urban competitiveness and livability affect the kind of strategic decisions that leaders have to make, and the impact of these decisions on the daily lives of people. Both livable and competitive cities need high-quality inter-urban transport and telecommunications. In the logic of inter-urban connectivity, some sectors or districts in two or more cities may have a higher degree of functional integration than they enjoy locally. In a networked global economy, the frame of reference is not the local labor market, but extended personal and professional contacts locally, regionally, and, for some, globally. The same things matter to both livable and competitive cities but the quality is often better in livable than in competitive cities.

Transport congestion, over-crowded airports, unaffordable housing, pollution, and other correctable negative externalities which eat into productivity and reflect a lack of long-term planning figure conspicuously on list of the shortcomings of competitive cities. Strangely, governments don't try hard enough to reduce the problems that burden competitive cities. This is an apparent paradox: surely successful market economies should be better able to reduce collective costs and project a long-term strategy that alleviates bottlenecks before they become critical. It is however a commonplace of political economy that the constituency for improving services and reducing the negative effects of congestion, pollution, and other factors that detract from the quality of life and efficiency of daily living is simply too diffuse and weak. Those who would suffer a higher cost from change lobby effectively to preserve the status quo; those who would benefit from reform lack the means to organize constructive interventions and practical solutions, or to put pressure on governments. But even this explanation is too simple.

The concept of trade-offs can help illuminate the paradoxical reluctance of governments to tackle the problems of competitive cities. Trade-offs are assessed at the regional or national level on the assumption that productivity gains on the part of firms and the people they employ more than compensate for environmental, transport, and social costs. Governments may scale back investments in competitive cities, which usually are net fiscal contributors, conveniently overlooking that their wealth and productivity reflect accumulated endowments which must be maintained and replenished. Governments inevitably try to encourage the development of sectors likely to generate the highest returns in a competitive city, based on a given level of public investment.

In a logic of trade-offs there are always losers who need to be compensated lest they block a decision – probably a major consideration affecting the expansion of London's airports. From a macro-economic perspective which treats the nation as the unit, a competitive city that contributes more to the treasury than is spent by government on it makes sense; investments to improve productivity may only cost money, especially if the result is an even larger city which needs more investment. Firms that have to make locational decisions in competitive cities will just put up with overcrowded airports, antiquated public transport, schools which fail to train people for the workforce, strained power generation capacity, over-stretched emergency services, the list lengthens into a checklist of the disadvantages of competitive cities which those who value competitiveness tolerate. An apposite example comes from the efforts of Singapore and Hong Kong to enhance their competitiveness by improving their cultural offerings and facilities as well as their airports: what once looked superfluous in cities where the work life dominated all became integral to their image as places where people would want to live to work. In this case, Hong Kong has to match Singapore as both strive to become known for their orchestras, theatres, and festivals, as well as their airports, restaurants, and container ports.

If a competitive city's main competitors are treated no better, its relative situation is not unduly compromised. Chicago's freight congestion was a local problem until port developments on the Pacific and Atlantic coasts and the widening of the Panama Canal created new competition. If the financial sectors in both New York and London continue to compete against each other even though both cities are famous around the world for their inadequate airports, it doesn't matter. If New York improved its airports, London would be bound to follow, and vice versa; put another way, as long as one doesn't act, the other need not. But even if the government of the United Kingdom that is elected in 2015 decides to expand Heathrow, there will be no improvement in service for the better part of a decade. And by then the growth of air traffic could mean that Heathrow's expansion will be a palliative, storing up problems for the future. (It takes as long to design and build an airport as it does to design and build a new model of aeroplane.)

The differences between competitive and livable cities, their respective challenges as well as what they have in common, relate to governance. Governance best describes the simple fact that neither the private nor the public sector is fully in control. Many of the things that get done every day to sustain life in cities – food supplies, waste removal, transport, energy, etc. – are handled by firms and individuals who coordinate in regulated markets. The public–private interface therefore should be a matter of collective responsibility, engaging stakeholders, the public at large, and elected and appointed authorities. Livable cities have often become so after a long period of sustained reform and change based on effective and far-sighted political leadership, civic-minded business, and public support. Is livability a top-down goal, elitist, or does it enjoy broad public support? To what extent are these validated through elections? Competitiveness implies technocratic decisions based on cost-benefit analysis for the growth of particular sectors (a form of picking winners), large-scale infrastructure projects and major urban services. Which decisions should be a matter of expertise? Consensus? How should the public be consulted? Many key decisions in transport, environmental management, and the like require solutions co-ordinated across many local and regional jurisdictions, but often in the absence of a clear decision-making structure or of a way to compensate losers without burdening winners. How can central governments cope with the political tensions surrounding the allocation of expenditure among regions, some declining, others leading? Livability, by contrast, implies a more holistic and comprehensive urban vision – often reconciling different positions and needs, giving the word "compromise" a positive connotation. This is not easy, but neither is a competitiveness strategy. How do policies and political processes affect progress toward livability? What happens when accountability and transparency must be managed across different levels of government and multiple jurisdictions, and in public–private partnerships? Answers probably have to do with the mix of public goods provided, with specific regulatory guidelines for design, with long-term visions and strategies for housing and transportation.

Mega-events such as the Olympic Games, Formula One racing, the World Cup, but also programs such as European City of Culture, highlight the challenges in governance and the tensions between short and medium term inherent in strategies for urban development (Gold and Gold, 2011). Cities competing to host mega-events want to validate and improve their standing in a universe of cities based on a package of criteria. Increasingly electorates in cities where livability is a high priority are hostile to mega-events which, it is argued, divert resources that could be better applied to improving the city; other criticisms relate to the environmental costs and security issues for events which do not yield sustainable gains, even in investment and employment. The fact that few local residents will participate in and enjoy these events is an additional negative factor. There is little evidence that mega-events improve the economy: the short-term boost to jobs in construction, for example, is often followed by a fall once the event is over; events often deter tourism rather than increase it; cities such as Atlanta and Los Angeles which hoped to improve their international attractiveness for business and investment found little measureable difference years later. "The lack of any substantial aims other than to make money will result in the failure to achieve even that objective" (Clark, 2008: 43). This is not to say that important infrastructure investments in Sydney, Athens, Beijing, and Rio were a waste; they might not have been made had the cities not had the Olympic Games to deliver, but they should have been anyway.

Urban marketing and branding, the construction of corporate buildings, and the use of corporate or philanthropic money to erect public facilities such as sports arenas or museums all contribute to a sense that the city is a commodity, and does not belong to those who live in it. Because mega-events usually involve huge cost over-runs, leaving debts that take years to pay off and stadiums that have to be rebuilt to find a market, only autocrats or private sponsors can escape public criticism of the mismanagement and corruption that often accompany them. The great exception remains Barcelona's 1992 Olympic Games, but then the infrastructure investment and urban renewal efforts were inscribed in a long-term strategy whose inception began years before as part of the post-Franco move for greater autonomy for Catalonia and whose trajectory extended well beyond the Games. Governments elsewhere eager to imitate Barcelona have focused more on winning the right to organize a mega-event, which is itself a kind of competition among cities, than on having the right long-term strategy which a mega-event could boost. To quote Clark (2008: 165), hosting "a global event can accelerate projects of urban transformation … It is at the earliest stages of planning a bid for a global event that city authorities must consider which goals to prioritise and how to implement them. Even if the bid is subsequently not successful, being forced to go through the bid process will produce a much clearer set of urban development targets."

Delivering an event on time, and even on budget, is not enough. Governments therefore have advanced the argument that a mega-event will yield a legacy for the city; this was in fact formally adopted by London for the Olympics of 2012 and by Glasgow for the Commonwealth Games in 2014. Itself a slippery term which suits the purposes of people in different political and cultural contexts, "legacy" has entered the mainstream vocabulary of politicians, civic leaders, and managers. In London, legacy referred to the regeneration of Stratford and the East End, largely in the form of housing, parks, higher education and transport facilities, and retail in a mix of public and private investments. The real regeneration challenge for London's East End – jobs, housing, education, cultural activities, etc. – began after the Olympic Games were over, helping to rebalance London's growth.

Glasgow has taken legacy further, to help train people to deliver, not only future mega-events, but a post-Games regeneration agenda. The focus in London was on traditional physical change; the focus in Glasgow was on the attitudes of people toward themselves and their community, to help cope with the disparities and poverty that have characterized the city's East End for too long. Those who prepare for a mega-event must learn how to make close public–private co-operation and cross-sectoral co-ordination work, and this in a multi-level local-national-international framework. By capturing this knowledge acquired on the job, so to speak, and under unique pressures of time and resources, others can gain from their experience to apply the lessons to other challenges critical for social and environmental development over the medium term. By embedding legacy planning from the beginning, Glasgow's evaluation frameworks were more comprehensive. Education, health, housing, transportation, as well as employment and investment, all have a place within a legacy agenda that focuses on the needs of people and places.

The institutions where research can be grounded and training provided are the universities in the cities where mega-events have been or may be held. To this end, after a successful Commonwealth Games in 2014, the City of Glasgow and three universities, Glasgow, Strathclyde, and Caledonian, have launched an international legacy network of cities and universities. The very term "common wealth" after all embraces those things that help people develop their potential. There may well be a tension between project-focused managers who want to impose a strict organizational discipline, and the kind of flexibility, inclusiveness, and imagination which any new, big project demands. Research that combines policy and practice can help limit risks while opening opportunities to take advantage of a one-off, unique chance to do something different. Governance, once again, is at the core. Design and delivery of programs that bring change for the better in a regeneration agenda call for the same commitment to a goal as delivery of a mega-event, the same willingness to work across or outside familiar and safe sectoral and jurisdictional boundaries, the same honesty to admit that not everything can go as expected, the same openness to criticism and evaluation. After all, decades will pass before a city may ever hope to host the Olympic or Commonwealth Games again, but the goal of livability remains.

There is a good reason why universities should be leading. In the search for new institutional forms of co-operation on future issues which run the spectrum from fundamental research, data collection, and applied research to education and professional training, the university, one of the oldest institutions in the western world, may actually have a lot to offer. Universities have specialists who understand how cities function, who train the next generation of professionals, and who often practice inter-disciplinarity which is so critical to successful policy design and implementation. Globalized, universities work abroad with satellite campuses, and draw students in larger numbers from around the world. (The number of foreign students in universities in the OECD area has increased 90 per cent since 1998.) Universities look beyond political and economic cycles; they can afford to introduce and test innovations. Moreover, many leading institutions now feature community engagement or regional co-operation as one of their core missions, and are engaged in long-term projects to expand by redeveloping precincts and districts that border on their urban campuses, with the potential to transform parts of cities where innovation and regeneration are needed. A wealth of knowledge generated by these efforts has largely focused on the immediate needs of the city or region where the main campus is located, but with a little more strategic foresight and stronger links to their internationalization efforts, universities in different cities and regions could extend their efforts at connecting teaching and research to local needs wherever there is demand, sustaining networks and flows of people and ideas, providing the basis for certification, quality assurance, and benchmarking, and testing the validity of existing knowledge against new challenges. *Unlearning* outmoded and obsolete beliefs and behavior is almost as important as *learning* new ones. There is huge potential to give university–community engagement an international dimension in ways which are more neutral politically than many intergovernmental efforts. No wonder several major universities are adopting "the city" as a cross-disciplinary theme to inspire the next generation of research. What a contrast to the 1960s when the impact of social unrest in western countries and the development agenda in the Third World led to the creation of academic centers and some changes in the curriculum, without affecting the vision and scope of the university as a whole.

As is so often the case, however, a strength contains a point of vulnerability. Public sector austerity measures are expected to intensify in the next few years, generating a new agenda to reform public services. Universities must remain at the cutting edge of research and knowledge about priority setting, modes of delivery, regulation and competition, technological innovation, intellectual property, and governance that are critical to successful reforms in health, education, the environment, and everyday services on which the well-being of people living and working in cities depends. Research and reputations may be benchmarked globally, but universities remain grounded in specific territories and cities. Universities, which together with comprehensive hospitals, institutions in the justice system, and arts and cultural centers are among the most important employers and landowners in cities, will not be exempt from the harsh impact of austerity. In sixty-six of the hundred largest American cities, these institutions are the largest employers (Inner City Insights, 2011). How they survive in an increasingly adverse fiscal environment will in turn affect how the cities of which they are a part will develop. The relationship is reciprocal: a university in a city in decline is itself less able to attract and retain the students and faculty who are its very *raison d'être*.

Getting things done differently, and better: place-based strategies

The key questions are everywhere the same: how to translate a city's assets and potential into a coherent, plausible vision; how to transform disparate interventions into a strategy whose whole is greater than the sum of its parts; and how to sustain investment to transform the city across electoral and economic cycles.

Where to begin? On the waterfront, where historically cities were founded and developed. Given their differences, down to the scale and texture of the everyday urban experience, what do livable and competitive cities have in common? In many cases, a waterfront, be it a river, a bay or harbor, or the sea itself. This can be, literally and figuratively, a bridge across to other issues. Above all, people share the pleasure of being near the water – Chicago and Milwaukee simply sparkle at the edge of Lake Michigan; San Francisco Bay or the inlets of Vancouver are cherished sights; the banks of the Seine are Paris's contribution to UNESCO's world urban heritage; the beaches of Sydney, Tel Aviv or Rio symbolize a unique lifestyle: from this perspective, waterfronts are a great common denominator. And in many, there is work to be done. Rio has a magnificent natural setting, but its older commercial piers have needed regeneration for a long time. Venice, once the mistress of the seas, and ever since a prime tourist destination, needs protection against high water. Belfast's Titanic Quarter and regeneration along the Lagan River however demonstrate how a waterfront can create a new civic space.

People want to live near the sea. The last two hundred years have seen a progressive relocation of population from upland to lowland sites, from the interior to the coast. This trend appears to be irreversible; forecasts of more frequent storms and floods could lead to the relocation of settlements, but do not appear to have deterred people from moving to vulnerable areas. In the early Middle Ages people moved from the coastal plains to elevated places and the interior; the expansion of Europe in the eighteenth and nineteenth centuries involved settlement in and competition over the vast rural spaces from Eastern Europe to Ukraine and beyond; the twentieth century saw a reverse flow to coastal regions, first for recreation and then for industrial and metropolitan growth. It is as if a tidal pull exerted over centuries, depopulating land-locked hinterlands, draws on some deep urge to be near water: *hydrophylia*.

Of the twenty-five most livable cities on the 2013 Monocle rankings, all but Vienna, Munich, Kyoto, and Madrid have ports, and a few – Hong Kong (twelfth), Singapore (sixteenth), and Hamburg (seventeenth) – are among the largest and most efficient in the world. Clearly the industrial port city is not an oxymoron from a livability perspective, in part because the logistics of handling containers has been displaced from the city center to the outer reaches with deep-water access. Diversity across competitive and livable cities brings out the potential for learning among cities, especially about the quality of design, decision-making, and financing mechanisms. Melbourne remains high on annual livability rankings while maintaining commercial waterfronts around Port Philip Bay and deepening the channel between the city's port and Australia's link to maritime routes. The huge cost of port expansion and the complexity of environmental regulations combine to restrict competition among ports: few countries can support more than one highly competitive, efficient port, especially when shipping lines (not shippers) dictate the terms of trade. Introducing competition in port services probably matters more in Australia or Japan for national competitiveness and productivity by lowering costs and raising efficiency than helping Sydney compete against Melbourne, or Tokyo against Osaka. New York's port may no longer be as important to its competitiveness as the efficiency of its land links which connect it to more efficient sea ports on the Pacific and Atlantic coasts, but the regeneration of the west-side High Line into a spectacular linear park is suggestive of what many cities intent on improving their livability could do with an obsolete and abandoned piece of infrastructure. The regeneration of rivers in Portland, Seoul, and Munich and the transformation of the waterfront of Barcelona and Helsinki are linked to their ambitions as centers of innovation in design. The differences between livability and competitiveness can also be seen more sharply at the shoreline. London's renewal of its docklands highlights tensions related to unemployment and inequality which compromise growth across the metropolitan region.

Waterways and waterfronts impose their own discipline on cities as climate change complicates decisions that must be taken about their management. The settlement of coastlines also exposes more people and more assets to the risks of flooding on a regular basis, and to catastrophic events which may occur more often in the future. (See Chapter 6.) Coastal zones, areas within 100 kilometers of a shoreline and below 100 meters of elevation, are home to 1.2 billion people, or 20 per cent of the world's population. The population of coastal zones is increasing faster than the world average; here, population density is three times the world average. (This phenomenon is swelled by population trends in India, South East Asia, and China.)

The coastal zone is the next policy frontier, where economic, cultural and environmental objectives will prove difficult to reconcile. Precisely because there are competing uses for the waterfront, there are competing visions of its future and different historical perspectives on its past. In every city ranked for livability or competitiveness, the ability to manage the interface between commercial, residential, environmental, and recreational demands along the waterfront should be a key criterion of success. The list of challenges is daunting, and especially in governance terms because each one of these is cross-sectoral and multi-jurisdictional. The coastal zone is so complex that the OECD has not yet undertaken comparative studies of policy effectiveness for its management. The consequences are especially critical in city-regions such as Chicago and Melbourne where the pressures from a backlog of deferred infrastructure planning and investment, if not alleviated and corrected, will make it almost impossible to restructure the metropolitan region to guide the next phase of growth. To manage the transformation of the waterfront, there is no alternative to comprehensive planning. It remains to be seen whether the organizational and conceptual techniques that are successful on the waterfront can be translated into urban strategic planning for the rest of the city, blending a liberal approach to economic change, open to trade, investment, competition and migration, with the social and environmental concerns of people in the places where they live.

Integrated planning – there is no alternative but to learn to do it better

Area-based, cross-sectoral strategies call for making a vision of the future easier to nurture, articulate, and act upon. What will it look like, people want to know. Public debates about what should be built what should be preserved or demolished, and what should not be built are shaped by aesthetic concerns. This can be inspiring to some, threatening to others. "Make way for progress" is still a rallying cry, often sweetened by the promise of jobs and investment. Projects left incomplete, buildings that age badly, and changes in values help to explain why highways, housing projects, and shopping centers that were proclaimed as the salvation of the city are torn down within decades. And their example then becomes evidence in the hands of people who want to kill projects in the design-stage. Questions about beauty will not go away, because people do care about what they see. Aesthetics however often serve as a screen for issues about community preferences and aversions, reflecting social fears as well as cultural values. In the NIMBY ("not in my back yard") and BANANA ("build absolutely nothing anywhere near anybody") era, the challenge is to improve the social acceptability of change.

We can stumble into the future, the Micawber-like equivalent of waiting for something to turn up, or we can try to guide change toward the realization of broader objectives As things stand, however, the city of tomorrow will emerge out of a haphazard process, ad-hocery. Missing is a vision of how different efforts, different elements can be put together more coherently through a territorial project that encourages investment.

City and regional planning – not just about physical form but also about the interaction in space of the economic, social, and cultural elements of cities, the most complex form of social organization – was once part of the progressive agenda of every advanced western nation. A future-oriented, risk-management approach is not radically new in historical terms. This task has been managed twice in the past 150 years. The first phase came during the period 1880–1920 when the modern fire-resistant, cholera-free metropolis was constructed at a time when land was available for outward expansion, and existing buildings could be easily demolished, to be replaced by larger and taller ones, thus taking advantage of a set of new technologies: rapid public transport, electricity, telephony, elevators. This phase was largely under the control of strong local and regional governments, whose policies were enriched by a wealth of proposals from engineers, planners, and architects and by discussion in the press, in business circles, and in community organizations. It was at this time that the modern regulatory framework of zoning, planning, building codes, and public services was introduced. The second phase came after 1945 to reconstruct cities that had been destroyed, or to rebuild existing cities. This phase was driven by national policies and drew heavily on national resources, redistributive in many cases, but also in the form of fiscal measures and direct expenditures or subsidies. A complex regulatory framework gave bureaucrats considerable control at every level of government. Not to plan, or to plan badly, was condemned as a failure of politics and administration in the era that ended in 1939. Postwar reconstruction extended the prewar planning tradition, but by the 1970s the growing industry of property developers captured debates about how much regulation markets needed.

To rebuild cities as they are, neither process can be replicated. Local governments are too weak and local economies too limited in their resources to carry out today what was managed over a century ago, when far less of the city was fixed and permanent, and when local elites in commerce, higher education, and public administration had more influence and capital. And national governments are now constrained by demands on their resources and policy-making capacity. The collapse of centrally controlled economies in 1990 coincided with an ascendant belief in the superiority of markets, defended by both philosophical and economic theorists; planning was discredited in the public mind and starved by the public purse. As argued in Chapter 3, the modest impact of various stimulus packages since 2008 can be partly explained by the simple fact that the there was so little in the drawers of planning departments, and so many regulatory barriers to be overcome whenever an ambitious plan is proposed. Falling back on the market was once an ideological commitment; in the fiscal crisis it is now a policy by default. This policy vacuum has become an urgent priority to fill.

The objections to planning are deeply held by people who simply do not know or fail to appreciate the achievements of planning in the post-Renaissance era of the seventeenth and eighteenth centuries, the industrial era of the nineteenth, or between the 1880s and 1960s. Because the future is unpredictable, or so the argument goes, planning, which commits resources for the long term, is likely to over- or under-provide what people need, and guide development to the wrong places. It is not enough to say that cities thrive because they are messy or because they attract people who would be worse off if they lived elsewhere, or to celebrate cities where diversity encourages tolerance, and talent receives its reward; all true, but the future of cities cannot be taken for granted. The spontaneity of life in neighborhoods may generate a higher level of social capital and support small businesses, but it does not deliver public services, collect the garbage, run the public transport system or health clinics, keep the streets safe and run the prisons, or increase the power supply, all of which call for sound public governance and far-sighted planning that function in a civic culture which also respects the value of neighborhoods and the intermingling of people. The market alone cannot create a credible set of strategies.

A forward-looking strategy however complements the market: it can and must anticipate how change can be accommodated in already built-up parts of cities, and in areas where development will take place. Above all, planning can discriminate among different parts of cities, and their respective contribution to productivity, growth, innovation, and the quality of life.

Why is there no rational alternative to strategic planning? The question is not theoretical; the answer is not idealistic. The crisis has shown the limits to "business as usual" when the search for new sources of growth remains as compelling and urgent in 2015 as it was in 2008. As discussed in Chapter 4, part of the reason why national governments are attracted to a coherent territorial approach – policies that are not the simple addition of spatial planning, urban, rural, and regional policies – is to reduce the burden on the national treasury at a time when ageing, unemployment, and security, make increasing demands. Much of the drive for territorial policies has been the realization that subsidies and other means of compensating lagging and promoting leading regions focus too much on exogenous investments and transfers, and not enough on endogenous assets. No, the urban lobby has not hijacked the agenda, but yes, the future of cities can shape a medium-term strategy for investment.

Three years into the crisis, the OECD (2011: 13–14) looked at the impact on and the role of the crisis, deficit reduction, and stimulus packages through the lens of multi-level governance. The OECD guidelines "for designing and implementing public investment strategies across levels of government" broadly fit the agenda for territorial development – or spatial development policy – more generally:

- Combine investments in physical infrastructure with the provision of soft infrastructure, such as skills and other innovation-related assets.
- Exploit the value added of *place-based* investment policies
- Improve co-ordination mechanisms for the design and implementation of investment strategies across levels of government
- Enhance horizontal co-ordination across local jurisdictions
- Build transparent management processes to improve the selection and implementation of investment projects at all levels of government
- Address risk through robust budget procedures
- Diversify sources of financing
- Conduct regular reviews of the regulation with potential impact on public investment decisions and strengthen regulatory coherence across different levels of government
- Focus on capacity building; and
- Bridge information gaps across levels of government.

The word "planning" does not appear in black-and-white but it is impossible to execute this agenda without it. In March 2014, the OECD adopted "Principles on effective public investment across levels of government," a higher-level form than guidelines because they become part of the Organisation's *acquis* to which any new members must subscribe. All these measures were needed before the crisis. High levels of debt, combined with the need to boost investment in and for cities, make this agenda imperative in a low-growth economy.

Planning is critical to translate strategy – especially to redevelop an area as a whole – into the kind of information that developers, owners, builders, officials, and citizens need. "Planning in a dynamic and changing world," wrote Patsey Healey early in the twenty-first century in a report for the OECD, shapes the "process of invention and innovation, rather than the production of investment blueprints for proposed urban forms .... The key strategic 'trick' is how exogenous and endogenous forces can be linked together to contribute to both the flourishing of the wider context (of national and supra national economies and societies) and the well being of people within localities" (Healey, 2001: 153). This statement already incorporates certain values and choices consistent with democracy and market economies; other societies would make other choices. It is not that far removed from Lewis Mumford's definition of "genuine planning" as "an attempt, not arbitrarily to displace reality, but to clarify it and to grasp firmly all the elements necessary to bring the geographic and economic facts in harmony with human purposes" – in contrast to drawings and images which Mumford criticized because they "cover all the tough knots of reality with coats of esthetic paint" or plans such as that made by the city commissioners of New York in 1811, now often praised, which imposed "a limited order of reality" (Mumford, 1938: 375–6). To succeed, it is important to tap the knowledge in society: neither the planning team, nor the public sector, nor the planning authority can any longer imagine that they are "in charge." This new emphasis on collaborative processes matters because, at a time when trust in government is low, "a spatial development strategy, to be legitimate, needs to show that it is not just the work of the old technical experts and politicians carrying on 'business as usual'" (Healey, 2001: 154).

The main focus of creative, adaptive policy delivery should be to improve sectoral policy and projects more likely to have a sustained territorial impact (OECD, 2014). There have been false starts in the recent past: "joined-up" thinking is but one example. Admittedly, the specific ideas and techniques to make cross-sectoral action effective are not yet in training manuals and handbooks. Conservative bureaucracies, regulatory barriers, cynical communities, rigid budgets, and indifferent elected officials all conspire against it. The chances of success are probably better now that the crisis itself affects the structure and strategy of the public sector, making a fresh examination of how government works and what skills the public sector needs timely. If an austerity drive cuts even further into planning capacity at the national and sub-national levels, however, a sustainable recovery will only recede.

There are three sets of problems: first, to carry out a coherent program that crosses existing jurisdictional boundaries, even when change would dilute the power of one jurisdiction and expand that of another, or when local interests could hold up progress toward an objective that serves the larger population (or put another way, how to secure political support when different levels of government are in the hands different parties, and when different jurisdictions are in competition for resources); second, to align national and local priorities and budgets, synchronizing timing across budget cycles and the time needed for capital projects; and third, to get departments set up on sectoral lines to work together. Making a vision of the future seems achievable; the transformation of the public sector in its political and administrative forms seems a harder task.

Inventing the city of tomorrow calls for innovation in governance. We are at a crossroads between intervention in the short term to remediate problems which are already costly and complex, or proactive strategic planning to focus on the assets which underpin a city's – and nation's – strengths and tackle the threats to them. The goal is to lift overall output by developing the assets of all regions, strengthening the link between firms and territories. That there is a tension between place-based regional and a-spatial macro-economic policy reflects two different approaches to enhancing performance and the efficiency of public intervention. There is nothing wrong with tension: it can release creativity. But creativity applied to institutions and policies has been in short supply. Complacency and its handmaiden, muddling through in times of crisis, are a poor substitute for policy innovation and leadership. There are bigger problems ahead, shaped by a risk agenda that reflects our greater ability to learn from past experience, understand complexity, and anticipate the future.

References

Alexander, John W. (1954), "The basic-nonbasic concept of urban economic functions," *Economic Geography*, 30 (1954): 246–61.
Allam, Matti and Martin Thompson (eds), "An international framework of good practice in research and delivery of the European Capital of Culture programme" www.liv.ac.uk/impacts 08/complementary-programmes/EC_cultural_policy_group.htm.
Art Newspaper (2014), "Visitor figures 2013", special report, April.
Clark, Greg (2008), *Local Development Benefits from Staging Major Events*, OECD, Programme on Local Economic and Employment Development (LEED). ISBN: 978-92-64-04206-3.
Financial Times (2009a), Tyler Brulé, "The city of your dreams," 13/14 June.
Financial Times (2009b), Michael Skapinker, discussing a study by A.T. Kearney, Foreign Policy Magazine and the Chicago Council on Global Affairs, "There is more to city life than convenience," 30 June.
Financial Times (2011), Tyler Brulé, "Why easy living can be so hard," 11/12 June.
Financial Times (2014), Michael Skapinker, "Move to life than livable cities," 11 September.
Gold, John R. and Margaret M. (eds) (2011), *Olympic Cities: City Agendas, Planning and the World's Games, 1896–2016*, 2nd edition (Milton Park, Oxon., and New York: Routledge).
Gordon, John C. and Helen Beilby-Orrin (2006), "International measurement of the economic and social importance of culture," unpublished paper, OECD Statistics Directorate, 9 August.

Grattan Institute (2013), *Productive Cities: Opportunity in a Changing Economy* (Melbourne: Grattan Institute).

Healey, Patsey (2001), "New approaches to the content and process of spatial development frameworks," pp. 143–59 in OECD, *Towards a New Role for Spatial Planning* (Paris: OECD), edited and supervised by Atsushi Koresawa and Josef Konvitz. ISBN: 92-64-18603-4.

Helliwell, J. F., Jaifang Huang, Shawn Grover, Shun Wang (2014), "Good governance and national well-being: what are the linkages"?, OECD Working Papers on Public Governance no. 24, OECD Publishing. Dx.doi.org/10.1787/5jxv9f651hvj-en.

Inner City Insights (2011), "Anchor institutions and urban economic development: from community benefit to shared value," working paper v.1, no. 2; Initiative for a Competitive Inner City.

Konvitz, Josef W. (2001), "Jobs for people and places," *European Urban and Regional Studies*, 8:3: 257–64.

Mumford, Lewis (1938), *The Culture of Cities* (New York: Harcourt, Brace).

Norris, Emma, Jill Rutter and Jonny Medland (2013), "Making the Games: what government can learn from London 2012," Institute for Government.

OECD (2006), "International measurement of the economic and social importance of culture," by John C. Gordon and Helen Beilby-Orrin, Statistics Directorate, unpublished paper.

OECD (2011), *Making the Most of Public Investment in a Tight Fiscal Environment: Multi-level Governance Lessons from the Crisis* (Paris: OECD). DOI: 10/1787/9789264114470-en.

OECD (2012), *Compact City Policies: A Comparative Assessment* (Paris: OECD), OECD Green Growth Studies. DOI: org/10.1787/9789264167865-en.

OECD (2014), *OECD Regional Outlook: Regions and Cities: Where Policies and People Meet* (Paris: OECD). (Chapter 5 contains sections on the problems governments confront when pursuing integrated policies, pp. 138–62). DOI: 10.1787/9789264201415-3en.

PART II

Making cities safer

6

The vulnerability and resilience of cities

The crash of 2008, more damaging than any recent earthquake, tsunami, forest fire, industrial disaster, flood, or storm when measured in income lost, unemployment, deferred investment, and mental distress and illness, was the biggest cross-border peacetime systemic crisis since the 1930s; it will not be the last. If the global financial crisis has not been enough to provoke a reassessment of policies for cities and growth, what could? Perhaps more crises of which cities will be the epicenter in energy, the environment, social cohesion, or the economy. States may have no choice but to be drawn into urban policy under the pressure of events over which they have no control.

In the final analysis, the ultimate test of how well prepared a society is to cope with and recover from a crisis is another crisis. By this standard, the crash of 2008 and its sequel, the post-crisis crisis which in 2014 has not yet ended, have found us wanting. If stronger measures were not taken in the run-up to the crisis of 2008 to check asset inflation and credit risk in the housing sector in several countries when there was clear reason to do so, what confidence can there be that adequate measures are being taken in advance of other natural or human-made catastrophes? And what can we learn about how to incorporate the lessons of experience into pre-disaster planning from the effort to introduce reforms in banking and finance since 2008, a process that is still incomplete and is taking longer than expected? What matters is not the scale of any single catastrophe but the accumulation of crises for which societies are unprepared. Impotence, incompetence, ignorance transform even single crises into something else, in a downward spiral.

Government policies for disasters are based on two assumptions: that disasters are infrequent and exceptional, and that economies recover, making good the loss at least at the national level, if not at the local level where a disaster is usually most intense. Both assumptions are based on extrapolations from historical trends because it has been possible in peacetime to contain the costs of disasters and catastrophes at manageable levels. From this perspective, incremental improvements for disaster prevention and post-disaster recovery which incorporate the lessons from disasters as they occur may be sufficient. This chapter however is grounded on a different set of assumptions, that catastrophes have become more frequent and more damaging, that the systemic links between different parts of the global urban economy are more visibly exposed to risks, that the sheer scale of urbanization changes the calculation of risks and costs, and that the long-term impact of the crisis of 2008 cannot be so casually set to one side when considering the potential damage of other crises not of an economic nature.

We face a choice between doing little or nothing now to prepare better for disasters that could occur in the next few years because there is neither sufficient time nor money, and preparing better for catastrophes that could occur in coming decades, adopting sound strategies for risk assessment, preventive measures, and resilience-enhancing efforts supported by adequate financing. Conscious of future risks, but without wishing to alarm the public, well-informed governments which see their liabilities escalate in the future may question the capacity of the insurance industry to provide adequate coverage. Some risks occur suddenly, and, as with earthquakes or tsunamis, with only seconds of warning; other "slow-onset risks ... provide more time for society to adjust, react and mitigate" (OECD, 2011: 15). The costs of major changes in domestic economic and social arrangements as part of a risk-management strategy to reduce loss of property and life in the event of a catastrophe may burden domestic economies. If the worst-case scenario does not materialize, governments will be accountable for having wasted public funds and introduced unnecessary reforms; if however there is worse to come and preventive, adaptive measures were not taken when it would have been comparatively easy to do so, governments will be blamed. Then all eyes turn toward elected leaders, even when government could have done nothing to prevent a disaster. The political scale of a disaster may matter more than its material or human costs. The Bush administration recovered from Hurricane Katrina; Fukushima contributed to the defeat of the Democratic Party government then in power in Japan and to the revision of energy policy in Germany; the Soviet era did not last long after Chernobyl. Indeed, crises can be rated according to their political impact, the destruction of a state and of its political culture being the most severe.

The agenda for better risk management is daunting. Consider that:

- Risk management for natural disasters calls for cross-border, cross-sectoral, and multi-level co-ordination to treat cities and regions as

the primary focus, but the structures of government and expectations of stakeholders are organized by sectors and within bounded territorial units.
- Place-based development, translating a territorial vision into coherent sectoral action, should reduce the exposure or vulnerability of cities, but few leaders are adopting this approach.
- Preparedness is cost-effective, but the will to bring change to reduce exposure and vulnerability is usually strong only after a disaster, not before, and dissipates quickly unless bold measures are taken.
- Changes in lifestyles and housing patterns could reduce vulnerability but public hostility remains a barrier to effective and efficient pre-disaster measures even as the public's aversion to risk remains high.
- Post-disaster recovery and reconstruction begin as soon as the disaster occurs, and are usually affected by how relief measures are carried out, but disaster–planning usually separates immediate relief from post-disaster recovery.
- Delegating authority to experts makes sense given the technical complexities of coherent pre-disaster risk-reduction efforts, but little can be achieved without strong, consistent political leadership.

As a strategy, resilience assumes that disasters are unavoidable but survivable. Grosvenor, a property company, has rated fifty cities from most to least resilient, resiliency being the combined score after evaluating adaptive capacity (governance, institutions, technical and learning facilities, planning systems, funding structures) and vulnerability (climate, environment, resources, infrastructure, community) (*Financial Times*, 2014). An armchair methodology is one thing; but the lessons of experience reveal how rarely events unfold as expected. Improvisation and initiative often make a critical difference, implying that people and institutions need to be prepared to improvise and innovate. Because urban societies can withstand a great deal more disorganization than theorists and social scientists earlier in the twentieth century had believed possible, resilience is receiving a lot of attention. But resilience does not come easily or cheaply: cutbacks in budgets which are likely to reduce public benefits and services will make it harder to enrich the stock of social and human capital and of public goods on which resilience rests.

The age of anxiety has been reborn; accepting that crises are normal goes against the deep-seated belief that, whatever "normal" is, it allows people to go about their lives without fear. There is an understandable human tendency to believe that, if this crisis or that disaster had not occurred, "things would have remained the same," the equivalent of the economists' trend line. Countries such as Canada and Australia whose banks were sound were nonetheless affected by the global financial crisis which originated elsewhere, the equivalent of being invaded when neutral. We are all exposed to cross-border risks. Two things follow. First, the a-spatial nature of most sectoral policies and budgets will be under pressure to become more sensitive to the spatial dimension of risk. And second, collective security (the subject of Chapter 10) will be tested by the international, cross-border nature of many risks to which cities, including many of the largest, are exposed.

What do we have to worry about?

Every year brings its own mix of catastrophes. The familiar categories "economic, social, environmental" break down when economic decisions about land use contribute to the risk of floods and fires, when environmental problems or externalities reduce welfare and raise the risks and costs to business, when economic disasters lead to the neglect of sound measures to protect the environment, and when social problems compromise public health measures. Any annual overview will show a similar pattern: very high casualties in very poor countries, often numbering a hundred thousand or more, usually following a flood or earthquake; rising property losses in richer countries, where investment in infrastructure, construction, and public services reduce the exposure of people. Some catastrophes stand out – Katrina, Kobe; others, which at the time transfixed world attention such as the tsunami that hit Indonesia in 2005, are less well remembered. Orders of magnitude are difficult to communicate: in proportion to the size of the Australian population, the devastating fires in Victoria in February 2010 were worse than the attack on the World Trade Center in New York in 2001, but the effects of the latter on public policy and private behavior were incomparably greater.

Rather than look at last year's disasters, it may be more instructive to revisit 1999, which came at the end of a decade when the cumulative effect of catastrophes had clearly broken the line on any graph, indicating both an increase in their number and an intensification of their impact.

In 1999, insured losses for natural disasters reached $28.6 billion, and $4.2 billion for technical catastrophes. This was the largest burden for insurance since 1992, when Hurricane Andrew (which cost the industry $19 billion) lifted the overall total to $32.4 billion. In 1999, seven events involved insured damages of over $1 billion. Two of the worst came at the end of the year: the winter wind storms Lothar (26 December, $4.5 billion) and Martin (27–8 December, $2.2 billion); the damage included the loss of 110 million trees in France, including a ten thousand in the gardens of Versailles. Storms of the magnitude of Lothar appear to occur once every ten years, but costs of $1 billion or more are more frequent, perhaps every two or three years. Fifty thousand died in earth slides in Venezuela, accounting for half the number of victims worldwide (and damages of $10 billion). This was however only the seventh-largest disaster in terms of loss of life between 1970 and 1999; far worse were the nuclear accident at Chernobyl (165,000 dead), tropical cyclones in Bangladesh (300,000 dead in 1970), and an earthquake in China in 1976 which left 250,000 dead (Swiss Re, 2000).

The events in 1999 with the greatest impact on public policies were the Izmit and Duezce earthquakes of 17 August and 12 November respectively ($20 billion overall damages, 600,000 homeless, 20,000 deaths), which led to major reforms in construction regulation and further opened the market in Turkey for private insurance. On a global scale between fifteen and twenty earthquakes annually register 7 or more on the Richter scale; there were twenty in 1999, meaning that the number of earthquakes was not greater than usual even though the losses were exceptional because of their impact which reflected not only settlement patterns in an industrialized zone of a rapidly growing, emerging economy, but past governance practices which compromised the structural integrity of buildings and tolerated construction in places known to be at high risk. The insurance industry covered only a portion of the losses of that year worldwide, which were estimated at approximately $100 billion, the largest since the Kobe earthquake of 1995.

So much for figures; what about underlying causes, not of catastrophes as such, but of the escalating scale of damages? Three are on a lot of lists: (1) greater population density, often in vulnerable areas such as coastal zones, leading to (2) more insured assets in vulnerable areas; and (3) the concentration of appreciating assets in industrialized countries. A fourth factor is less often cited: the reluctance of governments to take measures that restrict development in vulnerable regions, if those regions are otherwise attractive, thus privileging market-driven demand over other considerations. There is nothing necessarily wrong with this, especially if coupled with rising insurance coverage, but this is not always the case, and moreover and more important, the secondary or collateral effects of a disaster are usually far more costly than direct, insurable property damage. The costs in lost business activity, the relocation of firms and workers to other locations, or the loss of invaluable natural or cultural heritage, even the cost of lengthening the school year or providing medical coverage for people suffering post-traumatic symptoms years hence, are taken out of the general economy.

Anyone looking ahead in 1999 could have expected the next decade to be worse, and it was. The year 2010 cost insurers an estimated $36 billion, in contrast to $28.6 billion in 1999. The costliest disaster for insurers, at $8 billion, was the Chilean earthquake, with overall losses of €23 billion; the deadliest was the earthquake in Haiti in which some 223,000 people died; the second-deadliest disaster, the heat wave and forest fires in Russia, led to the deaths of 56,000. A 2012 retrospective to 1991 produced by AM Best, an insurance rating agency, ranked the five most costly natural disasters as the Tohoku earthquake and tsunami on 11 March 2011 at $210 billion, Hurricane Katrina on 25 August 2005 at $125 billion, the Kobe earthquake of 17 January 1995 at $100 billion, a series of earthquakes in China on 12 May 2008 at $85 billion, and the 2011 floods in Thailand which extended over several months at $46 billion. As the impact of deltaic flooding in Thailand in 2011 that shut down many factories in Bangkok made clear, a flood today can do a lot of damage to the industrial supply chain over a two-week period, more in fact than bombing of a single German city such as Hamburg by the Allies in World War Two. The Thai floods were the fifth costliest insured loss in the past thirty-one years, estimated by AM Best to total between US$15 billion and $20 billion (*Financial Times*, 2012). Insured losses amounted to approximately $110 billion against total economic losses in 2012 of $362 billion (*The Economist*, 2012). Hurricane Sandy is likely to cost between $50 billion and $100 billion. Port cities (already treated in Chapter 5 in relation to competitiveness and livability themes) are exposed – perhaps disproportionately so – to natural disasters. Tsunamis in Indonesia in 2004 and Japan in 2011, earthquakes in Turkey, Greece, Italy, and Haiti, hurricanes in Mexico and the United States all call attention to the exposure of coastal zones and their populations. Water, not fire, now appears to be the most significant and likely cause of widespread loss of life and property. With the exception of wild fires on the edge of cities – one thinks of Los Angeles and Melbourne – cities do not appear to be at great risk of fire unless attacked in war. The exposure of cities to floods is greater due to uncontrolled settlement patterns in floodplains and coastal areas, pressures on mangrove swamps, wetlands and sand dunes, groundwater extraction leading to subsidence, and flawed management of complex urban sub-surface networks and of waterways. And this list leaves out global warming, including the melting of the polar ice cap, and significant changes in ocean currents and rainfall patterns. Global climate change puts coastal zone management at the top of the urban policy agenda for the foreseeable future.

Port cities are not a subtype of city, one category among others, but the *ur*-type, without which life in other cities that do not have maritime functions would be all but impossible to understand in economic and social terms. It may sound as a truism that port cities are critical to globalization. The number of ships in global maritime transport has almost doubled and their capacity almost tripled between 1970 and 2004. The world seaborne trade of oil between 2000 and 2011 rose from 2.1 to 2.7 billion tons; container ships carried 630 million tons in 2000 but 1.47 billion in 2011 as globalization of manufacturing and distribution outdistanced, literally, the increased consumption of energy. Ever since the rise of the Portuguese, Spanish, and Dutch seaborne empires in the sixteenth and seventeenth centuries, long-distance trade in basic and exotic commodities, and the impact of contacts between civilizations, have been concentrated in great port cities. Istanbul, Antwerp, Seville–Cadiz, Lisbon, Amsterdam, and later Manila, Shanghai, even New York pulled away from their rural hinterlands, set apart from other cities by virtue of their size and rate of growth, the size and diversity of their markets, their mix of cultures and religions, posing challenges to rulers who wanted to tax their profits but could not control their trade. Today the owners of shipping fleets, and not the owners of the cargoes, determine the trade routes. In the long run, it is the ability of shipping to match supply and demand that helped land-locked agrarian economies overcome the constraints of seasonal variations in crops, and the high cost of storing and transporting perishable food commodities. The global network of port cities has changed with the expansion of economies in Africa, Asia and Latin America; volumes of shipping have increased massively following containerization and the development of specialized dry bulk and oil carriers; but some of the fundamental principles of how port cities and shipping networks operate today would be easily intelligible to a Dutch burgher investing in the East India Company or to a fleet owner in the late Victorian era placing an order with a shipyard on the Clyde.

Port cities function in networks, the great advantage of which is elasticity. The capacity of the network is affected by the number and size of port cities in the network, the travel time between them, and the number and size of ships on those routes. A port cannot operate in isolation from another port; congestion in one will usually lead to a diversion of shipping to another. This is especially the case with trans-shipment, when goods (or containers) move through a hub port as a link between two other port cities. When the port of Kobe was closed following the 1995 earthquake, spare capacity in Busan enabled that Korean port to take over some of Kobe's functions without disrupting Pacific trade. Problems are more likely to arise when congestion on inland transport routes makes it very difficult to move goods into or out of a port, as is increasingly the case in Africa. The worst problems come when inland congestion strangles a hub port which performs a unique role in the transport system: congestion in rail yards and a shortage of empty freight cars brought the port of New York to a halt during 1917–18, perhaps the archetypal example of this phenomenon; labor disputes on the Pacific coast are having a deleterious effect in the winter of 2014–15. A container ship with ten thousand containers – a size already surpassed by ships one-third larger in capacity – requires over five thousand single truck movements to clear its load. This example highlights the problems of connecting one transport system to another. Port-to-port movements are more likely to be affected, not by port operations directly, but by inland congestion in another port: as the saying goes, "the ship beats the quay." In other words, how a port city and coastal region are organized matters vitally to how well a port functions.

Most people who live in coastal regions do not work in or live near the port itself. Maritime commerce, like farming, enjoys huge economies of scale and makes modest demands on the labor force. We have already noted the preference for people to settle in coastal regions. Florida's 2.8 million people in 1950 are nineteen million today; most do not have any experience of the hurricanes of the 1950s. Experts in disasters at the Wharton School estimate that the value of insured and hurricane-prone assets along the Atlantic coast from Maine to Florida and around the Florida peninsula to Texas at $10 *trillion*. The Great Miami Hurricane of 1926, which cost $1 billion in 2011 dollars, would cause $188 billion now (*The Economist*, 2012). Two of the largest maritime cities in the world exposed to earthquakes are Tokyo and Istanbul: Tokyo's population is some thirty times larger than in 1923 at the time of the last earthquake that destroyed the city; insured losses for a major Tokyo earthquake are estimated at $1,000 billion. Istanbul has grown from a few hundred thousand in the mid-eighteenth century to approximately sixteen million people. The technologies used to create land for settlement in coastal areas give a false sense of security: reclaimed land from the sea will liquefy in an earthquake; dykes can be overwhelmed, or may increase water levels downstream. The proposal to build a new airport for Istanbul by 2019 nearer the Black Sea, included as part of the bid for the Olympic Games in Istanbul in 2020, is in fact a necessary solution to precisely the problem of having built the existing airport in a vulnerable zone, and not before time. The airport will be built; Tokyo however won the bid to host the Games.

All this by way of a prologue to the evidence that several of the world's maritime nations are exposed to extreme climatic events. Within 80 kilometers of the sea are the homes of two-thirds of the world's population. A crowding effect is evident: the French coast attracts only 10 per cent of the population (Paris, Lyon, Strasbourg, Toulouse are all inland) but at densities three times the national average, a phenomenon typical worldwide. Looking at 136 port cities with a population of more than one million, an OECD team considered the potential effects of coastal flooding due to storm surge and damage from high winds, together with population growth and waterfront construction. Already, about forty million people, or roughly 10 per cent of the population of the cities included in this study, are exposed to a one-in-a-hundred coastal flood event. Some are in developing countries – Mumbai, Guangzhou, Shanghai, Ho Chi Minh City, Kolkata, and Alexandria; others are not – Miami, Greater New York, Osaka–Kobe and New Orleans. Measured by potential property losses, the US, Japan and the Netherlands rank above emerging countries, which is to be expected. Across all cities, the OECD team estimated that the total value of assets exposed in 2005 is about 5 per cent of global GDP; this figure could rise to 9 per cent of global GDP in the next half century if the sea-level rose by 50 cm and the size of coastal populations increased at current rates of economic growth. (Nicholls et al., 2008).

More recently, a study by Stephane Hallegate and others (2013) arrived at a greater figure: if protective measures are not taken, the annual cost of property and physical damage (not loss of life) from the flooding of port cities by 2050 could be $1 trillion annually (€750 billion). By far the larger part of this sum reflects trends in the growth of population and of wealth linked to urbanization; a smaller share is due to climatic change and to the likelihood that new construction will be in more vulnerable zones. The usual suspects head the list of most exposed: Canton in China, Miami and New York in the United States, followed by Mumbai and Calcutta, but in forty years more Mediterranean cities will rank higher on this list than they do today. The figures change again when forecasts for the 2070s are run: the population exposed to a century flood rises to around 150 million; asset exposure reaches $ 35 trillion, or around 9 per cent of annual GDP. Population growth and rising levels of economic prosperity in developing countries account for much of the increase of flood risk expected over the next half century. But this is only the historical trend – not a prediction. Based on experience, those countries where the risks will increase most dramatically – by 2070, a rise in sea levels, storm surge, and subsidence would affect 21 per cent of China's population, 19 per cent of India's, 12 per cent of Bangladesh's, and 5 per cent of Vietnam's – are less likely to invest proportionally more in redirecting urbanization and in infrastructure protection: the gap between risk and prevention will widen over time as those countries become richer.

Preparedness is not prevention
It is a trick of the mind to assume that societies exposed to greater risk because their wealth is increasing will invest in better protection: very often a culture of proactive investment takes hold only after a catastrophic crisis. The Netherlands is a case in point; the shock of the flood of 1953 which put 9 per cent of agricultural land under water and killed 1,800 people led to a vast extension of dykes and the construction of defense works against high tides in the delta. This is why metrics based on probabilities of one in a hundred or even one in a thousand give a false sense of security: the OECD study estimates a 74 per cent chance that, every year, one or more of the 136 cities exposed to a hundred-year event will be hit by a major flood; for a one-in-a-thousand year event, the chances are 49 per cent that one of the 136 cities will be affected in any five-year period (Nicholls, 2008). The flawed relief effort in New Orleans when Hurricane Katrina hit in 2005, together with the experience of significant flooding in 1993 and 1995 (when 250,000 people across northwestern Europe had to be evacuated), provoked the Dutch to change their strategy to enhance the prospects for survival and recovery in flood-prone areas, even when this means letting high waters flood the land. Of course it is easier to allocate resources to improve physical defenses such as housing and infrastructure than to improve the community-based measures, including education and policing, that affect the capacity of a society to cope with a disaster if one occurs, and to rebound after. But both are needed.

Global mitigation and local adaptation and risk-reduction efforts could reduce the impact of disasters. Adopting a global carbon price may help reduce the impact of human activity on the climate in the future but it will do nothing to protect cities and coasts from changes already under way. The list of things to do includes upgraded protection, managing subsidence, land-use planning focusing development onto land less likely to be flooded, selective relocation from existing city areas, and flood warning and evacuation measures, especially as an immediate response in poorer countries. Who will pay? It is easier to reach the conclusion that annual investments of $50 billion to reduce exposure would generate larger social and economic returns than to develop a way whereby those in the future who benefit from the investments committed and sustained for more than a generation contribute their share. Of course expenditure today is an investment in better economic and environmental infrastructure that will be used in any case as well as protection against the costs of a disaster that may not occur. If the money is not spent on preparedness, the final costs of a disaster could be devastating: the political, economic, and even cultural consequences of mega-disasters are amplified if a disaster comes at a time when society and government can least afford one.

Investments of a routine nature made today and in years to come could help reduce the exposure of cities to risks and improve their capacity to cope with future emergencies. But risk-reduction strategies have proved difficult to normalize. Without better data and forecasts, capital-market instruments will be hard-pressed to cover the risk that people and firms – and governments – face (*Journal of Risk Research*, 2003). The OECD carried out a study of and methodological framework for disaster risk assessment and risk financing at the request of G20 finance ministers to help finance ministries in their efforts to provide adequate financial strategies for disaster risk management covering a government's contingent liabilities, giving incentives to the private sector to assume greater responsibility, and to accommodate a bigger role for insurance (OECD, 2012).[1] Analytical categories and estimates of the probability of a hazard occurring above a certain threshold however are largely retrospective; post-disaster impact analyses need to be repeated over the many years during which a recovery is under way; scenarios break down under a combination of long–term trends and of the sheer difficulty of projecting the spatial shape and social composition of urban economies beyond, say, ten years. The inter-connectedness of systems is another factor that escapes analysis: the indirect impacts may prove to be more significant than the direct ones, but harder to identify, let alone quantify, *ex-ante*.

It so happens that Hurricane Sandy hit New Jersey and New York on 29 October 2012 while this book was being written. Discussions about what to rebuild, and what changes on the coast and bay to introduce to reduce the impact and damages of a future storm, will have to cope with the complexity of regulation and politics: there are questions of federal and state laws, legal procedures on consultation, the imbalance between New York City's large municipal administration and the microjurisdictions in many coastal counties of New Jersey, not to mention problems of leveraging finance and the time needed to project into the future the compensation to people who will lose property. Political leaders, especially the governors of New York and New Jersey and the mayors of local jurisdictions, will want to handle the flow of funds and take credit for reconstruction which bring more visible results sooner than initiatives which could reduce the impact of future storms. What portion of funding and what share of political capital should be allocated to pre-disaster efforts? How can comprehensive, cross-jurisdictional decisions be made without abrogating democratic processes? If the payout from insurance firms takes years, and disbursement of public funds is likely to be slow and erratic, the pressures to rebuild what was lost will trump the impulse to bring about sustainable change. How can the added costs and incoherence of incremental decision-making be reconciled with the imperative to treat the entire region, *from the water inland*, as a whole?

One single book, *Paris coule-t-il?*, about the possibility of a devastating flood of Paris, puts this together. Geographer Magali Reghezza-Zitt (2012) begins, appropriately, with a lengthy discussion for the general reader about what it means to say that a given event, in this case a flood (of 8 meters above the banks of the Seine) equivalent to the 21 January 1910 event that isolated Paris from most of the rest of France but also from the United Kingdom, Italy, and Switzerland, has a one-in-a-hundred chance of recurring in a century, the point being to show how complicated preparedness is. First of all, the city of Paris and its environs are much changed, such that any modeling based on the 1910 flood can only be indicative, to be complemented by other more recent disasters such as terrorist attacks on metros in London, Moscow, and Madrid which highlighted the disruptive effects when public transport is out of service, Hurricane Katrina which dramatized the problems of rescuing the elderly and handicapped, the January 1998 ice storm in Quebec which led to the collapse of the electricity system, depriving Montreal of fresh drinking water, recent floods of 2001 in the Somme valley which showed how difficult the evacuation of people can be, and other storms and floods in France which drew attention to post-trauma effects among the population (Reghezza-Zitt, 2012: 39). Few records from 1910 survive: picture postcards, a map of areas inundated by the Seine, the odd marker on a building showing the height reached by the flood waters, but nothing which can touch the lives of people today who have only seen news reports of catastrophes elsewhere, an example of *schadenfreude* common worldwide.

Planning and preparedness are therefore complicated by the difficulties of forecasting a disaster, and thus also of giving authorities sufficient time to take precautions (such as the closing of the metro and securing hundreds of tunnels and passageways that could be inundated). If figures of the cost of damage to the economy could shock, one might think that a centenary flood in Paris would do it. But just as the precise course that a flood might take is impossible to predict, so are the economic damages, the one depending on the other. There are the direct costs to buildings and structures, and indirect costs due to the disruption of businesses which must close or relocate, perhaps for months after the flood waters have receded: these indirect costs could well exceed the direct costs by a factor of three. Huge supplies will be needed to secure underground tunnels; the people with the knowledge and the equipment have to be in place or on call, and able to get to where they have to go, under conditions which are likely to be anything but normal. Yet the speed with which the city's economy recovers depends to a large extent on how well protected the underground system will be. Between 140 km and 250 km of rapid public transport routes would be out of service; more than 1.5 million customers would be without electricity; more than five million might not have water on a regular basis. In a flood the entire city-region will be hit due to the inter-connectedness of urban environmental, transport and power systems, and to the impact of the catastrophe on what the public authorities can and cannot do.

Admittedly, it is hard for governments to know where to start without an overall strategy, but a strategy only highlights how difficult decision-making is. An OECD report on the risks of flooding in the Seine valley in Ile de France focused on governance for risk prevention (OECD, 2014). Business-as-usual has to change, calling for a different distribution of roles and responsibilities shared across more actors and agencies. But the current institutional framework makes a change of this order of magnitude difficult. A coherent risk strategy and risk culture are perfectly feasible but progress is uneven, even among businesses which already are more risk-conscious than the public at large. Much can be done nevertheless to make the region more resilient, but a strategy toward that objective would only be the beginning of an endless list of questions and problems which are difficult to answer.

Reghezza-Zitt focused on the problems associated with regulation before a crisis, and adaptation as a strategy from a preparedness perspective. Regulation sounds simple: interdict construction in flood-prone areas, for example. But many such areas are already built up. Should property-owners be compelled to invest in structural improvements? Should the state provide financial assistance? If new constructions are not allowed, the value of existing properties could fall; market prices will result in new patterns of social segregation replicating in developed countries what exists in the Third World: those with the lowest incomes and weakest voices occupy the most vulnerable spaces, or, put another way, those with the least to lose stand to lose most of what little they have. What does this imply for governments and their elected leaders, who will be under pressure to change the zoning restrictions so as not to penalize their electorate? For insurers? Regulations, especially those designed centrally and applied locally, absolve most authorities from having to think through whether any particular set of regulations is in fact relevant to local needs and meets local priorities. The task of applying rules and directives is another, and more complicated, matter for local officials, especially when practices that had been tolerated in the past become unacceptable. In December 2014, a court in Sables-d'Olonne sentenced René Marratier to prison for four years for homicide and jeopardizing life because, as Mayor of La Faute-sur-Mer, he had authorized the construction of housing in a flood zone where twenty-nine people died on the night of 27–8 December 2010 in the storm Xynthia.

Because natural disasters in developed countries lead to high property losses but few deaths, it is important to explore two dimensions of risk and regulation: building safety standards, and land-use planning and permission. Both call for a high degree of transparency. The public does not know what the risks of a flood or earthquake are, and for the most part has no living experience which can incorporate the lessons of past disasters, a classic case of imperfect knowledge: we trust the experts to determine the risks and set standards that ensure a high probability of survival. Safety measures that enable a structure to cope with unusual stresses may lead to overall higher housing costs if the amount of land for construction in desirable areas is reduced. In construction these costs are "built in" to the specifications and price, and passed on to successive owners. Compliance, to verify that the materials and methods used meet the required standard, can be enforced by independent inspectors and insurance firms, whose approval is needed for an occupancy permit. When it comes to land-use restrictions, pressure for development – including from local officials who want to attract investment and generate higher public revenues from fees and taxes – may result in plans which are more permissive, representing a compromise among stakeholders. Without a mix of pricing and fiscal measures, market forces and economic instruments may work against better regulatory performance and higher levels of safety. The wider public benefits of better regulation may well outweigh the initial costs, but those who stand to lose in the short term will be more vocal than the larger society.

An example comes from Turkey in the 1950s. At that time, Turkey politicized the mapping of geological hazards, principally earthquakes, changing the professional standards for maps and reducing their scale, making it all but impossible to identify whether a particular property is exposed to a fault line. In the absence of reliable maps, and at a time when government was unable and unwilling to regulate settlements and construction to accommodate a growing urban population, areas were developed that should not have been urbanized. To compensate for the risk to the public, the government was committed to replace any house that was destroyed or rendered uninhabitable in an earthquake. This commitment created a moral hazard problem for the state: without giving people the information to know where to build and where not to build, the state exposed itself to higher risks if and when an earthquake occurred. Conflict of interest on the part of inspectors who were hired by builders and contractors, sharp practices to inflate profits, compliant mayors eager to increase the population living in their jurisdiction even when people erected houses that did not comply with plans or codes, and the lack of insurance all contributed to the high loss of life and of property in the 1999 earthquakes of Turkey. After the 1999 earthquakes, people sometimes relocated without knowing whether they were moving to a safer or more exposed location. The government responded to the disaster by introducing radical reforms in the regulation of construction and by opening the private insurance market.

Access to information about risks concerning health, flood, earthquake, storm, etc. calls for up-to-date maps and databases generated and maintained by experts who take responsibility for the information they provide. The clue that the Turkish geological maps were flawed was easy to spot if you knew what to look for: they were not signed by a geologist. It is too much to expect that people looking to buy property in, say, Istanbul or Los Angeles will know how to read a geological map to see whether it was prepared according to high professional standards; they just want to know whether the property in question is near a fault line and what kind of fault line it is because they know that their city is exposed to a massive earthquake at some time in the future, and perhaps well within the time when they will be living there. The internet is making much of this information accessible. But in the final analysis, the officials who make decisions on a daily basis about what gets built where, and professional builders, must act with due diligence on the basis of the information at hand.

As the global economic crisis of 2008 and the post-crisis crisis have taught us, big numbers no longer scare: they become abstract units, admittedly of some interest for comparative purposes but not very meaningful. Simulations and maps are difficult for people to interpret, but give a misleading impression that everything has been thought of. Multiplying examples, piling up statistics, compiling documentaries in image and in oral history – the cumulative effect of reading annual reports on the human and economic cost of natural disasters, on the small measures being taken in large cities to learn from experience, on the huge governance failures especially but not only in low-income countries where people live in areas prone to floods, storms, mudslides, earthquakes – is numbing, breeding indifference. Perhaps it takes progressively larger disasters to shock people out of complacency. It is easy to reach the conclusion that the established, normative regulatory mode for urban development, based on economic/environmental trade-offs, is inadequate to cope with the economic and environmental challenges of cities in the twenty-first century; it is harder to know what to do about this.

Are cities really so vulnerable?

Analysis of the vulnerability of cities to collapse, it turns out, is hard to get right. The paradigmatic fires are London (1666) and Chicago (1870) because in their wake entirely new sets of rules were introduced, together with wholesale planning efforts. (Other major cities transformed after fire include Copenhagen, bombed in 1812, and San Francisco following an earthquake in 1906.) They set a model for rebuilding to replace existing smaller wooden or brick buildings with larger, taller, and better-built structures, and to impose new norms on areas being laid out and built up for the first time. Massive investment followed. The era 1880–1914 led to strict regulations, planning, inspection and compliance, insurance – but created a new set of fears, that the city's infrastructure would make it vulnerable to total collapse (whether by terrorism or crime, technological or systemic error, or war).

Stuart Chase wrote in *Harper's Magazine* in 1929 of two kinds of urban collapse: a social collapse born of the frustration and exhaustion of everyday life in the city, and a technological collapse that could follow the disruption of key systems of supply and control. The fact that infrastructure systems had not failed, argued Chase, is no proof that they are not susceptible to failure. And he emphasized how air raids could exploit the same kind of collapse that might come in peace. The British writer L. E. O. Charlton foresaw chaos in his 1938 book *The Air Defence of Britain*: "If it had been done deliberately," he wrote, "we could not as a nation have produced a social pattern, and a set economy, more favorable for aggression from the air. Our millions are bottle-fed, and all their needs cared for, by a system of distribution and supply so intricate, and so haphazardly evolved, that once dislocated beyond the power of immediate repair they would be as helpless as newborn babes to fend for themselves" (quoted in Konvitz, 1990). This assertion that people living in cities had lost the art of self-reliance went together with the efforts of social thinkers to define modernity in the 1920s in terms of how people in cities lived as individuals, and not in communities.

These were not the views of intellectual commentators alone; they were echoed in the June 1937 report of the National Resources Committee, "Our cities: their role in the national economy," an official government report submitted to President Roosevelt by a Cabinet committee supported by experts and researchers. The chapter entitled

"The problems of urban America" began with poverty, inequality, insecurity, and unemployment before covering a long catalogue of social, environmental, economic, and institutional problems leading to a call for a national policy for cities, the equivalent to one for rural development and agriculture. The third subheading was devoted to the vulnerability of city life, covering a modern version of the plagues which overwhelmed Pharaoh: epidemic, storm, accident, conflagration, war, internal strife, sabotage, strike or flood. Depicting the city as "a delicate mechanism which can be thrown out of gear and demoralized at a number of vulnerable points," the report specifically cited the risks associated with a breakdown in urban technologies, and called attention to the efforts of European governments to prepare cities and their inhabitants, including drastic steps to re-plan cities, for "the havoc that may be and actually is being wrought by military attacks on cities" (National Resources Committee, 1937: 56). People have long sought safety in cities; their security could leverage political support for planning when routine economic objectives might not.

The record of two world wars shows how these fears were translated into military actions, to destroy urban economies and social systems through bombing. The lesson that emerges from the history of air raids however is that even when the level of destruction approached totality, people coped, economic activity soon resumed: undermining the assumptions of aerial strategists, war proved how resilient modern cities are. This conclusion has obvious implications for crisis strategies today.

Two types of bombing strategy were developed during the years before World War Two. Strategic bombing theory was predicated on the belief that life in modern cities was dependent on the provision of basic services (power, transport, water), that this supply could be disrupted by the destruction of central command units and of distribution networks, and that these could be destroyed without directly killing many civilians. Precision bombing sought the destruction of electricity-generating plants, factories producing critical supplies, and key nodes in transportation systems. It promised a way to ration aircraft and crews to achieve maximum damage of an enemy's war economy, and also, but more subtly, it claimed to limit civilian casualties. Area bombing, favored by the British who lacked the better-quality bomb sight of the United States, assumed that the indiscriminate destruction of any part of a city would induce panic and perhaps riots, and that civilians subjected to such bombing would pressure their governments to end the war.

The British studied the effects of German air raids on their cities to better understand the theory of air war. German raids in mid-March and early May 1941 on Clydebank, a shipbuilding suburb of Glasgow, were typical. Approximately sixty tons of explosive fell per square mile, a high ratio, but fewer people were killed or injured per ton of high explosive than predicted in prewar forecasts, even though damage to housing was considerably higher. All essential utilities were knocked out, and transport links were severed. The complete loss of 10 per cent of the city's housing stock and damage to as much as half the rest seriously affected a city already suffering from residential overcrowding. Although most residents left Clydebank to seek shelter during the period of restoration, workers continued to travel back every day to work. Most factories lost between three and four weeks of production. About half the loss of production was due to damage to ships at shipyards, and about a third to damage to engineering works (principally of firms that made templates for ships). General disorganization accounted for the rest of the loss (Konvitz, 1992a).

Clearly the raids had not caused panic. The worst social problems involved incompetent municipal personnel and poorly led relief teams. Furthermore, people learned to cope with daily life in a city without vital services through the simple expedient of relocating to unaffected areas. From German air raids on British cities early in the war, the British learned that cities would have to be hit repeatedly if production levels were to remain depressed. And they also learned how such attacks could actually strengthen the nation by mobilizing its resolve against the enemy.

Prewar concern had focused on very large cities, on the assumption that life there could be disrupted more easily and effectively than in smaller communities. But experts at the British Ministry of Home Security drafting a report in May 1942 entitled "The total effect of air raids" concluded that the exact opposite was true: large cities can adjust better to the punishment of air raids because they have better transportation, larger housing stocks, and larger and more mobile labor markets.

The assumption that urban economies and societies are perilously dependent on a fragile technological infrastructure of supplies and services which rationalized the bombing of cities was disproved by post-bombing recovery, and this in Germany and Japan just as much as in France or the United Kingdom. People sorted out daily life for themselves, and returned to work as soon as possible; there was little desertion or signs of civil unrest. Even evidence during the war that cities continued to function did not however provoke a profound reassessment of strategic bombing, in part because the Allies had no other means to attack Germany directly until the invasion of 1945, and in part out of a belief that redoubled efforts would at last produce the intended results (Konvitz, 1992b). Some of the bombing in both world wars sacrificed lives without shortening the war or achieving military objectives, including social–economic ones. In the end bombing was effective against Germany, not as the cumulative result of the destruction of cities both large and small, but in combination with advances on the ground and following air raids in the winter of 1944–45 on the coal fields and rail networks of supply and distribution which brought German energy production to a halt two months before the end of the war.

The destruction of Halifax, Nova Scotia, on 6 December 1917 had some features in common with a rocket attack without warning. Two ships, the *Imo*, a Belgian relief ship, and the *Mont Blanc*, a French munitions ship, collided at 9:06 in the morning. (Although the captain of the French ship was found responsible for the accident, it seems that both masters were at fault.) The *Mont Blanc* carried 2,300 tons of picric acid, 200 tons of TNT, 35 tons of benzole and 10 tons of cotton wool. The power of the explosion set church bells ringing 60 miles away; a ship's anchor weighing half a ton was carried in the air and fell two miles from Halifax. Streets imploded, rail lines were bent, the superstructures of ships were torn apart; a 13-foot wave tore ships from their moorings and flooded streets; the aftershocks were felt by ships a thousand miles from the Canadian coast. People in Halifax were starting the day: 1,963 were killed; nine thousand were wounded; 199 lost their sight permanently (greater casualties than any single air raid against a British city in the Second World War). There were 25,000 made homeless, at least temporarily; of these, six thousand could not rebuild or repair their homes. A book on the social and economic effects of the explosion which appeared soon thereafter (Prince, 1920) told the story of how repairs and recovery began almost at once: telegraph service resumed, at least partially, after an hour of interruption, and was fully restored in a week; banks reopened the next day.[2] Although the explosion gave rise to rumors of a German invasion, there was scarcely any panic in a population that was unprepared for such an event. Relief efforts were mobilized across Canada and from New England almost at once. The rebuilding of Halifax included changes to improve the city which would have been difficult to introduce under normal circumstances.

It is not by chance that so many major attacks on cities in World War Two were on ports: London, Liverpool, Glasgow, Newcastle, Southampton; Rotterdam, Lorient, Brest, St Nazaire; Hamburg, Bremen, and the Rhine canal ports; Tokyo, Yokohama, Kobe, Nagoya, and yes, Hiroshima, Nagasaki. Clearly, urban residents – German, French, Japanese, British, Dutch, Italian, Austrian, Spanish – were not as disoriented or emotionally upset during air raids as had been expected. They coped because they were resourceful and adaptive in stressful situations. Although, in peacetime, city folk relied on technologically sophisticated networks, this dependence had not weakened the relation between individual and community. Confounding predictions, infrastructure facilities were quickly repaired or replaced: prewar strategists had overlooked the extent to which substitutes for elements of infrastructure could be found, or an existing resource base stretched. Incomprehensible, immense levels of physical destruction simply did not lead to proportional levels of social and economic disorganization. After the war most air strategists rationalized the limited effect of air raids on the German economy by citing imperfect target selection and technical problems with Allied air forces, implying that the practice of bombing cities could be perfected. The rhetoric of strategic bombing changed 180 degrees early in the era of the atomic bomb when predictions of the consequences of attacks against cities functioned as a form of dissuasion, the assumption being that one side would not attack another's cities for fear that its cities, too, would be destroyed.

An essential ambiguity remains about whether cities are vulnerable to destruction and what the consequences of a catastrophe might be: fear of destruction and of a breakdown in law and order is checked by hope that cities can tolerate disorganization and recover.

Resiliency: making reconstruction normal

Resilience is the current catch-all phrase, meaning that cities and indeed social and economic systems should have the capacity to cope with and recover from a major disaster, should one occur. The Rockefeller Foundation has launched the "100 Resilient Cities" initiative. On the one hand, macro-economists cite evidence based on past experience that national economies can absorb the shock of most disasters. On the other, experts in geo-science, insurance, and engineering are telling us that the cost of doing nothing about global climate change will be devastating. When better prevention would involve major expenditures over many years and politically difficult decisions about what should be built where, with no guarantee that in the end these measures will have been taken far enough in advance, indeed, with no guarantee that these measures will prove to be sufficient, resilience is a cautious, middle way forward, unobjectionable on its own terms. Resilience as a policy is realistic: it assumes that disasters will occur, that, even with a lot of good will, good planning, and good financing, measures to reduce the loss of life and property will be incomplete, and that measures to enhance resilience will increase the stock of public goods and build social capital.

Resilience is not however a cheap alternative to preparedness, but a costly complement. If survival is the most likely outcome, a resilience strategy must assume that the level of destruction will require substantial rebuilding. There is invariably an impulse to rebuild the city as an affirmation of life over death, not only as an expression of continuity in the face of tragedy, but out of a desire to make the rebuilt city better than the city as it had been, to redeem, as it were, something good out of tragedy. This is understandable, rooted not only in a deep attachment to a place (it is often the loss of objects of greater sentimental than material value that people feel most keenly when salvaging what they can from a flood, storm, or earthquake), but also in a belief, symbolized by Jerusalem, that a place is a way-station on a spiritual journey. It need not be a religious journey; the destination may take a secular form. What matters is the hope to realize something closer to perfection in this world. We do not want to suffer gratuitously.

It is false and misleading to separate relief and reconstruction into sequences, the one beginning when the other ends. Rebuilding begins with the disaster itself and how relief efforts are mobilized, and is affected by decisions taken then about what is further destroyed or saved, before all the damage has been assessed. All too often, however, manuals to be used in the event of a disaster separate immediate relief efforts from reconstruction, as if these can be spread out on a time-line, sequentially. In order to keep things administratively clear, relief and reconstruction are often assigned to different authorities, using different legal and monetary resources. This looks plausible on paper but always breaks down in reality. Laws, regulations, and insurance requirements may stipulate that property destroyed must be rebuilt in the same place and to the same value, thus adding to the financial and legal burden on the state if changes in street patterns or significant changes in land use and occupancy are to be introduced. Measures to reduce moral hazard have unintended, but often negative, consequences; bold plans get diluted as resources run out and as the pressure to get people out of temporary housing intensifies.

Nothing looks worse in the press than a figure which shows how many people are still living in tents or shelters a year or more after a natural disaster. The longer the reconstruction process, the greater the chances that firms will relocate to other places, that people will move away in search of work and housing. Such pressures lead to shortcuts which compromise the quality of reconstruction. We know the consequences of inaction before a catastrophe when combined with incompetence managing relief when a catastrophe occurs: people take their lives into their own hands, relocating, often permanently, seeking areas of greater security. Three examples: the center of Mexico City after 1985; Istanbul after the 1999 earthquakes in Izmit region; New Orleans and Katrina in 2005. In each case, the lack of trustworthy and reliable information about where the vulnerable areas of the city really are encouraged those who could afford to do so to relocate in areas that had not been destroyed, but without accurate knowledge of their underlying vulnerability.

A key lesson is the need for ongoing strategic assessments of a city's strengths and weaknesses well in advance of a disaster, and without regard for the probability that one will occur. In Kobe, some five-thousand people died, most instantly, when buildings collapsed in the Great Hanshin-Awaji Earthquake of a magnitude of 7.3 on the Richter scale in 1995. Most were elderly, living in older properties which did not meet current earthquake standards; many lived alone, or in areas predominantly populated by other elderly people. (Even a year later, a hundred thousand people were still living in temporary housing.) The city's only elevated expressway collapsed, showing how dependent Kobe was on infrastructure which lacked redundancy. Yet Kobe succeeded, where so many cities fail, in capitalizing on the desire to make the rebuilt city safer and better: older people were rehoused in districts characterized by a higher degree of multi-generational settlement, integrating the elderly with younger families; districts of up to ten thousand people were designed to be self-sustaining in the case of a future disaster. Fortuitously, just before the before the earthquake which brought to light some of the city's shortcomings in infrastructure, the city had carried out an assessment of its needs. Thus, the re-planning of Kobe's highways to provide more routes and greater capacity, and the creation and reorganization of its parks which can also serve as places of refuge, helped the city to realize strategic objectives that had already been identified before the 1995 earthquake.

The tasks of managing urban areas to reduce exposure to property damage or loss of life in the event of a catastrophe and to promote post-disaster recovery cannot be so easily separated from the basic problems of routine urban management, which are already compromised by overlapping jurisdictions which make a nonsense of functional areas, by inadequate or obsolete databases and maps, by problems of communicating with a public which itself is anything but homogeneous, by considerations of political consequences of taking any particular decision or any decision at all, and by a lack of coherence among different public authorities with different policy objectives. Put positively, the physical factors that promote resilience – polycentric urban systems, redundancy and spare capacity in infrastructure networks – need to be matched by social and organizational factors which contribute to the self-organizing capacity of society and leadership in government. Delays in rebuilding Kobe were minimized, partly because government at all levels worked together in a special taskforce under the responsibility of the prime minister, checking the outbreak of bureaucratic squabbles and jurisdictional disputes that otherwise would have compromised the reconstruction effort. In each district being redeveloped, an urban development council was formed – ninety-seven in all – drawing on dozens of experts who served as consultants at the community level (OECD, 2004).[3]

Regulations (the subject of Chapter 7) are essential tools in the armory of disaster protection. Like a wall, regulation erects barriers between good and bad behavior: within the precinct where the rules prevail, safety is, if not assured, at least more likely. The rules may be conventional and implicit, prevailing through community norms and vernacular standards of housing construction, for example, or explicitly elaborated in formal codes, enforced by law and decree. From this perspective, regulations designed to reduce risks become part of the everyday way of doing things, or, in other words, normalcy. The whole regulatory approach is based on assigning responsibility to different actors, meaning that it should also be possible to attribute mistakes and faults to individuals or to firms. After a disaster, however, the effort to assign liability can take years, may lead to financial settlements which leave the question of fault ambiguous at best, and lead to actions in anticipation of a future disaster which would only insulate an individual or firm from future liability for damages. Regulations cannot prevent a flood or earthquake or violent storm, but they contribute to the perception of government as omniscient and far-sighted. At the same time, regulations enable government to claim that, should a disaster occur, it had taken precautionary measures on the basis of the best available knowledge.

Adaptation starts from a different logic than regulation; it boosts a society's capacity for self-reliance, initiative, and co-operation, and assumes that the response of government cannot be programed in advance and will likely require considerable improvisation. Resilience calls for continued investment in and improvements to public health, education, infrastructure, and good governance – precisely those public goods that enable people to take more responsibility for themselves and more initiative to help one another. The disaster – its timing and amplitude – cannot be predicted; what can be forecast is that government plans will fall short of what is required. Geographer Kenneth Hewitt points out that the "key to vulnerability is found in *powerlessness*, and relative security in its opposite" (Hewitt, 1997: 151). By that definition, a passive society, waiting for government to "do something."

is both impotent and vulnerable. Regulation responds to the political and public imperative to reduce both risk and uncertainty. Both regulation and resilience are necessary, but they are fundamentally different. Resilience accepts a greater degree of risk and of uncertainty than regulation, or as Reghezza-Zitt wrote, "disorganization, given the current state of advanced techniques, is inevitable" (Reghezza-Zitt, 2012: 271). Fortunately, crises are not as chaotic as they appear; it is just that most people, who understandably have little experience of them, do not know that catastrophes, like normalcy, reveal an underlying structure and pattern. Before civil disasters attracted widespread interest among social scientists, forty years ago, Michael Barkun explored the differences between homeostatic, metastatic and hyperstatic disasters, concluding that "the declining ability to learn from past disasters militates against more rational responses to future catastrophes" (Barkun, 1977: 230). Maybe greater efforts are being made today to learn, but the good intentions to apply the lessons of experience dissipate quickly.

The case for resilience is political and cultural
An OECD report on "Future global shocks" highlighted the interconnectedness of the global economy. Just since 2009, the world has coped – badly – with a global financial crisis, the first declared pandemic in two generations (H1N1), the BP oil spill in the Gulf of Mexico, the closure of European air space due to a volcanic cloud, and the Tohuku earthquakes and tsunami in Japan. Potential global shocks include critical infrastructure disruption, financial crises, and social unrest (OECD, 2011: 27). Defining a disaster as "a rapid onset event with severely disruptive consequences covering at least two continents," the OECD notes that, although most disasters do not have such effects, some national disasters could be precursors to global shocks (OECD, 2011: 12). In an earlier age, people would have interpreted this convergence of different, separate damaging events coming at the same time as signs of divine wrath. Perhaps that reaction would, like the prophecy of Jonah, lead people to return to righteousness, which in this case would mean stronger compliance with rule of law, a higher sense of duty, and a deeper respect for what people owe to each other, including in social, economic and environmental policies. But first people have to want to listen and learn.

Jonah, to continue with that story, had to preach repentance to the people of Nineveh who were not Jews. The story does not indicate whether there were any particular problems of understanding due to language; perhaps they used an interpreter; perhaps Jonah and the people of Nineveh shared a second language. The message somehow got through because there was a willingness to listen to a stranger. Take this literally or symbolically. The fire on the *Normandie* in New York in 1942 which started when a welder's spark set fire to a stack of life preservers during the conversion of that luxury liner into a troop ship renamed the *Lafayette* could have been controlled had the Americans staffing the safety control panel on board understood the French in which the panel was written, and had the police authorities allowed Vladimir Yourkevitch, the ship's architect who was in New York, to gain access to the ship instead of keeping him off the pier because he was an alien (having emigrated from Russia and then from France). Communication – among actors, between the government and the private sector, between governments, and between governments and the public – remains a major challenge.

Nineveh is again in peril in contemporary Iraq, caught in the swirling ethnic violence that borders cannot contain. Other cities, at peace, nonetheless face a future shaped by exposure to risk. The people who lived in cities destroyed in World War Two were more resourceful and self-reliant than the experts of the time had thought possible. The implications of Robert Putnam's study of social capital in the United States (Putnam, 2002) are sobering: the interwar years and the immediate post-1945 decade marked the high-water point, after which the factors promoting the formation and use of social capital appear to have declined. What if people in and out of government reach the same conclusion as strategic bombing advocates nearly a century ago, that urban societies are unable to look after themselves, that the very factors that make cities attractive to people looking for opportunity also compromise the cohesion and co-operation so necessary to resilience?

The social agenda belongs at the core of a strategy for resilience. Society, already fragmenting into multiple social, economic, and ethnic categories, could disaggregate into groups trying to survive on their own or by taking advantage of others. This is why the debate about income disparities and the shrinking middle class is so relevant. It is sobering to realize that, in 1967, sociologist Daniel Bell forecast that "the society of the year 2000 … will be more fragile, more susceptible to hostilities and to polarization along many different lines" (Bell, 1967: 646). And so it has turned out. Writing as editor of the report of the American Academy of Arts and Sciences Commission on the Year 2000, Bell affirmed that looking to the future is rational, the basis for choice in a democracy. But the trends Bell anticipated have also contributed to the famous gridlock in many democracies, polarized around the extremes. The equivalent of 2000 in 1967 is 2047 in 2014; is it really that far into the future?

Resilience as a strategy may help reduce the level of fear when the level of risk can never be reduced to zero. Whether it will rebuild trust in government is another story.

Notes

1 The study enumerated a selection of regional and global databases on hazards (table 5, pp. 29–30), exposures (table 7. p. 35), and risk modeling initiatives and consequences (table 8, p. 38).
2 See also Evelyn M. Richardson, "The Halifax explosion, 1917," *Nova Scotia Historical Quarterly*, 7 (1977): 305–30; and Graham Meton (ed.), *The Halifax Explosion* (Toronto: McGraw-Hill-Ryerson, 1978).
3 This includes a summary of lessons by Reza Lahidji (9–24), chapters on economic recovery (27–32) and budgetary impact (33–6) by Patrick Lenain, and on housing and reconstruction by myself (63–70). A case study by Vedat Akigiray, Gulay Barbarasoglu and Mustafa Erdik on the 1999 Marmara earthquakes concludes the report (77–92).

References

Barkun, Michael (1977), "Disaster in history," *Mass Emergencies*, 2: 219–31.
Bell, Daniel (1967), "The year 2000 – the trajectory of an idea," *Daedalus*, 96:3, pp. 639–51 "Toward the year 2000: work in progress," *Proceedings of the American Academy of Arts and Sciences*.
The Economist (2012), "Briefing: natural disasters; counting the cost of calamities," 14 January.
Financial Times (2012), "Thai insurance sector still reeling from aftermath of floods," 6 March.
Financial Times (2014), "Cities at risk, the best ... and the worst," 8 April.
Hallegate, Stephane, Colin Green, Robert J. Nicholls and Jan Corfee-Morlot (2013), "Future flood losses in major coastal cities," 18 August, *Nature Climate Change*, pp. 802–6. DOI:10.1038/nclimate1979.
Hewitt, Kenneth (1997), *Regions of Risk: A Geographical Introduction to Disasters* (Harlow: Longman).
ICLEI (2011), *Financing the Resilient City, a Demand Driven Approach to Development, Disaster Risk Reduction and Climate Adaptation – an ICLEI White Paper*, ICLEI Global Report (Bonn: ICLEI).
Journal of Risk Research (2003), volume 6, special issue devoted to "riskworld."
Konvitz, Josef (1990), "Why cities don't die," *American Heritage of Invention and Technology*, 5:3 (Winter): 59–63; an abridged version of "Représentations urbaines et bombardements stratégiques, 1914–1945," *Annales Économies, Sociétés, Civilizations*, 44 (July–August 1989): 823–47. This research was supported by a Fellowship at the Wilson Center for Scholars in 1987.
Konvitz, Josef W. (1992a), "Bombs, cities and submarines; allied bombing

of the French ports, 1942–1943," *International History Review*, 14:1 (February): 23–44.

Konvitz, Josef W. (1992b), "Missing the boat: port city planning in Glasgow during World War II," *Urban Studies*, 29: 8: 1293–304.

National Resources Committee (1937), "Our cities: their role in the national economy", Report of the Urbanism Committee (Washington DC: US Government Printing Office, June).

Nicholls, R. J., S. Hanson, C. Herweijer, N. Patmore, J. Corfee-Morlot, J. Chateau and R. Muir-Wood (2008), "Ranking port cities with high exposure and vulnerability to climate extremes: exposure estimates," OECD Environment Working Papers no 1, OECD. The report can be accessed from www.oecd/org/env/workingpapers.

Nye, David E. (2010), *When the Lights Went Out: A History of Blackouts in America* (Cambridge, MA: MIT Press).

OECD (2004), *Large-scale Disasters: Lessons Learned* (Paris: OECD). ISBN: 2-64-02018-7.

OECD (2011), *Future Global Shocks: Improving Risk Governance* (Paris: OECD), OECD Reviews of Risk Management Policies. DOI: 10/1787/9789264114586-en.

OECD (2012), *Disaster Risk Assessment and Risk Financing: A G20/OECD Methodological Framework* (Paris: OECD), http://preventionweb.net/go/29524.

OECD (2014), *Etude de l'OCDE sur la gestion des risques d'inondation: La Seine en Ile-de France* (Paris: OECD). DOI: 10.1.1787/9789264207929-fr. Also available as *OECD Reviews of Risk Management: Seine Basin, Ile de France, Resilience to Major Floods* (Paris: OECD).

Prince, Samuel H. (1920) *Catastrophe and Social Change, Based upon a Sociological Study of the Halifax Disaster* (New York: Columbia University Studies in History, Economics and Public Law).

Putnam, Robert (2002), *Bowling Alone: The Collapse and Revival of American Community* (New York: Simon and Schuster).

Reghezza-Zitt, Magali (2012), *Paris coule-t-il?* (Paris: Fayard).

Swiss Re (2000), "Catastrophes naturelles et techniques en 1999," *Sigma*, 2.

Further reading

There is a vast literature on the bombing of cities in world war. Richard Overy, *The Bombing War: Europe 1939–1945* (London: Allen Lane, 2013) puts the contribution of bombing to the outcome in a wider context as an enabler. See also Conrad C. Crane, *Bombs, Cities, and Civilians: American Airpower Strategy in World War II*, Modern War Studies (Lawrence: University Press of Kansas, 1993); and Tami Davis Biddle, *Rhetoric and Reality in Air Warfare: The Evolution of British and American Ideas about Strategic Bombing, 1914–1945*, Princeton Studies in International History and Politics (Princeton: Princeton University Press, 2002). For a broader view of the question whether the physical destruction of a city also destroys its economic and social life, see Kenneth Hewitt, "Place annihilation: area bombing and the fate of urban places," *Annals of the Association of American Geographers*, 73:2 (1983): 257–84.

An introduction to contemporary urban warfare and security issues is Stephen Graham (ed.), *Cities, War and Terrorism: Towards an Urban Geopolitics*, (Oxford: Blackwell, 2004). Grounded in a retrospective look at World War Two and the Cold War, this volume covers Bosnia, Baghdad and Afghanistan, London and New York, with penetrating comments on the language and methodology of urban control and destruction. G. J. Ashworth wrote a historical introduction to the topic of *War and the City* (London: Routledge, 1991), with chapters on urban insurgency and riots, and on the physical artefacts of defense as historical heritage.

More books are appearing on how professional communities define urban risk problems and propose to treat them: Jennifer S. Light, *From Warfare to Welfare: Defense Intellectuals and Urban Problems in Cold War America* (Baltimore: Johns Hopkins University Press, 2004); and Scott Gabriel Knowles, *The Disaster Experts: Mastering Risk in Modern America* (Philadelphia: University of Pennsylvania Press, 2011). Kevin Rozario looks at the impact on culture in *The Culture of Calamity: Disaster and the Making of Modern America* (Chicago: University of Chicago Press, 2007). With the exception of Hewitt, this survey of the literature shows how difficult it has been to integrate non-military threats with state security issues. See also: Ari Kelman, *A River and Its City: The Nature of Landscape in New Orleans* (Berkeley and Los Angeles: University of California Press, 2003); Myron Echenberg, *Plague Ports: The Global Urban Impact of Bubonic Plague, 1894–1901* (New York: New York University Press, 2007); Lawrence J. Vale and Thomas J. Campanella, *The Resilient City: How Modern Cities Recover from Disaster* (Oxford: Oxford University Press, 2004).

7

Regulatory governance, risk, and the new security economies

Regulatory reform and risk management

When asked to do something, anything, the first instinct of an elected official or policy-maker under pressure is often to propose a new rule or regulation. Whenever people want to attack bureaucracy, they cite incomprehensible, stupid, or ineffective regulations, the sheer cost of compliance, red tape, regulatory complexity – the lot. Faced with more risks, responding to more accidents and crises, and concerned not to be found negligent in the future, governments have adopted more regulations to enhance security – whatever the threat, ideological, financial, industrial, or environmental. Chapter 6 highlighted a range of catastrophic risks, domestic, cross-border and global, which could put cities at the center of policies for energy, the environment, research, infrastructure investment, housing, education, even health for a generation. Other chapters have raised issues about regulation in relation to these sectors. Is more regulation indeed the way forward? How well suited is regulatory policy to meet the demands of society for preventive measures against catastrophes, and especially cross-border risks? Not well enough.

One reason why officials often regulate with a law or rule as the first or preferred option is because a regulation is supposed to be a clear, formal statement by government of what citizens or firms are allowed to do – or prohibited from doing. This formality is also a public good, a contribution to the rule of law which includes the restraint on government from arbitrary action. Problems start because there is no clean slate: all governments already have a stock of regulations, some of which are obsolete, some ineffective or inefficient, many overly complex; some countries have inherited regulations from past regimes (Israel, for example, from the Ottoman Empire and British Mandate). To the stock of existing regulations, there is a flow of new ones annually; regulations may also be required to comply with an international treaty or agreement. Governments make regulations more complicated by combining several policy objectives when regulating, from gender equity and support for small and medium enterprises, to environmental impacts and competition effects. (The broader meaning of regulation as a paradigm for economic governance to keep it functioning at its best, and to avoid breakdowns, is the subject of Part III.)

Regulatory inflation is what the public rails about the most, little understanding what its root causes are. When governments provided many services directly, fewer regulations were necessary. Paradoxically, deregulation and privatization in the 1990s actually generated a need for more regulation. In addition the complexity of modern economies and societies and the continual addition of new goods and services generate the demand for new regulations. Good regulation can become bad over time. It is however rarely possible to abolish all regulations and start from scratch. Even in countries where a wholesale culling (scrap-and-build) of the regulatory stock has been undertaken, where generalized reviews of sectors have been carried out, where a sunset clause has kicked in (cancelling a regulation after a fixed number of years unless a formal step is taken justifying its retention) or a guillotine has been applied (abolishing regulations unless they can be justified), the size of the stock of regulations soon grows again. Whatever method is applied, the results often fall short of expectations: many key sectors or issues are exempted from review, the regulations that are abolished were not being enforced anyway, reform fatigue sets in: people do not see any change.

Progress is being made to improve regulatory quality, although citizens and businesses often do not appreciate the results. In 1995, and ahead of most member countries, the OECD launched a program on regulatory reform. The 1995 OECD Checklist of Regulatory Decision-Making (appended to the Recommendation of the Council of the OECD on Improving the Quality of Government Regulation) became part of the *acquis* or formal body of agreements applicable in every OECD country. The Checklist puts the burden on government to ask whether a regulation is necessary: officials need to define the problem, and then assess whether government action is justified based on the likely costs and benefits of government action, including a realistic assessment of its effectiveness. Too often, however, alternatives to regulation are not given serious consideration.

Most OECD countries adopted regulatory quality standards and policies only since the mid-1990s. The 2005 Guiding Principles of Regulatory Quality and Performance and the 2005 APEC–OECD Integrated Checklist of Regulatory Reform rest on a unique series of country reviews, beginning with the United States in 1999: by 2012, this series had covered all but two member countries (Iceland and

New Zealand) at least once, and in some cases as many as three times. Recommendations also rest on thematic studies of impact analysis, administrative simplification, risk and regulation, and other issues, as well as stocktaking exercises that summarize progress achieved, and indicators of regulatory processes and of product market regulation (OECD 2002, 2011a and b).[1]

Notwithstanding cultural and constitutional differences among countries, there are certain common threads that give the fabric of regulatory policy its strength. Regulatory policy provides a single, comprehensive point of reference for the entire administration about how regulations should be drafted, enforced, and revised through evidence-based decision-making that is open to consultation and public scrutiny. Regulations likely to have the most significant impacts benefit from the most intense assessment. The time needed to carry out a sound process to assure regulatory quality should add only a few weeks to a decision-making process. Regulatory impact assessment is now standard in OECD countries; most have created a dedicated body with responsibility for promoting regulatory policy and monitoring on regulatory reform. A regulatory policy unit however has only so much leverage over line ministries. Regulatory reform involves a change in administrative culture: officials pursuing a sectoral policy agenda may be reluctant to have their work checked, and possibly blocked, by regulatory experts who may be attached to a more powerful ministry such as Economy, Finance, or Justice, or to a regulatory oversight body attached to the Presidency or Prime Ministry. Comprehensive *ex-ante* analysis of impacts, including on specific groups (small and medium-sized enterprises, the elderly, women) or factors such as job creation, investment, and competition – important as they are – should be complemented by *ex-post* studies which show the effects over time, which may turn out to be quite different. Almost all OECD countries carry out *ex-ante* analyses; comparatively few undertake *ex–post* evaluations.

The first driver for reform has often been a political leader who wants to reduce the influence of the state in the economy, sometimes in response to economic shocks leading to structural reforms and a reduction in the cost of regulatory burdens. Regulatory reform can lift the rate of growth even in countries where regulatory barriers and costs are already relatively low by enhancing competition, removing barriers to trade, facilitating innovation and its diffusion, and removing unnecessary burdens and procedures. Knowledge about what to reform is grounded in broad studies of economic performance, and comparative bench markings of the level of regulation in similar sectors in different countries (such as the OECD's product market regulation index and annual *Going for Growth* reports). If regulatory reform has such impressive and far-reaching benefits, why is it often so difficult to launch and sustain a regulatory quality program? Those who stand to lose in the short term are usually the most vocal and best organized, whereas those who stand to benefit, including the public at large, are usually less aware of what is at stake. Behind the successes and failures, there are stories of administrative battles, pressure on government from civil society and business interests often pulling in opposite directions, parliamentary debates, independent audits and reports – the whole machinery of politics.

If regulatory quality tools and policies are so good, why are so many regulations still being introduced that are below the mark? Perhaps officials carried out a regulatory impact analysis, but perfunctorily, without training or access to a database. Perhaps they considered the administrative burden (inspections, reporting) that would be required by the new regulation, but without making best use of burden-reduction techniques or of electronic tools (e-government). A list of shortcomings published by the OECD in 2002 highlighted important gaps in the coverage of regulatory policy, and in particular the financial sector and sub-national regulation; fragmented responsibility to support the policy, making resistance easier; and insufficient focus on monitoring, evaluation, and reporting progress due in part to a lack of resources. Some of these are more easily corrected than others. There will always be problems with statistical and analytical methods; few countries use impact analysis consistently for lower-level or subordinate regulations; compliance and enforcement practices are uneven. When poor-quality regulations are adopted, consumers and businesses pays the price, not the elected official or public servant. There is a steep learning curve, and it is almost impossible to tackle all the deficits on the better regulation agenda simultaneously.

In response to the crisis of 2008 and to the growing body of evidence about good practices and their limits, OECD countries adopted an updated set of Principles for Regulatory Policy and Governance in 2012. The operative term "governance" refers to the entire dynamic and continuous policy cycle, to strengthen the functions of regulatory institutions and their ability to work together for the public interest. The challenge therefore is co-ordination of regulatory actions, "from the design and development of regulations, to their implementation and enforcement, closing the loop with monitoring and evaluation which informs the development of new regulations and the adjustment of existing regulations" (OECD 2011a: 74).

The framework for regulatory reform took shape in the 1990s when risk was not a priority concern; it figured prominently in the 2012 Principles. In place of a single sentence on risk and regulation in the 2005 OECD Guiding Principles, the OECD's 2012 Principles included a separate section on this issue. Adopting an evidence-based approach, the recommendation states that governments should "evaluate the likely effectiveness of risk strategies against their capacity to identify and inform regulatory actions that will help to avoid or mitigate catastrophic or systemic risks and minimize unintended consequences and 'risk-risk' tradeoffs." (Risk–risk tradeoffs can occur when efforts to reduce risks in one sphere actually increase risks in another, as when efforts to control floods affect power plants.) Governments should "ensure that risk systems incorporate lessons from past events, including failures and close calls" (OECD, 2012: 279). There is much progress still to be made. When the political will to regulate is strong, will due consideration be given to regulatory alternatives, or to performance-based regulations? One of the key features of consultation should be the obligation for governments to report back to the public, specifically responding to questions and criticisms: is it plausible that issues related to security risks will receive the same treatment in this regard as those related to occupational health and safety, for example? Without a proper impact assessment *ex ante*, how can an *ex-post* evaluation be carried out?

This recommendation was consistent with the OECD's broader overview of risk and regulation which underscored that "the key regulatory management challenge for governments seeking to improve the governance of risk is to improve the evidentiary basis on which regulatory decisions are made and regulatory programs are delivered" (OECD, 2010: 32). Important factors for success are:

- systems to deliver sound science for the estimation of risk and to set regulatory priorities on an examination of significant risks
- risk assessment applied across the regulatory cycle, from data collection to the selection of regulatory instruments, the scheduling of inspection, and the allocation of resources for prosecution
- creative and flexible regulatory approaches that may achieve better outcomes than traditional, command-and-control ones, and design of policy institutions for risk-taking that encourage innovation, including within the public sector
- managing risk-risk tradeoffs, including the interconnected nature of government activities and policies, and trade and competition impacts
- communication.

This describes a more or less ideal configuration, put in perspective by the OECD when affirming that "The failure in financial regulation was an example of deficiencies in regulatory frameworks for the governance of risk" (OECD, 2011a: 92). The list of issues needing urgent attention in addition to transparency includes: guidelines to help risk assessors deal with issues in similar and consistent ways; measures to ensure that regulators give risk management the priority it deserves; techniques to build stakeholder participation and support public deliberation, and understanding of complex scientific and economic assessments in the process; and research that illuminates the cultural and institutional differences across countries that account for greater or lesser sensitivity to specific risks. Political support at the highest level is necessary if technical progress is to be made. Complacency, that current systems are working well enough, will only increase the chances that in the future there will be regulatory failures. As Julia Black observed in a comparative study of how different regulatory agencies work, "the key element of risk-based frameworks for allocating resources is that the starting point is risks not rules. Risk-based frameworks require regulators to begin by identifying the risks that it is seeking to mange, not the rules it has to enforce" (Black, 2011: 190).

Two major institutional issues, international regulatory co-operation and multi-level regulatory coherence, are especially relevant to the regulatory risk agenda. International co-operation is vital in relation to systemic risks which by definition are cross–border, and to other risks which originate in one country but can have significant impacts on another. The multi-level dimension is especially important because most economic and environmental regulations are applied and enforced at the sub-national, local level where capacity is most uneven, sometimes better than in central government, but usually less so. (Chapter 10 explores these issues further.) As the European reaction to the problems of the Eurozone demonstrates, constitutional considerations weigh heavily when designing and implementing measures that reduce risks. Institutional frameworks and legal traditions vary from one jurisdiction to another, but the challenge remains, to arrive at roughly similar outcomes using different means, taking account of the fact that compliance at the sub-national level is critical. Conflicts over who does what, between existing and proposed regulations, and about whether government has acted within the rules or arbitrarily are likely to go to the courts, to be resolved, perhaps after a lapse of years and at some cost, on the basis of jurisprudential or constitutional logics which are often a proxy for arguments over substance. A concerted effort to promote constitutional revisions to strengthen international regulatory co-operation and multi-level coherence is likely to incur immediate political resistance and arouse national and local sentiments, not only in Europe but in any other jurisdiction – the United States or Mexico come to mind – where domestic federal systems have functioned simultaneously with a strong, legal barrier against importing laws or legal standards from other jurisdictions or from international organizations. As things stand, it is difficult to see how a legalistic approach, to define who has responsibility to identify and assess risks especially those which cut across sectors and levels of government, will be sufficient: duplication, confusion, ambiguity – all add up to a lack of accountability, transparency and legal certainty.

The greater the perceived threat, when the gains of co-operation and preparedness could be huge, the greater the reluctance of states to share sovereignty or agree on joint and parallel measures. This is not quite the paradox it seems. After all much of the effort may be wasted, or may benefit only some of the jurisdictions whereas all have to make a sacrifice (or investment). Brummer provides a comprehensive overview of the impediments to better international regulation, including the challenge of extra-territoriality when capital and market actors are dispersed globally, the legitimacy of rule-making bodies, and the inherent difficulty in trying to write rules to be applied in different contexts. A legal scholar, Brummer concluded that an international regulatory framework which has adopted the wrong set of rules could put more countries at risk than a hodge-podge of well-developed and inadequate national systems (Brummer, 2012: 263). The time needed for routine procedures to screen and adopt regulations at the national level on international issues is compounded by the complexity of carrying out such procedures in more than one country at once, raising the possibility that the outcomes will be sufficiently different as to make negotiation necessary. Put another way, agreements which are close to current practice are unlikely to achieve results qualitatively different from what might happen in the absence of an agreement. For political reasons, it is easier to generate international agreements and to set up international regulatory bodies when the subjects are highly technical, easily checked by laboratories or other objective measures of investigation, and when the field itself is young, giving all countries an interest to co-operate in a new system from the beginning. Whether a subject is defined as technical, making it more suitable for treatment through international regulatory co-operation and even through delegated regulatory governance with private rule-making bodies and private-sector enforcement, or political, making it unlikely that technical matters will be resolved through agreement and negotiation, is itself a matter decided at the political level.

The appetite for risk and the capacity to handle it vary enormously within and between countries. This asymmetry generates its own problems, as when some countries push for agenda-setting, problem-solving agreements and others evade them. Incremental changes make sense when people are used to coping with and adjusting to uncertainty, a tense situation which "you can get used to." It may be pragmatic to avoid a major settlement which involves legally binding agreements when progress can be made at a more technical level that gradually creates a new status quo. But the absence of such a settlement adds an unwelcome degree of uncertainty, itself a risk factor for people who believe that legal agreements produce not only legal certainty but also a resolution of underlying conflicts.

Can the rate of progress be accelerated? Looking forward, this seems unlikely. Comparative studies of how different countries cope with similar problems show that, just as the sensitivity to risk varies, so does the selection of policy approaches. Focusing on "diversity in precautionary particularity," Jonathan Wiener observed that "Viewed across the array of risks, both the United States and Europe are precautionary about many risks (and both resist precaution regarding other risks), but they repeatedly differ as to which risks to worry about and regulate most or earliest" (Wiener, 2003: 262; see also OECD, 2010). Wiener detected a "dynamic process of legal hybridization, with interactive exchange of legal concepts occurring continuously. These patterns indicate a process of mutual legal borrowing," a positive example of how an international order can emerge out of a non-linear process, one that is not structured to reach a certain goal.

The OECD, which published a book on international regulatory co-operation as early as 1994, launched a fresh study in 2011 which highlighted the mis-match between progress at the technical and resistance at the political level (OECD, 2013). International regulatory co-operation is still in its early adolescence. And like many adolescents, it is struggling to shape its identity. Modes of co-operation have proliferated in parallel to the growth of the global economy, from traditional treaty-based models to trans-governmental networks which government hardly monitors. Regulatory flexibility and informal consultation may matter more in some fields which are less subject to law enforcement and criminal penalties; when the grounds for co-operation are strongest, compliance may pose fewer problems. There are examples of treaties which are binding in international law but are difficult to enforce: one study of trans-boundary water management found that enforcement was weak because agreements covered only certain issues, because governments fail to create enforcement mechanisms, or because there are free-rider problems (as when some of the countries that share a waterway are not party to the agreement). Because regulatory powers across levels of government and government agencies are often the result of constitutional and historical factors, responsibility for international regulatory co-operation is not clearly allocated; and without an explicit policy, there is no incentive to keep a database, establish monitoring, or even develop clear definitions. Analysis in this field is compromised by the lack of a common language or analytical framework. When institutions are broadly similar and the volume of trade is high, as is the case between the United States and Mexico, and between Canada and the United States, trans-border regulatory councils can identify regulatory differences which can be realigned to improve investment and trade. Examples include addressing third-country import risks, partnering on standards development, conformity testing, and enforcement tools, aligning risk analysis and approval processes, and even mutual reliance or recognition of testing and inspection. But there is a long way to go to identify specific problems or fields where international regulatory co-operation will be more efficient and effective.

Since 9/11 (with a glance back to the 1990s), governments have dramatically extended their extra-territorial regulatory power and their capacity to monitor and analyse information in response to terrorism. Cross-border regulation for cross-border risks is being generated unilaterally, through domestic legislation imposed on firms and individuals wherever they are based. Extra-territorial regulatory reach is *the* new development in the regulatory field; in different ways the European Union and the United States are both becoming global regulators by imposing standards on foreign firms and jurisdictions if they wish to sell their products to or use services in the EU or the US. There is little international co-operation in this when power is not shared.

Risk regulators would be the first to say that systems set up to control for domestic risks in, say, water quality or food supply or medicines, and even for some similar cross-border risks linked to global trade (product safety, counterfeiting, and phyto-sanitary risks, for example), were never designed to address other long-term risks to cities due to deeper social and economic changes, to exposure to natural or human-made disasters, emerging risks related to changes in science and technology, and to cross-border risks including terrorism, ecological disasters, epidemics, and cyber-attacks.

To address this agenda of global risks, governments need to assess the current set of regulations (the regulatory stock) and consider how to change from one type of regulatory mode to another (whether to use co-regulation, performance-based regulation, command-and-control regulation, or simply not regulate at all), when to relax or revise regulations to promote innovation, how much discretion to allow officials, what roles for different agencies and levels of government, how to evaluate compliance and enforcement, and how to cope with mistakes, because these there will be. Regulatory reform to cope with major social, economic, and environmental changes which may be necessary to address global warming or systemic risk in the financial sector will call significant bodies of regulation into question and for which modest, incremental revisions – adding new regulations here, deleting obsolete regulations there – will only lead to confusion, or, more abstractly, regulatory uncertainty. The problems may look the same globally, but affect different countries, and indeed regions and sectors within them, in very different ways. (In fact, similar routine problems that pose health and safety issues such as air quality or procedures to license drivers of long-distance trucks and check the safety of trucks are often regulated very differently in different countries.) Governments adjust regulations for competitive reasons and to accommodate domestic interests whose support may be needed to secure approval of a larger program of reform. They are likely to decide what to do and what not to do on the basis of deep-seated reflexes about how to manage the risk of policy failure and allocate responsibility between the private and public sector. Well might Gary Banks, when Chair of Australia's Productivity Commission, pronounce that a cost-effective climate change policy "is possibly the biggest regulatory challenge Australia has ever faced" (Banks, 2008).

There is a risk governance deficit. We are a long way from being able to rely on regulatory policies and institutions for normative activities (such as opening a business, property development and construction, food production, processing and distribution, waste management, and many economic activities) to handle significant systemic, cross-border, and emerging risks. Perhaps political leaders are not informed about or do not perceive some of the major risks facing their cities; at best, they delegate both the advisory function and responsibility for policy development to a technical body or level which, lacking strong political support, is under-resourced, and lacks traction with other agencies or units that have both technical knowledge and need to participate or contribute to any working plan. Austerity-driven cutbacks in the public sector will only aggravate the situation.

Blame-avoidance, weak incentives for co-ordination across sectors and levels of government, and unresolved questions about how much to communicate to the public and in what form, add to the list of difficulties. When catastrophes occur, people turn to the state for relief, but also question why so little had been done beforehand to prevent the catastrophe, to provide adequate warning, to provide assistance, etc. Leaders will be held responsible regardless of the cause: on 15 August 2003, when a major blackout of the Mid-West and North East in the United States and Ontario lasted for a couple of days, the press asked the Mayor of New York about the causes and expected duration and impact of the blackout, even though it had originated in western Ohio in a private-sector utility and, as is often the case, was preceded by circumstances and a series of accidents which, singly, would never have led to a blackout but together combined to do so (Nye, 2010). It is easy to understand how public pressure and political initiative combine to generate regulations that give the impression that a problem will not recur, that a gap in the public armor against disaster has been filled, even when experts may know that some such regulations are likely to be ineffective. No wonder Australian social scientist Patrick Troy was quick to spot that the growing volume of government regulations on buildings, the work place, and the environment are manifestations of low levels of trust and outright cynicism (Troy, 2004).[2]

There is worse: the low level of trust in government makes it harder for government to take risks in the political sense, to change policies to help mitigate future catastrophes. People may have more to gain from reform but fear that they will lose in the process, a phenomenon illuminated by Daniel Kahneman and others who have pioneered behavioral economics.

The public purpose of regulation is to achieve some larger objective, a more desirable, a better, safer future. This objective mirrors and reflects its opposite, embodied as fear of what will happen if steps are not taken, controls not imposed, goals not pursued. We are left with a seemingly insolvable problem: international regulatory co-operation is inadequate to the task of controlling cross-border risks, yet states themselves are unable to provide the level of protection and security their citizens demand.

- What does the agenda of risks to cities imply for a reallocation of regulatory roles and responsibilities among states, between states on the one hand and cities and regions at the sub-national level on the other, and between citizens and governments?
- By definition, systemic risks involve multiple jurisdictions. How can governments be assured that together they are providing adequate oversight of compliance?
- How can governments communicate more effectively when, as the impact of the Ebola epidemic on the United States showed, fear preempts facts?

- Should policies be designed to work with government institutions as they are? Or should capacity-building and institutional reforms precede a change in policies?

These are not theoretical questions. By the time some of these questions may be resolved in practical terms – theory-based, first-best approaches are unlikely – there will be less time to adjust policies in advance of major trends or events for which the clock is ticking – even if it is not possible to know when time runs out. This is why a strategy of preparedness that puts greater emphasis on resilience – that depends on the strength of the commercial economy which values co-operation, initiative, and innovation – is so critical. Paradoxical as it may seem, when the state tries to enhance security by tightly constraining the commercial sector, it may be working against its own objective, helping cities survive (Jacobs, 1992).[3]

The two security economies, state and commercial – resilience revisited

There were two new economies in the 1990s, both heavily concentrated in cities. The new economy everyone refers to is the global economy of innovation, communications technologies, falling barriers to trade and investment. This growth economy puts pressure on government to reduce the size of the public sector, decentralize, adopt regulations that pose fewer trade barriers and are at least competition-neutral, and improve public services. The World Bank's annual Doing Business report and other benchmarking exercises compare countries' legal and regulatory practices that affect investment and business creation. The new economy that people ignored, at least until 11 September 2001, is the economy of security, marked by tougher policing and a larger prison population, the spreading use of CCTV and other forms of surveillance, efforts to control money laundering, identity checks for travel, enclaves or privately owned and protected residential and commercial sites with restricted access, and improved measures to respond to disasters, all involving rising public expenditure as well as greater costs, regulatory burdens on citizens and the private sector, greater regulatory complexity, less transparency, and greater centralization.

The security economy is largely about protecting people and assets from threats, both natural and political. But even this description is an over-simplification. In fact there are *two* security economies. There is an urban security agenda for the state, and an urban security agenda for the private sector, *and they are not the same because they are concerned about different kinds of threats.*

To look further into the difference between the two security economies, we must look at hard and soft infrastructures. The word *infrastructure*, meaning the foundation of a building or engineering work, probably appeared in print for the first time in 1875, in French. It soon acquired additional meanings, referring to the permanent ground installations for armies or transport systems, and to the basic framework of social and economic organizations and systems. Perhaps it entered English during World War One, a linguistic transfer of sorts among the Allies who after all had to build and operate infrastructures in France.

Hard infrastructures are physical facilities for transport, power, water, and waste management. The infrastructures that support major cities often extend many kilometers into hinterlands, covering large water basins, for example, or coastal facilities. The City of Paris owns the land where the River Seine has its source, in Burgundy near Dijon. Network utilities for water, power, telecoms, etc. are often vertically integrated with many of the characteristics of natural monopolies, regulated to generate and sell the services they provide in non-competitive markets. *Soft infrastructures* deal with social and cultural forces that enable people to co-exist in cities, living in higher density among strangers. Public services in health, education, culture, the environment, labor markets – you name it – are the structural elements in soft infrastructure. The so-called third sector composed of civic and philanthropic institutions contributes importantly to soft infrastructures. Resilience is based upon both hard and soft infrastructures.

The hard and soft infrastructures which support urban economies and networks are exposed to two different kinds of risks, one set affecting the state, another the private sector. Hard infrastructures, which call for heavy maintenance, are limited by their capacity to handle peak loads. Business is concerned about a loss of competiveness, environmental damage, the supply of electricity and water; in addition business and citizens react negatively to a lower quality of service, especially coupled with higher prices; congestion and the complications of planning day-to-day operations weigh significantly as a cost. Business cries out for more investment in the kinds of infrastructures it uses. Government is more concerned about the risks associated with terrorism, crime, piracy, illegal activities, and smuggling and of course attacks on transport, telecommunications, and power systems. Governments respond by multiplying controls and checks, extending surveillance in public spaces.

Consider the respective concerns of business and government in relation to the social risks linked to soft infrastructures. Business, which speaks loudly about the need to improve skills and education for the workforce, and wants to attract the best employees without regard to nationality, is concerned about immigration and urban diasporas when social and educational services are inadequate, contributing to high unemployment, dependency, distressed neighborhoods, and poor housing. There is nothing new about what to do: improve education, target housing policy, adopt strategies of social integration. The state is concerned about the impact of the same syndromes on the political orientation of disaffected youth, on populism, on alienation: police control, tougher visa and immigration policies are brought into play. The tensions and contradictions between the one approach and the other, as when visa programs to screen for potential terrorists lead to a decline in enrolments from overseas students, or when those same programs force graduates to leave for their country of origin at the end of their course of study rather than join the workforce where they were educated, bringing their skills with them, are the stuff of editorialists.

Social welfare is another way to look at the different sets of risks in the commercial and in the state security economies. Ageing and health care will remain perennial issues for years to come. The commercial economy is affected by avoidable disabilities and lifestyles that translate into sickness-related absences and a shorter working lifespan, and that raise the costs of medical insurance. Preventive medicine, promoting healthy lifestyles, improving the quality of neighborhoods and the mix of transport modes, offering services to retired people, lifelong learning – all these and more go into the policy toolkit. Government is more concerned about virulent rare diseases, lifestyle choice which leads to costly medical care and/or early retirement, rampant epidemics, illicit and illegal substances to be controlled – that has to be the operative word – by regulating behavior, policing, mass programs for vaccines, etc. Hunger and malnutrition lead governments to adopt food security programs whereas a large part of the problem could be better addressed through a combination of trade deregulation, land reform, income supports, and other measures which work through markets and commercial sectors.

The same dual approach applies to environmental quality, which is more closely related to hard infrastructures. Water, after all, is a key input in many business operations. The commercial economy, more sensitive to cost, is also concerned about quality and supply. It asks government to provide greater regulatory certainty and better long-term planning especially on such questions as climate change – the familiar stuff of good urban management and progressive policy. Government looks at the disruption of a key service, or whether an attack on water or power could lead to cross-border conflicts. The risks to business call for long-term investment, better regulations, innovation, adaptation; the risks to the state call for hard protection, redundancy, rationing plans, and storage.

There is a massive deficit of infrastructure investment in all countries, developed, emerging, and in development. Each major system, whether for water, waste management, power generation and distribution, or transport, is inter-connected with other systems; each has a security dimension for states, and a security dimension in the commercial economy. It stands to reason that the private sector is more willing to invest in and join in partnership with governments to improve, expand, and maintain infrastructure systems that serve the needs of citizens and of business, either as end users or in the form of services which themselves are inputs to business. There is then a market; the areas that need servicing can be targeted for their growth potential; regulations can help assure universal coverage. When it comes to investment to meet the objectives and priorities set by states as part of the hard security economy, the mix of incentives and constraints is different. States can and do mandate what must be done by public bodies (agencies, different levels of government), by private operators (trucking and shipping firms, port operators, etc.), and even by households. These mandates, which usually take the form of regulations, in effect commit both public and private monies without discretion, and against a fixed deadline. The mandate-setting phase may give rise to negotiation with the private sector, but business is under no illusion that in the end the rules will be set and enforced. No prize to guess the answer to the question whether hard infrastructures get priority in policy over soft: they almost always do. We have yet to find the right balance between security to protect society and the economy, and state interests, two categories which often overlap but remain fundamentally distinct.

The new global economy of trade and production diminishes the sovereignty of the nation-state, promotes market-based decision-making, and, through the freer flow of information, gives people more control over their lives. The new security economy also reflects the diminished sovereignty of the nation-state but it restores – and in some respects expands – the intervention of the state, especially in the domains of travel, finance, and information.

It is one thing if the security economy reinforces and complements the commercial economy, but quite another if it becomes an end in itself with little restraint on its own growth. Hence a deep paradox at the heart of the state-defined security economy. Ultimately the power of a state – its capacity to project its influence and protect its interests – rests on an economic base. A country which fails to lift that base has no choice but to reduce its responsibilities and ambitions to a level proportionate to its means. Sometimes it can "punch above its weight," as the English like to say about the United Kingdom, but only up to a certain point: the UK has had to give up aircraft carriers, but still maintains a fleet of nuclear missile-launching submarines: it cannot afford both but may have made the wrong choice given the threats in this decade. The productive, market-oriented civilian economy which is the major source of wealth is itself a critical component of the state's security base. To improve productivity in the everyday economy of product markets, governments have removed many layers of fees, permits, and licenses, and have promoted a shift from "command-and-control" regulation to performance-based regulation, with risk-based inspections, impact assessments, consultant with users, and compliance mechanisms. To strengthen the security economy, however, governments have reverted to "command-and-control" regulation, imposing blanket procedures and restrictions and *ex-ante* measures which are the very opposite of what they are trying to do to lift growth by opening markets and raising productivity. Protection is partly responsible for the growth in the volume of regulation, in the extra-territorial extension of regulation, and in the increase in jobs and investment in the security field.

In an ideal world, the investment made in the security economy for the purposes of the state will have benefits – positive externalities, spillovers, to use the language of economists – for the commercial side. This does in fact happen: anti-terrorist measures in shipping, to check the contents of containers, for example, have commercial benefits as well. Insurance, fireproof building construction and codes to withstand the shocks of earthquakes, the repression of counterfeit goods, mandatory vaccination – the list of services and techniques generating jobs and improving welfare to reduce risks to life and property demonstrates problem-solving of a high order. These are examples of the kind of symbiotic relationship between two sets of values, two sets of responsibilities, which Jane Jacobs recognized as fundamental to progress (Jacobs, 1992). A more difficult task faces governments when tackling distressed urban areas where Jihadists and violent radicals may be recruited. The tactics outlined in Chapter 4 imply the integration of these zones into the city around them, and measures that meet commercial-economy needs. These things take time and coherence, which appear to be in short supply in the "war against terrorism." Getting the balance right means advancing toward short-term and long-term security objectives at the same time. This is not inevitable; it is urgent.

As things stand, citizens and firms are asked to assume more responsibility but in conditions that limit their initiative. Risk-sharing between the public and the public authorities is imposed from above, sometimes in unilateral decisions which are opaque and through procedures which are not open to much consultation or negotiation. Measures in the security economy that introduce controls on individual rights and privacy vitiate the sense of freedom which empowers people to act and behave responsibly, and encourages a posture of mistrust. Transparency could become a one-way mirror: government can see us but we cannot see government. Only by expanding the scope for innovation will the commercial economy be better able to generate solutions to problems which, left untreated or treated badly, risk undermining the foundations of cities – foundations which rest on both hard and soft infrastructures. Innovations depend on the free exercise of imagination and intelligence, access to markets, and a critical assessment of the status quo; what limits to security and surveillance can we accept if we want the benefits of innovation?

This is why risk, regulation, and responsibility are inextricably tied together in any discussion of the future of cities. Who decides what is vulnerable and what is to be protected? It does not take much mental effort to know which of these two agendas – commercial or state – gets the most attention in government. The events of 11 September 2001 did not so much create the new economies of security as increase the scale and scope of the state economy of security and give it new means to reinforce deterrent, potentially repressive measures. The tolerance of loss in terrorism in particular is very low compared to other urban disasters which cause death or injury: more people died in the 1995 Kobe earthquake than on 11 September 2001, but the media coverage and political consequences have been far greater for the latter than for the former. As always, there is an element of reality behind fear. But it is not terrorism alone that separates the twenty-first century of cities from the Cold War era when the threat of nuclear annihilation was never absent. Before 2001, terrorism ranked low as a concern of the American public; it took an attack to shift priorities. For some time thereafter, climate change continued to divide the American public between groups willing to accept significant policy changes even at some expense to growth, and those opposed to changes even if cost-free (Sunstein, 2006). It took successive storms, including Hurricane Sandy, to transform climate change into a national security issue, taking it out of the simple cost-benefit analysis which had defeated previous policy initiatives. Redefined as a security issue, climate change is repositioned in policy agendas and budgets. Taking collective security – a grand name for what in reality always has been based on the ability of each sovereign state to protect its people and territory – into the twenty-first century means coping with twenty-first century risks.

The state cannot do it all, neither can it do nothing. Finding where to draw the line can be a matter of theory and analysis, or of dividing the pie, that is, deciding who pays for what. Everything cannot be left to individuals, who do not have the same interests or means to cope; coverage would be incomplete, exposing people to the shortcomings of others, and society as a whole to free-rider problems. Equally, an assumption that the state will do everything leads to problems of moral hazard, meaning that people fail to take reasonable measures on their own. Of course the private sector spends what it must when directed by government mandate and regulation, transferring the cost to users in the form of higher charges when the state does not itself add fees: in either case, the equivalent of a tax. The private sector is paying for some of the costs of state security and for part, and perhaps a growing share, of the costs of security within the commercial sphere itself – the education, health and welfare of its workers, the safety of buildings and operations, etc.

So this is where we are. Risk scanning and early warning systems which focus on external, cross-border threats reinforce the illusion that nation-states can protect themselves – their *raison d'être* – because that is what the electorate wants to believe. Risk aversion and regulation are each reasonable but taken to extremes and in combination generate a vicious cycle which feeds on itself. More crises will generate more regulations, possibly compromising the social and cultural forces of resilience which historically have enabled cities to withstand and recover from sudden and high levels of disorganization or worse, destruction. There is of course the possibility that current and future threats to our well-being will turn out to be less destructive and more easily contained, but this book on cities and crisis assumes that would be an expensive bet.

We face the choice between fatalism – accepting the consequences of events that cannot be prevented – and forecasting – accepting responsibility to control what lies in our power. Fear can be rational if it guides responsible action. Or it can be irrational, a rejection of reason and a retreat into myth. On 11 December 1997 Leonard Slatkin, the distinguished American musician, led the Orchestre National de France in a concert that included Paul Dukas's "Sorcerer's Apprentice," Barber's "Summer of 1945," and Sibelius's elegiac but not optimistic Fifth Symphony. These compositions were about whether we can control our fantasies. We may try to grasp more power and knowledge than we can use wisely, but we must have the courage to see things as they are.

Democracy is distinguished as a political system by its tolerance of mistakes. Innovation and experimentation in politics – as in business, engineering, science – are encouraged by a philosophical stance that allows people to try, to fail, to learn from their mistakes, and to try again. In an authoritarian or totalitarian system, failure is impermissible, compromising the infallibility of the ruler or ruling body. Democracy, as a collective system in which the people participate actively, distributes both power and knowledge. When it comes to high-risk security issues, however, there may be no second chance for those in authority whose plans and policies prove inadequate. Failure in the private sector leads to nationalization, bankruptcy or merger. Failure in the public sector begins with the dismissal of a minister, proceeds to the removal of the head of government, and reaches its apex with the destruction of the state itself, and the introduction of a new constitution. Ultimately, the escalating scale of risks in politics puts the capacity of democracy for tolerance of mistakes under pressure. As the aftermath of the misguided invasion of Iraq in 2003 continues, it is clear that more space for learning from and admitting to mistakes can and must be made.

Notes

1 An excellent introduction is "Enabling regulatory reform" by Gabriella Meloni, chapter 9 in *Making Reform Happen: Lessons from OECD Countries*, OECD (2010), pp. 239–68.
2 Philippe Aghion, Yann Algan, Pierre Cahuc and Andrei Shleifer used the World Values Survey to explore the correlation between regulation and distrust, concluding that "distrust fuels support for government control over the economy ... even when people realize that the government is corrupt and ineffective; they prefer state control to unbridled activity by uncivic entrepreneurs." "Regulation and distrust," NBER Working Paper 14648, January 2009.
3 I am indebted to Allan Rodger who introduced me to this book which has informed my understanding of the roles of the private and public sectors.

References

Banks, Gary (2008), "Riding the third wave: some challenges in national reform," paper presented to the Economic and Social Outlook Conference, Melbourne, 27 March. Reprinted in *An Economy-wide View: Speeches on Structural Reform* (Melbourne: Productivity Commission, 2010), pp. 59–76.
Black, Julia (2011), "Risk-based regulation: choices, practices and lessons being learnt," pp. 185–224, in OECD, *Regulatory Policy and Governance: Supporting Economic Growth and Serving the Public Interest*. DOI 10.1787/9789264116573-en.
Brummer, Chris (2012), *Soft Law and the Global Financial System: Rule Making in the 21st Century* (Cambridge: Cambridge University Press).
Jacobs, Jane (1992), *Systems of Survival: A Dialogue on the Moral Foundations of Commerce and Politics* (New York: Random House).

Long, Bill L. (2000), OECD, *International Environmental Issues and the OECD, 1950–2000: An Historical Perspective.* ISBN: 92-64-17171-1.

Nye, David E. (2010), *When the Lights Went Out: A History of Blackouts in America* (Cambridge, MA: MIT Press).

OECD (1994), *Regulatory Co-operation for an Interdependent World* (Paris: OECD). ISBN: 92-64-14196-0.

OECD (2002), *Regulatory Policies in OECD Countries: From Interventionism to Regulatory Governance* (Paris: OECD), p. 65. ISBN: 92-64-19893-8.

OECD (2010), *Risk and Regulatory Policy: Improving the Governance of Risk* (Paris: OECD). DOI: 10.1787/9789264082939-en.

OECD (2011a), *Regulatory Policy and Governance: Supporting Economic Growth and Serving the Public Interest* (Paris: OECD). DOI: 10.1787/97892641116573-en.

OECD (2011b), *Better Regulation in Europe: Highlights* (Paris: OECD)(the individual country reports, including specific recommendations for remedial measures, can be accessed at www.oecd.org).

OECD (2012), "Recommendation of the Council on Regulatory Policy and Governance" (Paris: OECD).

OECD (2013), *International Regulatory Co-operation: Addressing Global Challenges* (Paris: OECD). DOI: 10.1787/978926400463-en; see also the series: vol.1, *Case Studies: Chemicals, Consumer Products, Tax and Competition*; vol. 2, *Case Studies: Canada-US Co-operation, EU Energy Regulation, Risk Assessment and Banking Supervision*; vol. 3, *Case Studies: Transnational Private Regulation and Water Management.*

Sunstein, Cass R. (2006), "On the divergent American reactions to terrorism and climate change," Working Paper 06–13, Washington DC: AEI-Brookings Joint Center for Regulatory Studies.

Troy, Patrick (2004), "Distrust and the development of urban regulations," in Russell Hardin (ed.), *Distrust* (New York: Russell Sage Foundation Series on Trust), pp. 207–32.

Wiener, Jonathan (2003), "Whose precaution after all? A comment on the comparison and evolution of risk regulatory systems," *Duke Journal of Comparative and International Law*, 13:3: 207–62. Wiener contributed "Risk regulation and governance institutions," in OECD, *Risk and Regulatory Policy* (Paris: OECD, 2010), pp. 133–56.

Wiener, Jonathan (forthcoming), *Recalibrating Risk: Crises, Perceptions and Regulatory Change.*

PART III
Cities and paradigms for economic governance

8

How the West overcomes crises, reduces risks, and copes with uncertainty

There is no historical evidence that macro-changes in time are the cumulative results of small-scale, linear micro changes. (Nisbet, 1969: 288)

Five ways to make cities safer in the twenty-first century, and five ways not to ...

The global financial crisis of 2008 introduced "systemic risk" into the public vocabulary and added economic shocks to a list including power failures, food and water shortages, natural disasters and epidemics that spill over borders. Cities worldwide are exposed to cross-border risks; there is what to worry about. If these assumptions for Part III are unfounded, the future will show either that current trends and forecasts exaggerate risks, or that national governments demonstrate the capacity to cope with them when and where they occur. The remaining chapters are of the nature of "what if": what are the implications for economic governance for cities if there are more, and more complex and potentially destructive crises; if a paradigm change in national policies to make cities safer does not come early enough; if national governments are overwhelmed by the scale of emerging risks but also limit international co-operation to cope with cross-border risks?

Climate change is the meta-version of cross-border risks because it includes the cumulative effect of past decisions, investments, and socio-spatial models, the threat of overwhelming disasters, the promise of transformational innovation, and the need for collective action. Look at the list of policy measures in the OECD's report on cities and climate change:

- Integrate climate priorities into the urban policy-making process.
- Improve inter-municipal and regional co-ordination to overcome barriers to effective local action.

- Exploit synergies between climate and other urban policy goals through systematic, multi-sectoral strategic planning.
- Adopt enabling national policies "to create a sound institutional foundation and knowledge base to help local decision makers engage stakeholders and identify and carry out cost-effective actions."
- Leverage existing financial instruments and explore complementary new ones.
- Make more use of fees and charges as instruments to influence behavior and thus mitigate climate change. (based on OECD, 2010: 22–8)

There is everything right about this list; missing is the key to unlock the chains of habit and routine, ignorance, and regulatory and institutional path-dependency. Too many policies already in place are in conflict with measures that need to be taken: for example, local governments which cannot raise taxes encourage greenfield development at low density; electricity market liberalization tends to discourage investment in new generation technologies, which are capital-intensive; new financial stability rules are less favorable to long-term infrastructure investment, including low-carbon infrastructure. It is not enough to show that tackling climate change will make us better off in the long run, or to argue that measures taken now will cost less than doing more later. Faced with the difficulty of understanding how any one policy initiative will affect others in a dynamic relationship, uncertainty breeds caution, or, more bluntly, procrastination. The sheer scale of tasks is a recipe, if not for failure, then for under-shooting:

- Must everything be done at once or are certain measures to be taken first, as preconditions for others to follow?
- How much will it cost? Who will pay? What about the scale of the benefits? And how might these be distributed?
- Will the over-representation of rural constituencies in many legislatures block or retard policy changes? Or can a shared concern to mitigate disasters that affect them both help moderate the traditional opposition of rural and urban interests?
- What is to be done if progress is not made? Or if newly elected governments reverse the decisions taken by their predecessor (as happened in Australia in 2014)?
- If some cities and countries pull ahead, will there be free rider problems, placing the more advanced at a competitive disadvantage?

It may already be too late to introduce gradual changes in patterns of urban development and lifestyles to reduce the impact of global warming and climate change or the potential cost of sudden catastrophic disasters. Radical shifts will be hugely unpopular and expensive; people will object that the state should not tell them how or where to live. More insurance may protect some businesses and homeowners but will do nothing to reform policies that contribute to the underlying problem. Are policy agendas equipped to reorient how urban issues are addressed in budgets and regulations? No; improving the economic, social, and environmental performance of cities is not the mandate of those who revise financial regulations or policy frameworks for energy. The scale of change necessary may inhibit radical reform. *The demand is for practical solutions, not radical reforms. But we may need radical reforms to get practical solutions.* A paradigm shift in how urban economies and societies are regulated will help make practical solutions more attractive and feasible.

What does "business as usual" look like? And why is it not good enough?
Let the market shape land use, property development, and housing. It is difficult to factor risks into the price of land or property, or to update the maps and zoning documents which show where people should not build. Poor people may have no choice but to live in areas where construction should be illegal, but some of the best properties are also exposed. And hazards change: places once thought to be safe may become at risk. People are notoriously poor judges of the risks they run. Anxious for investment, local authorities are too eager to grant permission to build, or retroactively grandfather structures built where they should not have been. Many people cannot afford insurance, or choose not to buy it. In any case, government cannot afford to expropriate property in a high-risk location, especially when risks were not known at the time of construction.

Share the risks and the costs. Modern states have disaster prevention and relief policies and agencies – all very good on paper. But too often, projects advance slowly due to administrative and regulatory complexity, and low levels of funding. Government does not set a good example: commitments to safeguard schools, hospitals, or essential public services are not backed up by an accelerated funding program, or by an evaluation and performance mechanism. Risk-sharing is another way government has to reduce its commitments in the face of skyrocketing obligations. Treasury will say that to provide more safety will cost too much in terms of lives saved, and will divert spending from other, more immediate needs; vast sums spent on disaster prevention may be wasted, or diverted through corruption.

Regulate. Risk reduction – look at climate change – becomes a partisan, polarizing political issue, compromising the public interest. When major policies or new laws are not possible politically, governments regulate. Anyway, the first reaction of politicians when a disaster occurs is to propose regulations. Of course, many rules only apply to buildings erected in the future; firms usually have years to comply. The growing volume of regulation protected by the security label represents an administrative tax on the private sector, thereby increasing costs without burdening the public budget. Moreover, existing regulations can act as a barrier to innovations. Bad regulation creates its own problems: people opposed to disaster planning argue that it will lead to a further expansion of government, and to more regulatory constraints on individual choices.

Pretend it won't happen – or any time soon. The call to do things differently is always loudest immediately after a disaster. With time, memories fade; people rebuild, or move away. Risk competes with other priorities which are likely to appeal to more voters. Highly polarized, voters are unlikely to endorse radical policy shifts. Paradoxically, although the public's appetite for risk continues to decrease, its fascination with disaster is unabated. Films and novels can make disasters rather banal. There is a kind of one-upmanship when each disaster film has to use more spectacular effects than the last. These apocalyptic spectacles tell us something about ourselves: we like to feel fear, sorrow, and pity, especially when we have escaped a tragedy that has hit others. People believe that technology, which often runs amok in disaster films, may yet provide reliable solutions: something always turns up.

One option, denial that there are problems which must be addressed at all, is attractive to some. This is not so improbable: the House of Representatives of the State of Tennessee – which censured the teaching of Darwinism, leading to the Scopes trial in the 1920s – passed a resolution attacking the United Nations Agenda 21 program, asserting that Agenda 21 and the entire effort to promote sustainable development would impose limitations on private property without due process of law, pre-empting the authority of state governments. This resolution echoed another adopted by the Republic National Committee on 13 January 2012 which lumped smart growth, resilient cities, regional visioning projects, and other "green" or "alternative" projects as a threat to the American way of life. This indirect attack on the evidence of global climate change comes close to state-sanctioned ideology, repressing dissent, scientific evidence, and experimentation (Sustainable Liberty Now, 2014). These and other similar measures cannot be so easily dismissed as extreme statements of opinion with no legal enforcement: they evoke the scale of resistance at sub-national level where most of the changes needed to make cities safer have to be realized.

Business as usual is not good enough. Disasters always contain elements that had not been anticipated. The very nature of a disaster is to be overwhelming, disorienting, confusing, upsetting pre-disaster relief plans. Every time there is a disaster – even something as sweeping as the global financial crisis of 2008 or as dramatic as the attack on the World Trade Center in 2001 – reports and inquiries find major flaws, some operational, some embedded in policy assumptions. We no longer believe that catastrophes are punishments for sin, or the result of some evil force; suffering is painful, not cathartic. Priorities will change when leaders tap into popular support for "future-proofing" cities.

What would a preventive, pro-active approach to manage cities and space better look like?

Recognize there is a problem. Crises are the new normal. The trend since 1990 seems ever upwards: more disasters at higher cost. Highly urbanized regions are vulnerable to more complex syndromes, from epidemics to power failures. Poor countries typically have high loss of life, and wealthy ones high loss of property; as more countries become wealthier, the economic cost will rise, and so will sensitivity to even modest numbers of deaths. With urbanization, more of the world's cities – and especially more of the key cities in the global economy – will be exposed to floods and storms: average global flood losses in 136 of the world's largest coastal cities could exceed $50 billion in 2050, up from $6 billion in 2005. Major fault lines are overdue for earthquakes, threatening California, Japan, Turkey, Mexico.

Spend the money differently. Both the OECD and McKinsey estimate that approximately $60 trillion must be spent over the next couple of decades to modernize and expand infrastructures for transport, water, energy; more than half will be spent in developed countries. These eye-blinking numbers do not take account of additional costs to adapt to climate change. Assuming the money is there when business is hoarding cash and interest rates are at historic lows, investment that has to be made to keep infrastructures in repair and cope with demand could be combined with measures to reduce the vulnerability of city-regions to catastrophes and help them recover more quickly if a catastrophe occurs. To make progress, the rate of urban rebuilding has to double, to 2–4 per cent a year. A forward-looking paradigm will generate a new wave of innovation, supporting economic and social development for decades.

Use existing knowledge better. When a disaster does occur, people always want to know "why wasn't more done to save lives." We know what to do, but not how to implement. It is often necessary to combine environmental and transport projects, for example, or to build in a measure of redundancy, or to bury or elevate essential facilities as a means of protection. Regional decision-making may have the right spatial scale, but the political incentives are greater for national leaders to take the initiative and claim credit with the electorate. A crisis strategy is the chance to reform the vertical silos in government which often get in the way of getting things done, and to generate incentives for different levels of government to co-operate, backed up by the right regulations. So much comes down to governance.

Commit to adaptation and resilience. Every day without a catastrophe should not breed complacency. Some societies cope better with disasters than others. The shock effect of a disaster fades within a decade; preparedness is difficult to maintain. Societies that have a higher stock of social capital, urban districts that function as communities, places with well-maintained public spaces and landmarks all have the potential to help people cope better when a disaster occurs. Investments in health, sport, culture, education pay dividends. A thorough analysis of community and regional assets and needs will help when decisions about what to change – or rebuild – have to be taken.

People need a message of hope. A policy for cities must be forward-looking, focusing on the opportunities they hold – and the risks they face. The great urban fear in the pre-industrial era was religious conflict, threatening social order and rulership; in the nineteenth century, people focused on crime, disease, a breakdown in family life, radical politics; mass unemployment and its social and political consequences drove policy in the twentieth century as population shifted from rural areas to cities. Security in our era means living in a society which acts to prevent catastrophes, or at least their worst effects, and strengthens its resilience, or its capacity to recover should a disaster occur.

These seemingly simple steps amount to a change in paradigm to redefine security, domestically and internationally. Notice that this list does not include anything specific about air or water, health, housing, transport, etc., but focuses instead on the main lines to set priorities from which the details for specific sectors follow. The change to take place is of a mind-set. The threat of war – and the reality of terrorism – remain uppermost in policy today, but security as a concept must also reflect the likelihood that other disasters can have the same effect as an attack, wiping out capital, weakening social structures, and destabilizing governments.

The problem we face is the sheer number of problems, without a clear way to set priorities. By 2010, as the post-crisis crisis succeeded the global financial crisis of 2008 and the recovery receded after several false dawns, the preconditions for a new paradigm became manifest, even if its outlines remain blurred. It was one thing to say that there would be no going back to the way things were in 2008, and another to hazard a prediction about how things may be in, say, 2020. We return to a point made at the beginning of this book: crises may produce benefits but the benefits of the crises we face are yet to be defined. How will the crisis produce a better society, a more stable order, a more productive economy?

Part III is about what may come next. It is unlikely to avoid the shortcomings of such chapters in books of this kind, which are usually stronger on the historical record as an analytical framework for a discussion of contemporary problems than on solutions, opening up options for the future. All too often, authors give up at this point, preferring to elaborate on the way things should be at the expense of the transition from here to there. And the practical next steps, when set forth on paper, are often so modest, either out of a belief that they will get done if they look easy, or out of a belief that anything more radical and ambitious will appear totally unrealistic and impractical. How often one puts down a book at the end of a lengthy and convincing explanation of why things are wrong with the feeling that the last chapter, on the way to set things right, is the weakest part. If these chapters are not written, however, does their omission betray a lack of imagination or simply excessive caution and modesty of the part of the writer, pretending that he or she has not thought about what may come next? Between hubris, the great seventeenth-century sin of overweening pride when people do not know their limits, and humility born of an awareness of how little they know, is honest doubt.

Economic regulation as a meta–paradigm

The process to develop a new meta-framework of economic governance for the urban world that now exists may look impossible today in view of the many obstacles ahead; once completed, however, it will have the look of inevitability. Why do paradigms change, and when they change, why is the process abrupt and dramatic? Some understanding, however inadequate, of the process by which periods of regulatory stability follow periods of profound disruption is indispensable to those few today who must act during the crisis, to the greater number who comment on current events and offer advice, and to the large public witnessing a unique period of transition, and wanting to know what kind of world will emerge from it.

When the principles for action and policy which seemed to work in the past are no longer effective, something happens to make it possible to evolve a new set which work reasonably well for long enough to become an established paradigm, pushing back the limits to growth. Meta-paradigms of economic regulation and governance evolve when their power to provide solutions is thwarted by deep changes in the environment in which they must be effective. Brilliant, creative transformations of the paradigms that regulate the relations between society, the economy, and the state take place during crises *and help to resolve them*. These critical periods erupt at long intervals at least a century apart and most recently early in the twentieth century; the transition from one paradigm to another is over in less than a generation; more than one generation will pass until the next paradigm shift.

Regulatory regimes are relatively stable sets of rules that are utilitarian and instrumental, helping people make decisions in the normal course of their professional work or daily lives. Regulation has two meanings in English, corresponding to two different levels at which regulation functions. The more conceptual, abstract meaning of regulation refers to policies and instruments by which governments try to regulate the economy as a whole, keeping the system intact and performing along a trend line toward a desired goal, for example, low unemployment. The common, everyday use of the word refers to a rule, usually specific to a particular task, and usually in written form which directs moral or physical persons to act in certain ways, to achieve an objective: continuing with the example of unemployment, this might take the form of rules on hiring and firing workers. As discussed in Chapter 8, the power of a governmental body to issue and enforce regulations is granted by law; private bodies also issue regulations within the sphere of their powers. The French language makes clear the distinction between the two forms of regulation used in English: *régulation* refers to what can be called meta-regulation, economic governance of the most sweeping kind which in the twentieth century meant macro-economic and sectoral policy (e.g., competition, energy, labor, etc.) at national level. *Règlementation* by contrast refers to specific, legal rules. The use of regulations in the legal and administrative sense of *règlementation* in modern states applies general principles to specific cases and policy objectives. Governance as a general subject is easier to communicate in English than in French, but, in terms of regulation, French clarity is conceptually more rigorous and helpful.

Regulation in its more profound sense, as *régulation*, is an over-arching strategy to align the short-term, erratic, and unpredictable character of daily life and markets with an independent, predictable and stable standard based on principles and beliefs about how societies function and about the purposes of institutions, and about why economic, social, political, and indeed environmental systems are imperfect and liable to fail. Economic regulation includes more than just the economy, as Chapter 2 on housing policy illustrates. Behind the rules there is a source of authority which provides the intellectual foundation on which the rules rest. These bodies of rules may be nested in larger value systems – the rule of law being the most conspicuous when it comes to regulations of any sphere promulgated and enforced by government – but those who need to know what the rules are do not need to think about the larger political construct, any more than nineteenth-century navigators, triangulating a position at sea, needed to think about whether the heavens on which they rely to set course prove the argument by design, or a car mechanic the laws of thermodynamics. Practice is what counts; theory can be taken for granted.

Regulation, or *régulation*, is therefore the expression of the power that issues rules and laws, but it is more: it is a purposeful effort by legal authorities to create harmony – what today is called coherence – between what exists in everyday terms, and a deeper structure of values. These values and goals may remain stable for decades but then are stretched to accommodate new problems and circumstances. The price of incoherence is then reflected in increased transaction costs, friction, unresolved conflicts. In the western scientific and philosophical tradition, regulation refers to the ability of a system, indeed of civilization itself, to remain coherent and stable over time. Problems, anomalies, emergents can be expected, but what matters is the balance between continuity and change, between what worked in the past but is no longer "fit for purpose," and innovations that can be tested, improved and normalized. Finding the right balance is easier said than done, as the records of both Keynesian and monetary policies over the past half-century have shown.

A "new common sense": modeling the paradigm shift

Like crises, paradigm shifts can be analysed and modeled. Carlota Perez grasped this point in a study of regulatory reforms to stabilize disruptive technological changes and financial innovation. In *Technological Revolutions and Financial Capital: The Dynamics of Bubbles and Golden Ages* (2002) Carlota Perez depicted a sequence of five technological revolutions beginning with the early Industrial Revolution of the nineteenth century, followed by the age of steam and railways, the age of steel, electricity, and heavy engineering, and the age of oil, the automobile, and mass production, before reaching the age of information and telecommunications.[1] Each involved a new technology whose diffusion "involved profound changes in people, organizations and skills in a sort of habit-breaking hurricane. Each led to an explosive period in the financial markets ... within an ever-expanding bubble." When it collapsed, as eventually it had to, a changeover happened: "new industries have grown, a new infrastructure is in place; new millionaires have appeared; the new way of doing things with the new technologies has become 'common sense.'" One crucial thing was still missing: "a systematic articulation of the new regulatory framework and of the appropriate institutions, capable of steering and facilitating the functioning of the new economy in a socially and economically sustainable manner" (Perez, 2002: 4).

The paradigm shift can be managed, but you have to know where you are when you start. The process involves both *unlearning* and *learning*. Some people will continue to look backwards, applying ideas and methods which have become obsolete; others will try to embrace change, including new institutions "to fit new conditions" (Perez, 2002: 165). During the process of institutional creative destruction, attention tends to concentrate on the destruction half of the process. "A society that had established countless routines and habits, norms and regulations to fit the conditions of the previous revolution, does not find it easy to assimilate the new one" (Perez, 2002: 154). What it needs to usher in "a period of synergy, convergence and prosperity" is "*adaptive regulation*" consisting of self-regulation in the area of finance "precisely to avoid the need for government supervision" and a "new framework for banking and monetary practices. Next, rules of the game are established to condition business, labor relations and so on, as well as regulatory innovations on the international level .... Some rules help strengthen firms; others reinforce market growth and social cohesion" (italics in the original, Perez, 2002: 128–9). Regulations codify accepted practice; but they also help to introduce and normalize social innovations which become indispensable to the well-functioning of the market economy and its productive agents during the new cycle, for example social welfare systems introduced early on in the expansion of mass production.

Five points in Perez's thesis deserve emphasis. (1) The process is embedded in the nature of capitalism. (2) The breakup of an established order and the transition to a new one is wasteful, marked by widening inequality and disparities. But (3) this cannot be helped, although the effort to analyse "what went wrong and how it can be prevented from happening again" is constructive. Following a crash and recession, "the more practical task of setting up an adequate regulatory system and a set of effective safeguards is soon undertaken" (Perez, 2002: 5). (4) What had first seemed impossible or unnecessary becomes the new "common sense," a new paradigm which is largely taken for granted. But (5) it too will not last indefinitely because, as a phase of maturity lengthens, sustained in part by inertia and the logic of the prevailing status quo, it creates the conditions favorable for the emergence and rapid diffusion of something new, fueled by "idle capital desperately looking for alternative investment" (Perez, 2002: 82). In the mature phase, therefore, the deep adaptation of the socio-institutional framework to each paradigm eventually becomes "an obstacle for the introduction and diffusion of the next technological revolution." From this perspective, the period 2008–15 appears to follow the first, second, and third of these points.

Each paradigm is unique, because each technological revolution is different. As a result, "each specific mode of growth ... involves a set of ideological values" which in turn influences the choices that people will make (Perez, 2002: 170). Perez illustrated the model which explains historically recurring processes and highlighted how they can vary in social terms. Because each techno-economic era generates a distinctive institutional and political context in specific countries, the model is not mechanistic. The outcome of the crisis at the turning point "is very much determined by politics, ideologies and relative power. Therefore the length of the recession or depression does not depend on economic factors only, not even on economic policies and measures narrowly understood" (Perez, 2002: 126). "What is significant, in terms of the value of the model, is that there are causal chains and identifying features" (Perez, 2002: 123).

Perez's periodization is based on the introduction of big technologies, not on the transformation of urban economies or of their capacity to support ever-larger numbers of people. From that perspective, however, the shift away from the basic economy of export production to the non-basic economy more characteristic of services stands out as a trigger of change on its own, calling into questions assumptions and models which worked well enough until this shift took place. This would be consistent with the remarks of many economists that the service sector and productivity are still not well-enough understood. Information technology, big data, etc. in relation to "smart cities" will effect spatial as well as socio-economic change in cities, but it is too easy to fall back on a kind of technological determinism with causality running from the machine to the activity the machine facilitates. The automobile changed mobility as housing and worksites decentralized and the spatial footprint of labor markets spread well beyond jurisdictional boundaries, but the automobile did not "invent" mobility, or suburbs, for that matter; both owe something to streetcars; nor did it "invent" the Fordist mode of mass production. IT systems form networks of a different kind, but again tying the providers and users of urban services together. The spatial impact may take years to become apparent (as was the case with the automobile – a half century separated the mass production of cars from the mature system of highways and suburbs).

Perez was concerned about market regulation affecting firms; in this book the focus is on how urban economies are regulated. In the Schumpeterian concept which informs Perez, firms can disappear in a process of creative destruction that allows new ones to take form. The process is ongoing: people in business school learn how to cope with this, and acquire experience on the job. In the territorial world, cities may shrink but rarely die. Meta-paradigms that help in the process of adjustment to external shocks and urban problems associated with the growth and complexity of cities evolve perhaps once per century. Clearly the process by which one paradigm succeeds another is not automatic, nor is it learned: at intervals of a generation (or more), no one goes through this process more than once, and the rules or techniques by which the process is navigated call for different mental skills and political talents than competitive survival within an established paradigm. This is why it is so difficult, why resistance and skepticism are normal, why *unlearning* is as important as *learning*.

The five points in Perez's thesis about the stages or phases of a paradigm shift driven by technological change and finance are applicable on a bigger scale to a higher or meta-level of values and concepts, when paradigms for *régulation* change. Extrapolating from financial-technological regulatory paradigms to urban transitions is instructive: a series of major regulatory reforms for finance, the environment, energy, space and the built environment, transport, housing, health and education may all be needed to adapt cities for the twenty-first century. But the process is not smooth; following the normative cycle of incremental reform, the shift will not happen in a coherent or co-ordinated way, nor will it take place fast enough. Both kinds of paradigm shifts – the financial-technological shift analysed by Perez and the kind that is evoked here on a larger scale of a civilization – begin with a crisis that is resistant to policies which worked in the past. And the new regulations can only be tested if another crisis occurs, and they are not found wanting. We need crises, both to provoke a paradigm shift and then to consolidate it.

The paradigmatic study of paradigms by Thomas Kuhn in his studies of the Copernican and Newtonian revolutions (1962) showed how the accumulated evidence of facts that could not be entirely accounted for by Ptolemaic astronomy caused a rethinking of theory. Kuhn's treatment of scientific revolutions dealt with some issues relevant to any great paradigm shift: how new paradigms retain "much of the vocabulary and apparatus, both conceptual and manipulative" of their predecessors, but in unfamiliar ways such that they "fall into new relationships one with the other"; why "communication across the revolutionary divide is inevitably partial" (Kuhn, 1962: 149) because people begin with different assumptions; why in the end what changes is a world view. In the final analysis, a paradigm "works" because it reduces the level of uncertainty and doubt: it seems a safer option. A new paradigm ultimately triumphs, Kuhn showed, because it is demonstrably better at solving problems. But this in turn raises questions about what problems are worth solving, and who sets the criteria and tests.

Today, the level of uncertainty – if such a thing can be measured – appears to be at an unprecedented level, notwithstanding the considerable advances in economic theory and applied economics and in the social and natural sciences more generally. If a new paradigm emerges, it must reduce the level of uncertainty, enabling people to make problems more manageable. The critical objective of each paradigm for economic governance is to give confidence to people that what they are doing is right, and going in the right direction. Put in terms of economic governance in an urban world, the most basic test of a paradigm as a code of behavior and set of beliefs – meta-regulation – is whether it helps people solve the problems that come from living together in cities where social mobility, economic exchange, political power, and cultural creativity are most intense. This is the keystone in the arch of a paradigm, transforming the parts that might fall down into a stable structure.

As the final chapter will argue, a new paradigm for economic regulation for cities in the twenty-first century, however desirable, is unlikely to emerge solely through rational discourse and evidence-based decision-making: changes of this order of magnitude are usually associated with other, dramatic events and geo-political crises. This is why the combination of the global crisis which has lifted uncertainty to unprecedented levels, and the demonstrable incapacity of the post-Cold War state system to cope with more instability than we have seen in a generation is so pregnant for the future. The lack of co-operation among nations on new financial regulations, the frustrations of the Eurozone torn between deficit-reduction rules and supply-side strategies to develop infrastructure and investment, and the tensions within the West on how to confront radical Islam, Russian nationalism, African insurgencies, and global environmental threats – all major issues in 2014 – more than hint at a loss of direction and of priorities, raising questions about the post-1945 symbiosis of intergovernmental agencies, international treaties, and sovereign decision-making. This is exactly the climate in which a new meta-paradigm can emerge.

Paradigms of economic governance – between fear and hope

Three epochs of economic governance, or *régulation*, in the West since the Renaissance can be distinguished, each shaped by a frame of reference directed toward a particular set of problems to be avoided or controlled and goals to be pursued. What differentiates one epoch from another is less its techno-economic component than the over-arching, transcending values it embodies and which helped direct and guide public intervention and private initiative. The relative emphasis on economic activity and its outcomes in each epoch itself reflects larger ideas common at the time about how best to achieve social, economic and political change consistent with the degree of stability which is necessary for families, firms, societies to adapt to change, or, in other words, how best to regulate.

Each paradigm for economic governance encapsulates knowledge about the limits to behavior that is essential to the rule of law. Why? Each paradigm is a form of rules which when followed lead society in the right direction, and when violated jeopardize that goal. The knowledge which takes form in a paradigm is believed to rest on valid, timeless principles which have been discovered and demonstrated: a form of truth, if not truth itself. It does not make a paradigm any less powerful if those who follow and act on it know that in the past there have been other paradigms and that there will be others in the future. What matters is that at a given time there is one dominant paradigm; a system composed of diverse parts or competing paradigms could not hold together.

Each successive meta-paradigm for economic and social regulation is based not only on the hope of something awesome to achieve, but also on fear of something awful to avoid. This pairing of hope and fear is the mechanism that holds a synthesis of regulatory governance together, making it coherent: regulation in the French sense of *régulation*, not specific rules and laws directing how specific situations should be handled, but over-arching conceptual frameworks – paradigms – which guide decisions about what should or should not be regulated by government in the effort to keep the economy, society, and the polity itself moving toward a shared goal. This pairing of hope and fear runs deep. "There can be no hope without fear, and no fear without hope," wrote Spinoza. Maurice Lévy, chief executive of the Publicis Group, used this quote in an op-ed essay in the *Financial Times* (2013) to argue that fear of economic decline and of a widening gap between northern and southern Europe might be enough to "inspire decision-makers" to introduce structural reforms and renew "the political drive for reunification" in Europe. Spinoza suggested that we want to believe in what we hope for, and resist believing that what we fear may be true. But what if our hopes are vain and our fears are real? There is a fine balance between fear and hope: it may in fact be the case that fear more than hope encourages people to do what they must rather than what they may want to do. It is not enough to define the aspirational goal in positive terms; the key to knowing the goal to which a society aspires is to know what it most fears.

Every era is defined by its aspiration:

- In the sixteenth and seventeenth centuries, the pursuit of salvation in the after life transcended other objectives.
- The Enlightenment pursuit of progress toward an ever more perfect society on earth dominated the eighteenth and nineteenth centuries.
- In the twentieth century the goal of prosperity – and not for a few only – held sway over private and public decision-making.

Each goal, each aspiration, is matched by a terrible fear, its nemesis:

- in the sixteenth and seventeenth centuries, of heresy, damnation from sin and prideful disobedience.
- in the eighteenth and nineteenth centuries, of deviancy, obscurantism, and reaction which undermine social and political progress and arrest the perfectibility of society; and
- in the twentieth century, of depression and inequality, unemployment and technological collapse which reverse economic gains and put prosperity out of reach for the majority, breaking down democracy and destroying capital.

When salvation was the social ideal, priests and clerics had the power and authority to say what was right and wrong; in pursuit of progress, critics became the voice of conscience, reminding people what remained to be done; experts and professionals have been the elite guiding prosperity in the twentieth century.

Each paradigm is a delicate assemblage of beliefs and practices based on assumptions about how much individuals can be trusted, and how much systems to channel behavior are needed. A paradigm can endure as long as people retain unqualified faith that it works: follow these precepts, do not violate certain rules, and the goal can be attained, its threats kept at bay. When one paradigm succeeds another, it does not entirely supersede or eliminate its predecessor. Thus, religion remains important even though tolerance of religious minorities and non-believers, once highly dangerous, are now the mark of civilization; the twentieth century has seen the normalization and acceptance of behaviors once considered anti-social during the age of reason and progress; care for the unemployed and the social safety net will survive the eclipse of prosperity by another goal in the twenty first century.

We need paradigms. The self-made individual, happy peasant, wise hermit, noble savage, bohemian eccentric, all dear to romantic philosophers, poets, and composers, cannot discover all the rules for living completely on their own early enough in life to live by them. No one can think through a complete philosophy or create a framework of rules and codes by which to live. The value of a civilization is precisely to transmit a framework which is roughly adequate for the times, and to assimilate the lessons of experience so that the framework remains relevant.

And that is what cities do. City-building is the continual process of adapting cities to meet current and anticipate future challenges. The urban environment takes shape within "a system of consistent choices ... based on the application of certain criteria which may be explicit, but are commonly implicit and unstated, so that many alternatives are never considered at all being, as it were, eliminated through major cultural constraints .... The question then becomes how, and for what reasons, choices are made, and criteria based" (Rapoport, 1977: 16–17). This decision-making framework functions as a series of norms, perceptions, procedures, and techniques that have prima facie validity which people internalize in their behavior and expectations. Think of it as a meta-language which directs the energies and resources of societies, transmits skills, and promotes attitudes and values about urban living (Konvitz, 1985: xv–xvi). The art of city-building is no mere utilitarian undertaking; it is endowed with a higher purpose because ultimately the city, or at least great cities, function as moral regulators of sorts, reminding residents and visitors alike of the need to find the right balance between the past, present and future, and between the needs of individuals and of society. Paris had this effect on Henry Kissinger as he took a solitary walk in the city centre on 8 October 1979 at a crucial juncture in talks between the United States and North Vietnam (Kissinger, 1979: 1346).

Unfamiliar though we are with the experience and practice of undertaking a paradigm shift, there is nothing mysterious about it because such transformations of knowledge and power have happened before in western civilization. Because hardly anyone has direct experience of a paradigm shift in economic governance, history becomes instructive, complementing improvisation and creativity. This capacity for the transformation of paradigms at critical junctures has helped the West grow economically, adapt socially and culturally, invent technologically, and expand politically when compared with other civilizations over five-hundred years. Knowledge that this transformation appears to be a recurring western phenomenon should give us confidence that the process at hand is normal, and can be better understood precisely because there are historical precedents.

Conjoncture – a once-in-a-century phenomenon

Western inventions and institutions figure in sweeping histories and detailed analyses of how Europe, a mere Asian peninsula in Paul Valéry's memorable phrase, became a global power in the sixteenth century and remained so for over four hundred years. All the talk about whether China will dominate the world scene and about the causes of the West's relative decline are predicated on the assumptions that the future of the West lies largely with the United States and that the influence of Europe will continue to contract. "Decline and fall" scenarios which focus on economic capital and military resources however seem to ignore the potential of Europe as well as America to generate and diffuse the next global economic paradigm. Implementation will always reflect economic and military power and institutional capacity, but the sheer impact of ideas that help redefine problems and identify viable solutions cannot be under-estimated.

As Jane Jacobs reminded us in her last book, *Dark Age Ahead*, civilizations need "beneficent spirals, processes in which each improvement and strengthening leads to other improvements and strengthenings in the culture" (Jacobs, 2004: 175). Her concern was that the West was in danger of a vicious spiral because it was blinded by its very success to interlocking problems "in the face of new realities." To avoid a vicious spiral which could feed on itself, she argued, the West had to remain self-aware of those values which have given it "competence, adaptability and identity" (Jacobs, 2004: 176). The capacity to overhaul policy frameworks is a huge, historic asset at such a time.

Our situation is an example of what in French is called a *conjoncture*, the effect of simultaneity when long-term and short-term phenomena coincide. This lies at the intersection between analyses which focus on the strengths and failures of macro-economic policy in recent years, and those which look instead and beyond at long-term trends, such as declining productivity, climate change, or ageing in the population, which extend over decades. Rarely are these two perspectives brought together beyond the columns of economists. Long-term trends are usually structural, evolving within their own logic; short-term ones are more likely to be the result of individual or collective decisions, usually taken without regard for the deeper structural context. (It is ironic that *conjoncture*, a French term, is helpful to understand the 2008 crisis of globalization, a phenomenon most often discussed in English. The number of French speakers however is rising rapidly, thanks to demographic growth in Africa).

The differences between the short and long term – and their connection – can be illustrated by two newspaper articles which appeared on the same day, 23 September 1999. The *Financial Times* called attention to the need for Japan to increase its money supply, a matter of short-term intervention; the *Frankfurter Allgemeine Zeitung* featured an article about the size of the world's population, which had doubled since 1960, to some six billion, a long-term trend. The *FT* article dealt with actions that could be taken today by very few people, essentially central bankers and treasury officials, with long-term consequences, whereas the *FAZ* article dealt with the consequences of decisions taken by individuals and families over the space of a generation. In a sense, these two articles between them define the problem of planning for the future: What are our options? What will make a difference? And who can make a difference? We know better what needs to be done than how to do it. Perhaps nothing much has changed since – Japan's money supply is still the subject of attention – and there are now seven billion people on the planet, and still growing. But deflation has become a threat in Europe as well, with consequences for the global economy; population ageing and the impact of public policies on population growth complement concern about the global size of the population.

As Perez pointed out, to cope with a shift in paradigms, you have to know where you are in the process. The explanatory concept of the *conjuncture*, which combined long-term structural patterns that constrain action with short-term opportunities and options, emerged from structuralism in the early twentieth century. In the hands of historian Fernand Braudel, history was a matter of how the *longue durée*, the long-term trend, coincided – or collided – with the short-term play of armies and rulers in the fourteenth to seventeenth centuries. This was no mere heuristic device, but a powerful analytic tool just as relevant for the era of central bankers and investment funds as for that of Philip II of Spain and Louis XIV of France (Voth and Drelichman, 2014). (And indeed, it was directly relevant to questions about how France could recover from the human cost of world wars and the economic cost of the Great Depression, issues in the background of Braudel's great work published in 1949).

In the preface to his magisterial two-volume work *La Méditerranée et le monde Méditerranéen* (1966), Fernand Braudel explained the relationship between three temporal frameworks. The first is geographical time which advances slowly and imperceptibly, defining the space which is inhabited and exploited. Using the metaphor of layers, geography represents the foundation on which everything else rests. Above it is social history about the groups whose organization and functions support the economy, the state, and, indeed, civilization. Their evolution is faster but still slow, marked as much by economic cycles as by intellectual currents. Braudel highlighted the importance of commercial, urban capitalism to transform the Mediterranean world of the Renaissance, like a young bird breaking out of its shell. To use Lewis Mumford's term, the city is an "emergent" whose very presence precipitated changes in the world around it (Mumford, 1961: 29). The major commercial, capitalist cities of Braudel's sixteenth century were in fact unique in their day: Seville, Venice, Antwerp grew rapidly, attaining unusual size, and established trade routes that linked Europe's interior to East Asia and the Atlantic and Pacific coasts of Mexico. The third and final layer belongs to the individual, whose experience of time is defined by events at a scale that is lived. Efforts to increase wealth and power take time to show results. Political leaders are therefore limited to what they have available, or can commandeer or borrow. They rarely have the time to prepare for future eventualities by deliberately undertaking to add resources. Yet until they are committed to a course of action, they do not know whether the resources at their disposal are adequate. The distance separating reach and reality, or, to use contemporary terms, between objectives and outcomes, found its echoes in the essays of Montaigne, the plays of Shakespeare, and the writings of Cervantes which are still contemporary. Using another metaphor which was common at the turn of the twentieth century, Braudel also wrote of deep currents barely visible on the surface, which is agitated by the winds and tides (or in other words, events). The impact of this structural approach on political history has been enormous. The archives of state which record the efforts of political leaders to direct or react to the course of events must be complemented by other records which bring to light the economic and social trends which we can understand better than they ever could.

From our perspective, these three temporal patterns have changed, and perhaps space the most. For years now it has been fashionable to talk about the acceleration of time, meaning the rate at which economic, political, and cultural events occur and succeed one another, elevating the short over the medium or long term. Global warming as well as global urbanization and the exploitation of natural resources have *accelerated geographic change*. Compare the shrinkage of Arctic ice or of Swiss glaciers through maps and photographs since 1950, or the expansion of London, Paris, Los Angeles, Tokyo, Singapore, Mexico City, indeed most cities. The earth that was mapped in the 1950s, illustrating text books and encyclopedias, was assumed to be known definitively; how wrong. I do not believe that we have yet absorbed what this means, partly because the fixity of things geographical appears to be "natural," partly because we do not know yet how to cope with the consequences of rapid geographical change in political, cultural, and economic terms. As argued in Part I, macro-economic and sectoral policies to regulate urban economies and their development retain assumptions that space is not a key variable and does not matter; now it matters very greatly. This goes to the heart of the argument why managing space better has become the new imperative: *the temporal evolution of space has caught up to the pace of political and economic change.*

The limits in the twenty-first century may be more easily stretched than in the eighteenth or sixteenth, but limits there are. The challenge which we today face, even with vastly superior means to collect and analyse information, is still to understand what are our options, what may be the consequences of our actions (including the decision to do nothing), and what new opportunities we can create. There are many reasons why historians so often concentrate on crises: by definition, they are complex, giving rise to different and sometimes conflicting interpretations; they generate unusually large and varied sources of documentation, which historians need; they are lived and remembered by many; and, critically, they turn around questions about "what if": because the decisive changes wrought during a crisis are usually not inevitable, we ask how things could have turned out differently, and if so, with what consequences.

When people in the future look for the origins of the phenomena they recognize as their reality, their status quo, they will look back to our present, to find the seeds, the origins, of the world they inhabit. They will see the confusion, the conflicts which divided political opinion, the convictions that people held which committed them either to the status quo or to change. And they will see the turning points, the roads taken and where they led. The danger for historians lies in giving an air of inevitability about what happened, and in endowing the victors in a struggle or contest for political or ideological or economic supremacy with superior virtues; the narrative structure of the march of progress and the triumph of the right owes more to the Bible than its exemplars in the eighteenth and nineteenth centuries would have wished to admit. In some ways historians, with access to more evidence than any actor can marshall, can know more about ourselves than we do. Yet history, to be truthful and compelling, must not do damage to the complexity and uncertainty that characterize periods of change. We who are living through this dramatic period without knowing when or how it will end also know some things about ourselves and our times that will elude people looking back from the future, making it more difficult for them to comprehend the situations people today face.

In one sense history as a discipline, as Vico and Voltaire and their romantic successors such as Hegel knew, is indispensable to progress. With hindsight comes wisdom: historical insight teaches us how to act on imperfect knowledge. Today, when people are undecided what course would be best, options are needed, together with the courage to try them. Tomorrow, when a new economic, geo-political, and institutional framework has emerged and looks likely to endure, people will ask why solutions which will someday be taken for granted were resisted for so long, why time and energy were spent on some issues which in the end did not matter.

Note

1 I am indebted to Catherine Schenk for calling my attention to this work.

References

Braudel, Ferdinand (1966), *La Méditerranée et le monde méditerranéen à l'époque de Philippe II*, 2 vols, 2nd edition (Paris: Armand Colin).
Financial Times (2013), Maurice Lévy, "France should face up to its fears of a somber future," 16 May.
Jacobs, Jane (2004), *Dark Age Ahead* (New York: Random House).
Kissinger, Henry (1979), *White House Years* (Boston: Little, Brown and Co.).
Konvitz, Josef W. (1985), *The Urban Millennium: The City-building Process from the Early Middle Ages in the Present* (Carbondale, IL: Southern Illinois University Press.
Kuhn, Thomas (1962), *The Structure of Scientific Revolutions* (Chicago: Chicago University Press, revised 1970).
Mumford, Lewis (1961), *The City in History: Its Origins, Its Transformations, and Its Prospects* (New York: Harcourt, Brace and World).
Nisbet, Robert (1969), *Social Change and History* (New York: Oxford University Press).

OECD (2010), *Cities and Climate Change*, pp. 17–28 (Paris: OECD). DOI: 10.1787/9789264091375-en.
Perez, Carlota (2002), *Technological Revolutions and Financial Capital: The Dynamics of Bubbles and Golden Ages* (Cheltenham: Edward Elgar).
Rapoport, Amos (1977), *Human Aspects of Urban Form: Towards a Man-environment Approach to Urban Form and Design* (Oxford: Pergamon).
Sustainable Liberty Now (2014), www.sustainablelibertynow.org/nationwide-resolutions-against-agenda-21iclei.html.
Voth, Hans-Joachim and Mauricio Drelichman (2014), *Lending to the Borrower from Hell: Debt, Taxes and Default in the Age of Philip II* (Princeton: Princeton University Press).

9

Paradigms for economic governance: how cities grew bigger and better

The making of a new synthesis or paradigm as a form of crisis resolution in the seventeenth century led to the Enlightenment with its hope of the perfectibility of society, and a similar shock during the era of the French Revolution advanced the Enlightenment agenda by extending civic rights and scientific and engineering projects, further expanding markets and the stock of useful knowledge in the nineteenth century. By the end of that century, the adoption of city-wide networks based on technology became compelling; the modern regulatory state emerged with centralized planning and co-ordination by corporations and the state, shaping innovation and investment. At the same time, radical changes in science and the arts built confidence that enhanced powers of perception and understanding would be up to the task of coping with social and economic changes. In the twentieth century, prosperity became equivalent to progress. A third paradigmatic shift in economic regulation and governance may be at hand. But first let us look at the paradigm that preceded the Enlightenment and at the transition to it.

From the pursuit of salvation to the pursuit of happiness

The regulatory epoch that led to the Westphalia settlement is important on its own terms, and instructive given the enduring importance of Westphalia and its implications for global governance in the twenty-first century, the topic of Chapter 10.

The Bible, prophetical literature, psalms, and proverbs expressed a clear correlation between the fitness of certain laws for society to provide care for the poor and destitute, give respect to strangers, protect property rights, and enforce truthful and fair dealings on the one hand, with the beneficence of God who would preserve his people from war, famine, flood, disease. Failure to obey such laws would lead to divine sanction in the form of economic and political catastrophe; a loss of self-control manifest as immoral behavior and a disregard for law would incur a collapse of state power; but salvation was the reward for faithful obedience.

The practical ordinances regulating markets, the size of a loaf of bread, weights and measures, the discharge of wastes, the lighting of fires, and the like, justified as utilitarian measures for public welfare and safety, were also tied into a mesh of laws and regulations which covered family and social behavior and morality, and the rights of different individuals to participate in various civic bodies. These laws and ordinances drew their authority from civic institutions whose privileges were granted or confirmed by rulers. The plethora of rules for markets, guilds, weights and measures, and even over what people could wear, can easily give rise to criticisms of how such rules interfered with social mobility, competition, trade, innovation. What is of interest is not the content and specificity of the rules but the fact that people lived within a framework of rules which was inseparable from the social and political order.

The rules that determined who was a free citizen of a community, able to participate in the full range of civic affairs, varied widely across Europe: what did not vary was the system itself.

Keeping peace and good order were the highest objectives of those who exercised power. If the direction of life was toward salvation after life, then disobedience to the law and to norms of morality was not only a threat to the individual at fault, justifying that society should try to correct or punish them "for their own good," but also a threat to society, which erred if it tolerated such misconduct. Civic leaders might try to enlarge their autonomy and independence from higher political or ecclesiastical authorities, but without challenging the fundamentally nested or hierarchical nature of the larger political system, or the assumption that this system was itself the bulwark against social instability, or, worse, a breakdown of law and order.

The idea of a perfect city, which emerged as a major theme in western culture at the beginning of the sixteenth century when in 1516 Sir Thomas More published *Utopia*, shaped the context in which the metropolis would be interpreted throughout the early modern period. By describing a utopia, More and other philosophers who followed his example tried to work out the problems that had to be solved if the gap between the way things are and the way they should be were ever to be bridged. (Even today, people need to visualize the city of tomorrow.) Utopia, which literally means *no place* but represents a perfect society, was understood in Renaissance culture in urban terms. People who imagined what a utopian society would be like almost always conceived of it as a city. There were religious antecedents for doing so, for the prophetic literature of the Old Testament frequently referred to the physical development of Jerusalem and the moral development of the society inhabiting the city in interchangeable terms; the Platonic tradition contributed a similar line of thought.

Utopian society would be highly regulated, its citizens free. The authors of utopian visions tried to anticipate laws and regulations covering a wide range of everyday situations, as well as procedures to follow in cases of individuals who violate community norms. The economy of the ideal city would provide adequately for everyday needs, thus eliminating the social consequences of poverty, but overabundance was itself suspect as deviating from the principle of moderation which the philosophers who drafted utopian projects so admired. Utopian cities were supposed to be places where people could live in greater freedom, but as philosophers in the post-Renaissance understood it, a certain conformity would prevail, not from fear or external constraint inhibiting individuals, but out of their desire to please one another and contribute to an overall harmony: this was the essence of Rabelais's "Abbaye de Thélème." The spatial layout of a utopian city, its straight streets of even width, would give a graphic impression of symmetry, uniformity, and proportion. The architect-planner became, therefore, a kind of law-giver with the power to shape society. Many descriptions of utopia contained measurements of the size and principal features of streets and public buildings, adding the illusion of reality to what was obviously an imaginative exercise. But such details also expressed the growing importance of measurement in practical affairs as a means of planning and control. The measurement of space itself was taken by contemporaries as a metaphor for self-examination and self-knowledge which has survived in our culture through the metaphor of the map as a tool of knowledge.

In the perfect city there would be congruence between the values by which people lived, their institutions, and the appearance of the city itself. The utopian city would neither grow nor change. This ideal stood in contrast to the pattern of development of the great capital cities and metropolises of early modern and modern Europe – of counter-Reformation Rome, Amsterdam with its rings of canals, London rebuilt after the great fire of 1666, and Paris transformed under Henri IV and Louis XIV, unfinished cities whose spatial form opened the way to further growth. Could the tension between an ideal of permanent perfection and the reality of change as the nature of things be reconciled?

The reality of change in Europe following the Reformation defied efforts to impose the degree of conformity necessary to realize the ideal of a harmonious society. Religious pluralism following the Reformation of the sixteenth century gave rise to a tension in the very relationship between society and state on which the political framework rested. Laws and the protection of the law applied to Christians; Jews and Muslims had to negotiate rights and duties separately with the ruler where they lived. But as Christianity split into Protestant and Catholic churches, and further, into different Protestant sects, the notion of unified Christendom was undermined at the Continental scale, only to survive at the level of and within kingdoms, principalities, city-states where presumably the faith of the ruler and the faith of the society were one and the same. The wars of religion ultimately took their toll, exhausting Europe's elites, displacing families, impoverishing peasants, killing millions. The combined shock of depressions, civil wars, and international conflicts that marked the Thirty Years War and inspired Jacques Callot's graphic images of brutality also set the context for Descartes to affirm the power of reason and Pascal the legitimacy of doubt. In 1689, John Locke published his Letter on Toleration, about which Paul Hazard wrote that, for Locke, tolerance was the very essence of Christianity. By taking the matter of religious conscience away from the ruler and closer to the responsibility of the individual, John Locke's political philosophy made possible a distinction between the private and the public spheres which has remained essential in regulation.

The transition that marked the shift from salvation in the world to come, to happiness in this world as the over-arching goal of the polity in the western world began with the resolution of political crises in the middle of the seventeenth century when the modern nation-state as a rational entity aware of its interests and powers emerged. T. K. Rabb rightly emphasized that the essential change was a matter of perception: "Long-standing problems were not really solved forever (with the one exception that ... religion did cease to affect foreign policies), but the elite stopped assuming that the problems were insoluble" (Rabb, 1975: p. 79). This transition – as much social and cultural as political – was largely a matter of a couple of decades in the middle of the seventeenth century. To be sure, it had antecedents and after-effects when turbulence and reactionary tendencies seemed to re-open issues: acceptance of Louis XIV's absolutism (c.1661) did not prevent the king from revoking the Edict of Nantes in 1685. More telling was the Sun-King's support for the Academy of Science. It was within the Scientific Revolution that the next regulatory era would develop, eventually transforming the state and expanding the capacity of science to serve it.

The role of economic developments in this transformation of paradigms or settlement of crisis continues to provoke debates among scholars. Economic circumstances during the Little Ice Age, compounded by the human and material cost of the Thirty Years War which left Germany devastated by losses unequalled until the second Thirty Years

War of 1914–45, aggravated the problems of rulers trying to maintain their armies and fleets while repressing rebellions sparked in part by repeated tax levies (Parker, 2013). But the crisis of the seventeenth century was not primarily an economic crisis; it was a crisis about the organizing principles of states whose social composition was no longer so easily aligned with the principles of faith-based order on which the rule of law had until then rested. The problem was socio-intellectual, and so, in due course, was the solution. This does not mean that economic issues were marginal, only that the relationships were often indirect and multiple.

The organization of the rational, bureaucratic state after 1648 – a critical element in the new synthesis or paradigm – contributed significantly in several respects: its own needs for finance made fiscal reform more necessary, and tax collection to be more centralized; equally, the need for exceptional resources gave governments an interest in circuits of lending controlled by bankers, in enforceable contracts, and in negotiated tax levies; and, last but not least, governments, beginning with the most enlightened, in France, Prussia, Austria, and England, took a very great interest in the substantive nature and codification of laws which could affect commerce, trade, and invention, key sources of current and future wealth.

This meant projecting into the future. John Nef noted a remarkable example of what this implied in language and thought when, to illustrate the turn towards quantitative precision, he cited an example from 1598 of an exchange between Lord Buckhurst in London, who was about to succeed Lord Burghley as Lord Treasurer of Elizabeth I, and one Fanshaw, a customs officer in Newcastle, already the principal coal-exporting port and hence the source of important taxes. Buckhurst requested Fanshaw (or his deputy or chief clerk) for a statistic for the past seven years: "How many caldron of coal have been carried out of England to any port beyond the seas as likewise how much has been brought to London or to any other port in England from New Castle." The answer he received was a global figure for the entire seven–year period: 95,558 chaldrons shipped overseas, 418,201 shipped coastwise. This figure, useless for Buckhurst's purposes, provoked this reply: "Mr Fanshaw this is a certificat of confusion more tending to blind than to inform ... I require you to set downe every of the said seven yeares in particular, according to the request of my note unto you." This Fanshaw and his staff did, but noted that the total could have been divided by 7. But Buckhurst did not want the yearly average. As Nef pointed out, "the distinction between the average traffic and the *rate of increase* was still meaningless to these customs officers.

But the distinction was obviously clear to Buckhurst" (Nef, 1958: 12–13). A century later, Vauban provided Louis XIV with a comprehensive picture of the composition of the economy of France and its sources in land and in commerce, with recommendations about how to promote its increase with a view to enlarging the tax receipts so essential to maintaining the motor of war and the magnificence of the monarchy. Vauban, moreover, and to his credit, also understood the depressing impact of repetitive cycles of military campaigns and weather-related crop failures which capped the capacity of the economy. And therein lies the difference between the sixteenth and eighteenth centuries: Vauban's composite picture of the economy, imperfect though it was, provided the elements against which different options for policy could be assessed, their outcomes weighed.

The age of progress: 1648–1918

After the settlement of Westphalia of 1648, a new set of rules was needed for a Europe divided by religion, if not to live in peace, at least to live without fear that religious difference alone was a sufficient reason for one state to attack another. A scientific synthesis based on reason and facts grounded in observations of nature that was neither Catholic nor Protestant provided the foundation for a common European culture which had previously rested on a single Christian church.

The making of the Enlightenment was called by Paul Hazard, and not without reason, "The Crisis of the European Conscience." To speak of the Battle between the Ancients and the Moderns at the end of the seventeenth century is to give the wrong impression that, at a time when all Europe was at war, society and culture were highly militarized. The intellectual battle was fought with pens and with wit, and, when over, it ushered in a period famous still for its irony and satire (Defoe), its celebration of love with a touch of vulnerability and transience (Watteau), and its civility, or the arts and manners of politesse.

The intellectual issues were however serious. Did the ancient philosophers possess a full stock of knowledge and wisdom? And could this be so if they were not given the revealed Christian faith? Did the understanding of nature by Newton and his contemporaries demonstrate that the scholars of his age possessed greater powers? If the answers were affirmative, the implications were twofold: that the sum of knowledge could be expected to continue to increase in the future, and that unlearning, to alter received ideas and facts, could be positive. The test of whether a new phenomenon or explanation could be accepted and assimilated would be the test of experience.

Elevating experience over dogma or received knowledge was fundamental to the Enlightenment and to the program of scientific discovery which it launched. The importance of experience – and thus of experimentation as a way of generating and advancing knowledge – dominated science until the rise of statistics in the twentieth century. Common to both methods to validate facts was – and is – the practice of publication, that is, of publicly exposing the results to critical scrutiny by peers. Let us take this further: it is humbling because to go through it, either as the proponent of a new idea or fact or as its critic, is to admit the possibility of error; it is democratic, because the finding of an error does not lead to a sanction either against the individual whose work is being corrected or against the critic who found that the work needs correcting. This ethos, therefore, provides the basis for learning by doing. Explicitly, the sum of knowledge tomorrow must be different from the knowledge of today. The thrust of historical writing, from Bayle through Voltaire, Gibbon, and Hume, showed the human record without divine intervention as a story of beliefs and facts once held to be true to be corrected in the light of new evidence and ideas: not only is our knowledge of better quality as a result, but also our understanding of the past may be superior to that of contemporaries who witnessed it. Bayle's radical article on the biblical David in his historical dictionary, treating David as a historical and not as a biblical figure, opened the breach.

The search for knowledge founded on reason, science, and experience – and not on revealed truth – led in turn to economic regulation based on greater freedom and belief in progress. Tellingly, regulation was also a term used in watchmaking, to denote the correct and continual beat of the mechanism independent of fluctuations caused by friction, foreign objects and dirt, humidity, temperature, altitude, and movement. Ultimately, as we shall see, this sense of regulation as a stabilizing, active force is essential in economic and social affairs. Diderot used the metaphor of time-keeping devices to illustrate the principle of harmony in the *Encyclopédie*. Harmony was defined as "the general order that prevails between the various parts of a whole," such that they "work together as perfectly as possible" (Mayr, 1986: 80). The more complex a system (of which the watch could be a model), the more it is necessary to understand how the different parts that make up a whole work with each other. The eighteenth-century constitutional model based on checks and balances illustrated this dual concept of harmony and system, what today would be called coherence between the way things work and a foundation of values and principles.

The mechanical clock "was a creative achievement of high intellectual rank. Nothing of comparable ingenuity had ever been invented before, and up to the advent of the steam engine, it remained Europe's intellectually most demanding mechanism" (Mayr, 1986: 27). Their numbers, produced by craftsmen with the best talent, masters of rare and complex devices, exceeded practical need, and were preserved and transmitted as objects worthy of great care and respect. Knowledge of time as the unique, unwavering standard for all measurement gave time-keeping devices unusual authority in culture, to be adopted for metaphorical purposes, illustrating other principles of life, idealizing "the qualities of regularity, order, and harmony." The clock became a "physical illustration," a "prototype for the world, with regard to both its creation and its normal functioning." By implication, the clock supported the argument by design because the complex, interlocking parts of the world could not possibly have been assembled otherwise: evolution, the equivalent of chance and ad-hocery, could not have produced this result (Mayr, 1986: 120).

Otto Mayr contrasted two approaches to the clock metaphor for politics and economics, one, more authoritarian, Continental, and the other, more libertarian, English. If checks and balances operate naturally, so to speak, in individuals and in society, there would be less need for state intervention. But do they? Can a self-regulating system function in something as complex as the economy? Does even a self-regulating system, like a clock which over time becomes less reliable and accurate, depend upon an external agency to keep it going, if not God, then the monarch? A vital tension existed in the Enlightenment between trusting individuals to do the right thing, and relying on systems to prevent people from actions and behavior that would deviate too far from the correct path. Advocates for either view – or their antagonists – had to weigh the consequences of erratic or dangerous behavior, and consider what corrective measures would be necessary if control mechanisms broke down. Into this intellectual opening stepped Adam Smith.

Clock metaphors are essential to understand "the invisible hand" introduced by Adam Smith in mid-eighteenth-century England, and with it a concept of regulation in the broad, conceptual sense which would inspire liberal politics thereafter. The intellectual consequences were immediate, the economic consequences slower to become manifest. The invisible hand refers to a form of checks and balance based on self-regulation fed by a continual flow of information. As a historian of technology in search of early examples of feedback loops, Mayr made a special point of the concept of self-regulation as "the unacknowledged heart" of Smith's effort to introduce liberalism into the practical workings of government in place of burdensome state controls which mercantilism required (Mayr, 1986: 171). A well-designed system will keep all the players, all the parts, in equilibrium, perpetuating itself. The choice between determinism (everything had been thought out in advance, order built in by design) and free will (by acting and choosing) was not just metaphysical, to be decided on the basis of philosophical preferences and tight logic. Making people responsible for their actions rested on the assumption that they will exercise liberty in ways that contribute to a better order and society. Citing Hume, Otto Mayr focused on the "idea that was a central element in contemporary liberal doctrine, namely the idea of *self-interest* as the source of energy behind successful self-regulating social systems" (Mayr, 1986: 65).

Benevolent self-interest was elaborated by Smith in *The Wealth of Nations* (1776). In its base form as the profit motive, self-interest had long been recognized in the eighteenth century for its economic utility. As Mayr succinctly put it, "For the loose slogan of laissez faire to develop into a fully articulated economic theory, an important question had to be answered: precisely what was it that harnessed the chaotic activities of countless self-seeking competitors on the market place into the service of the common good? ... The answer was to be supplied by Adam Smith in terms of the concept of self-regulation" (Mayr, 1986: 165). Mayr quoted Smith: "Every individual is continually exerting himself to find out the most advantageous employment for whatever capital he can command. It is his own advantage, indeed, and not that of society, which he has in view. But the study of his own advantage naturally, or rather necessarily leads him to prefer that employment which is most advantageous to the society." He is, so to speak led by an invisible hand (Mayr, 1986: 175, n. 28).

Smith also referred to the guidance "by an invisible hand" in *The Theory of Moral Sentiments*. The context is different from that in *The Wealth of Nations*, and the difference is revealing of the larger difference between the objective of the paradigm of the Enlightenment with its focus on happiness and the perfectibility of society and that of the twentieth century with its focus on prosperity. The phrase "invisible hand" appeared in a paragraph in which Smith acknowledged appreciation of the beauty and pleasures associated with wealth and luxury. What followed was an apologia of sorts for the economic consequences of the highly unequal distribution of resources, natural and acquired, within society and among nations. In common with other students of political economy, Smith argued that this unequal distribution generated trade and manufacturing, such that to gratify "their own vain and insatiable desires," the rich "divide with the poor the produce of all their improvements. They are led by an invisible hand to make nearly the same distribution of the necessaries of life, which would have been made, had the earth been divided into equal portions among all its inhabitants, and thus without intending it, without knowing it, advance the interests of the society, and afford means to the multiplication of the species." Everything balances out, Smith argued; there is a leveling, not of income but in the "ease of body and peace of mind" which "constitutes the real happiness of human life." There is much to comment upon: the points to emphasize are that the workings of the economy generate the result which the political system intends, with less direct intervention by the state; and that the quantum of goods which people possess is not the measure of happiness.

Ultimately, much depends on the political system. What motivates people to improve laws and institutions? The superiority of a political system is not to be measured by how much better housed, clothed, and fed are the people who benefit from it – precisely those measurements and comparisons which shape comparative tables and rankings and fill political speeches today. Civic mindedness, the "public spirit," Smith argues, is instead more likely when people are inspired by *a desire to perfect the system as a system*. A superior system will enable people as economic actors and social beings to improve the economy, but to build such a system, it is necessary to appeal to something other than material betterment. The passage is worth quoting verbatim:

> You will be more likely to persuade, if you describe the great system of public police which procures these advantages, if you explain the connexions and dependencies of its several parts, their mutual subordination to one another, and their general subserviency to the happiness of the society; if you show how this system might be introduced into his own country, what it is that hinders it from taking place there at present, how those obstructions might be removed, and all the several wheels of the machine of government be made to move with more harmony and smoothness, without grating upon one another, or mutually retarding one another's motions. It is scarce possible that a man should listen to a discourse of this kind, and not feel himself animated to some degree of public spirit. He will, at least for the moment, feel some desire to remove those obstructions, and to put into motion so beautiful and so orderly a machine.

Political studies, Smith concluded, "serve at least to animate the public passions of men, and rouse them to seek out the means of promoting the happiness of the society" (Smith, 1976: 187).

The problem, as always, is that the slate is never clean. Not only did the pursuit of progress and the perfection of the system of government move forward in the eighteenth and nineteenth centuries at different rates in every country; some seemed to fall back while others advanced.

In the process, the Renaissance ideal of utopia, the city that represented how things should be, took on a more concrete form as cities from Dublin to Dresden, from Sweden to France, underwent significant change, putting liberal values into practice.

City-building practices coherent with the Enlightenment program benefited from advances in surveying and engineering methods. Graphic artists learned to depict topographical and spatial features in map or plan form with greater control, showing the difference between the city as it is and as it could become; mathematicians undertook the study of probability and statistics, analytic geometry, and advanced geometry which by the mid-eighteenth century began to transform the practice of architecture and engineering (Perronet built a bridge across the Seine at Neuilly between 1768 and 1772 by calculating the size of the piers according to the loads to be carried, thereby reducing the width of the piers to half of what traditional methods would have required). Large-scale engineering works, mostly carried out by military officers, combined the refortification of national frontiers (thereby enabling garrisons with barracks and parade grounds to house hundreds or thousands of soldiers – six thousand in Strasbourg – at a convenient distance from the civilian population which previously had been subject to housing requisition) with the demolition of medieval city walls which had constrained cities in the past, raising density within and promoting suburbs without. The enclosure movement in England, the rebuilding of cities in Italy and Spain, the reclamation of land from the sea in the Low Countries, colonization of the Baltics, French urbanism (Bordeaux, Lyon, Marseille, Nantes, Rennes) which combined royal grandeur with an agenda to stimulate manufacturing and commerce, all encouraged municipalities to concern themselves more with public order, and property owners to maximize returns on investment. By combining maps and censuses, it became possible to arrive at probable estimates of population density for the first time, indicating which cities were underpopulated and which were overpopulated (Konvitz, 1985: 91–2).

With hindsight, we see that city builders were groping toward answers to such questions as how municipalities could gain access to capital for improvements, how to assess expropriation costs and how to analyse plans in relation to economic and demographic trends, and how to tax the profits of private investments that also created public benefits. Cadasters, introduced during the French Revolution, and the application of scientifically rigorous surveying to the production of maps of cities, gave officials the tools they needed to make the system work and, more important perhaps, to enable engineers to plan deep structural changes – to fill in streams, channel rivers between embankments, enlarge canals, build aqueducts, drain land. The Enlightenment paradigm of progress brought light and air into more parts of the city, improved the supply of water and the drainage of land, created parks and greens, facilitated the construction of multi-storey housing block-by-block.

But the obstacles to a more perfect system, economic and social as well as political, were not so easily overcome by an appeal to reason to design perfect institutions. Hope and fear co-existed, and in ways that applied pressure from the one on the other. Must a society be ready to accept a new political framework, or is the adoption of such a framework a precondition for social change? What were the fears which drove – or checked – a belief in progress? Who defined collective and individual threats to progress? Huge questions, which have come back in current discussions about growth, reform, and institutions.

In the era of religious cohesion, the source of authority was essentially priestly in origin and religious in nature. In the era of the Enlightenment and the nineteenth century, *philosophes* and critics called attention to the flaws in society and the state which if removed or attenuated would represent progress toward a higher level of existence. The charitable impulses of a more religious age were replaced by humanitarian movements and sentiments directed against illiteracy, slavery, the ill-treatment of the insane and disturbed and of prisoners, and on behalf of helping people with a handicap – blindness and deafness – anything which would keep individuals from benefiting from more rights and opportunities. The acceptance of Newtonian science at the turn of the eighteenth century preceded several decades when urban revolts virtually disappeared, and when the physical consequences of war, in terms of material destruction and loss of life, diminished significantly. Happiness did not seem so vain at a time when everyday life seemed indeed to be getting better. Civic and legal institutions (including courts and legislators), following written constitutions, would interpret and apply the rule of law. Academies and universities would increase secular, rational knowledge drawn from theory and experience. Thus the lecture hall, the theater and the opera, the academy, the café and the restaurant drew people toward knowledge and provided places where it could be heard, discussed, enacted.

The role of the critic was to bring out embarrassing truths, to show in image or in action the consequences of behavior that decent people would prefer to overlook, averting their gaze, stepping over an inconvenient puddle. Well might the Rousseau romantic believe that city life bred immorality, degrading people. Hogarth's wildly popular prints of London's gin houses and filthy streets, Reynolds's touching and sympathetic drawings of people in prison-like asylums, Beccaria's treatise that spurred prison reform, Hauy's study of deafness, the invention of the Braille alphabet – these examples, which could be multiplied, balanced the attack on abuses, often exploiting satire and popular culture, with programs of reform, typically through a combination of education, legal revision, and the establishment of institutions. Suffering, which religion justified as inherent in the nature of humanity as sinners, no longer seemed necessary. People who violated laws and norms could be reformed; the problem of the backslider however remained, especially in the form of deviant behavior, willfully anti-social and inimical to the family which was the social unit *par excellence*. This helps explain why immoral behavior in family life so often formed the backdrop of fiction and painting, and why so much classical and romantic opera and music was about how to reconcile the passions which incline people to the object of desire with their responsibilities to others.

On a more political level, the fear of deviancy became fear of subversion, of secret plots and conspiracies, of assassinations and barricades, conflicts driven by desperate fantasies or dreams rather than changes supported by reasoned arguments and open persuasion, the principles on which the liberal ethos rested. It is not surprising therefore that the mystery novel began almost with the French Revolution itself, or rather in the hands of Balzac in the early years of the Restoration looking back at the Revolution. *Une ténébreuse affaire* (1843) took place in the country of Champagne near Troyes in 1803 but the real action, as the reader learns only at the end, was in Paris in the form of a conspiracy against Napoleon. The novel in fact contained two mysteries, with action in the French countryside with its mix of riding paths through forests and thickets of brush which conveniently hid abandoned quarries suitable for hiding, to the edge of the great battlefields of central Austria. The message of so many mysteries is of the inherent stability of society. One could say that the nineteenth century ends with Conrad's story *The Secret Agent* (1907), of the Verlocs and their pathetic and doomed effort to blow up Greenwich precisely because it was the symbol of universal time on which the co-ordination of commercial contracts, maritime navigation and astronomical calculation all depended.

To one side, dirty lanes, shabby dwellings; to the other, straight streets lined with shops and houses with large windows and air. It was this contrast, this tension which lay at the heart of moral and social discourse for the middle and upper classes who had the opportunity and the means to benefit from modernity. They could see progress being made. But the conditions of life for the majority of people – peasants in the country or day-laborers in the city – still exposed those who were better off to the problems of poverty: prostitution and venereal disease which undermined families; epidemics which spread out of control or, like tuberculosis, remained endemic; fire, which also threatened to engulf all property (the London fire of 1666 which destroyed 13,600 houses, and the Chicago fire of 1870 which left ninety thousand homeless and the 1877 fire in Saint John, Nova Scotia which left fifteen thousand homeless sit like bookends on this period); and revolutionary ideology, or just civil unrest when employment dipped and the price of bread shot up.

Slum removal was an insoluble problem as long as people had to meet the cost of housing out of income, leaving "betterment," as it was called, to philanthropy or municipal socialism, neither of which could cope with the scale of the problem of overcrowded and unsanitary housing. The backlog of environmental and social conditions to be remediated, combined with the sheer pace of demographic pressures of growth, compromised any sense that enlightened civic leadership could get ahead, the very definition of progress. In the absence of redistributive tax systems, without large public expenditure supported through a tax base drawing on income, without a bureaucracy to manage everything from the public school system to the water system, the poor would remain poor, income disparities would remain wide.

Invention of course was the most visible sign of what people in the eighteenth and nineteenth centuries called progress. The legal protection of the rights of inventors was recognized early on in the Enlightenment as essential to promote invention; the US Patent Office occupied one of the most impressive buildings in mid-nineteenth-century Washington DC. Inventions helped improve the speed and safety of transport: roads, canals, railroads, large sailing ships, then steam-powered vessels and finally ships with steel hulls, marked with the Plimsoll Line to indicate a safe loading level (made compulsory in the UK in 1876) and sailing to coasts protected by lighthouses; communications (telegraph, telephone, postal services); the means to project firepower through standardization and mass production of weaponry and the organization of supply chains for armies and navies; the application of energy from coal, water, and oil to production and comfort; and institutions to educate the public and bring people interested in "improvement" as well as invention together. One can speak of the invention of a system of innovation. But the impact on health and longevity was constrained by social conditions of housing and income – critical constraints on growth. The limited capacity of the economy of the industrial age to reduce the scale of poverty or the frequency of depressions became acutely apparent in the 1890s: the Hamburg cholera epidemic of 1892 in which ten thousand people died; the depression and crash of 1896 (OECD, 2014). The modern infrastructure system for urban living – building fixed networks that extended public services uniformly across the metropolitan territory – became possible only as part of a new paradigm.

Space, time, and co-ordination – urban networks and the goal of prosperity

Social promiscuity, epidemics, poverty, illiteracy, and pollution which could subvert progress were abated only when a different regulatory regime with the potential to transform social and environmental conditions was introduced at the end of the nineteenth century, extending public utilities for energy, transport, water, and waste management and imposing standards on housing based on networked utilities and infrastructures. The construction of turnpikes, canals, and then railroads, culminating at the end of the nineteenth century in integrated networks of overland and maritime transport of valuable and basic commodities alike, was accompanied by the extension of national power over remote rural districts and sprawling metropolitan zones. This transformation, which also altered the role of government, was based on assumptions about professionalism and efficiency, defining modernity in terms which technology reified, or made manifest, as the application of science to practical living. The key to the solution of urban social and environmental problems was seen to be – and still remains – the extension of a uniform level of services across the entire urban region, in theory without distinction between places where rich and poor live. This regulatory regime, based on the authority of experts and the integrity of public bodies through which they exercise power to achieve prosperity and rising incomes and to prevent sustained economic recessions, survived into the twenty-first century.

Space – how to arrange it, how to conceive of it, how to represent it – was central to the paradigm shift at the end of the nineteenth century. The spatial frame of reference for the age of progress was the earth itself, mapped and measured according to scientific laws derived from the universe itself, as mastered through physics and mathematics. The spatial challenge in the industrial era of canals and railroads lay in trying to co-ordinate and synchronize the movement of commodities used in production from their source, through intermediate points of storage and warehousing (hence the grain elevators of Canada and the Great Lakes, the vast fireproof depots of London and Hamburg, etc.) to the final point of production and assembly, and thence into distribution channels. Much of this co-ordination was the work of myriad firms; government intervention was a matter of tariffs and prices. The so-called second age of globalization that began at the end of the nineteenth century extended these networks and expanded their capacity dramatically. The role of merchants and bankers in this complex process was matched by corporations, a stellar example of "the invisible hand" in operations that no government could master without seizing control of the vast apparatus itself.

Geographic theorists and imperialists changed perceptions of the importance of space during the last phase of territorial expansion, reflecting the capacity of different peoples or, as Ratzel, author of *Anthropogeographie* (1882) and *Politische Geographie* (1897) put it, of an instinct for expansion inherent in individual organisms and in nation-states (Kern, 1983: 224–5). Size alone was not the only variable; the quality of space also mattered. But as lands to control were assimilated into geo-political spheres shown on maps as grey, pink, etc., communications within the developed world took on greater importance. Russia's defeat by Japan in 1905 not only showed that wealth and power did not correlate directly with the number of square kilometers under a nation's control; it also highlighted some of the advantages of sea as against land power in extending its interests.

The idea of the seas as a space that could not be claimed by a state dated back to the seventeenth-century legal theories of Grotius, which fitted well with the maritime ambitions of the small and newly independent state that was the Netherlands, and with those of the larger but still weaker kingdom of England. The freedom of the seas counterbalanced the extension of land power on the continent which accompanied the construction of fortifications on national boundaries and the maintenance of standing armies. On land, armies were under the control of centralized commands. On the seas, the power of states was effectively constrained by the impossibility of communication with fleets. This began to change with the extension of underwater telegraph cables; the radio revolution early in the twentieth century put ships in contact with each other and with the land while at sea. Further evidence of the shrinking maritime frontier comes from the growth of large merchant fleets which were subject to national standards for insurance, licensing regimes for officers, and for safety equipment. The space where state regulation did not apply had shrunk progressively in the nineteenth century, an example of intangible territorial expansion, visible only in legal texts and in lines on maps and charts. Writers who talked about the closing of the frontier and artists who painted the encroachment of western civilization on the great plains of North America or the outback of Australia correctly captured the sense that the relationship between society and space – territory – was undergoing a fundamental change.

French geographer Camille Vallaux promoted the concept of distance measured in time as a check against measuring space linearly. In 1906 he produced an isochronic map "showing the world marked in zones determined by the number of days' travel between them and London or Paris" (Kern, 1983: 227). The modernity of Vallaux's map highlighted the growing importance of ship lanes. Port cities, which since the Renaissance had been the largest and fastest growing cities in the Atlantic world, supported shipping with minimal state intervention until the end of the nineteenth century when the expansion of shipping took on new proportions which overwhelmed systems based on private firms and corporations to handle port operations and expansion. Ships increased in size and speed, necessitating continual enlargements of port facilities. The British shipping fleet, the largest in the world, nearly doubled to 19 million tons between 1890 and 1914; its nearest rival, Germany, had a fleet of 5 million tons in 1914. (Today, London is no longer a port but Hamburg remains one of the largest in the Atlantic world.) Ports could not keep up, nor could cities respond to the pressures to enlarge them. Statistics – which were rarely synthesized at the time, so few were the studies devoted to port cities (the first comprehensive descriptions of the port economy of New York appeared in 1918 and 1920, and of London only in 1932) – tell the story. A covered slipway in England 1,000 feet long and 100 feet wide cost £150,000 in 1914, exclusive of working machinery. Yearly capital expenditure in England and Wales increased from about £2.3 million to £3.3 million in the period between 1892 and 1906–7, only 5 per cent in the form of direct public spending, a level of private investment that was unsustainable. The creation of new docks to enlarge a port precipitated changes throughout the port district as the movement of goods and workers was restructured. Local conditions differed, but similar pressures highlighted the limited capacity of local capitalists and governments everywhere to cope (Konvitz, 1994). Nation-states intervened in response to bankruptcies and strikes in stages which culminated in the *de-facto* or *de-jure* nationalization of ports during World War One.

Electrification, networks, and the era of prosperity

Electrification is not only key to the operation of modern regulated utilities on which contemporary urban life depends; the demands of electrification helped shape a new approach to regulation; and electrification came to symbolize comprehensive territorial networks and the seemingly automatic regulation of the economy, both in the safe hands of experts. Because there is no way to store electricity efficiently, to regulate the flow of power in an electricity system comes close to achieving a true balance between supply and demand across space in real time.

This book began with a question: if cities are the motors of the economy, what drives them? This metaphor owes much to the electric motor which whirs and hums, providing power on demand when and where it is needed. This metaphor tells us that, like electricity, monetary and fiscal policies are supposed to power urban economies, smoothly delivering inputs in the form of credit, pricing signals, and other instruments that allow economic actors – all of us as citizens, consumers, employees, and employers – to make choices which optimize the benefits of living and working in cities, another example of the invisible hand. Only it doesn't quite work like that. Electrification reminds us that urban markets are created, as much as the buildings, parks, water mains, and streets of the city. And more: electrification matters because all other technological systems in cities depend on it. It is the ultimate model of regulation because it depends on the fine balance between supply and demand. Electricity is managed within time frames of a few seconds; the network adjusts for the needs of different places at the same time. But the system – from feed stocks (gas, coal, nuclear, etc.) to generation, distribution, and consumption – calls for long-term investment.

Electrification became the chief symbol of modernity, transforming social conditions and work, tying communities together in ways that dissolved many of the traditional differences between country and town, and creating the basis for new spatial forms in cities, at unprecedented densities. For decades the construction, enlargement, and operation of electric generation and distribution systems remained a key instrument of government, with social or national ownership as a quasi-public good and essential utility. The privatization of power generation and distribution late in the twentieth century to achieve greater efficiency and lift investment has been part of the creation of the regulatory state, defined by the use of regulatory agencies, competition principles, and market conditions within a legal framework when the state withdraws from direct provision of a service.

To put this in an urban perspective: the coal-fired, gas-lit city of the late nineteenth century had its dark spots, physically and metaphorically, showing up like tubercular shadows on an X-ray of the slum-dwellers whose physical condition made them unfit for military service in the age of mass conscription. Poverty had often been taken as a given when as much as half the urban population, largely composed of migrants from rural areas, were engaged as unskilled workers or as day laborers living with their families or as lodgers in overcrowded and unsanitary dwellings, unable to save money when daily wages went on basic food and fuel. Only an economy that could grow on the basis of a better-educated workforce, better able to increase productivity, benefit from organizational structures, and use technology, could reduce poverty. Electrification became a key instrument to achieving wider, deeper changes which symbolized progress. The Paris Exposition of 1937 and the illuminated night-time skyline of New York were equally emblematic of the transformation of the city through electrification.

The process of electrification called for a break with laissez-faire ideology, enlarging the role of government in both peace and war justified no longer by the pursuit of progress but by the goal of prosperity. Electrification in the pre-1939 era prefigured the configuration of electricity grids and networks for the rest of the century, including critical issues of regional inter-dependence, centralized control, the ability to plan ahead of demand, and the competence to take decisions at the interface between technology, politics, and investment.

There are certain characteristics of electricity which helped shape its development as an industry. It cannot be stored, meaning that demand and supply have to be in balance at all times. This balancing is a form of continual regulation – that word again. Because demand fluctuates by the hour, the day, and the season, capacity must be there in a latent form, to be amplified when need be. This can be costly to provide. Incremental increases in generating capacity can be less efficient than the construction of generating capacity in advance of anticipated need. To help rationalize the investment, producers both of electric power and of the appliances that draw on it had an interest to promote consumer use, often by promoting the attractiveness of clean electric stoves and refrigerators, for example. The extension of power networks on a regional scale raised questions about cross-subsidization because the higher cost of connecting villages and farms to networks could never be recouped from those who benefited from the network, but, if the costs of rural electrification were shared with city users, then urban consumers would be paying more than they would otherwise. Given the quasi-monopolistic nature of electric systems – a power producer would want exclusive jurisdiction over a territory – regulation of prices went hand-in-hand with electrification, but could lead to problems either when prices were set too low to raise finance in anticipation of demand, or to run systems efficiently when there was over-capacity. Problems of this kind which existed in the pre-1920 era are as familiar today as then.

As historian Thomas P. Hughes set out in a path-finding work, *Networks of Power* (1983), electrification began long before the regulatory framework appropriate to its particular characteristics and potential was developed. Its early technology was essentially accommodated within the laissez-faire system of the nineteenth century because it involved small-scale generation for on-site use or for distribution in a very small perimeter. With direct current, there was no option. Only the adoption of alternating current allowed for the distribution of electric power over a wider area, extending far away from the generating plant. Hughes was primarily concerned to describe different systems in Berlin, Chicago, and London as the outcome of different managerial and engineering solutions to the technical limitations and potential of electric power, and the transfer of solutions from one place to another.

Electrical systems as they developed were unstable, not in scientific or engineering terms, but as an assembly of different parts which had to function coherently and in balance – and it was the adjustment of the different parts that called for continual modifications, change in one part leading to changes in others. (Steam turbines, for example, took less space in city generating plants, whose land costs were high, than reciprocating steam engines.) No system, however well built to last, was immune to change, but, as Hughes showed, a high degree of path dependency began to affect their evolution, not only due to the phenomenon of sunk costs which made retrofitting existing systems increasingly difficult and costly, but also because systems, as they evolved, incorporated legal and regulatory frameworks which made change difficult, and embodied concepts of what a system should look like and how it should function. The ability to navigate the political and regulatory sphere became critical. Consider that in the 1920s the "transmission system included overland steel transmission towers, copper or aluminum lines with costly insulators, and a complex array of lightning–protection apparatus, circuit breakers, switches, transformers, and synchronous generators" and it is no surprise to learn that at that time in the United States, when many regional systems were being built, "the capital demands of the American utilities … exceeded those of the railroads during the decades of their most rapid expansion" (Hughes, 1983: 365). The theories of system management that evolved, Hughes claimed, were the most sophisticated innovation "since the formulation of complex railroad management concepts in the nineteenth century" (Hughes, 1983: 371).

Networks were critical to electrification in several respects. They allowed systems to draw on several sources of power which were dispersed spatially, such as water, or delivered centrally, such as coal; they enabled power to be distributed to a mix of industrial, commercial, and residential users whose needs and demands varied temporally; and they could permit systems to inter-connect, thereby transferring surplus power to areas where demand exceeded generating capacity. We owe the term "grid" to Charles Merz, who observed "that the network of high-voltage transmission lines that would crisscross the [English] countryside took the shape of a great gridiron imposed upon a map of the country" (Hughes, 1983: 353). Control of such complex systems called for "increasingly complex information networks and remote controls, ... equations describing the essential parameters, variables, and functions of the different power systems, ... analog computers to solve the most tedious of these, ... [and] the keeping of historical records, especially load curves, and information about changes in population, transportation, industrialization, and social patterns, and the weather" (Hughes, 1983: 367). In other words, the management and planned expansion of an electric power system had to internalize as much information about the region it served as would have been necessary for its very governance. "In the 1920s, engineers increasingly used concepts such as 'coordination,' 'integration,' 'control,' 'flow,' 'concentration,' 'centralization,' and 'rationalization'" (Hughes, 1983: 368). Of these, rationalization was, in Hughes's considered opinion, the most important "governing strategy for regional utilities in the 1920s. It carried many shades of meaning, but generally it signified obtaining the optimal combination of economic gains with a minimum input of economic resources, including capital and labor" (Hughes, 1983: 369).

Who was in charge? Experts, professionally trained and certified or licensed, became the guardians of the twentieth century, succeeding the critic in the eighteenth and nineteenth centuries, and the clergy before, setting the parameters, codifying the rules, warning of the dangers of excess, in this case in economic and social policy, excessive debt, underinvestment and insufficient capacity, and of the weak links between systems that create systemic risk. The central command control of a power system became the visual and literary metaphor for regulatory power in the Detroit murals of Diego Rivera, in the novels of Vassily Grossman, in the film *Metropolis* – but always with the misgiving that the system itself is fragile, liable to collapse within a narrow range of tolerances. The defining image is of the operator in front of a wall of instruments, dials, switches and telecommunications equipment, with the frequency meter prominent. Control as a process and as an objective was located in the dispatching center where the dispatcher, using telephones and telegraphs, and information captured by specialized instruments, observed color-coded lights on a control board and operated remote-control electric signals (Hughes, 1983: 372–3).

It took time for the political sphere to grasp the potential of electric networks as an economic regulator, expanding the power of the state to expand the capacity of the economy and assure its growth. No longer was electricity a private good; it had become a basic public service on which people depended for everyday necessities whether at home, traveling to work, or at work. The creation of networks was transformative, altering the relations between the state, society, and the private sector. This story is critically important to understanding economic regulation in the twentieth century and its implications for the current crisis. First, regulation of any utility system or network, which was absolutely essential to its performance and growth, was a matter of internal organization, management, and control, an example of the interaction of the human and the technical. Second, and consistent with Perez's model of paradigm shifts, there was a time lag between the development of the sector, the capacity to project its growth in the form of concrete plans for systems and networks, and the formalization of government regulation in institutions and rules – without which systems and networks could not be built and function. Third, it took great crises to change political norms and behavior such that regulated planning could leap forward. And fourth, without a vision embracing social needs, environmental development and economic potential, the imagination needed to develop systems and networks would never have nurtured a working partnership between engineers, financiers, and politicians.

Electrification was so essential to the twentieth century that we tend to forget its nineteenth-century origins and the impact of World War One on economic governance, accelerating incipient changes. Would the Enlightenment meta-paradigm of progress have remained dominant had World War One not erupted? Or would it have been eclipsed even if the forces leading to war had been diverted and contained after Sarajevo? The pressures of rapid technological innovation, of increasing the capacity of systems of production and supply of commodities, and of the growth of cities and of new metropolitan city-regions where industrial production and consumer consumption were concentrated, to unprecedented size, straining networks of supply, were already testing the limits of the regulatory paradigm through which progress was pursued. What came next?

Having expanded control massively in war, governments after 1918 sought to return to some *status quo ante* at least in part in order to reduce the size and scale of government itself, burdened by huge debts. What followed was a depression so sharp and prolonged that it swept away democracy in Germany, Italy, and Spain, and made communism a credible alternative to capitalism in the eyes of many. When governments faced a similar challenge after 1945, rather than withdraw precipitously, they remained committed to greater intervention, even at the cost of extending credit internationally in a successful effort to break with a cycle which only years before had reignited national passions, overthrown governments, polarized extremes on the Left and Right, and triggered World War Two. This second Thirty Years War (1914–45) shaped the transformation of government and its relations to society and the economy, increasing enormously its scope for intervention and the means to do so, and providing a new rationale for using its powers based on two principles: that prosperity insures against social and revolutionary upheaval, and that the sacrifices of war entitle people to the material benefits of peace.

Exceptional crises are decisive in generating paradigm shifts in economic governance, or meta-regulation. Establishing the role of world wars in the history of urban economic regulation is important when the centenary of World War One has sparked debates about the nature of that conflict and whether it mattered in the end who won and who lost. The twentieth century was shaped by the knowledge that the barriers erected by grand strategy that kept society from the abyss had quickly collapsed, that the ascent from the abyss took decades, and that tens of millions remained buried in the abyss. The pursuit of prosperity as the over-arching paradigm of the twentieth century was driven by the imperative to contain forces which otherwise threatened to destabilize society, lest radical ideologies on the Left or Right capture an enlarged, newly enfranchised electorate, and force nationalism into destructive, aggressive channels. Cities were at the epicenter of these great issues. The massive investment to build and maintain urban infrastructures and their tentacular reach across the countryside to dispose of waste, to supply power and water, to connect cities to each other, far exceeded the capacity of cities themselves to finance. The organization of agencies and departments in government at all levels – driven by top–down policies – to design and operate such systems quickly became one of the fundamental characteristics of the modern bureaucratic state. The regulatory paradigm that evolved combines control over land use with control over the rules which keep investments in long-term infrastructure projects (and housing) reasonably safe, assuring that investors receive interest and recover their capital. The strengths of this paradigm help explain why it has lasted for decades.

When the paradigm for progress was dominant, the implicit signs of failure were suicide, prostitution and vagrancy, radical or ethnic politics, and even subversive, and revolutionary activity, or, in other words, evidence that the ideology of progress had limits. When the paradigm for prosperity reigned, signs of failure were high unemployment or non-participation in the workforce, breakdowns and capacity constraints in services, closed access to credit, recessions, widening income disparities, stable or rising percentages of people in poverty. The electoral slogans,

"You've never had it so good," or "Are you better off today?" tell it all. The narrowing of disparities and the widening of opportunities maintained belief that the economy is indeed working as it should; the widening of disparities and the narrowing of opportunities are therefore the contemporary equivalent of more sin in the Baroque era, or of more deviancy and revolutions in the eighteenth and nineteenth centuries, phenomena which undermined collective faith in the system. If the goal of security – economic, social, political, and environmental – is taking priority over prosperity, it is because confidence in twentieth-century macro-economic, sectoral regulatory paradigm has been undermined, not just by the crisis of 2008, but by the post-crisis crisis which shows no sign of ending.

It may be a coincidence that the inception of each paradigm coincided with a point of rupture in urban growth, that is, a point defined by the potential for a large city to grow to reach a size that no city had previously attained. The importance of such points of rupture cannot be underestimated even in a world which counts the number of mega-cities by multiples of ten. It was always thus; there is still an active debate about whether cities of very large size, of ten million inhabitants or more, generate problems which smaller cities do not have, or which are much more difficult to manage in very large cities. Put in historical perspective, in the sixteenth century, no city in Europe, not even Paris, London, or Naples, the largest, quite reached 300,000 inhabitants. By 1800, London was coming close to one million, Paris some 660,000; Vienna, which had been 20,000 in 1500, contained 230,000. The average size of a medium–size city such as Bordeaux, Seville, Edinburgh, or Antwerp in 1800 would have been that of a large city three centuries before. Between 1800 and 1900, the size of the largest city increased from one million to nearly ten million inhabitants. That the result was not anarchy, that the growth of cities accompanied and reinforced enormous gains in education and material welfare for many, that large and powerful cities the size of many smaller nation-states were assimilated into and did not destroy the institutional fabric of republics, monarchies, and empires – these might not have happened had there not been commensurate transformations in economic regulatory governance.

This compressed history shows the intellectual scale at which a meta-paradigm operates. It includes ideas which perhaps only an elite understand, but from which concepts and techniques can be applied in everyday life. Each meta-paradigm in successive regulatory epochs has not had the well–being of cities as its main objective, but each was vulnerable to problems that could be accentuated and concentrated in cities, and aspired to goals that could best be realized in cities. Each was grounded on assumptions about the nature of urban economic and social systems, and each offered the means to cope with urban growth in ways which enabled the size and number of cities to expand, lifting the limits to growth.

It is inconceivable that urban growth in the eighteenth and nineteenth centuries could have advanced through a pre-1650 economic governance paradigm, or that the modern networked city of the twentieth century could have taken shape according to the rules of the previous regulatory epoch. Given what we know – or assume – about the challenges of the twenty-first century, why should we believe that the twentieth-century paradigm of prosperity is capable of guiding the development of cities in a more inter-dependent world where the rate of change of space – the environment – appears to be accelerating?

References

Hazard, Paul (1935), *La crise de la conscience européene* (Paris: Boivin, translated as *The European Mind (1680–1715)* (London: Hollis and Carter, 1953).

Hughes, Thomas P. (1983), *Networks of Power: Electrification in Western Society, 1880–1920* (Baltimore: Johns Hopkins University Press).

Kern, Stephen (1983), *The Culture of Time and Space, 1880–1918* (Cambridge, MA: Harvard University Press).

Konvitz, Josef W. (1985), *The Urban Millennium: The City-building Process from the Early Middle Ages to the Present* (Carbondale, IL: Southern Illinois University Press).

Konvitz, Josef W. (1994), "The crises of Atlantic port cities, 1880 to 1920," *Comparative Studies in Society and History*, 36: 2 (April): 293–318.

Martin, Kingsley (1929), *French Liberal Thought in the Eighteenth Century: A Study of Political Ideas from Bayle to Condorcet* 1929, 2nd edition, revised, edited by J. P. Mayer (London: Turnstile Press, 1954, p. 277).

Mayr, Otto (1986) *Authority, Liberty and Automatic Machinery in Early Modern Europe* (Baltimore: Johns Hopkins University Press).

Nef, John U. (1958), *Cultural Foundations of Industrial Civilization* (Cambridge: Cambridge University Press).

OECD (2014), *How Was Life? Global Well-being since 1820* (Paris: OECD), DOI: 10/1787/9789264214262-en.

Parker, Geoffrey (2013), *Global Crisis: War, Climate Change and Catastrophe in the Seventeenth Century* (New Haven and London: Yale University Press).

Rabb, T. K., (1975), *The Struggle for Stability in Early Modern Europe* (New York: Oxford University Press).

Smith, Adam (1976) *The Theory of Moral Sentiments*, in the Glasgow Edition of the Works and Correspondence of Adam Smith, ed. D. D. Raphael and A. L. Macfie (Oxford: Clarendon Press).

Spinoza, B, (1677), *Ethica Ordine Geometrico Demonstrata*, Part III: On the Origin and Nature of the Emotions, translation of Definition 13: Explanation.

10

Cities and nation-states in the urban age: will inter-dependence reshape rules for the twenty-first century?

Hope: putting cities first in policy to make cities safer

In this last chapter, the nation-state, which has been almost as visible as the city in a book about cities, takes on greater importance. In the twentieth century, governments and their policies arguably had a greater impact on cities than cities had on governments; in the twenty-first century, cities and the challenges they face may turn out to reshape international relations and national governments.

The fact that governments did not adopt urban strategies to cope with the crisis of 2008 and build the foundations for a sustainable recovery was the point of departure for a book-long exploration of how cities can survive in the twenty-first century. Neither the public nor the private sector appears to have a strategic framework or vision (beyond "smart" or "green") to commit vast sums for transport, water, waste management, and energy to 2030 and beyond, most of it for cities. This is a troubling conclusion, suggesting that the crisis is a crisis of decision-making.

We have been there before. In the 1930s, the legacy of poverty and the impact of slums defined an agenda for and around cities which helped leverage massive public investment. Destroyed in war, undermined by the depression, the rebuilding of cities was the only way to rebuild the economies of Europe after 1918 and 1945, and after 1945 in Japan, as well as in the United States. The regulatory paradigm of the twentieth century was shaped by the failures of nineteenth-century industrialization to improve the prospects of life for the bottom half of the population and by the shock of the Great Depression. Today cities around the world are iconic landmarks of how much the postwar era achieved, setting the foundations for the growth in world trade and investment. But unless they are rebuilt – and rebuilt differently in many ways – they will be less fertile, less likely to generate the ideas, inventions, and firms that will help us all cope with social and environmental problems which are often phrased in apocalyptic terms for a good reason. There is a stalemate: without obvious solutions, why change? Yet without change, how can solutions be found? What can be done, starting with cities as they are? What should be – and can be – changed, to help advance transition to the next paradigm?

The goal of prosperity helped people feel that they had a stake in society and a future, justifying personal efforts and sacrifice to pursue education, secure housing, hold a job, engage in community activities. It enjoyed a very long run to the start of the twenty-first century, an impressive achievement. But its social and political gains have been damaged by the crisis and its aftermath; confidence in its assumptions has been badly shaken, and perhaps not to be recovered for many. The great fears of millions today for their future – those who risk sliding out of the urban middle class, those who may never become middle class, and those who are in the middle class but fear that they will never enjoy adequate security as they live, work, and age – cannot be waved away with graphs of economic cycles.

The test of any regulatory paradigm is *how to cope with uncertainty* – a human dilemma – whether for a devout Christian in the seventeenth century uncertain whether he will be saved, or for an ardent advocate of social and political change during the Enlightenment or the nineteenth century uncertain whether change means progress, or for a macroeconomist or policy-maker after the world wars anxious to promote productivity so that society can afford a high level of social and environmental benefit, but uncertain how to cope with crashes and recessions. Uncertainty today appears to have reached levels not seen for decades. Trans-boundary risks, insidious risks which erupt after a period of gradual development, and global risks for which a range of predictions can be established were always there in the past, but two things are now different: our ability to make calculated estimates of probabilities is greater, and there are more channels of transmission from one country to another, and from one sector to another.

Living with uncertainty is deeply human, but it need not be paralysing. Each paradigm since the sixteenth century has tried to give people a way to achieve individual and collective goals, even when success could not be assured. It is the lack of control over outcomes which heightens awareness of risk and feelings of insecurity today, magnifying uncertainty. The threat is not uncertainty as such, but unmanageable, paralysing fear of crises in an era which is more conscious of non-military risks than was the twentieth century. The risks which are uppermost in the twenty-first century – environmental, social, and economic – are defined differently from those of the past; this reflects not only objective change, but a profound evolution in our values, social structures, and intellectual capacities. Today and for the foreseeable future, many risks are all the more terrifying because we know how little we can do about them. It is this sense of loss of control that dis-empowers people. There are two unacceptable options: a fatalistic belief, more in keeping with premodern traditional cultures than with one liberated by science and engineering, or risk-obsessed measures, pursued single mindedly and often taking the form of command-and-control regulation, exempted from cost-benefit analysis under the blanket of "security."

What is needed is a framework to help people adapt to and cope with problems that connect their individual lives to global forces of change with greater confidence. To reiterate, the tens of trillions of dollars or euros needed to rebuild, modernize, and extend urban infrastructures is a governance challenge: a challenge for how banks and insurance companies invest and are regulated, a challenge for how land uses, spatial development, transport, housing, and public works are regulated and co-ordinated; a challenge for governments to set strategies for the connections between and within cities; a challenge for citizens to accept changes in living patterns. The advantages of a liberal, inter-connected economy must reinforce, not compromise, the social and environmental conditions of the places where people live. And most people live in cities and urban regions.

If we are at a turning point, it is because we do not see solutions to problems. And when problems accumulate, and appear intractable, the resulting situation itself becomes critical. The crisis of 2008 revealed and exacerbated economic governance shortcomings which the regulatory mode of the twentieth century cannot easily resolve or contain:

- The sectoral framework whereby the components of policy regulating urban development, fiscal and monetary policy, transport policy, environmental policy affecting land use and resources, energy policy affecting the supply and distribution of power, housing, health, education policies, etc., are disconnected from one another, and distributed to different agencies which guard their prerogatives, rules and resources.
- The assumption that local decisions matter only to local residents and stakeholders, ignoring the spillover costs when local actors do not engage in cross-jurisdictional co-operation. This mis-alignment in governance which limits multi-level co-ordination and often leaves the national level in the role of arbiter complicates investment especially in infrastructure which has the potential to affect urban form and land use for decades. Subsidiarity and public choice theory have not reduced the democratic deficit, symbolized by the very low rates of voter participation in local and regional elections.

- Declining trust in government to historically low levels partly due to regulatory and policy failures to anticipate or adequately cope with systemic risks and endemic and recurrent environmental and social problems. Rising inequality and widespread corruption legitimize the public's view of unfairness. The electorate is polarized, torn between an atavistic desire to enhance control over the forces of change by reducing the inter-dependence among countries, and a progressive impulse to turn inter-dependence into a source of strength.
- Regulation caught between complexity and certainty, carrying along the accumulation of rules and decisions which have built up in response to problems large and small, and to innovations which no one in the past had – or could have – anticipated. The modern regulatory state hardly existed when the modern city developed in the decades before World War One. Today and for the foreseeable future, regulatory complexity compromises transparency and compliance, and makes many long-term decisions about large-scale projects hostage to extensive, time-consuming, and costly consultations at several, different levels of government. Facing yet greater unprecedented challenges such as global health problems linked to lifestyle and diet, climate change, and natural disasters in the world's largest metropolitan centers, there is neither the resolve to adopt better economic instruments in the form of prices and taxes, or better regulatory instruments for land use, construction, insurance, etc.
- The eclipse of cities in national policies, meaning that national governments no longer try to guide urban development explicitly, and may not necessarily possess the technical capacities to do so if they so desired. Urban policy is narrow, associated with severe disadvantage. The interests of central governments of nation-states, and of their cities and regions are asymmetrical. Nation-states generate laws and regulations on the principle that space is uniform. People in Colorado and Oregon however do not respond to problems of air and water quality in the same way as people in West Virginia or South Carolina. Energy constraints in northern Italy are difficult to overcome when local authorities, the courts, and administrative procedures delay the construction of plants in southern Italy to process natural gas.

The crisis has added a new dimension because the manifestly limited scope of fiscal, monetary or regulatory policy to leverage a recovery calls the role and advice of economic and political experts into question. Understandably, it is not up to economists to recommend deep political changes, but many of the recommendations made during the height of the crisis between 2008 and 2012 and subsequently as other economic threats have emerged could not be implemented politically. When theory and practice conflict, the consequences can be dire for the legitimacy of both.

Regaining confidence and reducing uncertainty
Every paradigm, to be credible, links actions today to consequences tomorrow. The crisis of 2008 and its aftermath have shown the limits to predictability when it comes to forecasting how the economy will work its way through the collapse of credit and of confidence. The next paradigm must help people live better at a time when uncertainty covers everything from employment and health care to energy supplies and water that people take for granted, not to mention the risk of industrial and nuclear accidents, terrorism and war, natural disasters, and global epidemics.

Fear and hope are inseparable, but hope cannot be limited to the absence of fear. (Franklin D. Roosevelt proclaimed "freedom from fear" and from want as part of the Four Freedoms during World War Two.) Each paradigm is forward-looking, based on something essential to strive for – salvation, progress, prosperity – with some sense of how the effort is rewarded in the here-and-now even if the ultimate goal cannot be attained. (Sustainability, which delivers benefits to future generations, is a secular form of projecting beyond our lifetimes.) The goal of salvation and not just fear of damnation shaped the aspirations of the post-Renaissance era; the pursuit of progress and not just fear of social upheaval and reactionary forces guided civilization in the eighteenth and nineteenth centuries; the prospect of prosperity and not just fear of unemployment and economic chaos lifted society to overcome depression, war, and dictatorship in the twentieth century.

Bringing risks under control has always been the constant objective of economic regulation in the post-Renaissance western tradition. Each paradigm has sought to increase the level of safety in civilization: when moral issues dominated, by assuring salvation, then the highest protection against evil; when progress was the ascendant goal, confidence came in the form of well-designed constitutions with checks-and-balances and laws, reducing if not eliminating the causes of discord in society which could lead to conflicts and civil war; when prosperity was the objective, safety came in the form of steady employment and secure assets, including pensions, houses, health care, etc.

We are left with the question that framed this book: if cities are indeed the motors of the economy, what does this imply for the paradigm of economic policy-making to help regulate the economy, avoiding extremes, lifting hopes, and providing protection from what we most fear?

An economic governance paradigm for the twenty-first century will be shaped by the imperative to reduce the exposure of the world's urban population to global risks, and especially environmental, socio-economic, and health disasters which shatter communities. The first step is to recognize that inter-dependence defines essential relationships from the local scale of neighborhood and community to trans-border relationships, combining the economic, social, and environmental at all levels. Because they have a greater stake in each other's economic performance, environmental quality, and social welfare, inter-dependence changes the relations among states, and, for that matter, among cities and regions in different countries.

In the twenty-first century age of inter-dependence, safety will mean living in a society which acts to prevent catastrophes, or at least their worst effects, and renews its healing capacities, what is meant by resilience. Protectionism, autarky, efforts to husband sovereignty by withdrawing from treaties and international bodies will only make countries more liable to shocks, and less able to recover – the reverse of what presumably should be the goal of all who want to make their countries safer. Putting in place the social, economic, and political frameworks that transform fear into prevention, anxiety into preparedness, can inspire a vision of a better society: this has always been the goal of regulation since the Renaissance. Societies and countries which prove better at attenuating risk and at demonstrating their capacity to recover from catastrophes will show the way forward.

Managing space better is imperative because it is the key to solutions to so many problems, including that of lifting the productivity of cities. Putting cities first – and making space the operative and primary means of promoting cross-sectoral and cross-jurisdictional co-operation – will inevitably shift policy. Territorial policy is a means to an end, but it cannot describe the goal. To manage space better, territorial policy (for lack of a better term) has to generate a vision. For centuries since the Renaissance, territorial visions, usually centered on cities and what they may look like, have been essential to each major paradigm, even the paradigm of prosperity in the first half of the twentieth century showing how technology in the era of electricity and petroleum could transform the city. The reality may turn out to be different; it almost always is. But without a vision which inspires hope, mobilizes people and resources, and generates innovations, why invest?

Sectoral policy in the twentieth century improved the production of goods and services needed in cities, expanding trade in the process to create unprecedented networks of inter-dependency. A highly inter-dependent set of systems was not the intent, and indeed, to the extent that businesses and governments work side by side to enable cities to function, it is often more the result of the "invisible hand" than "by design." Nevertheless, *inter-dependency may be the biggest legacy of the twentieth century*, starting with the complex systems which make every part of the urban infrastructure dependent on every other part, from energy supply to waste management, transportation to health care. Every story about an urban disaster shows how the links between systems have widespread ramifications when they fail: cars cannot be refilled with gas when there is no electric power at the service station, eventually crippling the services needed to support the city (Nye, 2010). We must take care of inter-dependency, sustain and enrich it, because there is no rational alternative for cities to prosper if it collapses. Resist inter-dependence and see how far you get. Realism is a strong argument in its favor.

Inter-dependence implies that we are all affected by one another's actions or inactions, whether there is a high degree of connectedness or not. Inter-dependence internalizes and normalizes the condition of how dependent we are on actions and conditions both near and far, and how our behavior affects others. Inter-dependence, on which this book concludes, is the price worth paying to enjoy the benefits of cities as the home of humankind. The degree to which inter-dependency matters today and for the foreseeable future is both a challenge and an opportunity. Inter-dependence breaks down the legal fiction that a sovereign nation-state is master of its own house, and its corollary, that governments should stay out of each other's internal affairs as long as everything goes all right.

Inter-dependence helps the rule of law. It fits within the new era of mobile communications and social media, and the growth of civil society including corporate forms such as city alliances and networks, regional clusters, multi-stakeholder initiatives, foundations, and private initiatives. Just as criminal activities can be tracked globally, so can efforts to strengthen communities and rule of law. Legal and institutional commitments based on inter-dependence are far more transparent and traceable than ever before, as witness the impact on Wal-Mart of a disastrous 2012 fire in a Bangladesh textile contractor supplying the world's largest retailer. The ability of any jurisdiction to remain in "splendid isolation" is limited. International standards for what the rule of law means in practice are more likely to emerge, benefiting, not least, business. The law may lag but it will catch up; it usually does.

Inter-dependence works in favor of multi-level and cross-sectoral policy coherence. The constitutionally constricting distinction between what different ministries can or cannot do, what different levels of government can or cannot do, which had a positive impact during the expansion of national industrial economies and the growth of the public sector early in the twentieth century, stands in the way of the kind of co-operation and co-ordination that are imperative in the face of the risks that cities, regions, and states confront. For the time being the pressures are stronger to resist co-operation than to embrace it. This change of culture can be accelerated through incentives and rules, and new forms of association.

Finally, inter-dependence has a moral dimension, which for a paradigm is absolutely crucial. Every paradigm involves trust – that our individual actions matter to us individually, and contribute to a better overall outcome; and that others, because they are likely to share the same objectives, can be trusted not to take advantage of us, a form of fair play. Inter-dependence is consistent with sustainable development, linking one generation to another, and humankind to the planet. It implies stewardship as the hallmark of responsible behavior. And in a version of the Kantian imperative, it also means that we must be sensitive to how others behave, because relationships and trust in how people will behave reinforce the right behavior of ourselves. Just as we were all New Yorkers on September 11, we are all also Parisians, Venetians, Cariocas, Singaporeans, Sydney-siders, neighbors, though we be strangers (Tuan, 1988).

Inter-dependence is closer to the liberal economic synthesis, embracing trade, investment, and innovation which create more ties and diffuse power more broadly, to be preferred to more national control and less inter-dependence, which transfers decision-making power into the hands of those who control politics. Inter-dependency implies that we cannot do everything for ourselves – the basis for capitalism's invisible hand, specialization and division of labor, and comparative advantages. And to repeat, it implies that control is shared and diffused, the first essential in maintaining a system of governance checks and balances at any scale, bounded by rules. Governance is key, across sectors, across levels of government, and across jurisdictional boundaries within countries.

Simply put, inter-dependence highlights our mutual reliance on the rules made by and applicable to ourselves and to others and on their conduct. This calls for stronger collaboration, rewards and incentives for co-operation, compromises for inclusion which avoid a sense that there are only losers and winners. In an age that values inter-dependence, society will need mediators, people who can make connections between sectors and disciplines, across jurisdictional boundaries, and between the public and the private sector.

Of course inter-dependence, if it is the new normal, may not remain ascendant. It can even be unwound in a potentially disastrous effort by wealthier societies to retreat into protectionism, or worse, autarky, an economic version of the gated community, and to make gated communities the norm. And it may be difficult for states with weak institutions, fragile economies, and endemic civil wars to embrace it. A state that does not accept inter-dependence and what goes with it could exploit those that do (just as Russia and perhaps China in 2014 resisted the American-led system of voluntary alliances in Europe and Asia). Not enough is yet known about what factors, cultural patterns and values, legal principles and political objectives, economic conditions and technological systems are more likely to make inter-dependence attractive and rewarding. Learning by doing works; it usually does in democracies.

- What will inspire and motivate people in the twenty-first century? The hope that we can gain better control over the risks which are now and for the foreseeable future tied to the cities where we live.
- Why are these risks so threatening? Catastrophic crises can cause states to fail, economies to implode or suffer long-term depressions; societies and their value systems may collapse.
- What opportunities are created? Future-proofing cities will have dynamic effects, lifting the limits to growth by generating innovations, improving productivity, reducing patterns of dependency.
- What is the greatest threat to our hopes? Fissiparity, the fragmentation and splitting apart of things once whole; the inability of smaller entities to co-operate, be they social groups within countries, or nation-states. This way lies a form of chaos: paralysis from a lack of consensus.
- Virtuous behavior will be defined by how well people value the effort necessary to adapt cities and city–state relations to enhance their resilience and survive crises. States will try to sanction behavior that undermines the efforts of those who live by the rules.

This is as far as I can go. It might be possible to design the outlines of what a meta-paradigm for economic governance based on inter-dependence could look like but it would be an intellectual exercise. Too vague, critics will say; what will be regulated differently? How will multi-level governance be different? Detailed answers are too easily exposed to attack, for being either so radical as to be utopian or so conservative as to be worthless. Realistically, the next meta-paradigm is likely to result from pressures that accumulate during a period of crises which cumulatively overwhelm the current paradigm. It was thus in the mid-seventeenth century, and again in the early twentieth; the Ebola virus catastrophe in the summer and autumn of 2014, at the time of this writing, is an example of what may be a new series of crises which test the international order in an age of inter-dependence. And like other such crises, it reveals huge shortcomings in urban development, in this case in Africa where population growth and the growth of cities are most intense, as well as points of weakness in cities worldwide. Although a paradigm shift in economic governance for an urban century may seem both logical and inevitable, to most people, including decision-makers, it is not yet either the one or the other. If I am at all right, the process itself – the crucible of tensions that accumulate, evidence of failures to keep crises under control – will generate new ideas, new frameworks, new methods. But the lesson of past paradigm shifts is that the transition, which in retrospect happened relatively quickly in the space of a generation, was a wrenching experience.

Fate and fear: will cross-border risks overwhelm the Westphalian system?

The future of cities and international relations are linked through the Westphalian imperative that states do not intervene in one another's domestic affairs. Not only do cities face threats from abroad; domestic conditions also may pose threats to cities in other countries. These will be asymmetric: environmental and health conditions in, say, West Africa are a greater threat to cities in northern Europe than European cities are to cities in Senegal, Nigeria, or Mali. But cross-border risks are not a North–South issue, to be addressed in the fora of international organizations and with funds provided by the World Bank and through bilateral assistance. Epidemics, air pollution, the collapse of power systems, floods, and water management generally have been trans-border issues for years; cyber-attacks are just the latest addition to this list sanctified by biblical precedent and the language of myth. Nothing like the shift from military threats against states to economic, technological, and environmental threats against societies has occurred in recent history, exposing at one and the same time the limitations of states as protectors in the face of these threats, and the limited stock of tools – of policies, behavioral patterns and ideas, technologies and legal instruments – to face them. Can the international system based on the sovereignty of nation-states and their right to be free from intervention in their domestic affairs cope with the consequences of inter-dependence in the face of non-military cross-border risks to cities?

The growing importance and scale of cross-border risks to cities come at a time when the capacity of states to lead on an urban agenda is diminished, and when they must act more often in concert to achieve results, whether on public health, food and food safety, the exchange of information on financial transactions, or global warming. The crisis since 2008 is acting like a solvent, weakening the ties that have held centralized and federal system together. Consider how much has changed, and how fast:

- The sovereignty of all states has been eroded by the crisis; none can insulate itself entirely from imported shocks or prevent domestic shocks from being transmitted abroad, affecting others; most that borrow to cover fiscal deficits must do so in the international markets, which have been febrile.
- Small states can neither guide their destiny nor have much influence on the shape of social and economic regulations adopted in response to the crisis. Larger states which have assumed greater regulatory responsibility risk provoking fear of domination, and receive scant thanks for their leadership – or get blamed for making problems worse.
- A massive loss of wealth, equivalent to at least several years' output, has taken place without a collapse of international security as we knew it, even though considerable leverage has been handed to creditors, either in the private sector, or in foreign countries in other spheres of influence such as the Persian Gulf and China.
- Financial and fiscal laws are increasingly extra-territorial in scope, applying to persons or firms domiciled elsewhere.

The first lesson of the crisis of 2008 was the return of the state. In the face of an overwhelming threat, people wanted to know what government will do. Action covered two spheres: short-term measures to cope with the immediate consequences of the crisis, and measures to be taken to reduce systemic risks in the future. Before five years had passed, the jury of public opinion was in: the trend in trust in government has resumed its downward course. States are weaker now and for the foreseeable future, adding to the risk agenda because the international order itself needs a viable, strong system of states to check aggression and generate an adequate stock of public goods, both of which are in doubt. But this does not necessarily mean that states, to be strong, have to exercise power unilaterally; co-operation too can be a sign of strength, the basis for a new realism.

The erosion of sovereignty is not likely to be reversed soon. Previous crises, usually associated with war, solidified nation-states through democratic or revolutionary action, unifying the country, and through diplomacy which made the drawing of secure borders the basis for treaties and alliances. The nation-state is a fairly recent historical development, especially when viewed against the much longer history of cities. Its development remains a work in progress, especially in countries where it has not resolved long-standing tensions between regions within the country (Belgium, Spain) or is under pressure on its borders (Turkey, Mexico, Poland, Romania). The United Kingdom remains just that after the Scottish referendum on independence in 2014 which reminded many that until 1707 Scotland and England were separate, but the debate about a possible referendum on the EU has highlighted how different the interests of London are from the rest of the country, and how close London is to having many of the properties of an independent state. No one is expecting civil war: urban revolts virtually disappeared after the middle of the seventeenth-century in Europe. But there may well be highly politicized issues to be taken up by constitutional courts, parliamentary assemblies, and the electorate in referenda.

The Westphalian principle of non-intervention restrained hegemonic powers, the states most likely to take advantage of their superiority. It was the price paid by the more powerful states to secure the co-operation of all in the larger system. In terms of the kind of non-military cross-border risks which now represent the major threat to cities, this trade-off doesn't quite work: larger powers may be more exposed and vulnerable but they are better able than smaller ones to absorb crises. Smaller and less powerful states may benefit more from intervening to check or abate some problems before they become global threats, and can do so without arousing the same fears of domination as would accompany intervention by great powers; but small powers may lack the means if the great powers remain on the margins or actually oppose this kind of initiative. This conundrum redirects attention back to liberal intervention and governance for the collective good and not for exclusive advantage.

The interests of smaller states, who traditionally benefit from the Westphalian system which protects all states against non-interference, need not be compromised. They can benefit through a re-balancing within the international arena which recognizes that except for nuclear weapons (Israel, North Korea) size, the critical variable in balance-of-power and hegemonic relations measured in military terms, has less relevance in a global economy in which big states can be weaker, economically, and relatively speaking, than small ones. (Think Spain – Switzerland, or Italy – Sweden.) The factors that determined hierarchy and hegemony when armaments and the capacity to wage war defined the ranking of greater and lesser powers have been eclipsed by other indicators with a different rank order based on national accounts which show deficits and surpluses, tables of debt as a percentage of GDP, maps of regions exposed to prolonged drought or desertification and of cities exposed to devastating floods.

The Westphalian system, based on the principle of non-intervention and the independence of small states, will be tested to provide an adequate level of security against non-military risks that cities face. The idealistic belief in rational, evidence-based decision-making suggests that nation-states ought to co-operate to reduce cross-border risks and, in the event of catastrophes, to organize relief and reconstruction. What can one state do to put pressure on another, when the first is exposed to risks that may not be contained in the second? If governments deny themselves the right to intervene in one another's affairs, they need to find some way short of coercion to influence changes in policy and behavior to reduce risks: soft law, trade reprisals, even quarantine may not be good enough. This calls for a degree of co-operation and trust in a system of international relations which seeks to maintain the balance of power between large and small states and between different regions. If non-intervention is weakened, how will it be possible to prevent countries from interfering in the domestic affairs of others, to advance their interests and objectives? If intervention does become more legitimate, can force be used if there is resistance (for example, if Liberia had denied access during the Ebola epidemic)?

The international order today will be hard-pressed to adjust to greater inter-dependency. The Westphalian settlement emphasized that states – large and small, weaker and stronger – have a common interest in the survival of a state-based system with shared rules which cannot be violated with impunity. Security in the West in the post-Westphalia era (since 1648) has been grounded in international treaties on the one hand and on balance-of-power politics on the other, not the one in opposition to the other, but the two in tandem. Based on the principle that all states, however small or large, new or old, are equally sovereign and responsible for their domestic affairs, containment – of a hegemonic power, of a revolutionary movement – was the test of how well the system performed against collective threats.

This is where we were in 1989–90, when the formerly communist states of Central and Eastern Europe became free, democratic, and capitalist. American-led interventions in Afghanistan and Iraq early in the twenty-first century rested on the assumption that American motives were disinterested and benign. But this exercise of power to change regimes overstretched American public support, economic resources, and even political strategies and alliances. As a result, neo-isolationist opinion may well limit the willingness of the United States and of others to intervene even when the humanitarian grounds are compelling. The principal threats to cities now appear to come from natural or environmental and social change which may in turn alter the stability of a country or region, making aggression and conflict more likely, part of the scenario of climate change. Cross-border threats are not new. What is different is the extent to which the security of states is affected by risks to and sometimes originating in cities, risks which are increasingly cross-border because they reflect the inter-connected and inter-dependent character of the urban economy and of urban cultures. How states will manage the international order while protecting cities, and how they will manage urban affairs domestically to check problems at the source, are questions outstanding.

The fear that catastrophes such as pandemics or cyber-attacks could be triggered for the economic damage they would cause may be sufficient for states to wrap the security label around many types of catastrophe that have both human-made and natural dimensions, posing different challenges for those who must assess risks, prepare for disasters or cope with them should they occur, or rethink the spatial shape of the economy. Already, in the aftermath of 9/11 and through efforts to control money laundering, countries have had to adopt procedures – and submit them for verification – to gain preferred access to certain markets and services for their citizens and companies. But this is an old Cold War agenda for collective security updated for contemporary international aggression, not for the scale of economic, health, and environmental risks of the future.

This shift of focus is already provoking political tensions:

- How are environmental or health threats different from politico-military ones?
- When is intervention warranted?
- What are the responsibilities of states to protect their citizens and territories from the consequences of risks that get out of control in international space or in other jurisdictions?
- Can enough be achieved through soft law, regulations, and pressure?
- Should the international community act to strengthen the capacity of some states which may be unable to control or contain problems that pose hazards to others? Would such intervention create unreasonable forms of moral hazard by encouraging others to escape from the burdens of prudent leadership, knowing that in the end they will be rescued?

It is important to be clear-headed about future crises because the vast accumulation of pre-disaster government plans and private-sector initiatives can too easily give rise to the impression that governments have things in hand: preparedness is well-advanced, risk management is a priority, budgets are adequate, and research is targeting the risks which could be the most devastating. Yet, time after time, paper plans do not work as they were intended in real-life, real-time conditions: training was neglected, essential supplies were not ordered, manuals were out of date.

In 2003 the OECD published a report on *Emerging Risks in the 21st Century,* which began with an assessment of the shortcoming of risk management, noting that centralized risk management or command-and-control approaches which are most consistent with national sovereignty have become less effective in decentralized economies and societies characterized by increasingly complex operations. The report also highlighted a greater role for tort law and insurance associated with a "claim culture" which can turn disasters into profits for some (OECD, 2003:19). Noting that public perceptions of risk may not be objective, the report argued that education and communication call for measures that go beyond strict cost-benefit analysis. Improving the coherence of risk management, and developing synergies between the public and private sectors, will take time. Those who want to strengthen the capacity of governments to cope with crises must confront the need for stronger incentives and better policies and programs for greater co-operation within the public sector at all levels. This is not a debate about debt or about tax, but about how best to face the challenges of economic development in the context of the environmental, social and economic risks of the future.

A recent OECD report on *Future Global Shocks: Improving Risk Governance* (2011) illuminates a central governance challenge in cross-border risks which is incompatible with the Westphalian model as we know it. Efforts are being intensified to model what could happen in a crisis, to develop early warning systems, and to map zones at risk. These advances, which expand surveillance capacity enormously, reduce the time for decision-making and expand the spatial area that must be monitored in ways that are difficult to align with normative administrative and jurisdictional boundaries, especially when the onset of a problem in one country is detected in another. The spatial reach is global, the time frame a matter of days at most, sometimes minutes, even seconds. Disasters will happen: improvements come cumulatively, as the lessons of disasters are learned, but this too takes time. How much time do we have? With more information available sooner, do governments – or private or public agencies which are also gathering and interpreting information – have a responsibility to communicate when the risks are in another jurisdiction? What are the responsibilities of a foreign power which ignores the information it receives? At what point can one country act to prevent or attenuate risks in another jurisdiction which could jeopardize its interests, its people, environment, institutions? After a long list of pressing issues on which "traditional global leaders are unable to agree ... with emerging powers, and between themselves," the OECD report on *Future Global Shocks* concluded that "*co-operation between states seems to be breaking down when more than ever it needs to be strengthened*" (OECD, 2011: 113, italics added for emphasis).

The point of departure is recognition of the degree to which critical urban systems – and not just in finance – are inter-dependent. Global shocks can be transmitted through systems producing "wide-ranging and long-lasting secondary consequences that may have little to do with an event's initial trigger." Mapping and modeling therefore become important tools to "conceptualize where to reinforce the weakest of vulnerable points, where to prioritize limited resources and when to centralize, diversify or create redundancy in complex systems" (OECD, 2011: 56). But who pays for what has a lot to do with what gets done where, with the emphasis on place. Not surprisingly, even the production of maps and models will raise questions about policy responsibilities that cut across several disciplines and themes, ministries and levels of government. The OECD report refers to "emerging constructs" meaning trends in behavior "that are rarely noticed and never mapped or understood to the level of detail necessary for appropriate public policy interventions" (OECD, 2011: 69–70). Mapping is therefore both a metaphor – often it takes the form of a conceptual text or diagram or organizational chart, rather than a map – and the production and use of a true cartographic tool, enabling the spatial dimension in each case to become dominant analytically. As such, the text – for it is often words, not images, that the reader sees – refers to maps and mapping but does not actually provide a graphic example. The result nevertheless can give an illusion of completeness and clarity, obscuring problems in the acquisition of data and their quality, details showing the complexity of individual systems, and dynamic changes, making the dataset inherently unstable. Inter-dependence is not a checklist, a map, not even an inventory: it is a mind-set.

We are left with the paradox that urban development may benefit from greater decentralization and autonomy within nation-states, whereas international co-operation to reduce risks to cities depends on strengthening nation-states. Can these two objectives be reconciled in a sustainable balance? Or does that balance come only as the result of steering towards one objective and then towards the other? Some cities and regions are already trying to show how they can "go it alone," making progress on critical issues such as education, the environment and climate change, economic development, and transportation without waiting for new national policies or initiatives to set objectives and generate momentum. It may be easier for regions and cities to co-operate internationally on certain issues than it is for the national governments of their countries. As Nigel Harris perceived fifteen years ago, "decentralization within an open world economy implies that subnational levels of government acquire responsibilities that were formerly exclusively held by national governments, and correspondingly are required to begin to operate more like national governments – where the supply of information, monitoring and evaluating the performance of key sectors becomes a critical factor in public action" (Harris, 1997: 1702).

We often speak of cities as if possessed of an animate capacity to reflect and to act, without probing in what ways cities have powers to behave, or are manipulated by individuals or groups to spend, regulate, police, or even act against other private or public bodies (Orum, 1991). From one perspective this is nothing new: What about the city-states of the Renaissance? Boosterism in nineteenth-century America, and civic pride in Third Republic France or in Victorian England? The movement for direct election of mayors in London, Paris, Seoul, and Tokyo in the late twentieth century? What then is different?

The end of the crisis, when it comes, is likely to alter the relationships between regions within countries and their national governments. Indeed, these relationships are already changing. Some jurisdictions are ready to take on more responsibility; many, perhaps a majority, are not – and may not even understand how fast the change in city–state relations may occur. The boosterist school of local and metropolitan initiatives gives the misleading impression that, because cities can do a lot more on their own, governments need not intervene through policy changes or costly programs. There is much that cities can do; indeed, national governments may encourage greater urban initiative in order to reduce pressures to spend more and intervene (Barber, 2013). But municipal initiatives do not relieve national governments of their responsibilities in policy. The C40 urban initiative or other alliances of cities dedicated to a common effort to make progress on environmental, economic and social issues are exploiting the room for maneuver and flexibility which has expanded during the crisis. But, as their leaders are the first to say, urban initiatives are held back by the lack of progress and clarity on issues that only national governments can decide such as carbon pricing, taxation, labor migration, renewable energy, water rights, etc. Without greater regulatory and policy certainty, how will the $2 trillion a year be leveraged and invested to improve the world's infrastructure, or the $44 trillion increase estimated by the IEA needed between 2010 and 2050 to deliver low-carbon energy systems? How will that struggle over resources reshape politics? (OECD/IEA, 2014). Thus, the trend or movement among some cities to promote sustainable development may have only a marginal effect beyond themselves insofar as the number of cities embracing such strategies remains small (even if these include several of the largest), and in the absence of changes to national laws and regulations that affect the size of urban markets for energy, land and housing, competition, innovation and security. We are back to the problems of sectoral economic governance in Part I, and which cannot be remediated without huge changes at both sub-national and national levels.

Will cities and regions use their greater latitude to behave like autonomous mini-states, or seek alliances with other regions and states? If constitutional arrangements which historically have not kept pace with the growth of the urban population make policy change at the national level more difficult, should there be more formal, constitutional changes? At what point will some cities and regions try to seize the initiative, pressuring national governments to grant them specific legal and fiscal powers? Will federal states such as Germany have an advantage over highly centralized ones such as the United Kingdom? Initiatives by cities and regions which conflict with higher-level legislation and regulation will provoke legal challenges. In every system, rule of law means that constitutionality must be respected. Each nation's legal framework varies in the degree to which cities and regions have flexibility in this regard. In some countries where the status of cities is embedded in the national constitution (Germany) or where the municipal unit is the oldest surviving political institution (France, Switzerland), there never was any doubt that the country was composed of independent urban entities with legally recognized boundaries and a degree of self-government that antedate modern constitutions. In other countries cities are, literally, creatures of the state (the United States, Canada). But as the OECD 2014 Regional Outlook shows, seemingly permanent legal and administrative arrangements can be changed astoundingly quickly in countries such as France (where the number of regions drops from twenty-two to thirteen in 2016) and Denmark.

Often discussions about what gets done at what level of government come up against the evidence that regional and local authorities lack the capacity, are more prone to corruption, do not have the right incentives to co-operate, etc., but these arguments which amount to a defense of the status quo avoid the equally rich evidence that the national sectoral model is neither working properly nor being reformed dramatically either. The charge to free cities from the constraints of national policy is as dear to ideologues who want to reduce the size of the state in the economy and its scope for intervention as it is to mayors and their allies whose strategies for their cities are more advanced than policies at the national level, but it does not address how key cross-border risks can be addressed preventively, or in a crisis.

And so we come to perhaps the most difficult challenge linking public policy and governance, whether subsidiarity and public choice theory, or a combination of decentralization and budget cuts which is all but inevitable in the post-2008 age of austerity, can promote a more vibrant, participatory, and creative local democracy. The democratic deficit however exists: when more decisions about taxes, budgets, policies, and regulations are taken at the sub-national level, public participation is usually low, and the risk of capture by special or single-issue interests is high. It is just possible that, through their co-operation and networks, cities and regions can find more concrete and meaningful ways to involve citizens and stakeholders in the great issues of our times, issues which help define how we live on what is, after all, one world. Security and risk concerns however work in favor of greater centralization and top-down decision-making. As the risk agenda rises in importance, what will be the balance between national policy and leadership, and greater scope and initiative on the part of cities and regions, between reinforcing the points of vulnerability of states, and the weaknesses of cities?

Inter-dependence and nationalism
Disasters which transgress borders also define domestic political agendas. When natural or human-made disasters happen, countries and civic organizations want to help, but it is the natural instinct of governments to show that they are masters in their own house, and to assume more obligations than they can handle, keeping the outside world out by invoking the veil of sovereignty. The OECD report *Future Global Risks* was therefore completely right to include the global financial crisis of 2008 together with the H1N1 pandemic: whatever the differences in the nature of these two global shocks, it is the similar nature of state reactions, *putting sovereignty first*, which is underscored.

But this is not the whole story. If any proof of the potency of supra-national institutions and ideals to penetrate national cultures and precipitate reforms were needed, look back at two of the most momentous and successful transformations in Europe: the end of fascism in Portugal and Spain, and the collapse of communism and the fall of the Iron Curtain in Hungary, Poland, the Czech and Slovak republics, the Baltic states, Romania, Bulgaria, Croatia, Serbia, and Slovenia. In both cases, the integration into a wider economic region involved the adoption of laws, the *acquis communautaire,* which other nations had already passed, and the preparation to participate in a multi-national organization for which domestic reforms, including the creation of regional and federal structures, were necessary. Think for a moment how counter-intuitive this transformational process was. Limitations on sovereignty might have been the least popular option for peoples who had been denied free political expression, whose national identity had been repressed or perverted. And indeed, in many countries and regions, populist groups feed on the disenchantment accompanying the loss of traditional frames of reference and even of privileges when exposed to new currents of ideas and competition. But the course of change and the appeal of growth within Europe were stronger, promising greater security. Perhaps knowing that independence in the communist era was a fig leaf masking Soviet power helped newly democratic societies accept another supra-national jurisdiction.

Greater supra-nationality remains one path for the Eurozone, a way to handle intervention within a broader political and constitutional framework. In 2008–9, when the American origin of the economic crisis, triggered by the collapse of Lehman Brothers, was beyond dispute, and the euro a refuge, the path to institutional design at the supra-national level might have been easier but the impetus only came in response to the problems of the Eurozone which intensified in 2010–12. By then, it had become apparent that historical points of reference which were incontrovertibly strong when the single market and single currency were created had lost their potency due to the passage of time and the distance from the violence and destruction which it was the intent of leaders at national and European levels to avoid in the future.

In the debate about the future of the Eurozone, fear of a collapse of the euro is leading some countries to retain what is left of national supervision and sovereignty, and others to work towards European banking regulation and supervision and federal decision-making at the expense of nation-states. The former emphasize the flexibility of multiple currencies; the latter the beneficial discipline of a single currency. Sometimes one has the impression that economists of different schools want states to adopt their preferred model, whereas political leaders seem more inclined to chose the economic model which suits their political objectives and context best. The point is that the same fear of economic collapse is transmitted through *a priori* assumptions and preconceptions, ideology, history, and instinct into very different alternatives – greater integration for the Eurozone, or its unraveling.

Well might Mario Draghi, President of the European Central Bank, address journalists and policy-makers alike in his acceptance speech on receiving the M100 Media Award 2012 in Potsdam on 6 September 2012 with a plea for all to create "a genuine European public space, '*eine europäische Öffentlichkeit.*'" "Problems that cross borders require citizens to find consensus around common solutions," he said; everyone is affected by what happens in other member states, another way of defining collective security. On the one hand, outdated national stereotypes may be revived; on the other, a stronger sense of "belonging together and to care about decisions in other regions" may also strengthen. In a monetary union there "are limits to national discretion in economic policies that affect the area as a whole." Draghi of course was appealing to the press to help shape a "new consensus on economic policies that will reinvigorate the European social model and make it fit for the 21st century" (Draghi, 2012). When the citizens of one country are aware of decisions taken by their neighbors that affect them but are impotent to influence the decisions themselves, they are more likely to look for safety defensively, through greater autonomy. Conditionality, even by the ECB or the IMF, has its limits because it is not backed up by anything stronger than market power. But it was not the occasion for Draghi to take the argument one step further: how else but through the creation of a stronger supra-national institution can citizens be involved in a decision-making process for a cross-border economy?

Advocates of government intervention argue for a redistributive role for central government the better to assure an adequate level of public goods. Applied to the urban development agenda, this approach leads to the mutualization of costs and benefits. With a greater sense of common purpose, governments at different levels can try to co-ordinate to reduce the scale of risks that they face together. In any case the issue of moral hazard, often raised to control irresponsible risk-taking, is of diminished importance once a disaster has hit and it is too late to undue the damage caused by the mistakes of others. Strict accountability and liability then get in the way of the obvious, overwhelming need to face the consequences of the problem and find a way forward. The smaller-government camp is correct when arguing that people should accept more responsibility in the face of risks about which the state cannot do as much as people wish. But it misunderstands the shrinking appetite for risk-taking on the part of the public and it ignores the critical role that states retain, including during a crisis and recovery.

As Tomasso Padoa-Schioppa commented in his Per Jacobsen lecture of June 2010 at the Bank of International Settlements, the issue about how much government should intervene in markets is not a matter of too little or too much; "the defect lies in the *level* rather than in the *quantum* of government and has deep roots in the field of ideas rather than in that of practice" (Padoa-Schioppa, 2010). He went on to criticize the radical Reagan–Thatcher effort to strengthen markets for neglecting the need to build international modes of governance that would be appropriate to the enlarged scale of cross-border, international economic activity. Well might he ask why market ideologues would prefer a nationalist framework for regulatory governance rather than build a multi-lateral one closer to the global scale of markets.

Padoa-Schioppa attributed a nationalist stance to a rigorous defense of the Westphalia settlement of 1648 which erected the rule of non-interference in the internal affairs of states as part of the established order which gave each state, whatever its size, a full measure of unqualified sovereignty. It may be that the forces of globalization and liberalization give political leaders a stronger desire to resist creating new forms of international economic governance, preferring to retain control of what they still can, largely within their countries. National sovereignty however proved an inadequate bulwark either against domestic policy excesses or against the disruptive impact of international finance. Writing when the euro crisis was accelerating, Padoa-Schioppa clearly saw that the objective of those attacking supra-national regulation, and defending markets as both rational and efficient, was to halt the movement toward greater European integration. In the process, the international community was deprived of the opportunity to put in place institutional and regulatory frameworks which markets – and states – need.

Is not the prospect real of global fragmentation into two or more blocks *with different regulatory frameworks and capacities to respond to crises* – one directed to *more* co-operation, and the other toward *less*? What would this imply for international security, whether redefined in terms of economic and environmental risks? The likelihood is that in the face of similar risks, the prospects for coherent strategies to manage those risks will be compromised, increasing the vulnerability of complex economic and social systems to higher damages and costs. That the result will be a patchwork – illustrated in a map of the world with different colors for countries according to their orientation or policy – is fairly consistent with historical experience. After all, for decades, the western world was polarized between Catholic and Protestant countries, then between rival empires, liberal and autocratic regimes, and between capitalist and centrally planned economies. The world order may become polarized between hyper-sovereign and highly co-operative nations, *following two different standards for non-intervention in another country's domestic affairs.*

The central question is indeed about *control*, not efficiency or economics.

- Some believe that control is an end in itself, fundamental to the political order. Control has the character of an absolute: to the extent possible, the legal restrictions on what a state can control should be as minimal as possible. This way lies the defense of states from interference by others in their affairs. It is no surprise if some countries adopting this stance rely heavily on techno-military means.
- Those who see control as a means to an end are more likely to look at the outcomes weighed against costs and risks, and to adjust policies as conditions change. This is closer to maintaining balance through perpetual movement, like riding a bicycle without falling off. In this direction lie greater international co-operation and cross-border regulation, and greater reliance on a mix of economic incentives and moral constraints.

Some countries may choose greater international co-operation including supra-national decision-making, rather than greater autonomy and independence; others will try to reinforce national controls, even if this means trying to impose domestic limits on how open an economy would be to globalization; some may try a third way, to combine economic openness with resistance to supra-national decision-making. Which strategy, which set of values, is best suited to disaster preparedness and solidarity in the face of threats of catastrophic risks, as likely to originate abroad as at home? States with more sovereignty intact? Or states which work together, federate, or embrace some form of supra-national authority? The asymmetry between the value systems implicit in these approaches to control means that the tension between them can only be reduced, not eliminated.

No easy way forward: it takes a crisis to solve one
A concerted effort to address urban problems can succeed only if it leads to changes in the way governments function, in what is regulated and how, and in the benchmarks of outcomes. Historical experience however leads to a guarded prospect: a direct approach to improve international co-operation that is focused on improving the conditions of life in cities and on reducing the impact of disasters and crises on them is *likely to fail.* The arguments may be rational, the evidence overwhelming, but

the leap is simply too big, the counter-arguments difficult to refute: the time will never be right. The harsh fact is that a new paradigm for economic governance that will help cities function and grow is more likely to emerge from a prolonged crisis of multiple, overlapping causes which buffets nation-states and leaves them exhausted, after rather than before a series of catastrophes.

Inevitably, events, not singly, but concurrently, in complex patterns, will generate international tensions. How these in turn affect the international order will determine how and when states accept changes allowing one another to act together, including by intervening in each other's affairs, to address cross-border risks. If in politics as in comedy timing is everything, a preventive, forward-looking change in economic governance is likely at some time but not yet. How we meet the challenges of an era of crisis will shape the next paradigm, determining the fears and hopes that future generations will share, and the role of cities in that new order. Is there a strategy to cope with a succession of crises without losing sight of what could be achieved at their end for the betterment of urban humanity? Or is the alternative, to muddle through, improvise and see what happens next, more likely to shape the future of cities?

As Henry Kissinger reminds us in *World Order* (2014), the rule-based system of international relations known as Westphalia originated in specific European conditions. These no longer prevail, raising questions about whether the states in different regions of the world that adhere to this system can evolve a framework of rules better adapted to the multi-polar, inter-dependent, urban twenty-first century. I have argued that western civilization has transformed and revised paradigms as part of a unique way to resolve crises. If the West succeeds in this, will other mega-regions follow?

Perhaps, but perhaps not, because of differences between civilizations when defining and valuing the importance of cities. Why do cities matter? The basic global common denominator appears to be economic opportunity, even for the very poor, and especially for the very rich. This is not to be disparaged if the flow of people from country to city in so many countries gives hope toward the global objective to reduce poverty, illiteracy and eradicable diseases, and if the wealth and resources of cities can be harnessed to abate environmental degradation and check global warming. It is a remarkable achievement for the West to have transformed prosperity into a guiding vision for billions of people on all continents, linked to urban development. But to say that this is all – or enough – is itself a philosophical statement, giving greater priority to the material over everything else that cannot be quantified.

The lowest common denominator may be enough to unite peoples around the world; I doubt it.

In the western tradition the purposes of urban life cover the whole person, the development of the individual through participation in the social and political life of the city. Lewis Mumford, like his contemporaries Frederick Hayek, Jane Jacobs, Jean Gottmann, who wrote so much in the late 1950's that is still worth reading, feared that civilization would be badly compromised by the economic mismanagement of cities for political ends. They held that the higher social and political purposes that people can best pursue and fulfill in cities should be the point of reference for urban economic governance. This is itself a value-laden thesis, but it is central to western ideals of individual freedoms. In a sentence often quoted from the end of Mumford's *The City in History*, Mumford wrote: "The chief function of the city is to convert power into form, dead matter into the living symbols of art, biological reproduction into social creativity" (Mumford, 1961: 571). Leave to one side that in the age of Aristotle only part of society could aspire to this vision, and that urban politics generated conflict. The vision of virtue enhanced in the city has been transmitted through the utopian image of the city in the Renaissance, the Enlightenment ideal of the city as an instrument of progress, and the modern pursuit of prosperity to reduce human misery and other causes of social revolution, as it will be in cities in the future where inter-dependence is valued.

Will other societies with other priorities accept this legacy, this vision? Will they be as sensitive to and respectful of cities? Or will different and conflicting appreciations of cities – of what they stand for – come in the way of international collaboration to check threats to them, in whatever social and political system? Will the urban way of life, now that it is universal, be the next "clash of civilizations," dominated by competing and incompatible visions of what cities are for? This chapter began with hope; it ends with fear – fear that internal divisions, fragmented power blocks globally, and potentially divergent beliefs in different regions of the world about the importance of cities will focus energies on managing conflicts rather than finding solutions to them. *In other words, urbanization, which should unite us, also divides, and in ways that can drive nations apart.*

A prolonged period of heightened uncertainty and instability lies in front of us, integral to the paradigm shift that is already incipient. What happens after depends on how we define problems and learn from experience during this period. The transition to a paradigm for economic governance more suitable for the twenty-first century requires that we equip ourselves better to see our way through and beyond a period of greater volatility, instability, and uncertainty. This is the unique challenge of the generations that will live through the next couple of decades: the few from the pre-1945 era and many baby-boomers who share the memory of the Great Depression, the horrors of fascism, the Cold War, decolonization, and an era of "expanding liberties" (Konvitz, 1967); those who grew to maturity at the end of the Cold War and the start of the internet era during the third great age of globalization; those entering adulthood as the crisis of 2008 changes their prospects.

I have been arguing that sovereignty no longer provides adequate protection against a range of catastrophic risks to cities; that nation-states may have to intervene in one another's domestic affairs – if only by agreeing to new rules and objectives – to control problems at the source or to check their spread; that nations will have to find better ways of acting co-operatively; and that cities and regions will increasingly exercise more autonomy not only because they are in the front line, so to speak, but because there will be a policy space to be occupied. Taken together, this shift to put the needs and security of cities foremost in domestic policy and international relations constitutes the great readjustment to a new paradigm for economic governance.

Woodrow Wilson gave a refined and elegant an expression of the role of the state leading a change in regulatory paradigms based on protecting people in an economy transformed by urbanization. In his first inaugural address, 4 March 1913, Wilson, after praising the industrial economy for its achievements, called attention to its human cost, and attacked the misuse of political power by the few for the neglect of the welfare of the many. Linking economic and social regulation to justice as the "firm basis of government," Wilson proclaimed:

> There can be no equality or opportunity, the first essential of justice in the body politic, if men and women and children be not shielded in their lives, their very vitality, from the consequences of great industrial and social processes which they can not alter, control, or singly cope with. Society must see to it that it does not crush or weaken or damage its own constituent parts. The first duty of law is to keep sound the society it serves. Sanitary laws, pure food laws, and laws determining conditions of labor which individuals are powerless to determine for themselves are intimate parts of the very business of justice and legal efficiency.

In an appeal for objectivity and disinterested advice, Wilson, who spoke of restoration, not revolution, realized that progress to control risks without reform of regulation was not possible. The remaking of the state which he led helped to assure the dominance of a new regulatory paradigm.

Let us be clear: what makes the Wilsonian moment look remotely impractical is not the political and social situation of 1912, which after all marked the threshold of one of the greatest crises ever to shake western civilization, but the belief that a rational response called for broader rights, more democratic participation, and the application of sound principles of political economy to both public and private-sector governance.

Wilson, often called an idealist, tried to channel the social pressures at work in a society late in a phase of globalization at least as strong as that which has dominated the last two decades, and similar to ours as well in the extent to which it was marked by rapid urbanization and urban growth. To be sure, Wilson's effort to establish a new form of governance in the international sphere after World War One attracted more popular support than backing from other political leaders. But his insight underpinning the American entry into the war and the Fourteen Points that shortened it, that a vision must be coupled with *realpolitik*, has been validated over time.

In language that looks back at the post-Cold War era, in 2000 Henry Kissinger wrote that leaders "driven by short-term electoral pressure are ... tempted to go along with the conventional wisdom that treats economic phenomena as autonomous and self-correcting and essentially unrelated to the political process. Yet the great changes in history, almost without exception, were driven by mankind's need for some kind of political vision and pursuit of a standard of justice" (Kissinger, 2001:33). With foresight, Henry Kissinger wrote that "when vast amounts of capital move around the world in response to individual decisions, periodic crises of disequilibrium will almost invariably occur." Worryingly, Kissinger added that "a downturn of any length would wreak havoc with the international financial and political systems. What then would be the reaction of a generation that has never known economic crisis – much less a political one – and that has failed to prepare for it?" (Kissinger, 2001: 231). The crisis of 2008 and its aftermath gave us an answer – anger and resentment, more fear and less hope. "The industrial democracies must preserve and extend the extraordinary accomplishments that fostered globalization," he wrote. "But they can only do so in the long run if they endow the economic aspects of globalization with a political construction of comparable sweep and vision" (Kissinger, 2001: 233).[1] Often disparaged as unrealistic, at critical junctures idealism is exactly what the exercise of power and of *realpolitik*, based on an assessment of the interests, strengths, and weaknesses of countries, may require in the search for a peaceful outcome to a crisis.

Ultimately, the problem of policies for cities is about how political advances can keep pace with economic and social change. Each of the three major periods of urban development since the Renaissance expanded political rights and economic opportunities, albeit through a process of adjustment that was often highly conflictual. The late seventeenth and eighteenth centuries witnessed the creation of capital and commodity markets in the major metropolitan centers of the Atlantic world, but also checks on arbitrary government and on the dominion of the military over cities, as well as the emergence of individual rights enshrined in law. Urban growth in the period 1880–1920 accompanied the introduction of modern telecommunications, electrification, infrastructures for water and sanitation, and mass production, mass education, and the research university as well as modern social welfare systems and universal suffrage. The economic opportunities and environmental risks of our own era are fairly clear to see, but the implications of urban phenomena for the exercise of democratic rights, policy, and the internal workings of governments, and an international order based on nation-states, are difficult to grasp. This is a realistic, not a pessimistic conclusion: the resolution of past crises should give us confidence that solutions to exploit the potential of cities and urban regions and reduce the risks they face will prevail, even if new patterns of urban development and living – and the policies and institutions to guide them – will in due course almost certainly generate problems of their own; this is the proper working of our social and economic systems.

This inquiry into cities and crisis began with 2008, a pivotal year highlighting the limits to policy frameworks which, lifting growth and prosperity to unprecedented levels, and parrying economic shocks as different as oil in the 1970s, the collapse of old industries in the 1980s, banking failures and asset bubbles, carried the West from the era of world wars to the early twenty-first century. The crisis reveals a gap between the needs and potential of cities on the one hand, and the scope and objectives of macro-economic and sectoral policies on the other. This gap had not mattered so much when general economic and demographic trends coincided with a dramatic increase in the weight of cities in the economy; it matters now. The far-reaching implications of urbanization for national policies and international relations are too easily overlooked or marginalized at a time when many problems and issues are competing for attention and resources. Being clear-sighted means recognizing that cities are at the center of the great economic, environmental, cultural, and social changes which nation-states and their peoples must confront. Can our cities survive? The answer is of course yes; the real question is how.

Note

1 Quotations from Henry Kissinger appear with the permission of the author.

References

Barber, Benjamin (2013), *If Mayors Ruled the World: Dysfunctional Nations, Rising Cities* (New Haven and London: Yale University Press).
Davezies, Laurent (2012), *La crise qui vient* (Paris: Editions du Seuil).
Draghi, Mario (2012), "For a European public space," remarks on receiving the M100 Media Award, 6 September 2012, www.ecb.europa.eu/press/key/date/2012/html/sp120906.en.html.
Harris, Nigel (1997), "Cities in a global economy: structural change and policy reactions," *Urban Studies,* 34:1693–703.
Jacobs, Jane (2004), *Dark Age Ahead* (New York: Random House).
Kissinger, Henry (2001), *Does America Need a Foreign Policy? Toward a Diplomacy for the 21st Century* (New York: Simon and Schuster).
Kissinger, Henry (2014), *World Order: Reflections on the Character of Nations and the Course of History* (London: Allen Lane).
Konvitz Milton.(1967), *Expanding Liberties: The Emergence of New Civil Liberties and civil Rights* in Postwar America (New Yark: Vintage).
Mumford, Lewis (1961), *The City in History: Its Origins, Its Transformations and Its Prospects* (New York: Harcourt, Brace and World).
Nye, David E. (2010), *When the Lights Went Out: A History of Blackouts in America* (Cambridge, MA: MIT Press).
OECD (2003), *Emerging Risks in the 21st Century: An Agenda for Action* (Paris: OECD). ISBN: 92-64-19947-0.
OECD (2011), *Future Global Shocks: Improving Risk Governance* (Paris: OECD). DOI: 10.1787/9789264114586-en.
OECD/IDA (2014) "Energy technology perspectives factsheet" (Paris: OECD).
Orum, Anthony M. (1991), "Apprehending the city: the view from above, below, sand behind," *Urban Affairs Quarterly,* 26:4: 589–609.
Padoa-Schioppa, Tomasso (2010), "Markets and government before, during and after the 2007–20xx crisis," Per Jacobsen lecture of 27 June 2010 at the Bank of International Settlements, www.bis.org/events/agm2010/sp100627.htmesx3exexxexdss3xsex.
Tuan, Yi–Fu (1988), "The city as a moral universe," *The Geographical Review*,78: 316–24.

Index

agglomeration effects 8, 14, 21, 28, 32–3, 36, 53, 58, 88, 90, 94, 135, 142–3, 146
Alexander, John W. 134
Amin, Ash 118
Andrew, Chris 6
Australia 143, 200

Banks, Gary 200
Barkun, Michael 186
Belfast 125–6
Bell, Daniel 187
Berlin 11, 14, 124
Black, Julia 196
Braudel, Fernand 231
brownfields 9, 125–7
Brulé, Tyler 143
Brummer, Chris 197

Chicago 4, 7–9
cities
    attitudes toward 22, 46–7, 228, 283–4
    autonomy 31–2, 44, 275–8
    definitions and data 21, 30–3, 119–20
    future and untapped potential 4, 9–11, 29, 35, 37, 45–6, 72, 88, 95–100, 103–4, 118, 127–30, 138–9, 143, 151–4
    neglect in policy ix, 1–7, 13–14, 22, 27, 30, 33–5, 68, 72–3, 119–21, 215, 262–3, 282, 287
    see also policy levers
crisis
    economic (1992) x, 1, 6, 14, 119
    future 19–20, 163–72, 201–2, 219–20, 229–30, 260–1, 265, 282–5
    global financial (2008) vii–ix, 1–4, 27–30, 34–5, 37, 41, 51–3, 75, 86, 156–7, 196, 219, 260–3, 270, 279
    perceptions of 2, 6, 16–17, 165, 185–6, 217, 261–2

Davezies, Laurent 33
Delors, Jacques 10
Detroit 92, 104–11, 115–18, 130–1
disasters
    costs and trends 16–20, 166–72
    earthquakes 167, 176–7, 184–5
    floods and storms 5–6, 168–73
    preparedness 18, 163–5, 172–8, 185–8, 191, 215–19, 265, 274
disparities 6, 8, 40, 52, 96, 106, 113–22, 129–30, 187–8, 257–8
distressed urban areas 115, 119–27
Draghi, Mario 280
Drucker, Peter 5, 103

economy, urban 27–38, 43, 63–4, 95–6, 104, 117, 134–7, 142–7
electrification 27, 251–6
Europe and America, compared 9–12, 15–16, 80–1, 95–6, 198, 229

fear and hope viii, 4, 15–16, 22, 45–6, 182–3, 201, 208, 218, 226–8, 246–8, 258, 261, 264–5, 268, 283–4, 286

Glasgow 7, 96, 124, 140, 149–50, 179–80
globalisation 136–7, 140–2, 169, 205, 249–50, 266–7, 286

Gottmann, Jean 95, 284
governance
  free society and cities 22, 44, 46–7, 58–9, 93, 105, 118, 208–9, 283–7
  multi-level and urban policy 10, 34, 66, 52, 72, 78, 108, 130, 147, 157, 175, 196–7, 262–3, 267, 275–8, 285
  see also paradigm, economic
Greece 104–5, 111–18, 130–1
growth
  factors of viii, 9–10, 38–9, 43–6, 54–60, 103
  limits to 3, 29, 35–40, 43, 75, 94–7, 130, 258–9

Hall, Peter 89, 91–5, 104
Harris, Nigel 31, 276
housing 51–3, 59–66, 69–72
Hughes, Thomas 253–5

infrastructure
  investment deficit 4–5, 29, 34–7, 59, 75–89
  planning 136, 142–7, 154–9, 252, 262
  see also OECD; risk and security
innovation 29, 59–60, 75, 89–96, 98–100, 207, 219–24
interdependence, paradigm for twenty-first century 43, 48, 186, 265–8 273, 275, 281
international relations 18–19, 44–5, 47, 131, 197–9, 205–8, 225, 238, 250, 256–7, 269–73, 277, 280, 285
  see also risks, cross-border

Jacobs, Jane xii, 6, 99–100, 104, 128, 202, 206, 229, 284

Kissinger, Henry 229, 283, 286
Kobe 18, 167, 169 207
Kuhn, Thomas 225

Lange, Dorothea 107
Levy, Maurice 227
Locke, John 238
London 6, 32, 82, 96, 145–7, 149, 251, 271
Los Angeles 4, 14, 92, 103, 148
Luce, Edward 16, 80

McKinsey 36–7, 67, 85
Marshall, Alfred 94, 142
Melbourne 139, 143, 153–4
middle class 15, 54, 67–8, 187, 261
More, Thomas 237
Mayr, Otto 241–3
Münchau, Wolfgang 105
Mumford, Lewis xiii, 100, 158, 231, 284

New Orleans 168, 174, 184
New York 5, 28, 78, 92, 98, 106–7, 153, 170, 173, 251

Olympic Games 12, 111, 148–50
Organisation for Economic Co-operation and Development (OECD)
  climate change 30, 69–70, 90, 170–3, 213–19
  crises and risk, 41, 186, 274–5
  housing policy 53–4
  infrastructure investment 76, 83–5, 157–9
  mission xi, 12
  regulatory policy 192–5, 198–9
  urban and regional policy 13–16, 97, 107, 123–30

Padoa-Schioppa, Tomasso 281
paradigm for economic regulation x, 17, 27, 30, 43–4, 48, 200, 219–29, 235, 249, 257–9, 261, 264–8, 282, 287
  in history 227, 235–46
Paris 21, 39, 92, 136, 138, 140, 154–5, 228
Perez, Carlotta 221–5, 230, 256
Piketty, Thomas 37, 43
planning, spatial 7, 39, 55, 68–9, 87, 112, 123, 154–9, 184–5, 249–51
policy
  and cities 3, 6, 13, 33–6, 47, 100, 120–30, 142–8, 158–9, 184–5, 213, 224, 262–3, 276–7, 287
  levers 29, 31, 33, 42, 128–9, 191, 199–200, 206, 262–3, 269
politics and policy reform ix, 3–4, 10–11, 19, 33–5, 41–2, 64–6, 72, 81, 100, 105, 115–16, 123, 147, 175, 193–4, 200, 262–3

port cities and coastal zone 5–6, 18, 152–4, 168–72, 181–2, 251
Putnam, Robert 187

Rabb, T K 238
regeneration 15, 104, 109, 117–28, 149–51
Reghezza-Zitt, Magali 174–5, 186
regulation, macro-economic 27, 30, 33, 47, 52, 79–80, 86, 97, 220–1, 241–4, 252–8
regulatory reform 16, 52, 64–7, 79, 88, 90, 191–6
  and international co-operation 198–9, 201, 266–8, 281–2
Reinhart, Carmen 16, 38
resilience 165–6, 179–87, 202, 217–49, 265, 268
risk
  cross-border 19, 163–6, 196–202, 261, 265, 269–75, 279–80
  and security 19–20, 47–8, 176–7, 200–9
  see also OECD regulatory policy

Sachs, Jeffrey 29
Schwartz, Anna 3
Smith, Adam 242–4
space and change 20–1, 38, 56–7, 84, 97–8, 103, 107, 231–2, 259, 273

and macro-economy 27–30, 60, 63, 118, 134–6, 140, 159, 215
Spinoza, Baruch 227
Starr, Roger 107
strategy for cities 3, 14, 29, 33, 35–7, 39, 44–7, 64, 68, 71–2, 76, 83, 87–8, 97, 122–3, 126, 145–9, 151, 154–9, 164, 213–19, 256–61, 265
Summers, Lawrence 35

Troy, Patrick 201
Turkey 18, 167, 170, 176–7

uncertainty, and paradigm shift 4, 17, 43–4, 48, 76, 225, 261–73, 283–4
United Nations Conference on Human Settlements 14–15, 44, 58–9
United States
  and OECD, 13–14
  policies 61–2, 77–8

Vance, Cyrus 13

war 18, 178–82
Ward, Barbara 47
Westphalia Treaty 235
  see also international relations; risks, cross border
Wiener, Johnathan 198
Wilson, Woodrow 285
Wolf, Martin 51
World Bank 12, 88, 202, 269